Embattled Selves

EMBATTLED SELVES

An Investigation into the Nature of Identity
Through Oral Histories of Holocaust Survivors

Kenneth Jacobson

THE ATLANTIC MONTHLY PRESS
NEW YORK

Published simultaneously in Canada
Printed in the United States of America

FIRST EDITION

Library of Congress Cataloging-in-Publication Data

Jacobson, Kenneth, 1949–
Embattled selves: An investigation into the nature of identity through oral histories of Holocaust survivors/Kenneth Jacobson.—1st ed.
ISBN 0-87113-571-X
1. Holocaust survivors—Interviews. 2. Jews—Identity.
I. Title.
D804.3.J33   1994   940.53′18′0922—dc20   93-43719

DESIGN BY LAURA HOUGH

The Atlantic Monthly Press
841 Broadway
New York, NY 10003

10 9 8 7 6 5 4 3 2 1

To all those who told me about their lives,
for what they were able to learn
and what they found the courage to teach.

CONTENTS

INTRODUCTION

On an autumn day in 1973, not long after I had taken a job as a reporter in Amsterdam, two friends and I followed the Amstel River from the center of town to an old Jewish cemetery several miles upstream. The three of us had grown up almost without religion amid the ethnic blurring of California, and while our background did not keep us from feeling strongly about being Jews, it had left us unprepared for what we were about to see. We knew that the cemetery, established close to four centuries earlier by immigrants from Spain and Portugal, was valued for its place in Holland's Jewish history—so we were bewildered when we found the graves looking neglected, the lawn around them overrun by weeds. The assistant caretaker, having offered us a tour, recognized in an instant that the feeling of affinity which had moved us to visit was far deeper than our knowledge of Judaism. At times, the temptation to poke a little ironic fun at our ignorance proved too strong for this rather formal man to resist. But otherwise he gave his best effort to instructing us as he led us along.

When we were approaching the burial ground, the caretaker surprised us with the warning that any male whose last name points to the lineage of the ancient Hebrew priests must remain outside: Contact with death can defile the holy, who are thus required to stay clear. Nor had we known that the only prayer permitted in a graveyard is that honoring the dead; everyday worship, the caretaker explained, might seem to mock those no longer able to comply with religious commandments. But most exotic to us was the Sephardic insistence that the ground in a cemetery be altered as little as possible. The grass may not be cut or the leaves raked, and the caretaker saw to it that potted plants brought by mourners did not take root in the soil. With a shrug, he confessed that allowing visitors to leave flowers amounted to blinking at the rules: Adorning graves is opposed by the orthodox, who hold that a cemetery is not meant for the pleasure of the living. The caretaker had even gone so far as to say his daily prayers within the grounds until he was found out by others on the staff. "I told them my praying would not disturb these people who have lain here for hundreds of years," he recalled. "And it was so peaceful in the morning light . . ."

Shaken to discover that our Jewishness linked us to things we had never so much as imagined, my friends and I sat pensive on a bench by the gate. It was the caretaker who broke our silence, unexpectedly embarking on the story of his life. He was, it turned out, from a noble Protestant family. Born in Holland in 1915, educated in Germany during the 1920s, he had become a Jew in 1938, when he was a student of the fine arts in Antwerp. His brother, a member of the Dutch fascist movement from 1933 and a volunteer to the SS, was locked up after the war, converting to Catholicism while in prison. Their sister had been a Communist from 1933: "When my brother became a fascist, she joined the International," the caretaker observed, "to get even." Her role in the wartime resistance brought her wide notoriety—and a few years in concentration camps.

The caretaker himself returned to Amsterdam in late May of 1940, shortly after both Belgium and the Netherlands had surrendered to the German army. After living through most of the occupation hidden in a monastery, he allowed himself to be baptized, but only "for the experience"; this conversion had not been a matter of conviction. The war over, he devoted himself to Hebrew and spent many years studying, translating, and writing on important Jewish thinkers. When his inheritance ran out, he found the job as assistant caretaker and guide.

The shock of the cemetery's mystic strangeness faded for me over time, but the life of the caretaker remained a vivid and nagging puzzle. Here was a worldly and intelligent person who recalled witnessing anti-Semitism as a child in Germany, who had seen in his own family the bitterness to which political extremes can lead. Why should he choose to cast his lot with the Jews at such a precarious moment in their history? There seemed little basis in the caretaker's ancestry, in his family life, in his education, for a connection to anything Jewish. What could account for an identification so powerful that he preferred taking up its burdens to remaining apart from those who had no freedom to lay them down?

Nearly three years to the day after visiting the cemetery, I found myself in a ballroom on the edge of Paris, assigned to a luncheon sponsored by a French corporation. Drifting through a crowd of journalists and executives dressed in dark suits and chatting in important tones, I was stopped by a vivacious man of sixty or so wearing wire-rimmed glasses, a mustache, and a bow tie half hidden by a double chin. He had spotted the publication title on my name tag and, sending regards to a co-worker of mine, he handed me his card: "René Pommier." His pixieish eyes and apparent lack of affectation were winning; we sat down together to lunch.

As we talked—of economic problems, the food we were eating, what it's like to live in France—I felt a growing curiosity about René's background. I had an idea of where he came from and would have liked to hear about his life, but for some reason I was hesitant to ask. Finally, I took a chance: "Have you always lived in Paris?"

"Oh, what a question!" René blinked, but his expression remained cheerful. "Actually, I grew up in Germany."

Excited at the prospect of cementing our affinity, I exclaimed, "And, of course, you are Jewish!"

"Why—why, no," he said, discomfort creeping into his voice. "I, no, not at all. I mean, there could be some Jewish blood somewhere along the line, you never know about these things. But, no, I'm not . . ."

As his voice trailed off, I feared that I had smothered an enjoyable conversation and offended a gracious man. "Well, I myself am Jewish," I went on, hoping to smooth things over, "and I thought you might be, too. But do you mind telling me when you came to France?"

"In 1938."

"I'll permit myself one more question, then: If you came to France from Germany in 1938, and you aren't Jewish, did you come for political reasons?"

There was irony in René's words, but wistfulness in his eyes. "Let's just say that I was a student of history, and that the way in which history was taught in Germany in the 1930s was not of particular intellectual interest to me." His composure restored, René described fleeing before the blitzkrieg to the south of France and fighting in North Africa with the Free French. After the war he taught languages, then went into publishing.

The luncheon over, René suggested cordially that we continue at a neighborhood café. But when he turned from placing our order, his mood was changed. René's eyes seemed, suddenly, to burn; for the first time, his smile was gone. "What kind of a Jew are you, anyway?" he asked, peering.

It was my turn to be stunned. "I'm not sure I know what you mean. Do you mean, am I a practicing Jew? No, I'm not. But—"

"Of course I am Jewish," he interrupted. "But I've been a Catholic for nearly forty years." His voice grew a bit wild. "There was an answer given to the Jews! There's been a solution for the last two thousand years! Why haven't they recognized it? Why don't they see that there's a way out?"

Apparently sensing he had gotten carried away, René drew a deep breath, waving a hand before his eyes as if to brush aside unwelcome visions; no longer frantic or grieved, he wore a smile heavy with resignation. "Well, we can speak of these things another time. But how did you know that I am a Jew? After all, I converted decades ago."

I became very careful: "I realize that a person's own experience and character do much to shape his face. But certain things can show up in faces from one generation to the next, things that seem rooted in something passed on, things that may in fact be indelible."

This left René baffled, so I tried to dissect my intuition. "In the first place," I told him, "I didn't think you were a native of France."

Again there was amazement on René's face. "How can you say that? How could you think that? When my family sees me now, everyone says that in my appearance, my mannerisms, my habits, I have become perfectly French."

I felt disconcerted, because the notion of René as a Frenchman struck me as incongruous—and because, although I had figured *Pommier,* "apple tree," as a French rendering of *Apfelbaum,* it was beginning to dawn on me that the translation of *René* is "reborn."

I started over. "Foreigners, since they tend to be excluded, often recognize each other—it's a matter of survival." I meant to be delicate, and this last phrase, remembered later, would cause me to shudder. "Second, you spoke to me in English, which a French person would be unlikely to do. And, finally, when you speak English, you do not have a French accent."

"What kind of an accent do I have, then?"

"I don't know where you grew up, but I would guess you come from Berlin."

René gasped. Swiveling his elbow, forearm horizontal, he delivered a short, soft blow to my chest. "Remarkable!" he whispered, appearing oddly pleased. "But how could you tell?"

The answer was really quite simple: When he spoke, René reminded me of a Jew from Berlin who had long been a friend of my family. But I wove an elaborate explanation, embarrassed that my coup should rest on so flimsy a base. René listened attentively; by the time I had finished, however, his gaze was fixed upon the floor.

After a moment's silence, René shook his head, then looked up at me. Calmly, but in dead earnest, he said, "It just goes to show you: One can never be too careful."

At the end of our conversation, I said to René, "But it's all over now—it's been over for thirty years." René did not acknowledge my remark.

Upon reflection, I realized that "it" would never be over for René. I also began to wonder whether I had not met, in René, the mirror image of the caretaker. One had chosen Judaism in the shadow of Hitler, the other continued to hide his Jewishness three decades after Hitler's fall. One appeared willing to run grave risks to belong, the other seemed wedded to painstaking measures of escape. If one was bent on affiliation, the other was equally bent on denial.

In the wake of these encounters, I found myself haunted by a series of questions—questions that stalk all human beings, but most implacably those for whom identity becomes a matter of life and death. Which part of me is essential? What price will I pay to hold on to that part? How much can I change without losing it? Who will I be if I give it up? These questions, dimly perceived at first, burned ever brighter, until they stared at me with the intensity that I had imagined in the caretaker's prayers, and that I had seen in René Pommier's eyes.

In early 1978, I left my job to search for people who had struggled with their Jewishness during the Nazi period, my hope being that the accounts they would give of their lives might provide a new perspective on the nature of identity. I anxiously dialed René's office, only to learn that it had, after all, ended for him—with a fatal heart attack six weeks before. Reached at the cemetery, the caretaker explained that, although he considered himself close to the Jews and observed many religious laws, he had never formally converted to Judaism. Under the Nazi occupation, he had refused on principle to attest to his "Aryan" origins, thereby renouncing all possibility of employment as an artist and risking assignment to forced labor in the service of the German war effort. It was to avoid the latter that he had gone into hiding; the Nazis had never declared him to be, nor had they threatened him as a Jew.

In the ensuing forty-four months, however, I was able to tape-record the life histories of nearly three hundred men and women who had discovered, rejected, embraced, or concealed their Jewishness as a result of Nazi persecution. Fifteen of these stories form the basis of this book.

Under a decree issued late in 1935, the third year of National Socialist rule, Germany defined a Jew as anyone descended from three or four "Jewish" grandparents. Since grandparents were counted as "Jewish" if they had belonged to a Jewish religious community, it was the religious affiliation of a past generation that in fact served as the Nazi criterion for race. A similar principle applied to those descended from two "Jewish" grandparents, who were classed with the Jews as long as they had been enrolled in a Jewish community or married to another "Jew" on a specified date before the decree was issued. But even if the Nazi conception of Jewishness ultimately rested on institutional ties rather than blood, it had the practical effect of relegating a whole range of people— irrespective of how they lived, what they believed, or who they took themselves to be—to a single group whose limits were created by the Nazis themselves. Unlike at certain other moments in history, Jews could not escape persecution by renouncing the Jewish faith. Those subject to the "Final Solution" were trapped in their own skin: The sole fact of their origins threatened, directly and inexorably, their very existence.

For some members of this diverse group, being singled out for persecution purely on the basis of origin altered the meaning of Jewishness; for many, it forced the fact of being Jewish into a position of unaccustomed centrality. Whatever had defined them in the minds of their neighbors before the onset of persecution, their individuality often came to be eclipsed by their outcast status. However they themselves had understood its nature, Jewishness came to connote compulsory membership in the group seen as the principal enemy of the authorities.

And whatever importance they had attached to being Jewish, the fact of their origins came to dictate their circumstances and, even if not all realized it at the time, to determine their fate. Jewishness dominated two basic functions of their identity: the way others perceived them and the way they experienced themselves. And their predicament led them to ask, consciously or unconsciously, and to answer, in word or in deed, a number of fundamental questions: Am I a Jew? What makes me a Jew? How important is being a Jew to being who I am? Who am I?

Just how dramatically the experiences and feelings of individual Jews who lived under the Nazis highlight issues of identity depends, at least in part, on how much of a shift persecution occasioned in two important areas: the degree to which being Jewish shaped their lives and the significance that being Jewish held for their self-understanding.

Often, it appears, the contrasts were simply not that great. Unassimilated Jews, typically in Eastern Europe, had known cultural isolation long before the Nazis arrived and took for granted the frequently antagonistic attitude of those in whose countries they lived. Furthermore, the religious and cultural traditions that circumscribed their lives and marked them off from their neighbors had always been—and, despite what happened under the Nazis, tended in one form or another to remain—at the very heart of their self-understanding. Among the more assimilated Jews of Western and Central Europe and the larger cities of the East, the time was past when being of Jewish origin necessarily implied following Jewish religious practices or taking part in Jewish communal life. As legal and social acceptance of Jews had broadened, many had ended up deemphasizing their Jewish heritage, either in a deliberate attempt to remove what they feared might be an obstacle to full citizenship or as an incidental result of adopting the majority culture. Still, like their less assimilated fellows, most had grown up aware of their Jewish origins; had been known to the world around them as Jews; were persecuted as Jews; and, if they survived the period, continued to embrace or at least to acknowledge their Jewishness.

But members of an exceptional minority—among them, the 280 men and women whose lives I recorded—were in the position of having to choose between a Jewish and a non-Jewish identity or to find a way of making the two coexist. There were those who assumed a non-Jewish persona in an attempt to foil the Nazis, and those who revealed or insisted upon a Jewish connection even when it put them at peril. There were those who, turning their backs on the majority society, converted to Judaism once the Third Reich had fallen, and those who tried to loosen their ties to a Jewish past by taking a new name, becoming Christian, or simply getting lost in the crowd. There were those of mixed parentage, the legacy of whose birth might afford them the practical opportunity, but also saddle them with the psychological necessity, of deciding with whom they would identify: the majority, the persecuted, neither, or both. Finally, there were those who had Jewishness thrust upon them—who had been totally unaware of their Jewish background before being threatened because of it; or had known of it, but had wanted no part of it; or had acknowledged it, but had viewed themselves for religious reasons as Christians rather than Jews; or were first confronted with it, and with its implications for their own lives and those of their families, once the persecution was at an end. The conflict they faced, because it tested them so deeply and brought so clearly to expression the solutions they found, places their identity struggles in a particularly vivid light.

Such conflict was not unique to the Nazi period; it had been known to the Jewish people from its earliest days. Shadrach, Meshach, and Abednego had risked death in Nebuchadnezzar's furnace, and the Zealots had chosen suicide at Masada, rather than declare allegiance to an authority, divine or secular, other than their God. For them, as for Jewish martyrs of the Middle Ages, life seems to have made sense only as a vehicle for Jewish identity: Once they were no longer allowed to live as Jews, existence itself may have become inconceivable—while the purpose and meaning that derived from upholding Jewishness, now beyond their grasp in life, might find expression in death. But those who, faced with forced conversion, had chosen to go on living might have claimed Biblical precedent in the actions of Esther, who helped ensure her people's continuity by concealing her origins. Forced converts often tried to continue practicing Judaism in secret or to avoid or tone down those elements of Christianity that might offend their own enduring

Jewish sensibilities. To the extent that they cared about preserving their heritage, they had somehow to reconcile their new with their former condition, to make a Jewish past—and, perhaps, a Jewish future—compatible with a non-Jewish present.

Even if the dilemmas that it imposed were not entirely new, what made Nazi persecution such a keen threat to Jewish identity, besides its unprecedented scope, was that the identity of at least a part of European Jewry in the 1930s and 1940s was more susceptible to challenge than the identity of earlier Jewish populations had been. Only in the latter half of the eighteenth century had political emancipation and religious enlightenment opened the way to social and cultural assimilation. The accompanying erosion of Jewish communal life had been marked by a sharp rise in the number of nonobservant Jews, Jewish converts to Christianity, and children of marriages between Jews and non-Jews—people who, while they did often retain some tie to Jewishness, may have ceased to see themselves as Jews in religious or national terms. Those for whom the unity of faith and nation had broken down might have been left to wonder at the strength or even at the very existence of their bonds to Jewishness, and to ask what precisely it was that they felt bound to.

If Jewishness were no longer presumed to be assigned by God, where might it come from? Was it carried in the genes? Cued into the subconscious? Inculcated by teaching? Graven by experience?

If it no longer expressed the unity of nation and faith, what was it? A matter of religious conviction? Ethnic loyalty? Cultural heritage? Family custom? Shared condition? Common destiny?

And if it were no longer one with the meaning of life—or, in some cases, with life itself—how central was it to being? Did it stir the emotions or leave them indifferent? Was it at the heart of self-understanding or on its periphery? Could it determine choices, or was it irrelevant to choice?

Passed through the lens of Nazi persecution, these questions burned hotter and came into sharper focus. Those for whom the Jewish part of identity had been in the background sometimes found that it came to compete with other ways in which they had defined themselves, ways they may have regarded as more essential to their identity as individuals. Where there had been male or female, short or tall, young or old, dark or fair, now there was also Jew. Where there had been spouse, parent, sibling, child, now there was also Jew. Where there had been citizen of a nation-state, speaker of a language, member of a social class, resident of a neighborhood, now there was also Jew. Where there had been war veteran, civil servant, party member, nonconformist, now there was also Jew. Where there had been athlete, artist, laborer, intellectual, hoodlum, entrepreneur, now there was also Jew. And to those for whom Jewish identity had been foremost, the same conflict might present itself, but in reverse: Less assimilated Jews disguising themselves as "Aryans" might, like the forced converts of bygone eras, be confronted for the first time with the many-sided nature of identity as they sought to stay in touch with their Jewishness behind the mask.

Once the persecution had ended, those subjected to it could scarcely escape integrating the experience into their identity, irrespective of their conscious attitude toward being Jewish before, during, or even after the Nazi period. Since the experience of persecution must in itself have been among the most powerful experiences of their lives, it was destined to work changes both in how these people saw themselves and in who in fact they were. On top of that, it assigned them a place in history—a place which, at the same time that it positioned them within the Jewish historical tradition, marked them off from Jews of other ages just as it marked them off from the vast majority of their contemporaries, Jewish and non-Jewish alike. Finally, in the cases of those whose lives make up this book, a more explicit identity struggle influenced and perhaps complicated the need for personal redefinition by requiring an additional step: integrating the elements of an alternative identity, the dynamics of the struggle, or both.

From the outside, the experience of persecution and its implications for those who must cope with it have been viewed almost universally in a negative light. Perceived as a faceless mass and branded with new labels, these people have variously been pitied as victims, upbraided as whiners, venerated as martyrs, ridiculed as cowards, and shunned as pariahs. Their pain has sometimes been regarded as a sign of ill health rather than as an appropriate response to horror; even if such judgments often contain at least a grain of truth and more than a grain of compassion, they are apt to cause those at whom they are directed to feel that the validity of their emotions is being challenged and that the suffering that may attend those emotions is being disparaged as neither legitimate nor unique. More than a few of those interviewed said that, as the experience of persecution has played a part in making them who they are, they are inclined to view it less darkly than others tend to; but when they attempt to win recognition for the personal as opposed to the purely historical value of that which has become an inalienable part of themselves, they may be stigmatized, patronized, or rebuffed. Even when they are regarded as heroes, many live in a lonely double bind. "If people don't know that I was in Auschwitz," one woman explained, "they can't know me. But once I tell them, they are no longer able to see me for who I am."

Because of the emotional nature of the subject, I wanted to avoid taking my prospective interview partners unawares, as I had René. And specifically because memories of denunciation remained poignant for many, I did not want them to have the impression that details of their lives were being bandied about without their permission. I therefore preferred that they be contacted first by those who suggested I interview them, told something about my research and that their names had come to mind, and asked whether it would be all right if I got in touch with them.

A guarantee of anonymity rapidly became both a condition and a tool of the work. I discovered that many people felt embarrassed at having to ask whether they could count on me to protect their privacy; by declaring at the outset that all life histories would be treated anonymously in both conversation and print, I could spare everyone this potential awkwardness. This policy had a second advantage: I believe that it discouraged those few who seemed unduly eager to be named from trying to use the interview to glorify, justify, or even misrepresent themselves. The names of those who speak here have thus been changed, and in selected instances other names or details that might have led to identification have been altered or omitted.

Perhaps three-quarters of the people approached on my behalf were willing to have me look them up. Of those I actually met, all but a handful allowed me to tape-record their life stories. This still strikes me as remarkable, particularly in light of the upsetting nature of the enterprise: I sometimes found that my arrival had been preceded by a sleepless night, and it was not unusual for me to be greeted with apprehension—if not outright hostility—even by someone who had appeared eager to talk. People would try to convince me that what they had to tell was irrelevant to my research; claim that the work itself would be useless in informing the world of the horror of persecution or in preventing its recurrence; deride the question of identity as unimportant in the context of extreme danger and suffering; or declare that I, having been born after the end of the war, was simply too young to understand. Since I did not feel it was my place to debate the validity of these contentions, I would generally say that I myself didn't see things that way, then either try to help my interview partner through what I took to be an emotionally difficult moment or sit tight in the hope that the moment would pass.

A significant number of those I interviewed had rarely spoken of their lives under the Nazis, even with family or other intimates; in the years when the interviews were recorded, 1978 through 1981, the barriers of repression and taboo that had blocked discussion of the Nazi period both in public and in private were just beginning to come down. And of those who had talked about their experiences of persecution, few had recounted them in a complete and ordered manner or specifically addressed the question of identity. As their narratives unfolded, recreating an atmosphere that in some cases the mind had avoided for decades, many of my interview partners found themselves flooded with long-repressed memories that surged up in the context of events, as well as with feelings attached both to those memories and to the atmosphere as a whole.

Desiring to limit the stress to which they would be subjected, I generally requested only one taping session, a practice that also seemed to give heart to some who might have been frightened off by the prospect of going through such a trial more than once. Taping lasted anywhere from one to six hours, and the appointments consistently ran several hours longer than the interview itself. Time was almost always needed to work up to the telling, and it frequently took hours after the interview was over for the two of us—usually through chatting about family, travel, work, hobbies, current events, and other everyday matters—to return to the present. My interview partners were not the only ones to benefit from these periods of decompression; as a rule, I myself was strongly affected by both the events of the past and the emotion associated with relating them. On the rare occasions when I was shown the door immediately upon the conclusion of taping, I experienced acute disorientation.

Despite the taxing nature of the interview, most said when it was over that they were glad they had done it. Some, among them people who had had a difficult time, said they wanted to see me again—"but this time not for work"—and these later visits were always pleasant. Although word did now and then reach me that an interview partner had remained shaken for a time afterward, I never heard that serious harm had ensued. And occasionally I had the gratification of being told that the interview had done lasting good. A man who had asked for copies of his tapes once bumped into me on the street and, tapping his chest vigorously, he exclaimed, "Now that it's stored on the shelf, I no longer have to carry it around in here!"

But given the anxiety associated with the interview and the strain it seemed bound to cause, why, I often wondered, would anybody want to do it? Some undoubtedly agreed to the interview because the idea aroused their curiosity or their pride, others because they saw in it a momentary respite from boredom or loneliness, still others because they felt kindly disposed toward a young journalist or toward the friend who had made the introduction. A number hoped it would be good for them to confront the past head-on, while a few apparently took part so they could have a tape through which they might impart to their children things they had not found the strength to tell them directly. These largely personal motives were, however, often complemented by another that is inextricably connected to the theme of the inquiry itself.

An identification with the Jewish people and its fate seemed to impel quite a number of prospective interview partners to overcome whatever reluctance they may have felt. Many remarked that, although they had known in advance that the interview would be a disturbing event, they strongly believed that, if the persecution were forgotten, it would be more likely to recur. They thus felt it was their duty to bear witness before future generations—in fact, some saw in this obligation the very purpose of their survival—and they were willing to do so even at the price of considerable discomfort.

It was as if the experience that had affected their lives so deeply did not belong to them personally to do with as they wished: They had not chosen this experience but had been chosen by it, becoming in the process both tools of history and its living repositories. When they spoke into my tape recorder, they were not so much making me a present as passing to my safekeeping that which had been forcibly entrusted to their own; and I believe it was for this reason that so many, in expressing their pleasure at remaining anonymous, added that their names were "no matter" but that it was "the story that's important." The store set on keeping history alive thus seemed a reflection of a fundamental Jewish value: At times, I felt as if I were a child at the Passover table, asking the four questions that prompt the retelling of the Hebrews' bondage in Egypt and their subsequent liberation. The education of a younger person by an older one in the tribulations of the Jewish people is so hallowed by cultural tradition that my interview proposal may have been a difficult one for those who felt part of that tradition to refuse.

A motif running through the conversations I had was the extent to which the Jews of Nazi-dominated Europe lived in uncertainty. Particularly for those who, like myself, were born after World War II, it is sometimes difficult to bear in mind that an Allied victory was not a foregone conclusion—that, in fact, until the winter of 1942–43, the Axis appeared to be winning the war. The prospect that Europe's Jews saw before them was not one of simply holding out until a preordained liberation date set for May 1945 at the latest; rather, for most of the war years, their struggle either to avoid the Nazis' anti-Jewish measures or to withstand their effect appeared to them open-ended. Similarly, those of mixed parentage, while generally exempt from measures that were directly threatening to life, were beset by the fear that, should the war go on long enough for all those officially designated as "Jews" to disappear, their turn would come as well.

To compound this uncertainty, the meaning of the phrase *deportation to Poland* was never spelled out by Nazi authorities; on the contrary, the extermination program, which began officially in 1942, was designed specifically so that its nature and scope might remain unclear to the bulk of the non-Jewish population as well as to the Jews. Although an intention to wipe out the Jews was made plain in the public pronouncements of prominent Nazis and in the doctrine of the National Socialist movement, it appears that few had the foresight to take seriously—or, perhaps, the imagination even to entertain—such an unprecedented possibility. The Jews were not alone in rejecting the notion of the death camps: When descriptions of the camps reached London, officials there initially found them too extreme to be credible, and accounts ultimately broadcast over the BBC were discounted by many on the Continent—Jews and non-Jews alike—as Allied war propaganda.

The attitude of Jews toward the idea that Germany might be actively pursuing their extinction seems in many cases to have been somewhat contradictory: At the same time that many truly believed they were being sent to camps merely to perform hard labor, they looked upon arrest and deportation as spelling their end. This ambiguity may reflect the clash of two equally compelling viewpoints: Law-abiding people, prepared neither for their own outlaw status nor for the lawless behavior of the authorities, were reacting with a disbelief that could only have been reinforced by the general human tendency to deny the prospect of death; yet, while the ultimate terror remained hidden, the perceivable threat—to liberty, property, and, though in a less systematic way, life—must have been quite terrifying enough. That this ambiguity seems surprising today underlines the magnitude of the uncertainty in which those facing persecution lived and points up that, in order to understand their position, the contemporary observer must put aside the knowledge that time has brought.

Finally, the world in which the persecuted Jews lived was marked not only by uncertainty and incomplete knowledge but by restriction and chaos. Under measures in force in Germany and in many other lands under Nazi rule, Jews were prevented from holding jobs in the civil service, from owning businesses, from exercising their professions, from voting, from holding public office, from marrying or employing non-Jews, from remaining in their own homes, from holding driver's licenses, from using public transportation, from owning bicycles, from subscribing to many newspapers and magazines, from owning radios or typewriters, from using public telephones, from attending movies or concerts, from eating in restaurants, from going to public parks, from having pets, and from owning electrical appliances, optical instruments, woolen clothing, or furs. Their mobility was limited by curfews and travel restrictions, which the bold *J* stamped into their identity papers—and, in wartime, the yellow star they were made to wear—helped the authorities enforce. Once the war had started, they were, to a greater extent than the non-Jewish population around them, prey to cold, hunger, air raids, misinformation, and the breakdown of civil order. And all the while they lived under the threat that, at any time, yet unthought-of restrictions might jeopardize whatever comfort or security they had been able to maintain—or that a knock on the door might signal that they were finally being summoned for "transport."

The overall picture is thus one of helplessness and confusion, in which the individual's scope of action and freedom of choice were seriously eroded, and in which chance played an even larger part than it usually does in human affairs. Against this background, however, conditions varied greatly, with actions against Jews more effective or encompassing in some countries than in others. The extent of the persecution could depend on whether the German officials in place saw their primary function as that of implementing Nazi Party policy or administering a military occupation, on the level of their dedication to anti-Semitic ideology, and on their interpretation of the anti-Jewish policies emanating from the Party's highest echelons. It could depend on the ethnic, religious, and political background of the local non-Jewish population, on its consequent willingness for either practical or ideological reasons to cooperate with the Nazis, and on its affection or lack thereof for the Jews in its midst. It could depend on topography, demographic patterns, the availability of food, and the degree to which Jews' physical appearance tended to distinguish them from members of the surrounding population. And it could depend on the economic position of the Jews in question, on their level of cultural and linguistic assimilation, and on the clarity with which they perceived both the attitudes of their non-Jewish neighbors and the events in which they found themselves enmeshed.

Once deported, people might be confronted with conditions as diverse as the conditions they had known while still at home. There could be great variation from camp to camp, and even within a camp there were periods that were more dangerous than others, barracks that were more intolerable than others, work details that were more depleting than others, guards that were more brutal than others, national and age groups that were more vulnerable than others. The treatment of those whose origins were uncertain, or whose partial non-Jewish ancestry or marriage to a non-Jew exempted them from deportation to the ghettos and concentration camps, varied greatly from country to country as well. And, whatever variations existed across the broad landscape of Europe, variations were equally great, if not greater, from case to case—a fact to which the broad panorama of experience offered by this small collection of life histories emphatically attests.

What makes people who they are? What does their way of defining themselves make them think, feel, and do? What causes them to embrace or reject a group? How does their relation to the group affect their identity as individuals? These questions, which are posed by all the life histories and to which each life is its own answer, reach far beyond the narrators or their time and into the experience of most human beings.

Focusing on identity thus removes some emotional events surrounding Nazi persecution from the realm of the aberrant and unthinkable, allowing them to take their place beside experiences that are more easily recognized and understood. This book is set in an extreme period of history because that which is revealed by the extreme reactions such a period calls forth, although it can be crucial to identity, may remain hidden in more ordinary times. And the book spotlights extraordinary lives in the hope that these lives can provide extraordinary insights into familiar concerns.

Echoes of the world that we ourselves inhabit may sound for us in the narrators' words. Reflected in their stories may be sides of our own beings which, not having been so poignantly tested, have never been so eloquently expressed. Members of a stigmatized and persecuted group living under exceptional identity strains may thus be united in our eyes with the "average" citizen of today, facing no more acute crisis than the onslaught of pressures and influences that is simply a part of life in the global village—but that constitutes an identity challenge no less consuming because it is universal.

This is not to say that questions of identity have lost their power to shape political history or that human beings are no longer set apart, even threatened, simply for being who they are. It was hatred among

Serb, Muslim, and Croat rather than competition between East and West that brought war back to European soil. In the Middle East, intolerance daily claims the lives of Arabs, Jews, and Kurds. Skin color divides South Africans, religion Irish, language Canadians, ethnicity the peoples of the former Soviet Union—while all, in greater or lesser degrees, divide Americans. And the end of the Cold War dares countries on both sides of the defunct ideological divide to recast their national identities: No longer defined in contrast to their rivals, they can begin to examine more deeply what they themselves stand for—something they must do if they hope to learn who they are and to decide what role they wish to play.

Those who would resist being overwhelmed by such specific threats and challenges must make their stand in an atmosphere of routine and pervasive upheaval. In a world shaken by shifting loyalties to family, to class, to custom, and to place, the task of setting limits—to who we are, what we will do, how we can change—takes on an increasingly urgent cast. As the child leaves home and enters the marketplace, as minorities leave the fringes and enter the mainstream, as the roles of men and women are questioned and reshaped, as we wrestle with the change that intrudes upon our lives, each and all are continually faced with this task—similar in nature, although rarely in intensity, to that faced by the people who tell their stories here.

It is my hope, therefore, that those who read these lives will recognize themselves in the narrators, and will in so doing develop a more vivid feeling for—and a more vehement aversion to—the violence that persecution must do to the human soul. It is my further hope that they will recognize the narrators in themselves, and thereby gain something that may be of personal use as they struggle to find, and to remain true to, their own embattled selves.

The DYNAMICS *of* CONCEALMENT

"I did it to save my life. It was as simple as that."

To many Jews who assumed a non-Jewish identity in the hope of escaping Nazi persecution, the suggestion that living under another identity might in itself have been an experience of personal significance came as a surprise. Even those for whom the alternative identity had been not merely a name on a set of doctored papers but the foundation of an active life tended to see it as a practical tool, a means of defense much like a camouflage suit. And it was a suit that they had donned with the most straightforward of all objectives: physical survival.

But if the motive for putting it on appears consistent from one case to another, the experience of wearing it could hardly have been more varied. Some remained ever conscious that they were living under an unaccustomed name, that they had altered details of their biography if not totally fabricated a personal history—in short, that they were using a disguise. But there were others for whom the assumed identity became second nature; they could be immersed in it to the point that their previous lives seemed distant or unreal, to the point that being reminded of their past was a genuine shock. And there were a few who never quite let the assumed identity go, even when they had no further practical use for it, whether they retained elements of its content—the names or characteristics of the people they had "been"—or continued the process of pretending to be, or feeling as if they were, someone else.

Where is the line between role and identity? When does a persona remain a calculated device, and when does it become the object of an inner identification? Are there circumstances that favor one possibility over the other, individuals who are predisposed to one rather than the other?

Although each person's history is its own answer to these questions, outlining the stages people tended to go through when assuming a non-Jewish identity brings to light shared aspects of the experience. While some chose taking on a non-Jewish identity from among various possibilities for attempting to escape persecution, others were forced into it for lack of an alternative—a difference that, in itself, might not be without implications. But however they came to the assumed identity, Jews who led active lives in the guise of non-Jews were obliged to craft personas, and those personas were continuous to differing degrees with their cultural background, level of education, and place in society. Similarly, a persona might be in harmony or in discord with the overt personality of the individual who adopted it, or might even reflect an inner reality that had not reached the surface in prewar life.

Nor was this persona necessarily crafted once for all: It often evolved as life went along, and not only its outward manifestation but also its place in its crafter's personal universe might change. Some people had a conscious strategy for managing their personas and kept control of them, making deliberate use of them as tools. But others appeared to grow into theirs emotionally, to the point that the persona might compete with or even displace the "original" personality. To what extent this depended on circumstances—on the length of time during which someone was known to the world exclusively under the assumed identity, perhaps, or on the magnitude of the danger to which he or she was exposed—and to what extent on some inner match between the original and assumed identities can only be guessed.

Finally, behavior associated with living under an assumed identity, or features of the persona itself, could remain in evidence long after the danger had passed. Were some afraid to give up whatever it was they felt had saved them? Had the disguise, or the experience of wearing it, become so bound up with who they were that they could no longer cast it off? Or had the personas been representations, or provided completions, of who they had been in the first place?

Of the three whose stories make up this section, Maurits Hirsch appears to have taken the most care to maintain a distinction between the identity he had assumed and what was at his core. But even so, his program included moments when, as he puts it, "you took the liberty to think again as you had before—and, actually, to rebel." This rebellion— against his circumstances, the pressure of holding in his feelings, the reality of the persecution—took a symbolic form that suggests that, despite his conscious handling of his persona, he occasionally needed to bridge a gap in himself that living under the assumed identity had created.

Romulus Berliner seems also to have leaned on symbolism, but in a far less self-conscious way. No sooner had he assumed his disguise, in the shape of an SS uniform, than he revealed his original identity to a fellow Jew—after which, he says, he "turned around, and was gone." After three years of living exclusively under the non-Jewish identity, at the very instant that he no longer needed it to protect him, he informed his commanding officer in the SS that he was a Jew. Although at times Romulus made a deliberate effort to see himself as a German, a temperamental inclination not to notice conflict may have contributed more to the success of his persona.

For Gabriel Ritter, it was the possibility not of continuing but of breaking with the past—the past of a Jew whose entire life had been lived as an Untermensch*—that gave the non-Jewish identity its allure. But he also had compelling examples: Richard III and Hamlet, both of whom felt wronged by the corrupt behavior of the powers that be, and both of whom used role playing to seek revenge; and his mother, whose talent for deception could turn oppression into triumph. Becoming a stage actor after the war allowed Gabriel to make the "transformation," as he calls it, a permanent part of his life; it also put him in a position to make some unique observations on the relationship of role and identity.

------

*Untermensch: subhuman; a term applied by Nazis to Jews, Slavs, and others they considered inferior to the "Aryan race."

Maurits Hirsch

For Maurits Hirsch, as for many of the 80,000 Jews who lived in Amsterdam before World War II, being Jewish was an unquestioned fact of existence. Although his home and business were in a mixed neighborhood rather than in one of the city's more exclusively Jewish quarters, Maurits says his life took its rhythm from the Jewish calendar, with its days of celebration and of fasting, the way a country dweller's life takes its rhythm from nature, with its seasonal changes. The obligations of orthodox Jewish life never occasioned a second thought: "I had a store that actually should have been open on Saturday, but on Shabbat you absolutely did not do certain things, whatever the cost," he recalls.

During the mid-1920s, Maurits worked in a diamond factory. It was when hard times hit toward the end of the decade and the work dried up that he started a grocery store, reasoning, "People have to eat, even during a depression." In 1935 he married, and the couple had sons in 1937 and 1939.

Maurits says he felt "a certain uneasiness" when the Germans occupied Holland in May 1940 but that in general "people didn't believe that what was happening in Germany could happen here" and that he himself "just carried on" with his grocery business "as if nothing were afoot." By 1942, however, Jewish-owned businesses were being increasingly taken over by "Aryan" administrators, and although Maurits managed to hold on to his store, it operated under severe restrictions. Non-Jews were forbidden to patronize it, and what Maurits was allowed to sell he describes as "extremely limited."

At the same time, Maurits was put in charge by the Joodse Raad, the "Jewish Council" set up by the occupying authorities under the guise of creating self-administration for Jewish affairs in Holland, of procuring foodstuffs for the 3,000 Jews per week who were being sent on to Poland from the transit camp at

Westerbork in the northeast of the country. The rations officially allowed the deportees were "minimal," Maurits recalls, but he and his colleagues managed to supplement them through dealings both with politically reliable clerks in Amsterdam who illicitly provided extra ration coupons and with manufacturers who were willing to sell more than the group's supply of coupons could cover.

Although Maurits's status as an essential worker in theory protected him and his family from arrest, and although few at the time suspected the true fate of those deported to what were believed to be labor camps in "the East," the time of the roundups was one of enormous anxiety for the Hirsches.

You'd sit at home, and you could see the raid vans of the Grüne Polizei* come for your neighbors: Next door, across the street, the people were being taken from their homes. So what did you do? You went and packed your own rucksack with your most necessary things and had the rucksack standing in a corner ready to go, because when they came, you didn't get any time.

And you waited. You weren't in shape to do anything in the evening, because you just sat waiting to see whether or not you'd be picked up. Every evening, over and over again, my wife and I played backgammon—a game we can't even look at anymore—trying to distract ourselves from the fact that the bell might ring. And when the bell did ring, you were in mortal fear, thinking, "They've come to get me." The fear is a weight on you for your entire life, because of course it is no normal fear: It is a fear of people who are going to do something to you that you have no idea of.

When the German Security Police got around to those on the lists of persons officially exempted from arrest, the bell at the Hirsch apartment finally did begin to ring. Once, "feeling that something was amiss," Maurits "spread Lysol around so that the whole house stank of it" and came to the door bearing a scarlet fever quarantine certificate obtained through an acquaintance in public health. "The Germans were afraid of contagious diseases," Maurits explains, "so they left without taking us." On two subsequent occasions, Maurits's connection with the Joodse Raad saved him: once officially, when his status as an essential worker won release for him and his wife after they had been picked up in a street roundup,

---

*Grüne Polizei: green police (German); nickname in Holland for the German Security Police, from the color of their uniforms.

and once unofficially, when his whole family was allowed by Jewish guards who knew them to sneak away from a crowded detention area.

Although Maurits claims he "tried in every possible way, and for as long as possible, to postpone the moment" of arrest, certain steps were ruled out. He and his wife "neither considered, nor even discussed" going into hiding: "On the one hand, you had of course put too much faith in the idea that you were 'indispensable,' " he explains. "On the other, I always felt that going into hiding meant passing your own risks on to another: I was in danger of being picked up as it was, but anyone I went into hiding with would also be risking arrest for me, and I never wanted to drag down people who were doing me a favor." And at a moment when his exemption had suddenly become invalid, Maurits turned down a friend's offer to help him buy his way onto the so-called 120,000 List—purportedly the safest, but almost certainly the least savory of all exemptions lists, with places costing a large sum of money. Shortly after he and his wife had made this decision—they "couldn't see" providing the enemy with means "to further the conduct of the war," he explains—their exempt status was restored. Recalling the accelerating cycle of detention and release, Maurits remarks, "You'd say to yourself, 'Thank goodness I got out of that!' but you'd still sit there waiting for the next time."

Maurits temporarily survived the "sorting" of exempt personnel, one of the most controversial and heartbreaking chapters in the history of Dutch Jewry, ending up among the final few hundred of the 17,000 originally protected by the Joodse Raad as essential workers. But by the summer of 1943 there were scarcely any clients for the Joodse Raad's services, since most of the Jews living on Dutch soil—just over 140,000, according to an official list compiled in mid-1941—had disappeared either into camps or into hiding. Thus, this last list of exempted workers became an arrest roll.

I knew beforehand that they were going down the list and that I would presumably be included, but as we didn't want to go into hiding, we simply stayed at home, saying, "We'll get out, despite everything."

Across the street lived a former maid of ours, and when I suspected they would come, I went to see this young lady and said, "Listen, Jenny, it's possible we will be taken away this evening. Do me a favor: Keep an eye out, and go tell So-and-so when we've been taken away. Then they'll be able to take steps immediately and perhaps we can come back."

She began to cry: "Oh, how awful! You and the kiddies, too! I will certainly keep an eye out, and go straight to the person as soon as I've seen it. . . . But," she said, "it is of course possible that you won't be coming back. Couldn't you put that coal stove of yours outside? It's such a lovely stove, and then I can have it and the Germans won't get it." She was a first-rate girl, but that's just the way people thought: "If you don't come back, at least I'll have your stove."

This time, Maurits found no way out, and he and his family spent eight weeks in Westerbork, where they lived the emotions of the weekly transport selection.

Every Tuesday evening there was a horrible fear, because you never knew whether you yourself were going on transport. You had to get ready; then the Germans came into the barrack where you were and called off the names, and those who were on the transport were put into cattle cars. And if you experienced how cheerful those people were— their relief that it was over, their conviction that they would be rescued even before they reached the Dutch-German border, the jokes that they told! The family members stood there by the train weeping—it often took a while before the trains left—and the people in the trains were in better spirits than those who stayed behind. They were glad that the tension was past—that "yes/not yet" of Tuesday evening, that fight to get a place on a nontransport list from the camp commandant, whose actions were arbitrary—and they said, "Oh, don't get so worked up! Everything will be fine. Long before we get to the other labor camps, we'll be set free!" It was unbelievable when you realized, later, that these people were on their way to the gas chambers. And you would say that, if in such frightful circumstances they could still keep heart, then this people, this Jewish people, is not to be broken.

Maurits appealed for release on the ground that his services were still needed, and, in a move that was "apparently not entirely legal," he and his family were returned to Amsterdam. Upon arrival, the Hirsches found their apartment stripped bare—as a matter of policy, the Germans confiscated the belongings of deported Jews—and they accepted an invitation to move in with a close friend, Mrs. Porcelein, and her two sons. Mrs. Porcelein's husband had been deported after being denounced by a Jewish informer for violating currency regulations, and she had taken a lodger: a "good-looking" Austrian-Jewish immigrant named Spiegler, whom Maurits had observed "messing around" with German officers and who was now "shacking up" in her room with a member of the Dutch fascist party, the NSB. *"We knew it was a mortal danger,"* Maurits says, *"but I had no other address."*

Mrs. Porcelein and her sons owed their continued presence in Amsterdam to the sympathy of a prominent Dutch banker, who Maurits says "worked on both sides" and who had arranged a place on the 120,000 List for Mrs. Porcelein. Toward the end of September 1943, word came that the 120,000 exemption had become invalid—or, in the parlance of the time, had "burst."

Mrs. Porcelein immediately called the banker, who said, "Don't get upset. The exemption hasn't burst for you—they won't come to your place." But on the very night she called, they did come ring the bell.

We heard it was the Grüne Polizei. In great terror, Mrs. Porcelein rushed her two children, sleeping as they were, into our room. Then the Grüne Polizei entered the house, and everyone had to go: Mrs. Porcelein, who was on the list, and Mrs. Spiegler and the NSBer, whom they ran into by chance. Mrs. Spiegler was in good with the occupation authorities and made no attempt to stay out of the way; she had papers stating she wasn't to be taken in, but they weren't crediting anything and couldn't have cared less about her protests. Before they were taken out, we heard the police ask, "Are there any more people in the house?" Mrs. Spiegler said no—she was absolutely nuts about Mrs. Porcelein's children, and I figured that's why she had done it. Then, while the others were sitting in the van, the police came back to search the house.

If I'd had the 120,000 exemption, I would have been taken away at the same time, so not being on the list saved me; but I cannot explain how they didn't come into the room where my wife and I lay, on one twin bed, with the four children. It was one of the biggest rooms in the house—a suite with communicating doors, which of course were closed—and they looked through all the other rooms. They went to the veranda in back, and they even took things from the coal bin. They looked very closely at everything.

It took them an hour and a half to search the house, and to rob it—they stole a fur coat, the silver, whatever they could find—and we were just lying there. At that point, I was perhaps the most frightened that I was in the entire war: afraid that they might still come into the room at the last second; and that we'd have to go, too, and without taking anything with us, because we were not at all prepared. And people's fear is so odd: At a certain moment I said to my wife, "I can't hold out any longer. If they don't come in now, I am going to report to them myself, because I simply must go to the toilet." I didn't think at all, "I'll just do it in my pants." But by then they had finished.

Then I thought to myself, "That Mrs. Spiegler didn't inform on us because she's crazy about the children. When she comes back, though, she'll make sure one way or another that they don't take away those two, but she'll denounce us. So we have to leave."

Although Spiegler and her boyfriend were detained only a matter of hours, they would return to an empty apartment and a note from Maurits saying he had voluntarily reported for Westerbork. In the meantime, Maurits had arranged through a woman he knew as "an extraordinary underground worker" to have his wife and children, and Mrs. Porcelein's sons as well, brought into hiding. Still averse to passing on his own risks, he rejected an offer of an "address" where he could hide and struck out on his own.

Visiting a resistance connection in search of false papers, Maurits was offered a prized variety: the authentic identity card of a man who had died, on which Maurits's own photo and fingerprints were to be affixed. As it would take time to prepare the card and to sneak his fingerprints into the population files in The Hague—thus making the card "totally official"—Maurits was forced to stall. In the weeks that followed he ran through four hideouts, but when he was at last able to pick up the papers, he traveled by bicycle up the Rhine and "landed" in a town of several thousand inhabitants. Finding the setting "peaceful and pretty," he rented rooms at the home of the mailman, and, near the end of 1943, began life under the name of Rudolphus Johannes de Lange.

When I arrived they of course asked about my baggage. I told them that a suitcase had been sent from Amsterdam, and later that I had filled out a declaration that the suitcase had disappeared. But as my house had been empty when I returned from Westerbork, all I had were the clothes on my back and those in the rucksack; no suitcase had ever been sent.

They also asked me what I did for a living. I said I was a salesman for a large flour mill in Groningen* and that I would be away during the day. But where was I supposed to go? I could hardly go anywhere, and certainly not to Amsterdam. If the weather was at all acceptable, I spent the whole day lying around an outdoor pool in another town in the

---

Groningen: a city in the northeast of the Netherlands.

region. Then, with my briefcase under my arm, I came back home and said that I'd sold a lot that day, or perhaps that I hadn't done very well at all.

Although he was in contact with local underground operatives, Maurits was not active—"there wasn't much I could do for them at that time," he says—and lived uneventfully over nine months. In mid-September 1944, however, the Allies' Operation Market-Garden brought major fighting to Dutch soil, and evacuees surged down the Rhine from the area of Arnhem. Responding to a call for volunteers, Maurits—using, of course, the name of de Lange—took up a post at the town hall registering the refugees, calculating and distributing financial aid to them, and placing them with families.

You saw some really tragic things when the people arrived, because they had fled suddenly and brought only the barest necessities with them, but they hadn't known at that moment what the necessities really were. A man rode in on a bicycle carrying a few butchered rabbits around his neck because "it would be a pity to leave them for the Germans," and a chamber pot because "you never know when you might need a chamber pot," but for the rest he had nothing. These people were completely at a loss.

The plight of the refugees and the fact that municipal officials were themselves "at wits' end" trying to deal with them initially induced Maurits to offer his services; as he very quickly discovered, the town hall was also "a first-class place for information." When the Wehrmacht decided to establish a local garrison office, or Ortskommandantur, in the town, Maurits was asked by operatives connected with British Intelligence to report on contacts between the Germans and the municipal staff, so he spent as much time as he could at the town hall. He sometimes spent evenings there, including one that featured a reception attended by the "relatively high-ranking" Wehrmacht officer who was supervising the installation of the Ortskommandantur, as well as some local notables.

The Germans were reasonably lubricated by the end. The mayor and deputy mayor, both NSBers who had been named when the original mayor had gone into hiding, didn't open their mouths; this German officer disliked them for some reason, and he ignored them totally. Then, at a certain moment, the officer said, "There are three Bürgermeisters here—a blond one, a black-haired one, and a brown-haired one." The blond one was the secretary of the municipality, and an NSBer; the brown-haired one was a clerk of the civil registry, and an NSBer as well; and the black-haired one was me.

Drinking didn't do much for me—I've never been crazy about it—but I could hold it real well. And I spoke reasonably good German. The other two didn't speak such good German, and apparently weren't as quick-witted as I was; after a while they fell by the wayside, so that only the "black-haired Bürgermeister" was left. The next day, the German barred the mayor and deputy mayor from the town hall, and I was named to the office of mayor.

In his new capacity, Maurits set up a public kitchen and instituted a health insurance scheme for the evacuees within his jurisdiction. He occasionally traveled in an official Wehrmacht vehicle to the Finance Ministry in The Hague, where hundreds of thousands of guilders in refugee aid were handed over to him personally. His presence was required at all conferences on military matters taking place at the town hall. "All doors were open to me," he says, "and, of course, I could then plunge in on behalf of the underground."

Maurits capitalized on his position in a number of ways. Exempted from curfew, he smuggled messages and contraband through the streets after dark. He tipped off the underground to a particularly large cash shipment he was to receive, although the planned robbery was called off after a big bank job made Maurits's "crummy million" superfluous. When the Germans confiscated the specially adapted bicycle of a one-legged man—who because of his infirmity was one of the few in town still allowed a bike and who therefore generally functioned as a messenger for the underground—Maurits simply bellowed until the official responsible handed the bike back over. And he was more involved than ever in the task of gathering intelligence, which he passed on to London over a transmitter the messenger kept in his basement. "At a certain moment," Maurits notes, "his house was requisitioned by the German unit charged with searching out clandestine transmitters, which made for a really crazy situation: They were upstairs, and we had the transmitter down below."

But since we knew exactly when they were out searching, we kept on transmitting. When I heard at the town hall that the SS planned to set up a headquarters in a castle on the road out of town, I passed it along right away. Shortly thereafter, Lancasters flew over, but they missed; the bombs fell in the woods, and the castle was left standing. I was called in by the Wehrmacht and told, "Mr. Mayor, now that there's been a bombing, the SS headquarters will not be set up here. But there must be a traitor here in town, because so few people knew that a headquarters was coming. It's your job to find the traitor." Well, it wasn't all that difficult. . . . But when I went back to him the next day, I told him that

I didn't see any possibility of finding out who in God's name had been blabbing to England because with the suppliers and so forth there were, after all, quite a number of people who knew about it.

Relations between Maurits and the Wehrmacht captain who was given the job of Ortskommandant bordered on the cordial.

I went to see the Ortskommandant every evening. He was a very friendly fellow, and I got along with him fine. I had long talks with him, and the only thing was that he had a terrible dislike for the Jews. "The damned Jews!" he would say. "Filth! Swine! They are to blame for the war!"

"Why?" I asked. "I worked for Jewish people in Amsterdam, and I had fine experiences with them. How many Jews do you know?"

"Not a single one, thank God!" he said. "But Goebbels says they are bad, so they're bad."

"Well," I said, "I don't agree with you."

He was not really a bad guy—he was just a normal soldier, a pure Wehrmacht man who was only following his orders. Sadly enough, at the end he was transferred to the front, and he fell there.

The Ortskommandant's amiability provided Maurits a number of strategic advantages. During his nightly visits, he was able to listen surreptitiously to the BBC in the living room while his host was busy cooking dinner in the kitchen. He also obtained the Ortskommandant's unwitting cooperation in sneaking shot-down British fliers out of the district and toward Holland's liberated south.

I was responsible for getting the Tommies across the Rhine. They were given other clothes to wear, and were forbidden to speak, but they had to have papers to cross over on the ferry. Every day, there were municipal documents for the Ortskommandant to sign, sometimes a dozen pieces or more. When I came to see him I'd set them all out on top of each other, overlapping like shingles, and he'd take out his pen and say, "Do I have to sign?"

I'd say, "Yes, you have to sign."

"Whatever you put before me," he'd say, "I sign, no questions asked." And then he signed all the letters, and there would be two or three ID cards among them, personally signed by the Ortskommandant for the Tommies.

Things did not always go so smoothly. There were occasional reminders that the two men were not equals—as when the Ortskommandant, angered by Mau-

rits's evident obstruction of orders to round up men for forced labor, pulled a revolver on him and could have shot him down with impunity. Although Maurits was able to persuade him to put the gun away—"*You can kill me only once,*" *he pointed out,* "*and then all the things I do for you, you'll have to do for yourself*"—*he was not able with any consistency to avoid situations in which his conflicting responsibilities as mayor and resistance worker put him on a tightrope.*

At a certain moment, I got a message from the Ortskommandant saying that there were a number of SS arriving who needed shelter. As mayor, I was supposed to know all the houses and their inhabitants, and I was to requisition living quarters. Well, I had no desire to put the SS with the good people, and I had already requisitioned quarters with the NSBers and the pro-Germans and the other people whom we as underground workers didn't like. I gave those addresses again, and the Ortskommandant said, "You're always giving the same addresses."

"I don't know any others," I said.

Then the car of the Oberscharführer came to pick me up at the town hall, and I had to go along and point out where there was room. I indicated those same few addresses, but then we came to a large farmhouse just at the side of the road, and he said, "What about there?"

There were at least eight Tommies in a second farmhouse behind, and I didn't have the faintest idea what to do—not for myself, but for the farmers. "They don't have any space," I said.

"Well," said the Oberscharführer, "I'm still going to look."

There was no way around it, I had to go along. We ring, and the farmer's wife comes to the door and sees that they are SS, and she sees me, the mayor—she had no way of knowing that I was all right, she of course thought, "The mayor is also an NSBer" or whatever.

I say, "Madam, the gentlemen here are looking for living quarters and they want to have a look around."

She says, "I don't have any room at all."

Then he says, "We'll just have a little look for ourselves."

That woman was practically dead from fright. We walked through the main house to the back and suddenly I got an idea. "Oberscharführer," I said. "Watch out! This next house is not clean."

"What?"

"Be careful: This house is full of lice."

So he said to the woman, "Just forget it." And we left.

In the line of both his mayoral and his resistance duties, Maurits hid his true identity from everyone.

Of course, you have to have a background, and you can't tell it differently from one time to the next. Since you can slip if you make things up, I based my background as much as possible on reality, only I told everything in the third person instead of the first. I didn't say, "I had a grocery store"; I said, "My boss had a grocery store." And my boss was married—I was single—and my boss had two children. I could thus tell things from my own life, saying, "That happened to my boss," or "I know about that, my boss told me that once." And when I really had a longing to talk about the children, then I said, "Ach, that boss of mine, he had such lovely children! And did I get along great with those two kids—I was plumb crazy about them!" In this way, I could never make a mistake.

Maurits used a variation on this story in keeping a distance from the young woman with whom he let himself be seen in public in order to discourage the attentions of the town's social-climbing parents.

All the families who had marriageable daughters thought, "A mayor must be loaded with money," and they were extra friendly to me. It got to be rather a nuisance, so I decided to take a steady girlfriend. Now and then, I went for walks with her—no further—and people said, "He is going with that girl." But it wasn't true at all, and I had told her right off that she shouldn't get anything into her head, because I was actually waiting for the war to be over to marry a Jewish woman I had known in Amsterdam, a widow with two children.

She told me at times, "You are still young—I don't understand why you would take a woman with two children."

"Yes," I'd say, "but I love those children as if they were my own."

This strategy provided Maurits not only with a consistent and acceptable life history but also with some continuity between the past and present. In a similar way, he sought an equivalent for the religious life he had known before the war.

Living there as a non-Jew, you no longer belonged anywhere—you were a so-called Christian, although you weren't a Christian as far as religion was concerned. But even though you couldn't let it be seen that you were a Jew, you still had certain moments when you had a longing—not for God, but for a spiritual word, if I can put it that way. So, now and then, I went to the Reformed church.

The church itself didn't do much for me, although the Reformed church is very austere, just like ours; a Catholic church—with pictures all over, and kneeling, and other things that go totally against your grain—would have been a lot more difficult. But going to church, you translated a feeling into another language, actually; and once in a while you could have a talk with someone about it, which you had a longing for as well.

It was a matter of living your way totally into another role; and the better you could do that, the less risk you had that you'd get caught. There was a Jewish boarder in town who didn't live so much in his role, although he had not been orthodox at all before the war but actually stood quite a ways off from Jewishness. I knew him from the time before I was mayor or had much contact with the underground, and originally I didn't know he was a Jew; he didn't speak broken Dutch like the Polish-Jewish woman who was in hiding there with her son, and he wasn't from Amsterdam, so he didn't have an Amsterdam accent. But I once walked by the market when fish was being sold—a shipment had come in, which didn't happen every day—and when I saw him standing there buying fish, I thought to myself, "That man is a Jew."

Suppose you asked, "From what did you see that he was a Jew?" Simply the way he looked at and bought the fish made me think, "That's what I used to see by the fish stands in the Jewish Quarter." It was just a feeling; it wasn't as if someone else would have said right off, "He must have been haggling over the price," or whatever. Not at all. As I had had a store in a non-Jewish neighborhood, I could see the difference quite clearly: The Christian people aren't better and the Jews aren't worse for it, but Jews are more aware of what they are buying, and he was really looking intently at the fish. So you had to follow through even on little details, to the point that if I had been buying fish at that moment, I wouldn't have done it the way he did.

There were, in fact, 1,001 little things that you did differently than you were used to. For example, I couldn't get any kosher food and had to eat what there was, but for a very long time I kept up not smoking on Saturday without anyone being the wiser. When I became mayor, however, and had contact with people at the town hall and smoked the whole week, it would have been conspicuous if I had then suddenly refused a cigarette on Saturday. So that I had to do that also: that is, live as the others lived.

In the beginning, you of course paid attention to everything you did. You thought, "Be careful! I can't do that as I have always done, because I'll attract attention here. I am no longer among my own kind of people"—by which I don't mean Jews, but my own group, which included Jews and non-Jews—"but I am now in a totally different sort of world. And I am now going to do things the way they're done here, because that's what the people understand."

But after a while it was no longer necessary to pay attention; as you found your way into it, it gradually became easier. It's like someone who speaks a foreign language well: You think in the language, and you don't have to stop and say, "Wait a minute, I have to translate this word first." The role you played during those years was something you had to etch into your entire body. You actually changed color completely, like a chameleon.

And, in thinking just like the people around you, you switched your neshoma* out. Earlier, if you had been talking about health, you'd say, "He should live to 120 years," or "I feel very well, unbeschrieje, unberufe."† But of course no one knows those things among the non-Jews, so you just talked about illness and about death as was the custom there.

And when you talked about the events of the war, about the Germans, about the Nazi Party, you assented to certain arguments, whereas in your normal life you would have said, "Where do you get that? You're nuts!" People sometimes said, "Yes, the Jews are being picked up, but perhaps it serves some of them right." You started to argue against that and said, "I wouldn't know why—there are bad people among us as well, not only among the Jews"; but you couldn't oppose it as vehemently as you would have wanted to, because then they might have said, "Why is it that *you* are so opposed?" And when you joined in a religious discussion, you didn't say, "There's nothing original in all that, it's all been taken over from the Jews." You had to impose limits on your expression.

But that doesn't mean you imposed limits on your feelings. There

---

neshoma: Yiddish corruption of Hebrew word for *soul;* means "the Jewish side of one's personality" colloquially among Dutch Jews.

†*unbeschrieje, unberufe:* Yiddish equivalent of "touch wood"; used to take a jinx off.

were times when I said to myself, "All those people gone, separated from wife and children—how is it possible?" I didn't know very much at that point. I knew that people were being sent away to Poland, but we hadn't heard a thing about gassing, and we thought they would surely come back from the camps. I myself had been in Westerbork, and there people lived without freedom: They had to wait to eat, they had to wait to sleep, they were forced to do things they didn't want to do; for the rest, though, they weren't beaten, and they weren't done to death.

But once in a while you went for a ride on your bike, and then you took the liberty to think again as you had before—and, actually, to rebel. I very often sang a Yiddish song to myself; I no longer know the exact words, but it went something like this:

> *Gott und Sein mishpet sind gerecht.*
> *Man kann doch auch nicht sogen, 'Gott is schlecht.'*
> *Gott weiss was Er tut,*
> *Und wir sind Sein kinderlein.*
> *Und Gott und Sein mishpet sind gerecht.**

---

*As Maurits sang it, the song is more German than Yiddish. Literally translated, it means:
> God and His judgment are just.
> One can't say, after all, "God is bad."
> God knows what He's doing.
> And we are His little children.
> And God and His judgment are just.

This appears to be Maurits's recollection of a popular song that, according to a researcher at the YIVO Institute for Jewish Research in New York, was "known to [Yiddish] theatergoers throughout the world" earlier in this century. The transliteration of the song as quoted by YIVO goes:
> Az got un zayn mishpet iz gerekht.
> Men tor keyn mol nit zogn, az got is shlekht;
> Vayl got veyst vos er tut,
> Umzist shtroft er keynem nit;
> Got un zayn mishpet iz gerekht!

The translation differs slightly from Maurits's version:
> God and His judgment are just;
> One may never say that God is bad;
> Because God knows what He's doing,
> And punishes no one without reason;
> God and His judgment are just!

I sang that song as a way of expressing something. But maybe you're not convinced that that's how it is—after all, we cannot grasp that what God did to the Jews is good. You may be able to say it, and you may be able to sing it, but you can't really feel it; that's an impossibility. Still, that was a return you made now and then to the rebellion you felt in yourself.

Otherwise, you lived as if you no longer knew any other life. You had your occupations, you knew you were doing good work; and you lived alone, as a so-called bachelor. You had no idea where the children were or whether they were still alive, and while you knew somewhere far off where your wife was, you reasoned, "She'll have to take care of herself if she's going to make it through." The fear was not nearly as great as before, when you weren't afraid only for yourself, but also for your family—you now had no idea who would and who wouldn't make it through the war, and it left you pretty much indifferent. I actually have the feeling that I wasn't afraid at all—although presumably I really was, deep down. But I thought, "What more can happen to me now? Here I am, and I'll just have to take what comes."

Maurits claims that no one—not even his closest associate in the resistance—knew until after the war that he was a Jew. The one person in town who did have a suspicion was the man whose fish-buying gaze had betrayed him as a Jew to Maurits. On several occasions, he tried to draw Maurits out with references from Jewish culture—a greeting of "Sholem aleichem," or a remark comparing a string of eight empty machine-gun cartridges Maurits had found to a Chanukah menorah. Each time, Maurits pretended not to understand, something that he says the fellow held against him following the liberation.

Maurits's "principle of not telling anyone" was inviolate. Finding himself face-to-face in a train with a woman he knew well—and of whom he was "not particularly frightened," as he knew her to be a resistance operative—Maurits spoke of small-town life and of the profession of flour salesman. She later confessed that she had been completely taken in, although she had remarked to herself that her fellow passenger and Maurits "resembled each other like two peas in a pod." In The Hague on an errand, Maurits was spotted by a former neighbor from Amsterdam, a Nazi sympathizer who circled him three times on a bicycle before Maurits accosted him with an impatient "What's eating you?" Maurits then denied outright his true name and background, replying to the man's statement "I would have sworn that you were that Jew" with "Then you would have sworn a false oath," and finally convincing him to move on. "He knew that I knew that he was an NSBer," recalls Maurits, "so if I hadn't come up to him, or if I had run away, he would of course have come after me. It was a frightening moment, but one thing I had learned is that you have to look danger in the face."

Although Maurits describes himself as having been abstracted from the fate of his family, he did have periods of intense longing. Believing his sons to be in the area of Utrecht, he once made a bicycle trip of several days along the road to Amsterdam hoping to catch a glimpse of them. "My oldest son was six, so I stood in front of the schools, just close enough by to see the children go in and come out," *he recalls. "I wouldn't have spoken to him, I just wanted to be able to say, 'I see, he's there, he's still alive.'" Maurits's goal eluded him; by that time, his children had been brought to the province of Friesland in the far north of the Netherlands.*

In contrast, he had been able, through resistance channels, to carry on a regular correspondence with his wife, who had been in hiding with a family on the outskirts of Amsterdam. Although the family who hid her "did a great deal of resistance work," Maurits feels they exploited his wife "by having her work for virtually nothing" as a maid and governess; he was also incensed that, alerted to the possibility of a raid on their house, they fled without warning his wife and returned only when the danger was past. As the threat of raids increased, and as food supplies dwindled to the point that she began to develop edema from malnutrition, Mrs. Hirsch temporarily joined her brother in hiding back in town. Through "connections," Maurits had a letter brought to her there in which he suggested that he might be able to take better care of her himself.

On a snowy day in late 1944, following a raid on her brother's hiding address, Mrs. Hirsch put her rucksack on her back and, as hitchhiking was the only available means of transportation, positioned herself by the side of the road to Utrecht. She was lucky with rides—all of which came in Wehrmacht vehicles, the only vehicles on the road—and completed a journey she had expected to last several days by the end of the morning. She asked a boy she met in the street if he knew a Mr. de Lange—"Do you mean the mayor?" he replied—and gave him an unsigned note to deliver saying that she had arrived and was going to the house of the one-legged messenger, whose address Maurits had given her.

I got a note at the town hall, and I saw from the handwriting that it was from my wife. I said to the man from the civil registry that I had an errand to do and left the town hall immediately for the house of that friend. When I went in, there was my wife; I hadn't seen her, or heard anything from her, in so long.

"May I introduce you?" my friend said. "Mrs. van Hoorn, Mr. de Lange."

"Delighted, ma'am."

"A pleasure, sir."

She had false papers; her story was that she was the widow of an underground worker who had been executed in Vught.* I asked her if she had had a good trip, and she said, "It was all right."

"Well, ma'am," I said, "you have to be registered here in town, and I have an address where you'll probably be able to live, so just come to the town hall at one o'clock."

Only four or five people worked at the town hall, and all but one went home for lunch. I said to the municipal secretary, who was supposed to stay that day, "I'll be here through the noon hour, so you can just go home," and I sat down to wait. There was a knock, and my wife came in; that was the first time that I actually saw her and that we could talk. But she hadn't even gotten to the desk—because I sat in a kind of corner behind a really big desk—when the door opened and the Ortskommandant came in.

"I would like you to come by and see me for a bit," he says. "Can you come to the Ortskommandantur at two?"

"Jawohl, Herr Hauptmann!" I say. "Alles in Ordnung!"

My wife was standing there trembling; after all the times she'd been picked up, she was afraid of uniforms. Then he comes up to me, and puts his arm around my shoulders, and says, "Ach, my dear friend, mein lieber Bürgermeister, I see that you have a visitor. . . ."

Later, my wife said, "It was then that I knew that you really were mayor." I had written it to her, but she had more or less disregarded it; she couldn't get it through her head. And when I went to see the Ortskommandant at two, he said, "That was a good-looking woman you had visiting you. You know what I thought? That you two would make a good couple."

"I want to," I said, "but she doesn't"—at that point, we'd been married ten years.

Then he patted me on the shoulder and said, "Never say die! You'll win the day yet!"

Maurits lodged his wife with another Jewish woman living in town under an assumed identity and supplemented her rations with food he received from

---

Vught: concentration camp in Holland used extensively for political detainees.

farmers in the area who wished to stay on the mayor's good side. For the sake of caution, the couple kept open contacts to a minimum.

While neither of us looked obviously Jewish, and nobody asked either of us "are you a Jew?" or anything like that, we both had black hair, and I was afraid that if we were together, people might say, "They're the very image of a Jewish couple."

But I still wanted to speak with her alone, so she would go into the woods from one side, and I from the other; we would meet and walk a ways, and then go back to our own houses. At a certain moment I thought, "What kind of rubbish is this? I'm the mayor here, I myself have performed a marriage. I'll just marry my wife, and then we can go live together." We even entered our names at the registry office, but a certain time has to elapse, and the liberation came before I could marry my own wife for the second time.

The liberation did not arrive before Maurits went through a final and harrowing scrape. Among his resistance duties, he was in charge of producing documents London deemed "necessary for after the war": He would personally oversee the setting, printing, and binding of the material—as well as the destruction of the proofs—at a local printer's, then take it to a farm in the region where silver fox were being bred for the Germans' use and bury it alongside weapons and other contraband hidden by the local underground beneath the animals' cages. In April 1945, several weeks before the occupation ended, Maurits left the printer's carrying a packet containing twenty copies of "one or another of the silly books that had to be made up under orders from England—some kind of form that would have to be filled out after the war," and walked toward his home.

On the way, I saw a few SS on bicycles and thought, "I don't like their looks. They don't belong here—what have they come to do? It's …I don't know, it's dangerous." But I kept walking. I went to the baker's, which was across from where I lived, and the baker says, "There were a few Germans here, and they were asking after you." With the package under my arm, I head for home, but while I am in the front yard I see a glimmer of a German uniform inside and think, "Oh, jeez, this package I have on me is a mortal danger." So I walk around to the back of the house, and I put the package in the barn—just on a table in the barn— and I close the door.

When I come out, they're already waiting for me by the back door. They say, "Are you de Lange?"

"Jawohl!"

"Come inside!" Well, I come inside. He says, "What were you doing in the barn?"

"The barn? What are you talking about?"

"Yes, why did you go to the barn first?"

"Well, that's simple," I say. "I went by the baker's, and they told me that someone was asking after me"—which was the truth, someone *was* asking after me—"and I thought, 'I don't see anyone, maybe they're in the barn.' So I had a look in the barn, but no one was there."

I believe there were five of them, and he says to one, "Go see what he's hidden in the barn."

I think, "They don't have far to look, because that package is lying right there on the table."

In the meantime he made me come with him to my rooms, and it turned out that they'd gone through everything: cut open the mattresses, ripped up my clothing—in short, the place was a shambles. I had to strip naked and sit against the wall, and I got a machine gun in my belly. He says, "He'll be right back, and then we'll see what we've found. And we'll finish you off, because it's got to be weapons."

So I was actually sitting there waiting to be shot when the fellow came upstairs and said, "We've found it. So now tell us what it was that happened yesterday."

Hearing this, Maurits figured that "they can't have found it." If they really did discover the booklets, he reasoned, they wouldn't be bothering with trying to entrap him; and, as later appeared, the SS man had been so intent on finding weapons that, although he had started unwrapping the package, he'd set it aside without taking a close look once he had seen that it contained books. Lacking hard evidence against him, the SS then questioned Maurits regarding an incident of the previous day that had attracted their attention to him in the first place.

They say, "We caught a spy yesterday, and he said that you were the head of the underground."

"You mean," I ask, "that guy sitting there in the wood? I went riding by there"—which they had certainly seen—"but I don't know him." The day before, I had gone on my bike to another village in the neighborhood and on my way I had seen one of our messengers sitting against a tree. He was obviously being forced to sit there—they had put him there to see who would come to him—but I was sensible enough not to go up. I felt there was something strange in his sitting there, and

I just kept going. They then shot this young man dead; they buried him there also, and he was found later on.

All the while I was sitting there naked as a jaybird and, of course, frightened because I am circumcised. I was trying, through my impudence, to defend myself against the accusation that I was with the underground but, naked like that, I was thinking, "They'll see that I am a Jew, and then I can tell them what I will but they won't believe me anymore."

Not a word was said about it. "You have to report to the SD* in Zeist," they told me.

"All right," I said, "I'll go tomorrow."

"Yes, but what assurance do we have that you'll show up?"

"Well," I said, "I give you my word."

"Shit on your word!"

"Then confiscate my papers."

"You'll just have new papers tomorrow."

In the end, I managed to get them so crazy that they wrote in my papers, "This man has been declared outside the protection of the law and is banished to the west of the country as a danger to the state." Then he said, "You be at the SD tomorrow at thus-and-such a time."

Maurits's reaction to his unmasking recalled to him the feelings he had observed in those chosen for transport from Westerbork to "the East."

As long as you haven't been caught, you leave no stone unturned to avoid it, and that is what's so debilitating. But as soon as you have been picked up, then you have the certainty: "Now it's finally happened; that's the way it had to be, and I can't do anything about it anymore." And at this moment the fear was not so great, because I thought, "Well, here we are—it's all over, and now I no longer have to pass myself off as braver than I am." And I actually intended one hundred percent to report to the SD, until colleagues from the underground said, "You're nuts, you'll never get out of there alive. You know addresses, after all, so go into hiding." There was a house in the next town where they hid Tommies, and I stayed there a few weeks, until the liberation.

The war over, Maurits obtained the consent of his astonished landlady—

SD: Sicherheitsdienst; the Nazi Party intelligence organization, which worked in concert with the police.

who had never suspected that the dark-haired woman around the corner might be Mrs. Hirsch—to have his wife move in with him. Maurits soon bid his adopted hometown farewell to take a post in the provisional administration of the province of Utrecht. And shortly thereafter, armed with Canadian authorization to pass roadblocks and to use gasoline, which was in extremely short supply, the Hirsches embarked on a four-week drive through the Netherlands in search of their children. "Although we were liberated, these were not pleasant weeks," Maurits recalls. "Because it wasn't a question of knowing the children are alive and just having to look for them; we had to look for them to see whether they were alive." The Hirschs found forty hidden children and reported their whereabouts to relocation agencies before finally coming across their own sons.

After the liberation, Maurits found that he could not simply pick up where he had left off before he assumed the identity of Rudolphus de Lange; he needed some time to adjust.

Then you'd played a role, and now you were trying to become yourself again and to be yourself. Right after the war, you would do things and say afterwards, "Yes, but I can do it differently now." Becoming yourself consisted in realizing, "I don't have to do it that way anymore, or think about it that way anymore—I can, after all, just do it or think about it or say it in a way that feels normal to me." Those weren't big things, they weren't big decisions, but just the everyday things you had done differently then and could again do the way we were used to doing them.

Although Maurits's original habits and reactions gradually replaced those he had picked up during his time as de Lange, his level of religious practice never returned to what it had been before the war.

It was not a matter of "What has God done? He has murdered all those people," as you hear from time to time. It was that taking up again all the restrictions of a religious life is not so easy, particularly when you are building up a whole new existence, and conditions were a lot more difficult after the war as well. We had a kosher home and the children were raised properly, but you lost something for yourself. And I must say that I'm sorry about that, because before the war you lived more intensely as an orthodox Jew than after the war as a not-as-orthodox Jew.

At the time of the interview, Maurits, still active in business, lived with his wife in a comfortable house near Amsterdam's great museums. Two of his three sons—the third arriving after the war—maintain orthodox standards; the other is far less religious and, in Maurits's words, "laughs at us all." But while Maurits himself no longer practices quite as assiduously as in the days when he "went to shul [synagogue] as often as possible," he has no interest whatsoever in reform Judaism. "If you join the liberals," he says, "then this falls away, and you don't have to do this anymore, and that is no longer needed, and pretty soon there's not much left. And I'd find that really unfortunate, because, after all, the Jews have remained what they are through the centuries among other reasons because of their religion."

To sum up, Maurits calls on a metaphor that not only illustrates his point but also seems to recall the period during which his religion, his personal background, even his state of mind had to be adapted to the demands of an altered existence.

I consider the Jewish religion as a big building, built of stones. You might, at a given moment, pull down the top stones, and not a living soul would see it because the building would still be there. Then you'd think, "I can probably take another one off." But there comes a day when the building has disappeared, because you've kept taking more and more stones down.

If, on the other hand, you don't remove any stones—but you just don't use the building—you can always come back to it again. The building remains standing.

Romulus Berliner

Romulus Berliner was born in Transylvania in 1918, the year the Austro-Hungarian Empire was dissolved and that region, long under Hungarian rule, was incorporated into Rumania. The place of his birth—known as Cluj in Rumanian, Kolozsvar in Hungarian, and Klausenburg in German—counted some 10,000 Jews among its population of 85,000; it was a typical Balkan ethnic mixture that also included Rumanians, Magyars, and a small contingent of German speakers descended from the Saxon colonists of the twelfth century.

The Berliner household was strictly orthodox. Romulus's mother wore a wig in accordance with the married woman's obligation under Jewish law to cover her head; his father, though preferring modern dress to the caftan and broad-brimmed hat of the Chasid, was extremely religious. In addition to running the family's kosher restaurant, the elder Berliner devoted a great deal of time to the study of sacred matters and was considered a talmed chochem, or learned Jew.

Although Romulus, the Berliners' oldest son, accompanied his father to the synagogue every morning, he recalls this as a duty he discharged with neither conviction nor pleasure.

I don't know how it happened that, of six brothers and sisters, four were religious and two were not, but my older sister and I never had much feeling for the Jewish faith. My sister didn't deny that she was a Jew, but she had always been an "idealist"; and then, through people she met in school or some other way, she became a Communist, one hundred percent. I myself joined Hashomer Hatzair,* a left-organized

*Hashomer Hatzair: the left-wing Zionist youth organization.

group in which religion was regarded as something third-rate, but unlike my sister I wasn't at all interested in politics. I had exclusively Jewish friends, but my friends were nonreligious Jews like me who didn't keep Shabbat [the Sabbath] and didn't go to temple.

There is an episode I can remember that took place when I was seventeen or eighteen. It was Yom Kippur.* I went to temple in the morning, and at eleven o'clock or so I went for a walk with some friends. We paused in front of a pastry shop, and I was really hungry, so I looked left and then right and I walked into the shop. I sat down in a corner and ordered a plateful of cakes, but when I had taken one bite, I suddenly became so frightened that I left everything on the plate and went back to the temple. For days I lived with the fear: How will God punish me? But nothing happened, and from that day on I believed even less than before.

Whereas his brother and four sisters all went to Jewish schools, Romulus attended a Christian school from the age of eight or nine.

I had been a very naughty boy from early childhood—I didn't want to go to school at all and played hooky. There was a Christian school next door to where we lived that was very, very strict, and my father sent me there because he wanted to straighten me out and that seemed a possibility. I was the only Jew in this Rumanian Christian school, and occasionally someone said to me, "You stinking Jew." But that didn't bother me very much, and I never acknowledged it. I couldn't allow myself to notice it, because if I had, I would have had to hit the kid who said it to me—and then it would have come to no good.

Romulus left school in his early teens to work in a clothing store. In 1934, at the age of sixteen, he took a job as a salesman in Brasov,† about 120 miles southeast of Cluj, and quickly became manager of a clothing store. Things went well enough for him that, when his family ran into financial difficulties in 1937, he was able to help out.

Romulus was still in Brasov in 1940, when Hungary persuaded Germany

---

* *Yom Kippur:* the Day of Atonement, Judaism's most solemn holiday and a day of fasting.
†Although Romulus, speaking in German, used German-language place names, the names found on today's political maps are used here when there are no English equivalents. One exception, Stanislav, will be footnoted.

and Italy to move on its standing claim to Transylvania, and Rumania was forced to return a large portion of the territory it had received twenty-two years before. Because Cluj reverted to Hungary, whereas Brasov did not, Romulus was faced with a choice: "I had to decide whether I should stay in Rumania or go back home to my parents and my brother and sisters." He returned to Cluj, where he went into business for himself, opening a fabric store.

Neither the escalation of anti-Jewish measures in Germany nor the outbreak of war was seen as a personal threat by Romulus, who remembers "living normally" until 1941.

Up to 1940, we knew nothing at all about Germany, except that in '38 and '39 a large number of people from Poland and Czechoslovakia had come to Brasov and told us about the anti-Semitism and the pogroms. Still, we didn't pay much attention to that. There had always been anti-Semitism in Rumania, but it wasn't until the war started that there were pogroms—my young years had been lovely. Besides, I hadn't heard that much about the war itself—Czechoslovakia had been occupied and then Poland and part of Russia as well, but where I lived there had not yet been any deportations.

In 1941, however, Romulus joined the growing number of Jewish young men who, called up by the Hungarian government for "auxiliary service," were placed in camps run by the army and required to do heavy labor under the guard of Hungarian regular soldiers. Along with 1,200 other Jewish forced laborers, he was sent to Bretcu in eastern Transylvania.

We were in a huge camp in what had formerly been a tile factory. The conditions of life there were not so bad. There were gigantic structures that had been made into barracks where 200 people slept; there was no heating, of course, but we were dressed well and there were enough blankets, so it was all right. There were a few well-off fellows like me who were able to smuggle large quantities of food into the camp—farmers who lived nearby sold potatoes and chickens and so on—so that was no problem either. In comparison to what people went through later, it was a paradise. In comparison.

In the camp, the young men worked building roads, building bunkers—anything at all to keep us busy. When someone failed to carry out an order one hundred percent, he had to get down on his hands and knees on the floor of the toilet—practically lie on the floor—and, lying there, he had to clean out the filth. There were other, similar punishments, and some of the fellows were beaten.

Things went very well for me personally because I became friendly with the captain who was head of the camp and in whose office I worked as a clerk. As my parents sent a lot of packages and money to the captain's wife, who lived in Budapest, I was able to go home on vacation every two or three months. In the year I was in Bretcu, I went to Cluj at least seven times for between two or three days and a week.

After around a year in Bretcu, Romulus and his fellow prisoners were taken to the city of Stanislav* in southwestern Ukraine, which the German army was using as an assembly point for troops and matériel destined for the Russian front.

We made the trip in cattle cars, but there were only twenty people to a car, so it wasn't so bad. The problems started when we arrived: We were put in a huge camp, and the boys were taken out every morning at seven o'clock and had to build roads and bunkers until six in the evening. It was very heavy labor, but that wasn't so bad—what was bad was when supplies arrived from Germany by truck and they had to carry sacks of flour weighing ninety kilos up to the third floor. There were horrible scenes, because every three or four meters there was a Hungarian soldier standing with a whip in his hand, and those who couldn't carry the sacks were beaten horribly.

I was not involved in these scenes because I continued to work in the office. But then, shortly after we had arrived in this camp—that must have been in June or July 1942—my captain was called back to Hungary and another captain became the head of our camp. Someone had probably told him that I was the right-hand man of his predecessor, because the next morning I was taken aside after roll call and told that I was to report to the new captain in his office.

When I got to the office, the new captain asked me my name, and the names of my parents, and what kind of work I had done in the office. I told him what I had been doing there to help the captain, and then he told me to go on and to talk about something that was embarrassing to me and uncomfortable to discuss: the private affairs of my former captain. I said that I hadn't paid any attention to his private business—I had come in the morning and worked until four, straightening up, shining his boots, making his lunch. And, beyond that, I knew nothing.

---

*Called Stanislav in Russian and Yiddish, Stanislau in German, and Stanislawow in Polish, this city was renamed Ivano-Frankovsk by the Soviet government in 1962. Now in Ukraine, it is known by its Ukrainian name, Ivano-Frankivsk.

There were two enlisted men in the room, and he said to one of them, "Tell Berliner to go ahead with what interests me." They hit me from behind, both of them, over the head, back, and feet. And then he asked me, "Now will you tell me what I want to know? Because if you don't, they will help you along, until you leave here a dead man. In Bretcu, your comrades always had to work, even in the worst weather, but you just sat around doing nothing. What kind of gifts did the captain get from you that you stayed with him the whole time and didn't have to work?"

I repeated that I hadn't done anything—that he had probably taken a liking to me, or maybe because I was the oldest of our company he had given me some support, but otherwise I couldn't say. I was beaten again, until I collapsed, and then they brought me back to where we were living, 400 of us, on the floor.

I was brought in there around midday. The next thing I can remember is that I had to get up the following morning and go to roll call, and it was then that the punishment began for the past, when I had been on friendly terms with my captain. It was about ten kilometers from the camp to the work site, and the fellows all went in carts drawn by a pair of horses. While they sat, I had to walk—or run—behind them. There were about twenty guards for 400 Jewish laborers, but one of the guards—a Hungarian gypsy who was a soldier in the Hungarian army—was assigned specifically to me, and he stood over me from morning till evening so that I couldn't pause even for an instant.

There, in the worst heat, we were building roads. I wasn't used to the work, and going the whole day without a break was a catastrophe because, when I left off for a second, the guard jabbed me with his rifle. When someone had to go to the toilet, he could just walk across the road, and I remember one instance when I crossed the road into the brush, which was about half a meter high, and crouched down, and then sat a little to rest. Suddenly, there he was—he stabbed me so with the bayonet that the blood was flowing from both feet, and I ran quickly back to work.

In the camp, Romulus had become friends with a "half-Jew" from Hungary proper named Imre Kovacs.

I went up to him one evening, after I had been under the new captain for about a month, and I said, "Listen, Imre, I've decided to leave here. If you want to, you can come with me." Where we would go I had no idea, but I had to get out, because I knew that if I stayed there another week or two, I would collapse. Then they would beat me to death, or finish me off some other way. When I asked him, Imre said, "I'm coming with you."

We started making plans right away, but the question was, How do you get out of here? You weren't allowed outside the camp, and a number of guards stood watch in the evenings to make sure no one could escape. But they knew there was no great danger in any case, because there was nowhere to run to—where were you supposed to go in Stanislav?

Still, there was one possibility. There was a kind of toilet where they had dug a trench one meter or maybe half a meter deep, and you had to straddle it and, standing, do your business. Behind the toilets was a low wall, and it was no problem to jump over it and run away. We conducted a trial that evening: First I went by there, then my friend went by, and we saw how it would go if we did it. We made up our minds to carry out our escape the next day.

We wore normal civilian clothes in the camp, and the next evening we put on as much clothing as we could. Then we again went to the toilet, and we jumped over the little wall and left—without papers, without anything. There was a wood not far away, and we went into the wood and decided to walk all night so that we wouldn't be in the vicinity of the camp, because we figured that they might send a patrol to look for us.

We walked all night without knowing where we were going. The next morning we stopped in the wood, ate some bread we had taken with us, and sat and waited until it got dark and we could go on—we were afraid someone might see us if we moved during the day. We again walked all night, and when we stopped to rest the next morning, we saw a little village not far away. We walked toward it, and, terribly tired and filthy, we came to the town not knowing what we would do or what we would say.

We had tried to work out together that if we were caught—if a patrol or something caught up with us—we would say that we had been working and that our comrades had gone off somewhere and we couldn't find them again and had gotten lost looking for our camp. That much we had talked over, in case anyone asked us. So when we arrived in this village, we went up to a farmer and asked him if he hadn't seen Hungarian workers marching through in the past two days, because we had lost them. We didn't say that we were Jews, but that we were coming from a Hungarian labor camp.

These people were Poles, and since we couldn't speak their language and they couldn't speak ours, we tried in sign language to get across the why and wherefore. They were very nice people—they gave us something to eat and drink, and said that in another village there was a German commandant's office and that the best would be if we went there and reported. When we had eaten our fill and shaved and shined our shoes, we left the farmer's with the intention of going to the next village, where the German commandant's office was.

In the meantime, my friend and I had discussed what we would say. We knew that there was, in Stanislav, a labor camp for Hungarian Christians: thieves, bandits, murderers, and convicts who had been formed into a group and sent there to do forced labor. This camp was, of course, much better provisioned than ours, and they had uniforms; but it was a kind of uniform that didn't have a sash, so you could see right away that it wasn't a real soldier, just a laborer. We agreed we would say that we belonged to this group.

But there was another possibility. My friend told me that a law had been enacted in Hungary under which Hungarians could report as volunteers to an SS panzer division. These volunteers were sent, not yet in uniform, to Stanislav, where they were brought to a marshaling camp, mustered in, trained, and sent off to the front. We decided to say that we were from one of these groups of Hungarian SS volunteers, we made up a story, we went to the other village, and we asked where the German commandant's office was.

Someone showed us a house. I can't remember what was written on the door, but, in any case, we knocked. In the front room there were three enlisted men, or maybe NCOs, and they asked in German what we wanted. We had decided that my friend would speak. He spoke German very badly, but with a true Hungarian accent; my German was much better, but there was some Yiddish mixed in with it, so what we had agreed on was that I could speak only Hungarian whereas he could speak Hungarian and a little German.

My friend told them very briefly: "We were marching from Budapest to Stanislav with German enlisted men and NCOs, and around 300 Hungarian volunteers, when we came upon a German automobile that was standing at the side of the road. Two German officers and their driver, an enlisted man, were in the car. They stopped us and asked our commander whether he didn't have an auto mechanic, because they had a flat tire and the spare was flat as well. My friend had a car before the war and he knows how to fix a flat, so he reported, and I reported with him automatically. The officers promised our commander that we would be there only fifteen minutes or half an hour and that, when we had repaired the tire, they would give us a ride back to the group. So our battalion marched on.

"We repaired the tires, but it took us an hour and a half or two hours, and the officers were drinking in the meantime. After we had finished, they didn't take us with them in the car but said that we should just walk on ahead and we would catch up with our colleagues. We walked for a few hours, but we couldn't find them, and three hours ago we arrived in a village. We asked around, and people said that in the next village, not far away, was a German commandant's office and that they would know where our battalion was."

The German NCO asked very sternly for our papers. We had purposely thrown our coats away; we said that we had set them down on the car and that when the car was repaired, the officers had gotten in, the driver had stepped on the gas, and they had gone off with our clothes. The NCO started shouting at us: "What a lie! How do I know you're not spies?" And "That's rubbish," and "I'll lock you up," and so on and so forth.

In the meantime an officer had come out of another room, and the NCO reported what my friend had said. The officer asked him, "Why are you making a big deal of this? Give them documents and let them take the train to Szombathely.* They'll figure out what to do with them at the marshaling camp there. What do we care?"

We received documents. I changed my name: I didn't say I was Berliner Romulus,† I said I was Broda Romulus. We had a shoemaker

---

*Szombathely: a city in western Hungary, near the Austrian border.
†Berliner Romulus: Berliner refers to himself by his family name first, a reflection of Hungarian usage.

in the building; they were Saxons who had a son my age who had died. I don't know why I thought of that—maybe I was thinking that if they went asking after Broda Romulus in Cluj, people would say that he had existed or that the name existed or something. And as it was wartime, I didn't necessarily count on their looking into it so much. So I was given a paper: "Broda Romulus, born on thus-and-such a date, pass to Szombathely."

We were also given provisions—each one a loaf of bread, cookies, and two sausages—and we were overjoyed because we had made it out of there. Looking neither right nor left, we went to the train station, and we sat waiting half an hour or an hour for our train. After a trip that lasted, if I remember correctly, five or six hours, we arrived in Szombathely.

There, we again asked where the German commandant's office was, and we were sent to a preparatory marshaling camp from which people who had come back from furlough and the like were sent on to the front. We were brought into an office, and they didn't ask us anything at all, they said only, "Are you Hungarian SS volunteers?" We said yes. They sent us to a wash area, and we bathed.

Everything was going just fine until they said that the next morning we were to undergo a medical examination. At that moment, things looked black to me, because I knew the difference between being circumcised and not being circumcised; you can see it quite plainly and unmistakably. I didn't sleep the whole night, and I worked out that, should they ask anything, I would say that I had been operated on—I had a friend in Cluj who had been operated on for Spanish collar,* and he looked as if he were a Jew. Kovacs was not circumcised, and he and I agreed that we didn't know each other and would not speak with each other, so that if anything happened to me, nothing would happen to him. He had no problem at all with it and was not afraid.

The next morning at eight o'clock they brought eight or nine of us into a room, and a few minutes later an NCO in a white coat came

---

Spanish collar: paraphimosis; a condition in which an abnormally tight foreskin that has been drawn back over the glans cannot return to its usual position; generally corrected by circumcision.

in and said, "Take all your clothes off. When you've undressed, come inside." The fellows got undressed very quickly. I was the last one to pull off his underpants. I looked—I had a look at all of them—and there was a gigantic difference between my organ and theirs. The sweat was pouring off me, and, though I didn't see my own face, I can imagine that I looked half dead. I knew that these were my last moments, and I shuddered, thinking, "How will they kill me? How *slowly* will they kill me?" This was the only thing that frightened me; if they were going to shoot me on the spot, I wouldn't be afraid.

We came into the room, and they lined us up in a row. I was the fifth or sixth. The doctor came up to the first fellow and asked him, "Have you been ill? Have you been operated on?" The first one answered, "No. No." He had to hold his hands out to the doctor palms up, and then the doctor looked very quickly at his eyes, and with that he could leave. The second one then stood facing the doctor, and the third, the fourth, the fifth, and everything was done.

It was my turn. "Have you been ill?"

"No."

"Have you been operated on?"

"Yes."

"What did you have?"

I said it in Hungarian: "Spanyol galér."

He looked at it, then he looked at my eyes. "Passed."

Terribly happy inside, we left. Imre took my hands and pressed them in his: We had made it.

The same day, we got our uniforms. They were German uniforms with the pants tucked into the boots, those beautiful German short boots. We chose nice trousers and nice jackets for ourselves, and we went to the camp barber, who cut our hair very short, the way the Germans wore their hair at the time. I looked at myself in the mirror. I was a good-looking guy, and my friend was a good-looking guy, and we looked really great.

We had two days free, and the next day we went out for a walk in Szombathely. All of a sudden, we see a small group of Jews with three Hungarian soldiers guarding them. We stop on the sidewalk. There were twenty or twenty-five of them, you could see from a good ways off that they were Jews, and I say to my friend, "Hey, I know one of them!"

This man was a bookkeeper in the biggest drugstore in Cluj, and I had been in love with his sister's daughter. I tell my friend, "Come here a minute. I would like to see if it really is he, because this is unbelievable." We get closer, and I have another look, and I was one hundred percent positive.

This wasn't far from our camp, and that's where they were brought. We went back, and we wanted to see from a distance what they were going to do with them. At that time, we knew nothing about the crematoria and things like that. This group of Jews had to sit down in the middle of the yard, and one of the soldiers then went into an office while two or three other soldiers with rifles watched over them. I went up to one of the soldiers and asked, "Where are you bringing these Jews from?" The Jews didn't even dare to look, they were so frightened of the SS, and I could feel it. I told Imre, "Keep up a conversation with these soldiers"—the others had come over as well—and he chatted with them.

I went up to the man I knew and said, very quietly, "Look, don't answer back. My name is Berliner Ruvi"—my name is Berliner Romulus, but I was called Ruvi at home, and he also knew me by that name. I say, "Look, don't answer back. I am Berliner Ruvi, and should you ever get back home" . . . I am almost crying now, thinking back on this . . . "should you ever get back home, say that I was here, that you saw me." That was such a scene, I can't tell you. And I turned around, and was gone.

The next day, Romulus and Imre were inducted.

They put us in a vehicle. I don't know how many of us were sitting in this vehicle—thirty, forty, fifty people. By this time we were Germans, volunteers to the German SS. The others had no training either, they were exactly like us, except that they had come officially from somewhere, they had been brought from a prison or had reported on their own to the SS. We were driven to the train station and from the station to a small village where there was what was called an assembly camp, similar to the one in Szombathely.

There, they asked, "What can you do? What have you done? For which department would he be suited?" I could drive a car, and told them that I was a driver. My friend said that he was a mathematical genius—which is the truth, he has a gift for mental arithmetic, he sees the numbers before his eyes. Then they told us that we would have to leave for another village later in the day.

They brought us to the train station that evening, and we were put in a kind of cattle car with a layer of straw on the floor, and we undressed and lay down to sleep. Everyone there was Hungarian, and next to us in the car was a group of lowlifes. They were chatting among themselves, and suddenly my friend hears how one of them is saying to the others, "Say, those two aren't Hungarians. They're Jews."

I didn't hear it, because they were lying next to my friend, but my friend whispers in my ear, "Watch it! They've found us out!"

I said, "What can they have found out? We are Christians like them, and that's it. After all, we have papers and everything."

"No, it's no good," he said and became terribly frightened.

Suddenly, one of them asks, "Where you guys from?"

My friend answered, "From Szombathely," because he had been from there originally. They said something back, but I can no longer remember the details. We tried to speak as little as possible—my friend could really do the accent, but I couldn't speak as primitively as these ganoven,* so from my speech you could have told that I didn't belong to this band.

Also from my appearance. I wasn't a Jewish type in the sense that people would necessarily say right away, "He is a Jew, he has a big nose"—or big ears, or I don't know what—but I didn't have the primitive appearance of these guys. It was the lowest class of people who reported voluntarily for these SS panzer divisions; they were told that you could live well in the SS, and the only thing people were afraid of was the front, but there was war in the cities as well. So if they had lined up ten or twenty of us in a row, you could have seen that this one or that one didn't belong.

In any case, it was night, it was dark in the car, and everyone was sleeping. The next morning, we got dressed, and my friend and I agreed that we would try to get as far away from those people as possible. We arrived in a huge camp with thousands of people, and as soon as we left the train, we saw to it that we went one way and they went the other.

We had been ordered to report to an office. Just before we went into the office, my friend said to me, "Listen, Ruvi, don't be angry, but

---

ganoven: thieves, undesirables (Yiddish).

I think it would be better if we split up. I'm scared, and it's no use that if, God forbid, anything happens, they catch us both." I was very depressed, because he knew how to deal with Hungarians. I could speak Hungarian well, but, for all practical purposes, I was a Rumanian—I had been in Rumanian schools, and it makes a difference if you're from Transylvania, because it was only in 1940 that we went back to the Hungarians. I felt completely whipped, in a word, but I saw that there was no sense in it if he didn't want it.

Then we reported—you could report where you wanted—and they assigned us right away. Kovacs reported to a panzer division and was sent to the front. I reported as a driver, and I had enormous luck: I was assigned to a radio division.

There were about fifty people in the group. The staff, consisting of the Hauptsturmführer, the Untersturmführer,* and three or four technicians, were German SS. The rest of us, about forty fellows, were Hungarian SS volunteers. We were stationed in a little Polish village, somewhere five to ten kilometers from the front and totally out of the way. We received reports from the front, SS bulletins, and passed them along.

Romulus was assigned to a truck and became driver for the Hauptsturmführer, a role which expanded to that of orderly.

This was a stroke of luck, exactly like in the first days in the labor camp, when I met my captain and more or less became his manservant. My Hauptsturmführer lived with a farmer, and I lived with the same farmer—there was no room in the house so I got a bed in the stable, but it was really very nice. He would tell me, "Have the car out front tomorrow morning"; so I came to his room when he was still asleep, put his things in order, brought him his breakfast from the farmer, and drove him to join the others.

Officially, he wasn't allowed to have a servant, and he didn't really need one; I believe it was only because I took such care of his belongings. I spent hours shining his boots, so he had the most beautifully polished boots every morning. The women there washed his shirts, but I ironed his pants—I had never ironed pants in my life, and I didn't need to press

---

Hauptsturmführer: captain; *Untersturmführer:* second lieutenant (SS rank designations).

my own pants, but I pressed his. He was a good-looking young fellow, and he had a girlfriend from the village who either came in the evening or was there during the day. I was at her disposal, and I got everything ready for when he came home in the evening. My Hauptsturmführer never had to ask me for anything, because everything he would have wished was there waiting for him—and that really impressed him.

As I saw to it that he wouldn't need to ask for anything, and that I wouldn't need to say anything, we spoke very little. Still, I was afraid that he would call me in and start making conversation—it wasn't normal to be together like that and never once ask, "Do you have a brother, do you have a sister, do you have a mother? Have you written? Why don't you write?" Because I didn't write to anyone and I didn't ever wait for the mail. I would never have told him the truth, but I figured on his calling me in once. As luck would have it, he never bothered himself about me.

I had nothing at all to do with the other soldiers, neither with the Hungarians nor with the Germans who ran the apparatus. Every morning the staff met together and discussed the work before them, but I didn't have to go. I never even saw what they did—I don't know how they relayed the reports they received from the front. And while the others drilled and trained and played sports, I was home all day.

Romulus says that his unsociability, which had its roots in his natural reserve, failed to arouse anyone's curiosity—or, if it did, his proximity to the commanding officer of the division discouraged inquiries.

I can well imagine that the Hauptsturmführer himself believed I was a little nincompoop who looked neither right nor left and was good only for being a servant—who was incapable of doing any other kind of work. To the soldiers, I was a loner. Besides, they knew that I was the right-hand man, or the left-hand man, of the Hauptsturmführer, and in these groups the Hauptsturmführer was everything—that was the king, that was a second Hitler.

The only people I had anything at all to do with were the farmers where I lived. Some of them could speak a little German, but I didn't want to speak German, and I tried to have it so that no one would speak with me and I wouldn't need to speak myself. There was a girl in the house, and in the beginning she didn't even look at me—they were so frightened of us the first weeks—and I didn't want to talk to her either.

But then, one evening, I took her with me and I started in with her. I wanted to have it dark, and she didn't want to, and I didn't let her touch me down there because I was afraid. Ach, nonsense! Today I know it's nonsense, but at that time I was scared that she would somehow notice that things were different with me.

But that is just a kind of sidelight; it was not an important event. Most of the time, all I worried about was taking care of my Hauptsturm-führer's things. I didn't take walks because I didn't want to meet anyone, I didn't want anyone asking me questions. When I had nothing to do, I lay low—I sat in a corner or stayed in the yard. I didn't want to hear much, or see much, or do anything at all. That's how the time went by: without problems or adventures. Things went singularly well for me.

After the radio division had spent around half a year at its original position, it was restationed in a succession of small Polish villages whose names, like that of the initial village, Romulus no longer remembers or never even knew. In each new village, the Hauptsturmführer was billeted with a farmer; Romulus, who continued as his orderly, was given a bed in the kitchen or stable and managed to keep to himself. The villages were far enough from the front that Romulus saw no soldiers other than those of his own group—nor, he says, did he hear anything of the fate of the Jews.

When I was working as a laborer for the Hungarians, I had heard for the first time that there were deportations. At the labor camp in Stanislav I had gotten a last letter from my mother in which she told me that they were in a factory in Cluj and that "a transport is going to Germany in the next few days and they are deporting us." I understood deportation to mean that they were bringing the Jews to Germany and making them work in the factories while their own people were fighting in the service. Still, I knew it was no advantage to be a Jew, and I saw to it that I hid from them what I was.

According to the information we were getting, the Germans were going to win the war—it wouldn't be otherwise, it couldn't be otherwise. This is what I imagined: When they win the war, Jewry will no longer exist. Jews will exist, but as the lowest of heavy laborers, or street sweepers, or something like that—and that's all. I couldn't imagine that I would be able to go home and report as a Jew and say what I had been doing up to then—I never would have been able to do that. Besides, I knew that I would not find anyone at home, and that I could never go to Germany to look for my mother or my father or my brother and sisters. So I had to think, "Either live and give up on my family, or . . ."

I wrote them all off. And it wasn't so easy to put the family aside, because my entire life up to that time had been only for my family, in my youth I had had nothing else in mind but to help my family. But I knew that there was no other future than "You have to switch yourself out."

There were times when I asked myself: "What will become of me when we win the war?" When *we* win the war—we Germans. So that I wouldn't ever slip, I had to talk myself into that *we*. I tried, in my innermost, to convince myself, "When we win the war, I will be a German," and I thought, "What will you do?"

I would have to find somewhere to hide for the rest of my life, so that the time would go by and I wouldn't be found out and taken prisoner for not being who I was supposed to be. I racked my brain, and decided that after the war I would probably report somewhere deep in Russia and take up some post there—I don't know, mayor of a village or something. In this way, I would live out my life.

But then the whole situation turned around. We heard that the war would soon be over, that the Germans had lost the war, and we moved farther back almost every week. One fine day, in 1944, we began to hear firing, so we retreated steadily, moving closer to Germany by the day. When I was driving in the direction of Czechoslovakia, whom did I see marching but Kovacs! I shouted to him from the window of the truck, and he shouted back, "Take me with you!" But I simply was unable to stop.

One evening in April 1945, Romulus's division stopped in a meadow a few kilometers from Prague.

The Hauptsturmführer came up to me and said, "It's now to the point that if we sleep here, we will most likely run into the Russians tomorrow." He threw off his uniform and got into civilian clothes, whereupon I put on a civilian jacket I had—I didn't have any trousers. In the cab of the truck, he on the right, I on the left, we slept.

Suddenly, around three or four in the morning, there was gunfire. I awoke to find Russian and Czech soldiers surrounding us. There was shouting—"Hands up!" and "Out of the truck!"—from a loudspeaker.

They got everyone together, prodding us into a group. They had brought others, so there were 500, 600 Germans like me—well, not like me, but German enlisted men and officers. When we were assembled, they lined us up in rows of four—with every fourth or fifth row there was a soldier with a rifle—and they herded us along.

We marched into Prague, and in Prague people threw rocks at us, and "Pfui!" and "Pfui!" and "Pfui!" I wasn't hit by any of the rocks, but many must have been hit—cut open, fallen down. Now and then a shot was fired, and one person was left lying there.

They brought us to a big barracks. There were already a great many Germans—prisoners, like me—lined up in the yard with their faces to the wall and their hands above their heads. Above, there were soldiers with automatic weapons, and from the way they were standing I could see that they were waiting only for someone to come with the order to shoot us down.

It was eight or nine in the morning when they brought us in. We stood that way all day without food, and in the evening they said that each was to lie down where he was standing and sleep. I don't know how it happened, but I had ended up next to the Hauptsturmführer. He had a girlfriend there as well, although how she got there I don't know, because she didn't come with us in my truck. As it was rather cold, we were lying one against the other to keep warm; and, for the first time, I had a conversation with my Hauptsturmführer.

I asked him where he was from and what he was going to do, and similar chitchat. He didn't ask a thing about me, but I said to him, "What would you say if I told you that I am a Jew?" I can't remember the exact words, but I asked him more or less in that way. He didn't say a word in response, so that subject was exhausted. We chatted on a little, about what I no longer remember; our conversation lasted around half an hour. Then, all of a sudden, I felt him stand up, and he left. I never saw him again.

Telling him was spontaneous: for a laugh, and at the same time to let him know who he'd been together with, that his servant was a Jew. The war was over. I had nothing against him. I am convinced he didn't know that there was a crematorium—I didn't know myself. I knew that the SS hated the Jews, but that they hated them so much that they would destroy them—that, I didn't know. And I didn't believe that he was against the Jews—well, so terribly against. He lived his life: It was his duty to report to his staff in the morning; otherwise, he saw to it that the day went by quickly, and when he had the possibility, he stayed home and read.

After the conversation, I felt so upset. I hadn't said it angrily, but out of joy, as a surprise: that a Jew was there next to him. I thought that he would begin talking with me—"That's not possible!" and "How and what and why?"—but he didn't say a word. He asked nothing, he acted like he hadn't heard it, and he disappeared. Because of that, I believe he actually did know that they were killing Jews; if he hadn't known, he would have talked with me.

That was a horrible night in that they came with a lantern to look the girls over, and the ones that were at all good-looking they brought to their quarters, which were not far away, and you could hear how they were raping them. And there were shootings. We were lying there on the ground, and they were drunk, and they took some shots at us. We heard screams, and not far away someone was bleeding. I have no notion how many died and how many were wounded.

In the morning we stood up, hands high, facing the wall; I was already quite weak. All of a sudden, I hear a group of officers approaching. They're walking behind the prisoners, looking them over, and they're speaking Russian with one another. It had crossed my mind to say, if anyone came, that I was a Jew. But at the very moment that they were behind my back, without really having prepared or thought it through, I thrust myself away from the wall, stood there, and shouted: "Tam romanskii zhid!"—I am a Rumanian Jew. I don't know if that's Russian or Polish or Czech, but it was all I knew.

There are soldiers all around, and one of them is there with a bayonet trying to push me away before I've even spoken. But just then a Russian officer comes up and says, "Stoi!"—stay there.

He asks me something in Russian, and I say, "Nye pone mai russki"; and I didn't know Russian, either.

So he says, "Chaveri?"—what do you speak?

And I begin saying in Rumanian, "Eu sunt jidan din Romaniya"—I am a Rumanian Jew.

Then he asks me, "Do you speak Yiddish?"

"That goes without saying," I tell him.

"How," he says—now everything is in Yiddish—"how did you end up with this bunch?"

I told him that I was in a Jewish labor camp in Stanislav, and the SS came, and they were looking for a driver. My captain said that I was a driver, and they took me with them, and I had to enlist—I didn't tell him that I had reported voluntarily. They put me in uniform—German boots and pants and a jacket—and gave me a truck and had me drive behind another truck. Then, the day before yesterday, early in the morning, I was taken prisoner—as a German—and brought here.

"Bravo!" he said, clapping me on the shoulder. He took a Czech officer aside and said something to him in Czech, and the Czech said, in German, "Come with me." He gave me some chocolate, and asked my name—I said Berliner Romulus—and they gave me a document that said I had safe-conduct from there to Cluj. I took the papers and found a seat in the train.

I am sitting in the car, and we're standing in a station, and I see how two Czech soldiers are beating a man with a rifle. Then they force him to get down on his knees, and they shoot him. We were sitting there in a compartment in the train. Under my breath, I said, "Pfui!"

There, in a train station, after the war, was the first time I had seen someone die. There had been deaths in the camp at Stanislav, but I myself had never seen anyone being killed. I had heard firing from the front, but I never saw a battle and I never saw any dead. They had forced him to get down on his knees, and, with a pistol, they had shot him from behind. And I said, "Disznosag!"—how foul!—something like that. Because, simply, how could they kill someone that way?

One of the people in the car got out. I didn't even notice it; I realized it only later. He gets off, and I see below that he is speaking with two civilians who have armbands; I am standing by the window, and they are pointing at me. The two come up, grab me, and take me off the train. They lead me to a room, and I see one of them taking out a pistol. I knew that I was finished; I had seen how that other man had been shot down.

I say, in Hungarian—I didn't dare speak German anymore—I ask, "Mit akarnak?" What do they want from me? And in Rumanian: "What do you want from me? I Jew."

"You no Jew. You German."

"I Jew."

One of them says to me, "Take off your pants."

I take down my pants, and I show him. "You're lucky," he says to me, and he lets me go.

From that moment, I didn't speak with anyone anymore; I looked neither right nor left. When they had grabbed me, that was nothing—but when we were by the door and he pulled out the pistol, I saw that they were going to shoot me down. This was the biggest event that I lived through in the entire war—it was even more terrifying than when I went to the medical exam.

Romulus arrived in Cluj as the first Jews trickled back from deportation. He went straight home, where he had a joyous reunion with his father, who had spent the war years in a Cluj hospital posing as a non-Jewish patient; and with his younger brother, who, of those sent to the labor camps of the kind in which Romulus himself had been, was among the minority alive at the end of the war. Romulus's older sister, who had spent the war years in a Rumanian underground movement, remained in Bucharest, but his three younger sisters, who had been in Auschwitz, soon returned home.

My sisters had been deported together with Mama. When they came back, they told me how they had seen Mama taken to the left, while they were brought to the right. At that moment, they themselves did not yet know that Mother was being brought to the crematorium, but the next day they found out that she had been gassed.

With my sisters' return, the whole family was there. The next day I opened a store and we began a new life.

One day, about a month later, a Russian comes, along with a Rumanian Communist, and they request that I go with them. They take me to a villa—in Cluj, the Russian secret service was in a villa. They bring me in and conduct me below into a cellar, and an official is sitting there. I am to take a seat, and he begins very courteously, in Hungarian. I am to tell him what I was doing with the SS. "What? Where do you know that from?"

"You were seen. You were seen in Szombathely."

A few of that group had returned, and before I got home they reported—well, they didn't report, they were just blabbing—that "Berliner was an SS man." And I was to tell about it.

I say, "I saw to it that I saved my life." He stands up and gives me a gigantic slap in the face. I was strong, and I was not afraid—although we were afraid of the Russians, because we, as Jews, were not so popular with them either; they deported many Jews, people like me, after the war. In any case, I say to him, "Are you nuts?"

Suddenly, there is a knock at the door. A fellow my age comes in: "Hiya, Ruvi!" It is a certain Czerny, who was head of the police. I had been in school with him. I say to him, "This is not right. He popped me one in the face. Up to now, I haven't been hit in the face—but now I get it, and because I saw to it that I saved my life."

I had to tell the story. He gave me his hand. "I believe you that you didn't go to fight against Russia, or against America, or against the Jews."

At the time of the interview, Romulus Berliner lived on an estate near Vienna with the young wife he had married, almost on the spur of the moment, in early middle age and the couple's two children. Showing exceptional drive and commercial acumen, he had built up businesses in Rumania and France after the war before striking it very rich in Austria. Despite his wealth, Romulus was unassuming; his reputation as a large contributor to Jewish charities filled him with an incredulous pride, as did the fact that a road running by his family's Vienna warehouse had been marked with the Berliner name. He was also, by all appearances, a loyal friend: Imre Kovacs, who had lived in a small town in Hungary since the end of the war, was as frequent a guest in the Berliner home as travel regulations would allow.

Romulus says that his attitude toward Jewishness has in no way changed since childhood and that he is "completely switched out of" the identity of Hungarian SS volunteer Broda Romulus.

With this difference: I am not an opponent of the Nazis to the extent that some of my friends are. I simply didn't experience the things they did, and I couldn't imagine them. If my sister hadn't told me herself, "I saw how Mama was brought to the crematorium," if someone else had told me, I wouldn't have believed it. So I don't say that all of them were murderers—only eighty percent, or fifty percent, or forty. But not all.

Gabriel Ritter

Gabriel Ritter, who began life as Günther Ritter, was born in Germany in 1932, only shortly before the Nazis' accession to power. His parents, Jewish immigrants from Poland, had arrived in Chemnitz two years earlier with their older son, born in 1928. Just after Günther's birth, the family moved north to Berlin, where Mr. Ritter opened a fabric shop in partnership with a non-Jewish woman.

The household young Günther grew up in was a religious one.

My father was a rather orthodox Jew, and he gave us a rather orthodox upbringing. We had to go to temple every Sabbath, and my brother and I could read the Bible in Hebrew, which we learned from Father. We also went in part to Jewish schools until they were closed down.

At the same time, however, Mr. Ritter was an assimilationist.

He was very interested in German culture and felt a considerable link to it. He thought it important that I be brought up German, which means that I didn't understand Polish and that it was even hard for me to understand Yiddish—to say nothing of speaking it. Thus, he tried from the very beginning to have his children assimilate even though the Nazis were in power. I can still remember him saying, "Hitler will not be long-lived. He'll be voted out again in two or three years, or go under in some other way. It simply can't last; with a civilized people like the Germans such a thing is not possible." He didn't want to believe it; he couldn't believe it. Well, he was terribly mistaken.

In early October 1938, Polish authorities, fearing Germany might expel the 50,000 Jews of Polish nationality living under German rule, announced that Poland would begin denying reentry to Polish citizens whose papers lacked a special endorsement. Later that month, Günther's father found himself among

15,000 Jews shipped to the Polish border just as the measure was to take effect. But a last-minute compromise allowed around half of the deportees to stay in Germany, and Mr. Ritter was able to return home.

Scarcely two weeks later—just forty-eight hours after Kristallnacht, the "Night of Broken Glass," which saw the mass arrest of Jews and the destruction of synagogues and Jewish-owned shops—the Nazi regime declared the business interests of all Jews subject to "compulsory Aryanization." While Mr. Ritter had already taken a backseat in his business because of the economic pressure steadily mounting against the Jews, he was now forced out altogether. Unlike many in this predicament, however, the Ritters were not left entirely without means. Mr. Ritter's holdings, rather than being confiscated by an outside "administrator," were taken over by his "Aryan" partner, and she proved, says Gabriel, looking back, "very fair" to the family.

Then, in the early fall of 1939, Günther's father was arrested and taken to the Sachsenhausen concentration camp, just beyond the northern outskirts of Berlin. Günther's mother actively pursued her husband's release, even daring to go before high-ranking SS officials to plead his case. "Although it was horribly difficult," Gabriel remembers, "she managed to get him out." But four months in the camp had left Mr. Ritter close to death.

They had broken him down terribly. He went into the Jewish Hospital in Berlin, where he told about the hideous things that had been done to him; he wasn't supposed to tell, but he didn't care, he knew he was dying. They were locked in barracks—the windows were nailed shut, the doors nailed shut—where they were packed so closely together that they couldn't lie down and had to sleep standing up. They weren't given anything to drink. After three days the doors were ripped open, and it was announced, "Anyone who can drink a whole bucket of water is to report, but he has to drink it down completely." My father volunteered, hoping he would get pneumonia or something that way; the water was ice cold. He got two or three liters down but couldn't manage any more. Then he was beaten so terribly—his intestines trampled or his chest trampled—that he was gravely ill, and they released him. Three months later—it was, I believe, April 27, 1940—he died.

Mrs. Ritter approached the Jewish Agency, and before the year was out Günther's brother had left for Palestine. Günther and his mother stayed in Berlin, living in a furnished room; "we were no longer allowed to have our own apartment," Gabriel recalls. After the Jewish schools were closed, Günther worked as an orderly at the Jewish Hospital.

Life, if difficult, remained stable until the morning of what Gabriel remembers as February 28, 1943.

We were looking out of the window facing the courtyard—we lived in the front house of a typical Berlin apartment building with a garden house, a rear house, and so on—and we saw how the Jews were being taken from the rear house. My mother was then very resolute and tore off our stars. We got dressed quickly, and really catch-as-catch-can: I remember that my mother put on the wrong skirt with the wrong jacket, she actually wanted to dress in a suit. It was very curious, and it was a lot of fun for me.

At the moment we were going down in the elevator they were coming up the stairs—because the elevator was occupied—to collect us. We walked out down below, and my mother went up, quite bold, to an SS man standing at the entrance to the building. "What's going on here?" she said.

"Keep going," he answered. "See that you move along." And move along we did.

But we didn't know where to. We called various acquaintances, and one did hide us for three days on the understanding that we look for something else as quickly as possible, because they were really scared. My mother had some money stashed away, and through this same connection we found a family that let us hide at their place for pay and with whom we stayed for over a year.

Günther and his mother thus joined the ranks of the 1,200 Jews estimated to have lived in hiding in wartime Berlin.

The family was an older couple with three daughters. Since we couldn't show our faces outside at all, I was home all day and had to accommodate myself to the parents. That was very difficult because the woman was outrageously primitive. She talked the whole time about how much her daughters were making—these three daughters walked the streets to a certain degree—and about how we were paying her too little. She always let loose around me because she didn't presume to say it to my mother. My mother kept paying a higher and higher price, but even when she had just raised it this woman said, "That's still far too little." So it was extortion, more or less.

My mother and I slept in the same room with one of these "whores"—so-called, because they weren't really professionals. She dragged men up, and they transacted their business, and my mother

must have suffered terribly. It was interesting for me—although unpleasant as well—but I think my mother's nerves eventually gave out.
Still, we were glad we had these people because, despite it all, they
saved our lives.

Since I never went out onto the street during this time, I started
reading books insofar as it was possible. A friend of my father's, a Jewish
schoolteacher who was also in hiding, popped up at our place from time
to time; he would bring along whatever books he himself had been able
to get hold of and give me some lessons. But he couldn't do it more than
once every four or five weeks, because things were quite dangerous by
1943, and he could go out in public only at certain times—in the
evenings, for instance, when he didn't have to be afraid of roundups in
the streetcars.

This was also the time of the first big air raids. We were not
allowed down in the cellar and had to stay in the apartment. The
Americans would indiscriminately carpet the city with bombs, and I was
very frightened because the houses shook like crazy. There was a hit
right next to us—in fact, everything else in the neighborhood was
bombed to the ground—but this house was left standing. So we were
lucky.

*In the spring of 1944, Mr. Ritter's former business partner managed to put
Günther's mother in touch with a couple who offered to hide her and her son at
their home in Waldesruh, a suburb on the eastern outskirts of Berlin. The couple,
who had no children, lived with the wife's unmarried sister on a sizable plot of
ground that served the husband, a gardener, as a nursery. From what Günther
could tell, the man had been a member of the German Communist Party and was
"actively engaged in the underground, distributing literature and so on." He and
his wife gave the Ritters a room on the second floor of their house, for which, as
Gabriel points out, "they didn't take any money."*

*Whereas they had remained hidden at their previous address, Günther and
his mother were obliged to have contact with the neighbors in Waldesruh, where
their presence could not be kept totally secret. Their host represented them as
having been bombed out in Berlin; he also procured an old identification card that
had belonged to a woman killed in an air raid, and he replaced the original photo
on it with one of Mrs. Ritter. Although the card was meant to be used exclusively
in transactions with the post office rather than as a general-purpose personal
document, "people recognized it as a valid form of identification," Gabriel recalls.*

So my mother had another name—she was called Blomberg on the postal ID—and I was also called by it. They drummed it into me, saying over and over, "Your name is now Gabriel Blomberg. No longer Günther Ritter, but Gabriel Blomberg." And he was always telling my mother, "Please, leave him in peace. Don't tell him anything more about being Jewish, don't tell him anything more about Father. Let him forget until the war is over."

The man encouraged Gabriel, as he has been called ever since, to get to know the children in the neighborhood and bought him a pair of Hitler Youth pants with regulation belt to help him blend in. Dressed in the uniform bottoms and a plain shirt, Gabriel went out into the street and played with the other kids. Thanks in large part to his father's assimilationism—"something I don't totally understand today," he says, "but which at the time saved my life"—he never felt out of place.

It was so easy, because you'd grown up in this milieu, in this culture, and you were familiar with everything, you knew every reaction. In my gestures, my language, the whole way I expressed myself, I had always been a German; so I actually did what I had always done and I never had any problems with that. I just had to watch out that I didn't put my foot in my mouth.

I joined in everything. I took an interest in the airplanes and knew all the different types: whether it was English or American, whether it was the Lightning, the Spitfire, or the Hurricane, whether it was the ME-109 or the ME-110 of the Germans. I spoke with people about the planes, about the war itself, about what prospects we had. I absolutely did say "we"; I also said on occasion, "Yeah, we'll show 'em who's boss!"

Of course, the boys asked me, "Why aren't you with us in our district group of the Hitler Youth?"

I said, "I'm still in the group in the Warschauer Strasse"—that's where the Blombergs had lived—"but I haven't heard from them yet. You know how it is, people are bombed out." So one always found a way around it, and it worked out just fine.

Escaping the Jewish stigma proved quite congenial to a child who had grown up in an atmosphere of unremitting anti-Semitism.

As my first consciousness dates from the year 1934, I was underprivileged from the very beginning. In fact, I had always been, as one

heard day in and day out on the radio and elsewhere, an Untermensch*
—even though I didn't believe it, even though I always knew what
criminals they were. So it was a big relief not to have to talk about being
Jewish, not to have to explain that I was a Jew, not to have to put up with
being shouted at by children who called me "dirty Jew" and didn't want
to have anything to do with me.

I was suddenly accepted—suddenly, I was a German—and I experienced equal treatment from my playmates. I thought it was great fun
wearing those Hitler Youth pants; I was quite proud to wear the belt this
man had gotten me. It was like making up an imaginary life, a dream life
that you can never realize because the course of your own life is simply
different, and then having this dream life come true on the street: to have
equal rights, to be just like all the rest, to share in the fate of the German
people in this situation, to be integrated into a society that hadn't
expelled you. So basically I lived during the underground period the
way I would always have wished to live: without being persecuted.
Oddly enough, I was actually liberated.

*Gabriel says that through self-suggestion he got to the point that, "in the
presence of others," he "actually felt like a non-Jew."*

It did me good to be someone else; I felt good in it, and I forgot
completely that I was someone else. But I was living in a kind of
schizophrenia, because when I came home, when I was with my mother
again, I became conscious of who I was. The "I" always remained the
Jewish origin, always remained the family; I naturally felt that it was my
Jewish origin which, for me, was real—which was me. I also *wanted* to
be a Jew; at bottom, I didn't want to have anything to do with the others.

I myself didn't accept this society. Deep down, I despised and
hated it—something inculcated in me by my mother, by my teacher—
even if I wasn't able to grasp the whole scale of the crime, which my
mother kept from me to the extent she was able. Only, in public I was
protected—no one knew anything—and sometimes it was downright
unpleasant to be again, suddenly, one of the persecuted. I remember
very clearly that coming home was always like plunging back into true
darkness, because not till I was home did I know that I was a Jew.

Untermensch: subhuman; a term applied by Nazis to Jews, Slavs, and others they considered inferior to the "Aryan race."

Gabriel does not believe that his "liberation" was shared by his mother.

She passed herself off as very National Socialist in front of the neighbors, and people were even afraid of her sometimes because they thought she was a big Nazi. But though this gardener tried day and night to persuade her—*"Be* Frau Blomberg; the best thing you can do is to switch yourself into this role as well"—it was very difficult for my mother. She would weep in rage and despair when an American plane was shot down. And on the sixth of June, when the landings took place in France, for the first time I saw my mother drink; she got herself totally drunk, pouring down one brandy after another, and she began to dance czardas. What with the shock she had had with my father, it was harder for her to repress all that she had gone through than it was for me.

Nonetheless, Gabriel and his mother did share a condition which, though "disagreeable when you got home and felt like an outcast," could also be "very proud." Sometimes, says Gabriel, life was lived "on three or four levels" at once.

For example, the director of a labor camp there in the area often came to visit. He was friendly with an acquaintance of this gardener, and though he was a real Nazi and knew that the gardener was a Communist, he was not an informer. Except what he didn't know, of course, was that we were Jews; we were introduced as Blomberg, as people from the center of town who had been bombed out.

Once, he said to this man who saved our lives, "You can do what you want, but Russia is already kaput. Well, all right, it may last another three years, but we shall win." Then he turned to my mother—with whom, as it appeared, he was rather infatuated—and said, "Don't you agree, gnädige Frau, that we will win? You must also be of the opinion that we are going to win."

Whereupon my mother, glancing at me, told him, "Yes, *we* are going to win."

So you had pride in having shit on the world around you, just to make it absolutely clear. And the feelings we had, when we were able to make asses of them like that, were many-layered: You were tremendously relieved; and it was also an enormous pleasure, a great deal of fun; and it was a satisfaction as well; and, at the same time, you were proud that you could play it. But then again, you weren't *playing* it—at that moment, you *were* it.

Despite their prudence and their flair for impersonation, the Ritters were not able to remain totally beyond suspicion.

In Waldesruh, I was friendly with a boy two years older than I who always talked very strangely about the Hitler Youth and who didn't like to go to the meetings and rallies at all. I was invited to his family's house one evening; it had gotten dark, and we came home a little earlier than they expected us. As we came in, I heard a very, very distinctive sound coming from a closed sitting room: this rhythm from Beethoven's Fifth Symphony, "dah-dah-dah-DAH." That is, the signature of the BBC.

The boy shrank back and stared at me, while in the same instant the radio died out and the father was already tearing the door open and asking me, "When did you two come in?" He was very nervous.

"Yeah," I said, "just now."

"What did you hear? Tell me what you heard!"

"Nothing."

Whereupon he said, "You *must* have heard something—the door was ajar."

"I think I heard a radio or something," I said.

"Yes," he said, "but what?"

"Just a noise, I didn't hear any talking."

"Listen," he said, "I'll tell you this: If you denounce me, before I go, you're dead and your mother is dead."

So I said, "Why should my mother be dead, and why should I be dead?"

He said, "You know that I was listening to the British broadcast"—that, I will never forget.

To which I said, "So? I listen to it also."

Then he peered at me, and he pulled me into the room, and he said to me, "You people listen to the British broadcast?"

"Yes."

"You weren't bombed out, either, were you?"

"No."

"I don't want to know anything more."

Thereafter this boy and I were always together. I used to sleep over at his house until it was bombed out, and we were the closest of friends. And the father, a big antifascist, made out bit by bit that there was something about me that didn't add up, but whether he knew exactly what we were I don't know to this day.

When the Ritters' routine in Waldesruh was interrupted, however, it was not because they had been identified as Jews; rather, it was because their protectors were picked up as resistance operatives.

When the people came in to arrest them below, the sister came upstairs to us and said, "You have to jump out the window, there's no other way." My mother jumped first, down into the garden, and she landed wonderfully; but when I tried it, I badly sprained my foot. We then ran across the garden, and out over another lot, and into the next street. But what was fantastic was that she had also said to us, "I have an address for you in town. Please go there right away." They were so organized that even at this moment of mortal danger to themselves they were still thinking of us. So the husband was sent to Mauthausen, a horrible extermination camp in Austria; and the wife was sent to Ravensbrück, a women's camp; and we went to the Olivaer Platz in the west of Berlin.

During the four weeks we lived there, we went out quite a lot. One day, when we were walking down the street, a truck stopped suddenly in front of my mother; the door was torn open, and two Gestapo men in plain clothes jumped out. They stopped my mother and said, "Your papers, please." I was walking along behind my mother, and she signaled me with a movement of her hand that I was to walk into a kind of park there. I understood immediately and continued on, very calmly, into the park, which was lucky for us, because if I had come up as well, I think I would have put my foot in it.

"You are Frau Ritter," they said to my mother.

"Excuse me, but who am I supposed to be?"

"Elisabeth Ritter."

Whereupon my mother said "no," pulled out her postal ID, and with enormous indifference—which impressed me no end—said, "All right, look: I have only an old postal ID on me, and my name is Blomberg. I don't know what you want from me, and why I should be arrested. But, please, I'm registered here, and there's a police station right in the neighborhood. We can go over there, and you and I can inquire together at the police station as to who I am, and then we will have cleared this up."

They became very uncertain and hauled a man out of the truck. It was a Jewish gentleman my mother had known from before; he had pointed her out. Such people were told, "If you want, you can stay here, but you have to find your people for us"; and they did it, too, aiming to save their own lives.

They asked him, "Is that she, or isn't it?"

He looked her over and said, "Now I don't know; it looks like her."

"But are you sure, or aren't you?"

And my mother again said, "Look, I don't have a lot of time. My child is upstairs, and I have to shop. Please, let's go to the police station and straighten this out so I can go my way in peace."

Then they said, "Everything is in order. Please excuse us. Run along."

She said, "No. I would like to know with whom I have been dealing here."

"That doesn't concern you," the Gestapo agent said. "It's none of your business. Excuse us, please. And now get going."

I'll never forget my mother's doing that; for me, that was the greatest.

A few days after this, the sister of the arrested couple visited us and brought us home with her again. I found it colossal that we could live with her even though her sister and brother-in-law were in concentration camps. We stayed there until the end of the war, and we were actually never in need, she took care of everything. She fed us; we had our own garden, we had fruit, we never went hungry. Naturally, the nourishment was rather one-sided, and we broke out in boils on account of it. But it was always bearable, and we actually got through it in good shape.

In April 1945, Gabriel and his mother heard over the BBC that the Red Army was mounting an attack at the present-day Polish city of Kostrzyn, about fifty miles east of Berlin on the Oder River.

We figured on their arriving eight days later, but on the third day it suddenly got completely still. We heard nothing, and then all at once there was a really strange noise that we were hearing for the first time: tanks. They rolled through the streets, and it just didn't stop.

Since we were in the eastern part of Berlin, we were the first to be occupied. They went into each house looking for hidden uniforms and the like, and they hauled out everything there was to haul out. They forced our house open as well.

My mother spoke Polish and Russian, and that was her misfortune, because they said, "Wait a second! You speak Russian—you're a spy."

"No," she said. "I am a Jew and I was born in Poland. They have been hiding us here." Naturally, the Russians couldn't believe that they would still be running across Jews, because Hitler was supposed to have killed them all.

But then an officer came and said, "One moment—I'll handle this." You see, he was a Jew. "I'll check right away whether she's Jewish. She might have practiced up, so I won't test her, but the boy can't have rehearsed anything." He then told my mother, "You keep still now—I want to speak with the little fellow.

"Your father is dead, right?"

"Yeah."

"You are thirteen years old—that's what you said, isn't it?"

"Yes."

"Then you must be able to say Kaddish." The prayer he was asking me is one that not all Jews may know; most of the time, you ask a Jew to say the Shema, but you don't ask him to say Kaddish. "Do you know what that is, Kaddish?" he asked. Whereupon I recited the whole Kaddish for him. So it was my good fortune that we had been brought up orthodox.

The Russian army continued on right away, but what happened while they were there was truly frightful. They took the women from their houses and raped them. It was chaos; everything was in ruins. There wasn't much shooting, but they executed a few people who were known to be SS. My friend's father was a Nazi hater such as I've seldom seen, and the first thing he did was hand someone over to the Russians: a terrible Nazi who had continually denounced antifascist Germans who then ended up in concentration camps because of him. The Russians lined this man right up against the door of his house and they shot him.

We took a walk from Waldesruh to Koepenick, and there were some SS units that had been strung up from lampposts. I still see images of bodies lying around; for days you were stepping over bodies that hadn't been taken away, and it suddenly got very warm and it stank horribly. Once, I stepped on a glove that was filled: I tripped on a glove and looked at it because it felt so soft, and there was a hand in it. That, for me, was actually the biggest shock of the whole war.

Sadly, it was not the only shock. Shortly after war's end, Gabriel's friend, whose mother had died in an air raid, was blown to pieces by a land mine while collecting shell fragments in the wood near Waldesruh. In late 1945, news came that the woman whose house the Ritters had lived in had died in Ravensbrück.

The next year, her husband returned "a wreck" from Mauthausen. "They had beaten one of his eyes out," Gabriel recalls. "He was unrecognizable."

Attempting to get a fresh start following the collapse of the Third Reich, the Ritters ran into a bureaucratic obstacle: As they no longer had their original papers and the civil registry in Chemnitz had been bombed out, they were unable to establish their true identities.

My mother had terrible problems with that; she was called in again and again by the Allied supervisory authorities and asked, "Who are you *really?*" They could see, of course, that the postal ID was false, and they investigated, and they gave us provisional papers. But we actually lived for two years under the name Blomberg because we couldn't prove that our name was Ritter. Finally, the news came that the records from the registry in Chemnitz had been brought during the war to Annaberg and that our files had been found. Otherwise, it would have been difficult for us to get our real names back.

When they at last received permission to return to their original names, the name Blomberg went, but Gabriel stayed.

Although I wasn't born with this name, it became such a part of me that I accepted it unconditionally. My playmates called me Gabriel, my mother always called me by this name as well, and I so identified with it that my own first name became absolutely foreign to me. But I was always Ritter, that was never effaced. My playmates never said the name Blomberg; had I been older, had people called me "Herr Blomberg," I don't know how it would have been. But Blomberg was always strange to me, and I got used to it only in the way you accept something you know is not permanent.

My real first name has now disappeared; in my family I am exclusively called Gabriel, and the name is in my passport as well. I feel it is simply more suited to me than the other name; it is the name with which I identified more. This probably has to do with a particular phase in my development: I was called repeatedly by this name over a certain time and just couldn't detach myself from it anymore. But the name was also very likely associated with a certain freedom and gave me, each time it was used, the feeling of being someone with equal rights.

His formal education having been interrupted so early, Gabriel himself was faced with "much catching up for school" when the war ended. While his mother hoped that, once his schooling was finished, he would go into business with her, Gabriel was soon inflamed with a desire of his own. "I went to the theater for the first time and I saw Hamlet," *he recalls, "and from that moment on I wanted to become an actor and to play Hamlet." Gabriel moved on his own into a furnished room in Berlin and supported his acting studies by working as an extra and bit player.*

Gabriel sees a strong connection between his interest in the theater and his experience of persecution. "This profession is the only possibility, if you are not a writer, to help bring to the public certain things of a humanistic or political nature. And to oppose time and time again," he adds, laughing softly at the understatement, "the notion that fascism might have anything to do with humanism." But another aspect of the connection seems to him more compelling.

My main reason for taking up this profession was the transformation: that you can feel for four hours—or three, or two, or five—that you are someone else completely. The first thing I got hold of was, oddly enough, *Richard III;* this teacher happened to have it and brought it to me before I had seen any theater at all. It really is something to have this power for four hours, to have this feeling of saying, " 'Death to the children in the Tower.' Now I will build him up and make him a great man." To be someone with a completely different identity, with a completely different origin, attracted me enormously. But when I read *Richard III,* I didn't yet want to be an actor. The true initial spark was when I saw *Hamlet*—but that was probably only the outward motive, because otherwise I wouldn't have been able to decide so quickly or to keep going so long.

Gabriel did not return in the postwar years to his orthodox upbringing. His wife, a Czech, is not Jewish; their children have not been brought up in any religion and, says Gabriel, will "make their own decision when they come of age." But Gabriel has never ceased to be aware of his origins, nor has he distanced himself from those who share them.

I still feel myself to be a Jew—although more in the national sense—and I make no secret of that here in Germany, either. I am happy for all Jews who did not live through the persecution and who thus have been able to hold on to their emotional equilibrium. But with those who have been wounded by it I feel a close community, a strong and true kinship.

A play that brought together Gabriel's personal and professional lives—and thus provided him with a part with which he "had to identify in an exceptional way"—was George Tabori's The Cannibals.

I played a seventy-two-year-old concentration camp inmate who at the same time plays his own son,* who has escaped in some round-about way to America. Now, the play begins with the sons of the dead fathers coming together in America to talk: "How was what happened in Auschwitz possible? How could they let themselves be done in that way, without resisting? What actually took place? Let's act it out."

The prisoners are cooking a person, they have him in a pot. The SS overseer comes along with a camera and says, "What are you cooking in there?" He takes off the lid, and of course he knows right away. "Let's take pictures of it for the Red Cross," he says, in his cynicism. "Look how well they're eating. They still have everything." And he tells these thirteen people, "Serve it up. Eat."

But this old man says, "If you do that, you are no better than your tormentors." And by the end of the play, I have gotten them not to eat. They all say no, and they all go into the gas chamber—all but two, who eat. These two survive, and they are with this group of sons in America; they speak with these children and are the informants as to what really happened. I identified most with the role of this old man, because I of course knew all this from firsthand accounts and I felt along with him.

To do his job onstage, Gabriel says, he "must identify" with the role he is interpreting—although "it doesn't always work," he admits, "so sometimes you're no good."

When you begin working on a role, you test out approaches; some may work better than others, some may not work at all. Then, one day, the external attitude—an outwardly worked-out technical attitude—suddenly leads you to the inner attitude, the inner situation, the inner pattern of behavior of the entire character. The same thing can happen the other way around, when through an inner drive you jump into the character all at once and the external expression is determined instantly by your inner being. But a technical attitude always leads to a spiritual change; as technical as you may be about it, has an effect on you. You conduct yourself differently, your inner bearing is suddenly another—and whether you can ever shed it completely, I don't know.

But as fully as he has identified with some of his stage roles—among which,

---

*In fact, Gabriel played the son, who in turn plays his father in a play-within-the-play.

to his great satisfaction, he counts Hamlet—Gabriel Ritter recalls as "different" his feelings toward Gabriel Blomberg.

That was not a role. Rather, I *was* it. One had taken a certain identity—I had this identity—and it was not to be wiped away. I don't remember having had this feeling when playing a role.

The URGE *to*
BELONG

If it seemed a foregone conclusion that, for Jews living under the Nazis, a non-Jewish identity would have been little more than a means to an end, it may be equally easy to assume that the end itself—physical survival—was the one motive that overwhelmed all others. For, irrespective of persecution's specific trials, it would be difficult indeed to name a human characteristic more fundamental than the instinct of self-preservation. Millions of years of evolution speak for its primacy in shaping both our mental processes and the behavior that flows from them. While some elements of our identity distinguish us as a species from other species, and some as individuals from one another, the urge to survive defines us in our relationship to the whole of natural history.

But just as living under an assumed identity could stand as an experience of personal significance in its own right, departing from the path trod by the majority of Jews was, for certain individuals, a burden apart. This burden was often difficult to differentiate in the heat of the moment from that of living with an acute threat, and even in retrospect many rejected its importance or questioned its very existence. Their reason seems firmly grounded in common sense: They took for granted that their fear of concrete dangers mattered far more than the seemingly abstract feeling of affinity for a group. But, their objections notwith-standing, their stories often show that a need to belong to the Jews played a powerful role in determining their feelings, their perceptions, even their choices—at a time when life itself was at stake.

What happens when two elements of identity, the urge to survive and the need to belong, come into conflict? Can the pull of the group truly rival the instinct of self-preservation? And if the latter wins out, is its victory as complete—and as free from consequences for the individual—as the logic of evolution might suggest?

The influence that the feeling of belonging can exercise is not always entirely obvious. Among the great mass of those who were identified and persecuted as Jews were very many—most likely a major-ity—who had never made an attempt to escape the Nazis. Any one of a number of things may have accounted for their facing their destiny in the company of fellow Jews: They may have judged that to be the safest course; or they may have wanted to avoid separation from their loved ones; or they may have had no alternative. But also possible is that it simply did not occur to some that there might be an alternative—and then, perhaps, because it was not only from their family and other intimates but also from the larger group of the Jews that they could not imagine separating themselves.

Others' lives demonstrated what could happen when the two yearnings, belonging and survival, coexisted on a somewhat less unequal basis, and thus in a somewhat less stable form. Many Jews who had assumed non-Jewish identities encountered moments at which the desire to identify themselves as Jews proved irresistible—even when they were revealing themselves to people they had no reason to trust, even when this apparently irrational act might place in jeopardy a closely calculated strategy for survival.

For many, the feeling of being separated from the group may have emerged in its most poignant form after the persecution had ended. The ultimate separation—of those who lived from the vast number who died—has often proved an emotional ordeal. The Nazis had directed their threat against all the Jews. Those who survived may well have done so purely by accident—and even if individuals' efforts seemed in certain instances to have contributed to their survival, there was seldom a reason, discernible or otherwise, that one person had lived while another had not. Might a necessity to explain, justify, or make up for their separation from others with whom they identified have helped motivate some to such postwar acts as testifying at war crimes trials; writing, speaking, or in some other way working to keep the memory of the persecution alive; or even taking part in the founding and preservation of the state of Israel? Does not the fact that so many Jews who lived under the Nazis appear to harbor strong feelings of guilt—feelings they themselves may ascribe to surviving where their fellows did not—also point to the vitality of the conflict between belonging and survival?

Fate presented this conflict to Isaäk Feldman as a real-life metaphor: Separated from his fellow Jews by barbed wire, Isaäk felt a longing to throw off his German uniform and take his place among them. Survival required that he "postpone" the act of identification, that he "conquer" his need to perform it—but if he succeeded in the former, he ultimately failed in the latter. When events thwart Isaäk's repeated attempts to build a bridge to his Jewish past by aiding the threatened and oppressed, he is left a "Janus figure": Drawn to the Jewish community but unable to enter it, he remains in suspension, much as he was at the camp gates.

David Kornbluth appears to have lived a similar conflict but to have made the opposite choice. An orthodox Jew turned Protestant minister, he did not lack for offers to hide his family. But he and his wife declined them, deciding, as David puts it, "to bear the fate of our people." The hardship of the camps, even exposing his five children to a potentially heightened risk of death, somehow seems to have been preferable to following a path that—although it was taken by 25,000 other Jews in the Netherlands—David sees as separating him from the Jewish lot.

Actions taken by Hilda Dujardin seem at times almost beyond the realm of choice. Even though establishing her mother's "Aryan" ancestry held the promise of protecting her husband and her own child, it was a course Hilda barely considered. On the contrary: She twice ensured that the Nazi authorities, who might not have noticed her otherwise, became aware that she was a Jew. Possibly as a result, Hilda ended the war in a concentration camp, "on a first-name basis with death." But she "never regretted it," she declares, "even with all the consequences it may ultimately have entailed." To Hilda, those consequences appear to pale beside the need to make her stand as a Jew.

Isaäk Feldman

Isaäk Feldman was born in 1924, the first child of an orthodox couple living in the heart of Amsterdam's oldest Jewish neighborhood. Isaäk's father had been a young boy when his family left Russia in 1904; the Feldmans were hoping to reach America, but their journey was interrupted in the Netherlands, and they ended up settling there.

Isaäk's Dutch-born mother was of far less orthodox background than her husband, but it was the father's side that prevailed in matters of religion. Not only was practice strict at home but Isaäk and his younger brothers, Louis and Jacques, were forbidden to eat at their maternal cousins', where the dietary laws were observed with less rigor. And because their father was employed by the Jewish community, the boys were under pressure not to do anything that might bring criticism upon the family.

Isaäk often chafed under the restrictions his father imposed. He felt cheated at having to excuse himself when his cousins ate over at one another's houses. His grandfather's wish that Isaäk study for the rabbinate—which meant private lessons two evenings a week, as well as long days at a demanding religious school—was felt as an added burden. "I was an active, energetic child," Isaäk recalls, "and more given to playing with the kids in the street than to sitting around looking at books."

Nor was I overflowing with religion. Still, it was Shabbes morning, with your hat on and your tallis under your arm, to shul;* Shabbes afternoon, to shul; evenings, shul. Going to shul was more an obligation

---

Shabbes: the Sabbath; *tallis:* prayer shawl; *shul:* synagogue (all Yiddish).

I had to my family, and it was hard for me in that I couldn't do what children of liberal parents could do—I couldn't go along to the swimming pool, or roller skating, or join in other games on Saturdays. Instead, I had to walk up and down the street with my younger brother—just back and forth, aimlessly—dressed, summer or winter, in a jacket and a tie.

You had your private life more at school, at noontime and during recess. There were pranks you pulled, for which you often were punished. I lived in mortal fear when it got to the point that my father was called on the carpet and told about my mischief. Then I was in for it, and I don't want to go into what the consequences were at home.

So it went: The weeks passed, one after another, through the years. And I accepted it. Well, I don't know whether I should really call it "accepting"; it just was the way it was. I had nowhere to turn, because at that time life wasn't as it is nowadays, when young kids just run away or find other people who understand what they're going through. We lived in strictly orthodox circles, and there was no way out.

Still, Isaäk remembers the Sunday visits of his mother's relatives as lively and warm. And, religious obligations apart, he took comfort in his surroundings. "I lived in a selected society of Jewish people, in a Jewish culture with a Jewish atmosphere," he recalls. "You thought Jewish, because you were brought up that way—you learned everything that was kosher, everything that had to do with Jewish practice." In that atmosphere, Isaäk says, he felt "safe, protected."

Isaäk was not quite sixteen on May 10, 1940, when the German army invaded Holland. Although the bombing in Rotterdam was far worse, Isaäk remembers seeing a huge column of black smoke rise from the direction of Amsterdam's petroleum storage depots and hearing an explosion in the canal behind his house. On a nearby street corner, people were burning books and newspapers. Isaäk describes the atmosphere as "eerie" and calls his neighborhood's initial response one of "bewilderment."

Then the Germans came. It was the first time I had seen Germans, and I studied them the way children today would look at men from the moon. They were very strange. They all had close-cropped hair.

No one did anything, we weren't arrested, but you noticed that something was up because the atmosphere had changed. Everyone was tiptoeing around. There was a sort of apprehension: stage fright, not knowing what was going to happen.

My parents didn't react. They didn't talk about any of it and acted as if there were nothing going on. And since I come from a family in which nothing was ever discussed with the children, in which you were left completely on your own, you were all by yourself with your emotions and your fears, with all those feelings. So, for a time, we just lived on quietly, but we lived in tension and expectancy.

The silence ended abruptly in February 1941, when the military wing of the NSB, Holland's National Socialist Party, marched into one of Amsterdam's Jewish neighborhoods, touching off a riot in which one of the Dutch Nazis suffered fatal injuries. Later that month, the German Security Police—whose green uniforms inspired the nickname Grüne Polizei in the Netherlands—triggered an apparent booby trap during a check on a suspected Jewish resistance cell. German authorities retaliated by arresting 425 Jewish men, most of whom later died at the concentration camp Mauthausen in Austria. This first deportation occasioned a major strike, Holland's most impressive anti-German demonstration of the war. But martial law was declared, the movement was broken within several days, and more roundups ensued.

Caught in one of them were Isaäk and an older cousin whose parents owned a pastry shop around the corner from Isaäk's home.

Next to the bakery was a barbershop that was open on Sunday, and one Sunday morning I went with my cousin to the barber's. He was going in for the works: a haircut and a shave, to feel a little relaxed and refreshed. I sat against the back wall with a few other people. I no longer remember whether there were two barber chairs or three, but two barbers were working.

Suddenly, the Grüne Polizei came in shouting. All you had to do was see a uniform and you couldn't speak anymore, your knees turned to jelly; and we were so terrified that we couldn't make out what they were saying, or perhaps it just didn't register. It turned out that they had only shouted, "Ausweis!" Papers. "Ausweis, sofort!" Papers, right away; everything had to happen on the double. But by the time it began to dawn on people what was happening, the barbershop had turned into a kind of Madame Tussaud's. Everyone froze—the barbers just stood there holding their razors, and the customers couldn't react, from the fright.

But the Grüne Polizei thought we were resisting them, and a few people caught really nasty blows. They took a bunch of people with them; you see it but you can't make anything of it, you're just so paralyzed. They didn't ask me a thing, figuring I was still only a kid, but some adults among those waiting there were taken away. That was the first time I reacted, my first real moment of dread. But though I felt very threatened then, it's like with a disease: If its course is gradual, the longer it lasts, the more you get used to it.

Anti-Jewish measures soon became more methodical. In July 1941, Jews' identification cards were marked with the letter J; from May 1942, Jews were required to wear a large yellow star on the left breast of their outer garments. In the meantime, nearly half of the 140,000 Jews known to be living in Holland had been resettled in three of Amsterdam's Jewish neighborhoods, one of them Isaäk's, and the neighborhoods were marked with placards reading "Juden Viertel," German for "Jewish Quarter."

Slowly, it began. You had the call-ups to report for work camp, and you saw people leaving with knapsacks. But none of the things you found out later had occurred to you. You couldn't yet imagine it, you simply didn't know—you really thought that these people were going off to work. Then came the roundups. I myself didn't witness it, but you heard people say that in the east and south of Amsterdam they were coming around with lists and systematically taking people away.

The pace of deportations increased toward the end of 1942. That Isaäk's family was still in their home in the spring of 1943 seems to have been the combined result of his father's Russian roots, the Netherlands' never having granted the Soviet Union diplomatic recognition, and the Nazis' legalistic mentality. Nonnaturalized Russian-born Jews and certain of their descendants, regarded by the Dutch as Russian rather than Soviet citizens, apparently confounded the occupier's regulations for the handling of Jews, which could vary according to nationality. Thus they were, for a time, sheltered from deportation.

Others in our house were taken away, and it was terribly grim. On the second floor lived a woman who couldn't walk, but the Moffen* thought she was faking it. They grabbed her, and they shouted so. If you're sitting there upstairs and you don't know what's going on, your blood runs cold; I can't express what you felt, but you felt you were at the mercy of something horrible.

After, well, I don't know how much time, the street was totally

---

*Moffen: a pejorative Dutch term for Germans, roughly equivalent to the American "Krauts."

thinned out. There were hardly any people anymore; it was exactly as if we were living on a stage set. And because everything had been forbidden to the Jews by that time, you were just kind of knocking around. How my father put bread on the table, for the life of me I don't know.

Then, one evening—it was very late, and I slept at the front of the house, facing the street—I heard those boots again. It was so quiet you could hear the boots clearly from a distance; there was no one out, and with that march step it was as if there were just one boot, as if Bellefleur and Bonnevu* were approaching. They stopped before the door of our building. The light was out in my room, and I opened the window. It was pitch dark. I saw nothing but ghosts down there, and I ran out of my room and flew up to the attic.

From there I heard how they came up the stairs and into our apartment; there was no one else living off that stairway, we were the only ones still in the house. I was sitting there, shaking terribly in the dark. There was a skylight in the roof, and I was slender, and I felt so closed in. I thought, "Maybe they're coming to have a look in the attic also," so I climbed out onto the roof in a shirt, or in my pajamas, I can't in God's name remember anymore.

After a few moments, all I could hear was footsteps on the stairs: I was hearing my father and mother and my little brothers being taken away. I don't know how long I sat on the roof, I don't remember at all whether I was cold or warm, I had absolutely no more sensation. I couldn't think, either. I didn't know anymore what to do. It hadn't been discussed in any way that I should do what I did; it happened on impulse, just like that, spontaneously.

I can't remember anything else from that night. But I do remember that when I came to the apartment door the next morning, it was sealed with a kind of tape and there were stamps, half on the tape, half on the doorjamb. I broke the seal and went in. There was no family left, and I walked around in an empty house not knowing what to do.

I went out onto the street. There were some people walking whom I didn't know at all, but I must have been utterly beside myself and I

Bellefleur and Bonnevu: two giants from a Dutch children's book.

wanted to talk to them. Then, when I went to speak—that was the first time I opened my mouth—I discovered that I had lost my voice. I couldn't talk, and the people just stared, and shrugged their shoulders, and walked on. I felt so terribly . . . I don't know how to describe it. Powerless is actually not the right word, although I certainly was powerless. Anybody would have filled the bill as long as they had listened, but I couldn't express what was going on with me. I was at my wits' end.

One of Isaäk's cousins, Harry, lived beyond the confinement of Amsterdam's shrinking Jewish neighborhoods with his non-Jewish wife and their son. As a partner in a mixed marriage with a child, Harry was exempted from many anti-Jewish measures, most notably deportation. Isaac has no memory of going to tell his cousin what had happened, but he does recall the visit of Harry's wife, Anneke, to the empty apartment on the day following his family's arrest.

She took some knives and forks and some other things she said she could use. "These will be for you," she said. "You can stay at our place for the time being." And I just followed along like a dog, because I didn't know where else I was supposed to go.

That evening, I made my first acquaintance with pork. Anneke said, "So, did you have a good dinner?" And I said yes. I said yes to everything, because my mind wasn't on eating, it wasn't on anything, my mind was simply blank. I no longer felt at home anywhere; I was still totally wrapped up in my own home, that's actually what it was. Then she said, "You ate pork," and she looked at me.

I got nauseated, literally nauseated, and she thought that was strange. My cousin was also getting a bit of a laugh out of it; he thought it was kind of amusing in his way. For me, it was as if insult had been added to injury; not that they meant it personally, they had done it without thinking, but I didn't understand why they had done it. I was, of course, brought up to think that pork was unclean, that you're not allowed to eat it, and at that moment I felt exactly as if I had eaten spoiled food.

Isaäk remained with Harry and Anneke for several months. As his temperament was unsuited to staying cooped up, and his cousin's apartment was unsuited to hiding him away completely, Isaäk spent a great deal of time wandering around Amsterdam. He lightened his hair with hydrogen peroxide, kept to busy sections of the city where he could lose himself in the crowd, and carried a false ID card he had procured.

In the winter of 1942–43, Isaäk had been approached on the street by a pair of non-Jewish youths. Called up, as they told him, to forced labor in Germany, the young men had been provided with new papers and now wanted to sell their standard Dutch identity cards for pocket money. Fearing a trap, Isaäk brushed them off at first, but he ended up buying the documents. He resold one but doctored the other, in the name of Hendrik van Heerden, for his own use.

I had photos taken, and I steamed the seal completely off and put my own photo on the card. The two-and-a-half-cent piece you had then fit the outer edge of the stamp perfectly, so I simply ran a pen around it and wrote in the place of issue by hand. I changed the original birth date, 1922, to 1925, but the typeface of the 5 didn't match the other typeface at all. Anyone could have seen that; I had no idea what I was doing. I didn't change anything else, including the fingerprint, which you can't change, of course. But I took some of the egg yolk my uncle worked with at the bakery and smeared it on to conceal that I'd tampered with it; since the fellow was a factory worker, you could have expected the card to be dirty.

In the spring of 1943, Isaäk attempted to burglarize the abandoned bakery of his aunt and uncle, who had been taken away, in search of hidden cash that might finance an escape to Switzerland. The plan failed, but two daring flights followed. One got as far as Paris before a man wearing the lapel pin of the Dutch fascist party told Isaäk and two companions that their resistance contact had been arrested by the Germans. Not knowing whether this messenger was friend or foe, and not about to ask, the three boys—who had undertaken the voyage without so much as a forged travel permit—sneaked back to Holland.

At the beginning of June, Isaäk set out alone. He and two young men he joined up with en route were surprised by border guards as they tried to cross into Belgium; Isaäk remembers fleeing gunfire and dogs, then awakening to find that he had been taken prisoner. Interrogated on the spot by German authorities, he pieced together an explanation from details picked up in Paris and from a Dutch newspaper item: Isaäk claimed to be a forced laborer who had earlier worked in France but was being sent to Germany following a furlough in Holland. He had wanted to go back for his belongings, he said, despite a new regulation forbidding laborers destined for the Reich from returning to their previous work sites.

Ordered held while his identity and story were investigated, Isaäk was placed in a convoy of Belgian smugglers for transfer. During the trip he was reunited with one of his companions, who told him that the other had been shot dead at the border; "that was the first death," Isaäk recalls, "that I really felt inside." The convoy was brought to the southern Dutch city of Breda, where Isaäk was imprisoned on June 4, 1943.

I found myself in a dome-shaped vault. It was just like a space capsule, only with 10,000 people living in it. I was small, and I was still young, and I had never been in jail. Those footsteps on the floor that echoed through the entire vault with all those enormous, cell-lined galleries—that beats you down and strangles you. "This is it," I thought. "I'll never get out of here alive."

I went for a shower. I had to get completely undressed and I thought, "Oh, just don't let them look at me." That's what I was afraid of. But I didn't know that the guards there weren't all that sharp, that nothing would ever have crossed their minds. When I came out of the shower, my clothes were gone, and you got the familiar zebra suit. There was only one size: extra large. I got into the trousers—it was just ridiculous, I could have pulled those trousers all the way up to my neck—and I had to put that shirt on, and a cap, and I got wooden shoes. Then I had to climb an iron staircase, and the first twenty-four hours I couldn't leave my cell.

On the second morning the door was opened, and you had to come out. You had to look straight ahead with your eyes lowered, and they shouted, "Right face!" No one told you the house rules beforehand, you just followed along: You were thrown into a cage, then you came out, then you did right face.

You had to go down those iron steps, which were deadly danger-ous, and you came to a landing. On every landing stood a guard with a nightstick, but what I hadn't noticed was that you had to salute each guard you passed, or tip your cap. I was busy holding my pants up just as if I had been wading, because otherwise I would have tripped on the cuffs and broken my neck—and then, all of a sudden, I was lying on the ground. I had taken quite a blow from a nightstick, and I couldn't figure out why, and that guy was screaming so at me that I was frozen with fear.

Then I had to make sure I got back into step. We were aired outside in pens; you had to walk along the edges of the pens just like a wild animal. How long it lasted I don't know, but then you went back up, and you weren't allowed to lie on your cot during the day.

Meanwhile, the authorities ran their check. They located Hendrik van

Heerden's official records but failed to notice the discrepancy between the birth date on Isaäk's doctored identity card and the date in the file. After three days Isaäk was called in, scolded for his "dumb" attempt to sneak back to France, handed a train ticket, and told to report to the labor office in Amsterdam. Seeing his cousin walk through the door of the apartment, Harry exclaimed, "You're just like the weeds: They can't root you out. You come back every time."

Isaäk continued living with Harry and Anneke, who by this time were illegally sheltering two other Jews as well. Tipped off by the wife of a resistance operative living upstairs, Isaäk escaped a major roundup on June 20, 1943, using his false ID and fluent German—plus considerable bravado—to work himself and several others through police barricades blocking the bridges over Amsterdam's canals.

In August, Isaäk, who spent a lot of time with Anneke's brothers and sisters, joined a group of them for a Sunday outing to a nearby fishing village. Returning to Amsterdam after a pleasant day of sightseeing, they happened upon another sister on the street. Her face "deathly pale," she told Isaäk not to return to Harry and Anneke's: The police had come that morning, just after he had left, and arrested the two others who had been hiding there.

Well, I changed on the spot into a pillar of stone, because now everything was gone. I didn't know anymore what I thought; it was so unexpected and so incomprehensible, I simply couldn't get it. So many thoughts pass through your mind: Betrayal. Yes, betrayal. But by whom?

It was at that point that things started getting very tough for me. I couldn't stay with Anneke's mother. Her son Karel had been called up for forced labor in Germany and had reported to the Central Station, where he was marked "present"—but then he got into the train and climbed out the window on the other side. So, although officially he was in Germany, in fact he was in hiding at his mom's. On top of that, they had taken in a Jewish man who had originally been in hiding with the sister of Anneke's mother. They couldn't have me in the house as well.

I rented a room for five guilders a week but slept there only one night. I didn't dare go back, because I never knew what ideas people might get or who they were. I rented rooms in this way until I had no money left—and then, well, there I was. And I thought, "Where am I supposed to go?"

I went to Anneke's mother. I said I was just going to give myself up because the outlook was hopeless, and everyone began to cry. But then along came Jan, an old friend of Karel's whom I myself knew and used to bump into from time to time. Jan had been working in Germany but had returned to Amsterdam on furlough and gone into hiding. He said to me, "I may have a solution for you, but it'll take some guts."

"Well, what do I have to do?"

"There's a German labor office," he said. "If you report there for work in Germany, you don't have to turn in a ration card or coupons, which you do at the Dutch labor office." I couldn't have reported as an eighteen-year-old to the German labor office; they would have re-marked right off, "You should have reported to the Dutch labor office long ago." But I had already changed my identity card to say that I was seventeen.

So I went over there, and the sweat was in my palms. I stood there a moment; there was a man sitting behind a desk, and he looked up suddenly. He asked in German what I wanted. I said, in Dutch, "I've come to report for work in Germany."

The first thing he asked was "Ausweis." Papers, that's the first thing they ask. I gave him the false identity card. He looked it over and said, "You're still a minor, you have to have permission from your parents."

"My parents are dead."

"Then from your guardian."

"But my guardian is anti-German," I said. "He'll never do it."

"Well," he said, "go to the police station where you live and ask for a certificate of good conduct. Then come back, and you can go work in Germany."

I left the place perspiring heavily, and I went down a few steps somewhere, and it was as if I had rubber knees. Then I went straight back to Anneke's mother's, and I told the story, and no one knew what to do.

Since I couldn't sleep there, I slept for a while right across the street, at the apartment of a guy who rented rooms. But one evening I come in and he comes up to me—it's right before curfew—and he says, "Someone else has your room."

"How can that be?"

"A German officer came," he says, "and he had a look around and said, 'That's the room I want.' I said there was someone already in it, but he didn't care."

"But *I* don't have a room."

"You can sleep with me in my bed," he says.

Then I felt a little sick; I don't know what it was, but I got downright queasy. I sat all night in the stairwell, and I held out like that for a few days.

A week later, on August 31, 1943—Isaäk remembers it as the birthday of the Netherlands' Queen Wilhelmina, a day of clandestine patriotic gestures—he returned to the German labor office.

I was desperate, I no longer knew where to turn, and I thought, "I'll take the gamble, I'm a lost cause as it is." When I walked in, a different man was sitting there. He asked what I wanted. "I've come to pick up some papers," I said.

"Well, who are you?" he asked. "Ausweis!" I hand over the identity card, and he goes leafing through a whole stack of papers. And yes, indeed: It was all ready to go, it had only to be stamped. There was no letter or annotation that "a statement from the police must be attached"; in any case, he didn't ask about it. The only thing he asked me was "When do you want to go?"

I shrugged my shoulders, really nonchalant, as if to say, "Well, I couldn't care less." But I was thinking, "If only I were out of here already . . ."

He stamped all the papers, and I got a ticket, Amsterdam–Berlin. "You can leave tonight," he said. "At seven, from The Hague."

I went over the bridge toward the trolley stop near the Municipal Theater, and when I was just about at the stop, two plainclothesmen came up, one on either side of me: "May I see your papers?" I hadn't read any of it, in my emotion; I had just folded it all up and stuck it into a pocket.

I took out the whole batch and shoved it into their hands. They looked through it and offered their apologies—it was stamped in German, and I was on my way to Berlin. Everything was in order. They didn't give it a second thought.

I didn't go to Anneke's mother's; I took the train straight to The Hague. Since I got there early, I went to see a sister of Anneke's who lived there. Well, they stared at me with eyes like saucers; it was not to be believed that I was still on the loose. Then I went to the station, and at exactly seven o'clock the train left for Berlin.

We arrived at ten or eleven in the morning. I got off the train, and everyone you saw was in uniform. It was really awful—it was as if they were out to nab you, that's the feeling you had. But no one knew you.

I get on the subway for the address written on the papers. When I want to get off, the doors open, and who is standing there in front of me? Piet, one of Anneke's brothers! Just like that. Right across from me, exactly in front of the door where I'm getting out, whereas there are so many doors in the subway!

Well, that man's jaw practically hit the ground. He wasn't expecting any Jewish boys in Berlin—he couldn't fathom it, he couldn't speak at all. But neither could I, that's for sure. Because I didn't know that he was in Berlin, they hadn't ever told me. I'm thinking, "Gosh! He knows who I am!" And, "How is he going to react?"

He was on his way to the dentist. He asked, "Is there a certain time you have to report?" I said there wasn't. He said, "Come on, then. Come with me."

I said, "Sure, why not?" I was happy to have someone nice around, someone I felt a little bit connected to, and we went to the dentist in Berlin. But on the way back I started to fret. I'm thinking, "Is he all right, or isn't he? Because, if he's not, he'll turn me in. He can be friendly and kind, but if he says, 'There's a Jew here,' they'll come get me but they're not going to say who told."

"I couldn't be myself," recalls Isaäk of his first days in Berlin, *"and that's something I couldn't cope with."* That, coupled with his intense worry that Piet might denounce him, very rapidly took its toll on Isaäk, putting him in the infirmary for three weeks with stomach problems—"nerves," he says, "really bad." On his release, Isaäk joined the Organisation Todt unit to which he had been assigned at the labor office in Amsterdam. As the Reich agency in charge of construction, the OT absorbed a large number of forced laborers sent from the occupied countries to Germany as part of the labor mobilization, or Arbeitseinsatz.

At first, Isaäk worked helping an artist whose job it was to paint war scenes, a man with a comforting presence whom Isaäk found to be "a human being." But that arrangement ended overnight—"he was transferred or something," Isaäk remembers, "you weren't told what happened"—and the rest of Isaäk's stay in Berlin was far less pleasant.

On the one hand, Allied bombing was well under way, and the aerial attacks left Isaäk shaken; on the other, thrown in with a group of Dutch and Belgian OT *members, he was always on his guard. "I had rehearsed what was on the identity card," he recalls, "repeating over and over, 'I am Hendrick van Heerden,' and getting my birth date, my place of birth, and my place of residence down cold." He made, he remembers, a constant "effort not to be recognized, to remain anonymous."*

I was smaller than the rest, with a tiny little noggin, and they took me for a kind of tyke. The other fellows were all older, and three or four years make a big difference—they were all married or engaged, or in any case a lot more independent than I was. They thought of me as a kid, they didn't take me seriously, and I didn't really belong.

Isaäk believes that the others never asked him questions about himself precisely because they didn't take him seriously; "that was the only silver lining," he says. And he believes that no one other than Anneke's brother even suspected that he was Jewish. Still, describing his condition as one of "hiding away," he says, "I was never at ease, never secure."

I was the wandering Jew, and I would just keep going until I was caught. It was the same feeling I had had in the jail in Breda. I knew they were working to figure out who I was in reality, and whenever someone's glance rests on you an extra beat, you think, "That's it." I lived daily with the tension in the back of my mind: What if they ever find out?

In the evenings, the others began talking about home: what their mother had said, and their sister, and "then thus-and-such happened"—a little family chitchat. I had to be careful that I didn't say, "Oh, yeah, I know what you mean . . ." That could have been walking into a trap, and it would have been a trap I'd set for myself. I couldn't say any names, of course, because then I'd be talking about Louis and Jacques, and about Aunt Rivke,* and so on. What happens is that you don't talk anymore, you talk only when someone asks something of you: "You have to do this or that." You can never react spontaneously, from your own self.

You become completely quiet, you live like a deaf mute. You can't handle what happens around you because you're living submerged in

---

*The names *Louis* and *Jacques* might have had a Jewish resonance for Isaäk's Dutch comrades even though they are somewhat assimilationist in flavor compared with Biblical names. *Rivke* is the Yiddish equivalent of Rebekah.

fear. In my emotional life I had no sorrow, no happiness, I was totally anesthetized. You hear things much too late that others hear right away, you react too late. And then you're afraid that they'll take too much notice of you, which is what I wanted to avoid.

So nobody knows, and you hope that you don't run into anybody who knows you. I was waiting on a subway platform somewhere in Berlin when out of the train came a guy I had worked with in Amsterdam. He knew me very well, and he came out of the subway and called in a loud voice, "Isaäk!" Well, boy oh boy, I thought I would disappear from the face of the earth; I was stunned into paralysis. But then I started looking around behind me, and he said, "It's *you* I'm talking to. It *is* you, isn't it?" and so forth.

I started in German, saying that I hadn't understood a thing, and what did he want? I kept it up, and the fellow walked away completely disoriented; he was dumbfounded. I got out of that one all right, but it was really sad, because I would rather have chatted with him for a bit.

Piet's presence at the OT quarters never ceased to weigh on Isaäk, who was "happy, on the whole" to leave Berlin—and his cousin's brother-in-law—behind. Over the next few months, in part because of Allied bombing, the unit he was with bounced around among Berlin, Munich, and various cities in the western part of Germany. Along the way, Isaäk was twice assigned to domestic chores in German barracks, once in the barracks of a company of Grüne Polizei. His unit ended up moving from town to town in the Ruhr, a period Isaäk remembers as "a horror."

The houses all had holes blown in them, and the cities were bombed to the ground, and that was rubble, cleaning up rubble and more rubble. It was a nightmare: clearing the streets and . . . pulling out what was underneath.

I was there until the Americans landed in Normandy. There was an upbeat mood among the guys—kind of, "Just a little while longer, we're right near Holland, we'll be back home in a shake." But then we were loaded into a train in Duisburg—and three days later you arrive in Auschwitz.

The train stood still. It was dusky, between light and dark, and really nice weather. I think it was the end of June 1944, or the beginning of July; no, it was June. In the distance you see "Auschwitz," and on another signboard behind it "Oswiecim," in Polish. Two signs at a tiny train station.

Today I think, did I actually know about the gas chambers? Did I actually know? That is to say, I no longer know when I first knew. But you grow so lonely. It's unbelievable—it was just as if I had had a halo over my head, as if I kept being let off. But this? This, I couldn't comprehend: that I, a Jew, would turn up there, while the Moffen didn't know I was a Jew.

We got off the train. You see how many camps there are, and you see how the people there are working, and you hear that it's for IG Farben, there in the inner area, with the barbed wire. You leave the station and there's a dead end, so you have to go around. There was a dentist—I remember that, I went once myself—and there were baths and a shower room for general use. Then you turn the corner and there is a narrow, dusty alley with potholes, and all the camps are on one side. And there is a complex where there was nothing but rocks, I saw nothing but rocks from rubble heaps that the prisoners stood chipping away at. That was the first thing I saw.

We were brought to an empty camp in Auschwitz that bordered on a camp where there were military prisoners: Americans, Englishmen, New Zealanders, Canadians, Australians, all Allied pilots who had been shot down and were imprisoned there. We were just in front of them, and we were big friends with them immediately because they heard we were Dutch, and it started with the cigarettes—you know how it goes. Then the SS saw that we were getting along much too well and we were taken out of there. We had to go all the way to the back of Auschwitz, to the last barracks. Behind us was just barren ground—no farming or anything, simply wasteland. We were bivouacked there for a few months, until autumn. It was really terrible, a living nightmare.

Isaäk's unit was put to work filling in potholes in the roads around Monowitz, also known as Auschwitz III. The task was typical of those the Nazi bureaucracy found to keep its huge number of forced laborers occupied. One experience Isaäk had there had already become familiar.

We went through an awful bombing at Auschwitz. The Allied camp was hit. I don't have an overview—naturally, I couldn't survey the scene—but you do see, in the distance, those columns of smoke, and fire and stench and screaming, and you don't know exactly who, what, how, or where.

Although he was never within the compound itself, Isaäk was occasionally able to speak with Jewish prisoners who were in work details assigned outside. When he did, he sought information about his family.

I didn't know then that my parents and my brothers hadn't been brought to Auschwitz; I thought that Auschwitz was the only camp people were transported to. It was after the war that I found out via the Red Cross that they had already been gassed, in April '43, immediately on arrival at Sobibor. So when I came into contact with prisoners, I asked if they knew my brothers, whether they knew a Louis or a Jacques.

You keep searching. I asked about it all the time, but I didn't ask adults—I didn't dare—only children. I saw a lot of little boys around, and you think, "Auschwitz," and you didn't know, and you think, "Maybe the children know, the children ought to know." Some of these boys couldn't understand me at all, nor could they understand German. They were French and Hungarian and all nationalities, it was a Babel.

But they all looked like one another, they were all bald and all dressed the same. And all the women looked like one another, all the men looked like one another. It was unbelievable. It was absolutely awful.

I saw women shoveling. I found that so sadistic. The shovel blades were two or three times the size of the ones the men had. Everyone is shaved bald, and you have to look twice before you know if they are men or women. But you see it at a given moment: You see it from the posture, it dawns on you from the expression, from the whole movement that a woman makes when she shovels, and a man. I hadn't realized it because I had never seen a woman shovel, but it registers all at once.

Once, from a distance, Isaäk recognized the son of friends from home, and he sent a postcard to Amsterdam indicating that the man was still alive. "I wrote in veiled terms—about 'dirty Jews'—because it had to go through the censor," says Isaäk. "I said that I had seen him, but that's all I wrote. And that I was there." On another occasion, Isaäk actually spoke with a prisoner from Amsterdam.

I saw someone coming in from working in the fields. It was terribly hot, so hot the ground shimmered, and as this man came by, he collapsed. I heard him calling "Water!" in Dutch. So it was a Dutchman, and I went to the man and I asked him right away what his name was—well, that happened in my enthusiasm—but he was completely exhausted, he was just shouting, "Water!" And where were you supposed to find water?

There was a sort of little store nearby that sold vegetables which had been dead for about a month—they were all limp—and I got a cucumber. I came back with the cucumber, and what did I see? The man was being beaten horribly by a kapo,* and there were six soldiers there—guards, all old men who had perhaps been on the Eastern Front and who had been declared unfit but were still good enough for guard duty—and they were just sitting around, staying out of the way.

I picked up a piece of iron, and I rammed into that kapo something horrible. And what all he said to me I don't know, but he went back to work and the man didn't finish the cucumber. I still remember that he said his name was Katz and that he lived in the Blasiusstraat in Amsterdam. I didn't know him, and I couldn't tell him who I was either. He might not have believed it or understood it.

Isaäk claims he is unable to express what it was like, as he himself terms it, being "on the wrong side of the barbed wire."

It is simply a feeling of powerlessness. If someone were to ask me, "Why didn't you just turn yourself in? Then you would have had peace"—which is what I don't have—the only thing I could say is that you're young, and you think, "God damn it, you'll make it through, and maybe there'll be someone you know who comes out of it as well."

The nights above all, the nights were truly terrible. I lay there crying. Well, I couldn't cry spontaneously—because I was afraid that others would notice that I was weeping, and that they'd start asking questions—but when I had pulled a blanket over my head.

Do you know that feeling when you're in the car and you pass a truck? That you're being sucked along, you have the feeling that you're being pulled along by that truck? That's the feeling I had. I actually had the need just to say it, and to give myself up. That was so strong, and I had to find a way to postpone it, to conquer it. That was unimaginable, I just can't make it clear in words. That feeling . . . it breaks you.

Isaäk's unit was ordered to leave Auschwitz in the fall of 1944. As the German Reich crumbled, Isaäk was sent on an aimless railroad journey that took

---

*kapo: in the concentration camps, a trusty prisoner. Kapos were often put in charge of work details and were sometimes given authority over fellow prisoners in other contexts as well.

him deeper into Poland, through Czechoslovakia and Hungary to the Rumanian border, then back to Budapest. "The war was gradually coming to an end," Isaäk says. "The Russians were advancing, but you didn't know that, you didn't hear news. Why are you going here and not there? Nobody knows what is supposed to be happening." In December 1944, following a period of memory loss that he has never been able to reconstruct, Isaäk awoke—neither ill nor injured, so far as he could tell—in a hospital bed in the German city of Chemnitz.

With the new year, he was sent off again on a march that took him through war-ravaged landscape he describes as "out of Hieronymus Bosch." First heading north to East Prussia, the group Isaäk was with then crossed the frozen Bay of Gdansk on foot, reaching Danzig after several months.

In Danzig, you can't get on the ship, it's full. The next day you do get on a ship, and you hear that the ship you couldn't sail on the day before has been torpedoed and that everyone was killed or drowned. Just before we sailed, the SS came and we had to load them on. They were all badly wounded and bandaged with paper; it was a crazy sight, just like Carnival except that it was so sad. They were laid on blankets below, there was nothing else. The last load to come on was food for the wounded. And that, we stole: white bread and butter, we were beside ourselves when we saw that. That evening they were continually being thrown overboard, the ones that had died, and it stank below terribly.

During the voyage, Isaäk ran into a former prisoner from Auschwitz to whom he had given what was left of the cucumber he had originally brought for the spent Dutchman.

All the Jewish people came together, and a man came up to me, a real tall guy with a good-looking head of hair and a nice suit. "Hi, Henny," he said, putting his arm around my shoulders.

I looked at him, and I said, "My name isn't Henny, my name is Isaäk."

"Come off it," he said, "I recognize you."

"Where, but where do you know me from?"

"From Auschwitz."

I said, "I've never been in Auschwitz"—because initially I thought that he thought that I had been a prisoner there.

Reaching the German port of Swinemünde, the passengers walked off the ship and "into a pile of rubble."

It was all rubble, there were no people, you didn't know what you were seeing. When we got near Neustrelitz, the Moffen called out, "You can go home. The war is over, the Führer is dead." Not one of us moved a step, because we thought, "It's a trick." We thought as soon as we took a step, they'd shoot us down—because there was no longer any food, and we thought, "Now they won't have to feed us." Everything goes through your mind. But the Moffen just walked away and left us standing there, and we had no idea anymore of where we are or what we're supposed to do.

Then begins the march through Rostock and Wismar to Schwerin and Lübeck. On May 4 we came across the Americans. I wasn't happy at all. I wasn't relieved, and I didn't shout "Hurrah!" or anything. I was so knocked out, I had had it with everything. I was a little bit dead; all of us were drained. The Americans looked at us just like a herd of lost cattle; they had no idea what to do with all these people.

Isaäk had been lodged with a German family in Pomerania and had picked up a traveling companion, a girl one year younger than he.

Her mother asked me to be good to her, and I took her along. The mother was also making a run for it because anything in a Russian uniform was raping anything in skirts; that was the big fear, that's why so many people were clearing out.

I brought the girl all the way to Assen,* and then I told the truth: who I was. It was the so-called resistance, the Dutch Home Army, and I thought, "Now I'm back in Holland and I can say it."

They sent the girl back. I wanted to go with her but I wasn't allowed to; they were ready to beat the daylights out of me. She didn't have a German name, and I could have said with no trouble at all that she was Czech, because those people could hardly distinguish, they were such imbeciles. But that's what you get if you're honest, and it just strangled me, because I loved her very much. She was really sweet, and that's what I go for, someone who's sweet.

They raped her in the car as they were taking her back. There were a couple of people in front, and the rest who were supposed to be guarding her were in back. I could murder them. Not only the Moffen, for whom I have an eternal blood hatred, but I also hate those people, the "good patriots," the Home Army bastards.

Assen: a city in the northeast of the Netherlands.

After numerous delays, Isaäk was brought by truck and boat to Amsterdam.
Upon his arrival, he was put through an inspection designed to ferret out
collaborators who might have been trying to slip back into the country among the
returning refugees.

We had to strip to the waist. You walk into the Central Station and
go by a bunch of tables. You have to tell your story: where you're coming
from, and what you've done, and who you are. Everything is noted
down, and if you can document it, so much the better.

Well, I told what happened. "But I'm not this person, I'm So-and-
so."

"Yeah, sure."

Just as if I were nuts, that's the way they treated me: "Yeah, fella,
sure." I went from table to table, I tried everywhere. They thought I was
a little crazy from the tension and the tragedy because I sort of went on
and on. But in that sense I was perfectly fine. It was just that I was
terribly tired—I was worn-out and undernourished.

So you again meet up with people you can't get through to, who
don't take you seriously. They didn't take anyone seriously. What they
were keen on was whether there were SS among those coming in; as for
the rest, that was Arbeitseinsatz, and they were allowed to go through.

That's the category they put me in. If I'd been in a camp, then
you're brought together somewhere with all the people from the camps.
I hadn't been in a camp, but I had still gone through terrible misery. I
got the feeling that people didn't know what they were supposed to do
with me, or what they were supposed to say; no one had a clue. I was
treated just like someone who had done forced labor, who still had his
family at home. But I had nobody.

I stood outside the Central Station. I saw the horse-drawn car-
riages driving—they were the taxis—and the Victoria Hotel. It was
truly, totally strange: Everything was intact. I was used to living in the
ruins, with hunger and destruction, and then you arrive in this beautiful,
empty Amsterdam—it could have been a diorama. Well, that day was
the seventeenth of June: my birthday. Precisely on my twenty-first
birthday I was standing there. All I remember is that it struck me that
I couldn't find my way around town. I never really felt at home in
Amsterdam after that.

Within days, Isaäk saw a military recruiting poster containing information
which, he recalls, hit him "like a bomb": Fellow citizens in the Dutch East Indies

were being held in Japanese concentration camps. Isaäk "didn't think about it for a minute"—he went around the corner and enlisted.

I was inducted into the marine corps, but I had to wait for a call-up. And what happened? I was called up, and then in August '45 the atom bomb fell on Hiroshima and Nagasaki and the war was over. I thought, "Well, it's all over, we'll go home"; but nothing doing, no, sir. I did three years, and it was a kind of Vietnam in miniature.

Again horrible things happened: There were mass graves in Madura as well, and 200 liters of gasoline went over them and a match was held up to it, to burn the corpses. Yeah. It was necessary, but you never get used to it.

And when I was in the marines, I had more trouble with anti-Semitism than I had in the Organisation Todt. Because in the marines they *knew* I was a Jew: I was called Isaäk Feldman, and you get it automatically.

As Isaäk sees it, his Jewish perspective quickly brought him into conflict with the military authorities. When his bangs crept slightly below his eyebrows, he was ordered to have his head shaved—something he "didn't want," he says, "because that camp had left such an impression." Having refused an order to go to the barber, Isaäk was placed in detention and threatened with eight years in prison for "insubordination in wartime."

I didn't knuckle under; I resisted, I didn't accept it. I think I told the lieutenant colonel at one point that my whole family had died in the camp and that it happened without hair; but that wasn't his affair. Finally, though, the commandant thought, "I can't really do this," and climbed down a little, so I got out of it. He says, "I'll tell the barber to give you a 'regulation cut.'" I ask what that is, and he says, "Just short, not bald." It was done with clippers and he left only a little hair. I looked awful, just like a German soldier.

While in the marines, Isaäk learned that he would not be covered in the event he became disabled unless he assumed Dutch nationality; because his paternal grandfather had never been naturalized, the whole family was still considered stateless under Dutch law. Isaäk wrote to The Hague to apply for citizenship.

I get a letter from the ministry in which they say that I spell my name wrong. "Your name should not be spelled Veldman, but Feldman."

"Well, my father also spelled it Veldman"—I didn't know, that was the way it always was.

"Yes, but your grandfather spelled it Feldman, so you have to spell it Feldman as well."

That was their big worry: splitting hairs. You get the feeling—and not because the *V* becomes an *F*—but I had the feeling that I was nobody anymore, that I was actually being completely negated.

Upon his return to the Netherlands, Isaäk came down with malaria, which kept him hospitalized for more than a year; it was 1949 before he could begin building a life for himself. For some years he had difficulty paying the rent, but by the early 1970s he had carved out a comfortable existence working as a salesman, and he had a wife and two children.

The world is hard, but I kept going. And when at a certain point I had pulled myself up out of the financial misery—you have a house and you have a boat and you have a company car and your own car as well—then you go to pieces. I fell still, totally still. I didn't go out on the street anymore, I didn't go walking with my dog, I didn't go out in my boat. I just spent all day standing and staring.

Isaäk began psychotherapy, but he avoided revealing his personal history to his therapist for over a year—the result, he says, of an abiding fear of "betrayal."

When I'm in trouble, I don't call for help; I'd rather die. That is the anonymity which I never want to give up, which is my only security in life. Henny has been in me too long, the feeling will never go away. The name, yes; but that feeling, I still have it, it's still there. Even in therapy I couldn't be spontaneous. I changed sometimes from Isaäk—I'd begin by feeling like Isaäk, and then all of a sudden I'd hear Henny.

I was Henny in the marines. I was under my real name, but in my behavior I was still Henny. On Surabaja, a Jewish chaplain took me to get acquainted with the Jewish community, but there was nothing there for me. I remained Henny, I didn't become Isaäk. They saw me as Isaac: I was a Jew, Isaäk. But in my inner feelings I wasn't.

And that's how it is today. I've fallen away totally from the sphere of Jewish life. I'm a Janus figure: I would like to be taken into the community, but I can't find it in me any longer, I'm not up to it. Before, I was Isaäk; I was completely at home in that atmosphere, in those circles. I have such a warm emotional tie to it, but when I go to the Jewish community now, I no longer feel at home, because I go there as Henny.

I've survived completely alone. It's just as if there were no one anymore. When I walk, everything has gotten so distant, everything so far away, I'm a complete stranger here. I'm actually a stranger everywhere. Since that time, I've never really felt at home.

Isaäk looks back with "regret" on his tour of duty in the Dutch East Indies, where he went with the aim of liberating prisoners from concentration camps— "for that alone," he says—only to end up in a colonial war. During the 1973 Middle East war, he offered the benefit of his experience to the Israeli army, but the offer was rejected. "I was already nearly fifty," he explains, "and it was too late." What he would have preferred above all is to have fought in Israel's War of Independence.

During the Second World War, I did what I did in order to survive. After that, it wasn't necessary anymore—but they played false with emotions, the bastards. I went through so much: I saw people burned alive, I saw houses collapse, I had to clear out hospitals. I actually fought for anti-Semites in the Indies, for the interests of the plantation people, and that sticks in my craw. In 'forty-five, I shouldn't have signed up for the Indies, I should have gone to Israel.

Because if I had gone to Israel, well, friend, then I would have had pleasure from my fear. I know that sounds strange, but it's true. In the Indies it was just like the Organisation Todt in Berlin: You arrive somewhere, and this one goes to the tanks, that one to the infantry, and you never know where you're going, or what will happen to you. If you join the army of Israel, things happen, but you don't have stage fright anymore—*that's* what I mean. You know what is going to happen. You feel it, and you know it.

And if you die, that's not so bad. I know how that is from guys I was with. There was this kid with me in the tank in Madura. He was sitting up top on the cockpit adjusting the antenna and he fell down dead—damn it!—just like that, at my feet. It was a blow to his family— he was nineteen, and a conscript on top of it—but he died instantly, lucky for him. They don't feel it; it lasts only a second, and as soon as they start to feel it, they're already dead. That doesn't get to me so much.

What does get to me is people who are caught by surprise, but who aren't taken away immediately, who are just left there on pins and needles. At first they send them away with their knapsacks, and then they round up the rest, and there are more of them, more and more, and then they all go. Till I myself find out where they end up, till I myself sit three days in the train from Duisburg to Auschwitz; for them it also lasted three days and three nights, through Breslau and Ratibor to Auschwitz. I make the same trip, I see the camp, I see what happens there—only I am not gassed.

Here is the barbed wire: I was here, and they there. But I had the same feelings. In fact, I was in a worse spot, because they were all together, after all, and I was alone. And that was very dangerous, that was the feeling of being sucked along, of "Come on, out with it! Then at least I'll . . . then we'll all go together." For that helps you bear up: If you meet death together, it's gentler. You are less frightened than if you have to die alone.

But for me it's just the other way around, because I survived. You could almost say that I would have a guilt complex. The therapist tried to talk me into that, but the only thing I said was "You can talk about regret, that I didn't go along with my parents." Because beforehand, as a child, I didn't know that I would have to go such a route of suffering, that I would end up in Germany, I didn't know that I would flee up to the roof, I didn't know anything at all.

And suppose I had stayed in bed, suppose I had just lain in bed: I would have been taken away. They just come in all of a sudden and you go along. That is all pure chance, it has nothing to do with reason, only with luck, with circumstance; it's unbelievable. For the rest, I went along that same path of suffering that the others did, because I followed the people and saw what happened and how they were treated, and I can't get it off my mind.

In fact, I am the spokesman. And I'm not speaking in my own name, and I am no one—I am no one anymore since I'm alone. I speak with you as a representative of all those people who can no longer speak for themselves. I am someone who was just as frightened as all the other people, those who were dragged from their houses and who went to the gas chambers on such a horrible, unimaginable, ineffable road of suffering—except I can tell you about it, this road. I also traveled it, only I'm still alive.

So I declare it openly, and it's a terrible burden, I suffer a lot from it. If someone takes a swing at me, I can hit back—and how! But if someone calls out "Jew," then he calls that whole story back. I could handle it better in the old days, because as a kid you'd duke it out—and it was aimed only at me then, whereas now it's aimed at all those poor wretches. All that suffering—that's what "Jew" represents for me. People tell you, "Now, just forget it," but I can't forget, and what I want to do is to keep on thinking of them with love.

When we spoke, Isaäc had been separated for quite some time from his wife. He was living on the outskirts of Amsterdam in a housing development whose massive concrete structures have a deserved reputation for isolation, impersonality, and ugliness. "As Isaäk, I would never live out here," he reflects. "Here it's not normal. This is just like a barracks, a bunker, it makes me think of Berlin. As Isaäk, I would have looked for something back in the old neighborhood."

Beset by headaches and other ailments that had plagued him without letup for several years, Isaäk had not been employed for some time. Although he himself describes his ills as "psychosomatic," he had chosen to discontinue psychotherapy not long after meeting Yvonne, a woman perhaps half a dozen years his junior with whom he had begun to spend a great deal of time.

I have a lot to thank her for. It's unbelievable, the good one person can do another, making you feel what she means to you. I've never experienced anything like it, that someone was so kind to me. I find it very frightening; it goes together with intense emotions. In the war you did everything automatically, and now I do everything with feeling, and that's really tough.

It's so hard for me to give myself totally to someone, because then I get that closed-in feeling. It happened again a short time ago: I felt that I was losing consciousness, but I didn't call anyone. They say, "You have to trust." I can't do it, I don't dare with anyone, I have learned not to. I dare to trust only myself.

But now I'm trying to do something about it, even though it's so painful. And why? Because I can't go through my whole life so embittered. I had five years of war, four years in the marine corps, five years in therapy. Twenty-five years in a company where I worked like a dog, not because I'm such a hard worker, but just not to get fired. I always have the feeling that I have to achieve a little bit more than someone else, otherwise I can't stay around. And if your whole life has been in the service of another—figuring out the other's wishes so that the other likes you or the other finds you companionable or the other thinks you're a good worker—and the other thinks of it all what *he* thinks, I want for once to feel what *I* think, what *I* want.

I'm fifty-four now, and sometimes I feel eighteen. I still need the things where I actually left off—where the war plunged me into a life that I didn't want, that had nothing to do with me, that I had to take on, compelled by necessity, in order to survive. And the price was very high, looking back.

I talk about those things with Yvonne: what it is like to go out with a girl, to go to bed with someone, when you're grown up, twenty-one, and you have some money in your pocket, you're already independent. But I was still such a child. I have the feeling that I'm eighteen and still have the wish to do that, but sometimes I'm eighty—no, one hundred and eighty. When I look at myself, I'm a little boy walking hand in hand with an old graybeard, and in between there is no one.

Rev. David Kornbluth

David Kornbluth was born in 1902 in the eastern Polish village of Kotzk, famed among religious Jews as the home of the Chasidic leader Menachem Mendel. David's father was an orthodox Jew who understood his faith in the tradition of the Mitnaggedim, the opponents of Chasidism who, though no less deeply religious, emphasized rationalism, skepticism, and Talmudic study in reaction to the emotional style of the Chasidim and their charismatic rabbis. The elder Kornbluth was also a passionate Zionist and an admirer of Theodor Herzl, Zionism's founder. "As I was not yet three years old, I cannot remember it," says David, "but the other children told me that when Herzl died, my father wept, sobbing, 'The Messiah is dead.' "

Within a few months of David's birth, his father decided to leave Kotzk, whose population of 5,000 was two-thirds Jewish, for a larger city where he would be able to "give his children a general education in addition to a traditional Jewish upbringing." He found a job in Lodz, an industrial center on the western fringe of Russian-ruled Poland with a Jewish population of over 100,000. David was enrolled in a Jewish day school between the ages of five and nine; after that, he attended a secular school in the mornings, studying Jewish subjects during classes that met each afternoon. "My father died in 1913, when I was eleven years old," David recalls, "but I continued with the orthodox education he had laid out for me."

By the end of the First World War, however, it was their late father's Zionist leaning that was proving the main inspiration for the Kornbluth children.

Although I had been brought up very religious, my religious conviction was, at this point, relegated to the background. When I was sixteen, I became a member of the Poale Zion, a group within the

Zionist movement that furthered the cause of socialism and worked toward the founding of a Jewish national state on socialist principles. In an industrial city such as Lodz you are confronted with the misery of the working people—which is why, having begun with the Zionist perspective, I added socialism. My father had considered Herzl as Messiah, but he was well off, he had built himself a solid position in Lodz's middle class; we, as children, went further. In those days of czarist rule, there was a kind of socialist-Zionist cell in our home.

After finishing secondary school, David took an administrative job in Lodz. In April 1922, he was called up for military service and became "the only Jewish telegrapher" in the Polish army.

Poland had become independent in 1918, and there were a great many illiterates as a legacy of Russian rule, so someone with a proper secondary education like I had was not one of the masses but actually a kind of rarity. I was assigned to train as a telegraph operator and, after six months, sent to a radio post. But there you had the anti-Semitism that is still rampant in Poland today: "Jews at a radio post? They'll betray the whole works." So I was assigned to a clerical job in Radymno, the town where we were stationed, and never did work as a telegrapher.

In the battalion I belonged to, we were two Jews in the midst of at least 200 non-Jews. There was also a young man from a Protestant family—another rarity in Poland, where everyone was Roman Catholic. As a Protestant he wasn't at ease; among all those Catholics, he was in the same position that I was in as a Jew. For this reason he felt drawn to me, and I to him as well, and we became friends.

One day, he was reading the New Testament, and he asked me if I also wanted to take a look at it. He didn't have anything specific in mind, it was just between friends. I got the New Testament from him and began to read, and I was deeply touched by the figure of Jesus; the figure of Jesus began to captivate me. But when we were discharged from the army, he went his own way—he was the son of a rich textile manufacturer in Lodz—and I went mine, and all this receded into the background.

David was discharged in 1924 and moved to Radom, where his fiancée lived, taking a job as secretary of a Jewish tradesmen's association; the couple was married the next year. He also resumed his activism in Poale Zion, managing its campaign in Radom's 1926 municipal elections, in which it achieved unprece-

dented success. He remained politically active after moving back to Lodz in early 1928 to take a job as a bookkeeper.

It was then that I again picked up the New Testament—well, not only the New Testament, but the Old Testament as well. The unity of the two struck me.

Of the first five books—the books of Moses, or Chummash,* as it is called—my favorite was, and still is, Deuteronomy. That book captivated me enormously, particularly in its social import. For example, I read there that when a Jew harvests his field, he may not pick up the sheaves that fall on the ground, but he must leave them for the poor; and he may not harvest the corners of the field, which he must leave for the poor. If someone has borrowed from you and cannot pay you back, in the fiftieth year you must return his collateral to him on the theory that you have already gotten back what you lent him in the interest he paid through the years.† Deuteronomy is full of such social tendencies.

I've read the Bible a hundred times since then, front to back and back to front, and it continues to enthrall me for the very reason that I see in it the first social tendencies of humankind, a message that God chose the people Israel to propagate among the other nations. And I have always contended that if our Jewish people, at first in their own land and elsewhere thereafter, had lived according to the principles set forth in Deuteronomy, then Marx would not have been needed. Because there, in Deuteronomy, are to be found the principles of a socialism which began before all else, and which will remain when all else has passed.

Then I began to go through the long line of our prophets. With the prophet Amos there is again this social principle: Amos stands up against the ruling class of rich men and luxuriant women who exploit the others and who preen themselves at the expense of others' sweat and blood. Or take a man such as Jeremiah—or any of our prophets, for that matter. Our own rabbis say that if the people Israel had held itself to Moses' teachings, then the prophets would not have come.

And now we can take a big step: When I read the New Testament,

---

Chummash: the five books of Moses, from the Hebrew *chammesh,* "five."
†This last example is actually from Leviticus.

I was fascinated by the person of Jesus. Someone who stands up for the poor, someone who stands up for the oppressed, someone who speaks of self-denial and who lived it out to its most extreme consequences. He is no stranger to us—He is flesh of our flesh, blood of our blood. "Think not that I am come to destroy the law, or the prophets," He said. "I am come not to destroy, but to fulfill." And He did fulfill them, unto His own death.

The more I devote myself to the Holy Scriptures, the more convinced I am of the indissoluble unity of what are referred to as the Old and New Testaments, but which I would rather call Tanach* and the Gospels. They make up a whole, a chronological progression. If Israel had held itself to the words of Moses, we never would have had this whole to-do: no prophets, and no Jesus. The prophets, as the rabbis themselves have said, came to bring Israel back to the teachings of Moses. But since our people did not take the voices of the prophets to heart, did not attend to their teachings, there came, in his time, the Messiah, in the person of Jesus of Nazareth.

So it was that the person of Jesus came closer to me. Even while I was active as a socialist Zionist, and had a wife and child and a position in society, the Bible engrossed me; once I truly began to immerse myself in it, I couldn't get free anymore. The religious background that I had—the orthodox Jewish upbringing I brought with me from home, with its traditional and social elements—did not release me. It left its stamp on me; or, more precisely, it paved the way for what I was later to become.

In the meantime this began to get through to my family, and they felt, "He is on the wrong path." My mother was still alive then, as were my brothers and sisters, and since I was already married and leading my own life, I thought to myself, "Why must I cause them grief? I can live my life somewhere else."

Hoping to gain a foothold, David left his wife and child behind in Lodz and, before the end of 1928, settled in Paris. There he found work and, in his limited

---

Tanach: Hebrew name of the Old Testament; acronym formed from the names of the three parts of the Bible: Torah (five books of Moses), Nevi'im (the Prophets), and Ketuvim (the Writings).

spare time, became a regular at the meetings of a London-based missionary society, the Hebrew-Christian Testimony to Israel. What he heard there, David remembers, "connected to the thoughts I was having. It didn't seem foreign to me at all." Recognizing a kindred spirit, but unable to help David further on his way, the head of the Paris branch of the mission looked to his opposite number in the Netherlands.

Without asking me, he got in touch with him: "I have a brother here who is seriously involved, but his ideal is to go to Palestine." That was my ideal then: just as the apostle Paul, who worked making tents but at the same time preached the Gospels, to proclaim the Word in the land of our fathers. Thus, the Zionist ideal had not let me go, not for one second.

In the summer of 1930, David left France for Holland, where he was reunited with his wife—who shared his interest in the Christian faith—and their young daughter. After the family's request for permission to settle in Palestine had been rejected, a casualty of the restrictive immigration policy enforced under the British Mandate, David began a three-year course of study at the theological seminary of the Free Evangelical church at Apeldoorn in central Holland. In September 1933, he began work as an independent missionary—"a word," he admits, "that leaves an aftertaste."

I did my missionary work among the Jews, but I did it my own way: I first tried to impart a knowledge of Judaism—which I did very scrupulously, without any particular slant—because here in Holland you came across Jews who actually knew even less about Judaism than the Christians. I taught that the people Israel alone received a message from God, through Moses and through the prophets. That the people Israel is not to shut itself up in the synagogue, but to carry this message to the other nations. This is the task of the election of the people Israel—not in its own interest, but for the others, for the world.

The reason God chose the people Israel to carry out a message of humanity and social feeling among the other nations is that 3,500 years ago, when Moses brought the way, no one yet knew anything about the social side. I'm not talking only about the primitive peoples but even about the civilized nations such as Egypt and Babylon, peoples of high culture: They, too, had slaves! And the slave was lower than a dog. But, for Israel, a slave was not to be held longer than six years, and he did not have to buy his freedom—the seventh year, he was to go free.

So the people Israel was chosen to be the avant-garde. But being chosen is not easy—suffering goes along with it, as we have seen throughout history. Israel has suffered because of its election and suffers still, alas. The prophets have suffered at the hands of their own people— Ezekiel suffered, Jeremiah suffered, even Isaiah suffered. Amos was cast out. And, of course, Jesus suffered. That is what it is to be chosen: It is a responsibility, and we must bear the consequences.

"When we've spent two years together studying Judaism"—this is how I worked—"you can decide whether you want to go further and also learn something about Christianity." Some among them remained with the synagogue—I won't say they remained Jews, because I also have remained a Jew—but, fine, they had become good friends and at least they had learned something.

Others said, "Why did you, who know so much about Judaism, nonetheless become a Christian?"

"If you want to know something further," I said, "then we can go on: Then came Jesus as the promised Messiah, pointing everything out all over again—but for him there was only a place on the cross. And I bring the same message to the Christians: 'We reproach the Jews for not having fulfilled their mission, but we Christians have fulfilled it just as little. We have gone the same way as the Jews. We have Moses, and the prophets, and Jesus, and the apostles, but we don't act as they teach us.' "

Those who went the same path as I were not many, but I don't regret it—because those few who did said, "Only now do I understand why I am a Jew."

As the 1930s went by, David occupied himself with his church work, but he could not ignore what he felt to be a potential threat emanating from Germany. Already having seen Hitler's rise to power in 1933 as a danger signal, he was again jolted in 1935 when, following their annexation of the Saar, the Germans began to rearm.

I thought, "This is only the beginning; they won't let it go at that." But you couldn't talk about it out loud here, because the Dutch are a peculiar people—you can't tell them anything. "We have a waterline," they thought. "We'll let everything flood, and the enemy will be unable to pass." As if they didn't have boats.

Then the Germans began to move specifically against the Jews, and I saw the danger precisely because I am a Jew. With the infamous

Kristallnacht in 'thirty-eight, I said, "Now we know what we have to prepare ourselves for—there'll be the devil to pay." But even then you couldn't say to the Dutch that it could happen here—they still felt perfectly safe.

On a Sunday in April 1940, when I was to preach to a congregation in Zeeland, the news reached here that the Germans had invaded Norway. It then became such a torrent that there was no holding it back. On the tenth of May, the Germans invaded here. The first few months, it was quiet again: "They will keep their hands off the Jews here, because they know that we as Dutchmen stand behind the Jews." But how it went—that they by no means kept their hands off the Jews—the whole world now knows.

While Jews were deported from the Netherlands as early as February 1941, it was in the summer of 1942 that systematic roundups began. Until that time, David, who was living with his wife and five children in The Hague, had continued his work as a missionary.

At that point, my house was searched by the Nazis. They asked about diamonds and postage stamps* and suchlike, but they didn't get any because I didn't have any. They did take whole piles of my papers—the papers were not dangerous, fortunately, but because they were papers, they confiscated them all. And one of the two SS men who performed the search said, "From now on you may not speak with Jews about Jesus, because the Gospels"—this is interesting—"are not for the Jews."

I just stared at him. I wanted to ask, "Who *are* they for, then? They come *from* the Jews, why shouldn't they be *for* the Jews?" But you are sometimes better off swallowing it than spitting it out. In any case, I thus received the order that I was no longer to go on with my missionary work.

Although he had been ordained in the Free Evangelical church and was not to be ordained in the Dutch Reformed church until 1954, the latter had got wind of what had happened at David's house and, the very next day, gave him the special assignment of "tending to the affairs of Jews who were in danger." As a

---

*Like diamonds, collectors' stamps provided a vehicle for wealth that could be easily concealed and transported.

curate at the Dutch Reformed church in The Hague, he received and counseled Jews who turned to the church for help: at first mainly refugees from Germany but later those of Dutch origin as well.

Almost all were seeking exemption from concentration at Westerbork, a transit camp in the east of the Netherlands. A system of exemptions instituted under the German occupation shielded from deportation Jews working in industries judged essential to the German war effort; officials of the Joodse Raad, the "Jewish Council" set up by the occupying authorities to administer Jewish community affairs; and Jewish partners in mixed marriages. Deportation was also blocked in a number of special cases—among them were Jews of certain foreign nationalities and some individuals whose "racial" ancestry was unclear. Nevertheless, before the war ended, over 90,000 Jews were to be transported to the extermination camps at Auschwitz and Sobibor in Poland, and the vast majority were to die there.

The German administration also granted exemption from deportation to Jews who, as of January 1, 1941, had fit into one of five categories: (1) those born of parents who were members of the Dutch Reformed church; (2) those undergoing Christian education with the intention of being confirmed as members of that church; (3) those regularly attending the church's services and with whom its council had religious contact; (4) those baptized in the church; and (5) those confirmed in the church.

As the tempo of roundups increased in the summer of 1942, there was a consequent clamor for exemptions. Most of the exempted or "blocked" Jews, with the exception of those in mixed marriages, were ultimately to be deported, the coveted stamps in their identity papers notwithstanding. But as long as exemptions seemed to hold out hope of escaping deportation, David recalls, "Jews came in droves" to his office.

The Synod asked me if I would receive them, speak with them, and, insofar as was necessary, include them among those who were to receive a stamp. Everyone who showed up got an exemption—I really did not ask if they answered to the five conditions of the Germans. "Do you want a stamp? Here, you have a stamp, you belong to the church." It made no difference to me.

Well, I did ask, pro forma, "Have you ever actually been in a church?"

"Oh, yes," they said, "of course."

But it was a question of saving people—they thought, "Perhaps we can save or prolong our lives here with the church," and we didn't ask any questions.

On the basis of the five groups, we put together a list of around 1,200 Jews—the lists were drawn up, compiled, classified, and made up in so many copies. But the Germans saw through it. They said, "This is impossible—it's gone too far," and they began to purge the list. The fateful day of January 1, 1941, was no longer valid, groups fell away at every turn, and the list we had put together diminished apace. Jews holding an exemption from the church were being deported en masse.

My wife and I had many Christian friends, and, as happened in the case of other Jewish people who were taken in and hidden, they began to come to me and say, "Why do you have to go? We'll take care of you. Holland is big enough that we can find somewhere to hide you and your wife and the five children." The first was a grocer from the little town near Rotterdam where I had lived before I moved to The Hague. He came to see us and asked us if we wanted to give the children to him, saying he would take care that they come through the dangers no matter how long it all lasted. Then there were farmers from Zeeland and others who wanted to have my wife and me.

I talked it over with my wife, and do you know what we decided? We decided that if the Dutch Jews, and Jews everywhere, were undergoing this fate, we saw no reason that we should get ourselves out of it simply because we had the opportunity of doing so. On purely human grounds, of course, we would have been split up from one another if we had gone into hiding, and we would probably not have heard anything about what was happening to the others. But it was our shared feeling that we should not make use of the more favorable situation that we found ourselves in: that of being able to go into hiding without having to pay. Because our friends didn't want us to pay at all, whereas others did have to pay. I said, "If the whole of Dutch Jewry is going, we are going with them." We decided to bear the fate of our people, and we declined.

David continued to work in the Synod office until the spring of 1943. By that time, he and his family were among only 500 or 600 Protestant Jews who were still exempted—in the meantime, many others who had been on the list had been deported, while a few had gone into hiding. But then the Germans decided that The Hague should be made "Judenrein": free from Jews. On April 22, 1943, *the city's entire Jewish population—"among them," notes David, "the chief rabbi, and the other rabbis, and the shochet, and the chazzan,* and all the baptized Jews, including the ministers such as myself, and the unbaptized Jews"—were brought by train to the concentration camp at Vught in the south of the Netherlands.*

The day we arrived in Vught, it was Pesach,† and the Jews there had come together in one of the big barracks to hold prayers. There were a lot of Jews who didn't take part, and they were standing outside and making such a racket that those inside couldn't pray. I said to a group of my people, "Let's go stand there in front of the door and chase the others away," so that they could pray in peace. Of course, the Jews very much appreciated that. "Finally," they said, "we have a few watchmen at the door," because they couldn't take care of that themselves.

I had gotten an authorization from the Reformed Synod to care for the spiritual condition of the baptized Jews, but I couldn't put it to any use in Vught because the Germans didn't recognize it. They said, "A Jew is a Jew." Which is right as far as it goes—because I have never considered myself to be anything other than a Jew—but they didn't recognize that there could be different spiritual interests among the Jews. The rabbis were exempted from work in Vught because they had the spiritual care of the Jews; but I was not exempted as spiritual leader of my own group, which had, after all, a few hundred people. I had to do my work like anyone else, but that was fine with me. I dug ditches and dragged rocks around and so on, just like all the others.

My name was well known among the Jews—in an unfavorable sense, they considered me a gesjmadde‡—so, of course, I got the cold shoulder in Vught. There was even an incident that took place in the camp washroom; I wasn't there myself, but a man from our group was there and he told me about it. The rabbis were in the wash area, and there were other Jews as well, and they were saying, "That Kornbluth is sure to go into action now, because among the Jews like this he has

---

**shochet:* ritual butcher for kosher meat; *chazzan:* cantor (Hebrew).

†*Pesach:* Passover (Hebrew).

‡*gesjmadde:* baptized Jew. This is a noun formed from the past participle of *sjmadden,* the Dutch form of the derogatory Yiddish word for "to convert to Christianity, to be baptized."

his big chance." Which was not the case at all, I was not going to take advantage of the situation in any way—maybe they thought so, but I just went my way in peace.

Four weeks later we were brought to Westerbork, where we, as the baptized group, were placed in a different barrack from the other Jews and kept apart. I was immediately able to take up my duties on the basis of the Synod's authorization, so in Westerbork I did the work of a minister. During the week I worked just as I would have worked with a congregation outside the camp. I gave lessons to those who wanted them, but only those in my own group, I never tried to bring the others into it. Every Sunday I was able to preach for the people, though not in a separate hall, in the large barrack where 700 people slept. The pulpit was atop a triple bunk, and the people sat listening below. We even had our own choir, led by a well-known choir director.

On the first Sunday of each month a minister from outside the camp came before our group, something the Synod had negotiated with the occupation authorities in order to maintain contact between our group and the outside. After the minister gave his service, I could speak with him and tell him, "We need books for the children, we need toys for the children, we need more food packages," and he made sure that the church regularly sent us these things.

There was another minister who came, but he was not sent by the Synod. He was a German-Jewish minister so-called, but I never recognized him as such because he himself said, in a sermon from the pulpit, that his son was fighting at the front with the Germans. And he was saying that among Jews, nota bene; because, after all, we were there as Jews. "My son is fighting for the freedom of the Germanic people," he told us, with a sort of pride.

On Sunday, March 5, 1944, this man led the service. He was given the registration hall, in which concerts were held, and everything was all spick-and-span. When I came in, my wife on my arm, we saw a movie camera standing there. And when I saw that movie camera, a little red light suddenly went on in my head: In this lovely hall, where on Sunday morning the Jews are together—baptized Jews, but Jews all the same— they are going to make a film for propaganda. I said to myself, "I won't go along with this," and, in protest, I walked out.

The Wednesday thereafter, March 8, I was called in by the camp commandant, and he began reading me the riot act: that I had committed sabotage and that I knew what was in store for me. He asked me why I had left the service, so I said—you must, after all, say something—"As a clergyman, I could not sit idly by and watch as a service was being filmed." I myself felt that it wouldn't hold water, and the fellow wasn't born yesterday either.

He started to laugh like the devil: "Heh, heh, heh! You've certainly seen all the newsreels and magazines in which a congregation has been photographed during a service," he said. "How come they could allow it, but not you?"

I told him, "That's their decision, but I couldn't do it. That's why I walked out."

"No," he said, "you knew very well that I had ordered it, and you wanted to oppose me. I consider that as the height of resistance and insubordination, and you will therefore not escape your fate." He rang a bell, and the head of the guard came in right away and brought me to the stockade.

My hair was cut, and I got a kind of jailbird suit, blue overalls that had a red back, red sleeves, and red shoulders so that you could be recognized from a distance if you tried to escape. The stockade was a concentration camp within a concentration camp: There were three double rows of barbed wire, and it was electrified so that, in fact, escape was impossible. I was separated from my family; my wife was allowed to come speak with me on Sundays, but only for a moment before she had to leave again. So I stayed in the stockade and awaited my fate.

Almost immediately, David was told that he was among those to be sent for punitive reasons with the regular weekly transport "to the East."

The following Tuesday I was loaded onto the train, then pulled off again at the last moment and permitted to return to the stockade. That happened three weeks running, I didn't know why. Finally I received notice that I would not have to go on punitive transport after all, so I no longer had to be afraid. Because that punitive transport hung over your head as a sword of Damocles. Each time, you saw thousands of people—sometimes as many as 3,000—going on transport to Auschwitz. But I was allowed to come back, and the fourth week I was no longer on the punishment list and I stayed in the stockade.

It was in the stockade that I learned for the first time the fate of those who were deported. Every two or three days, groups of people who had been picked up in sweeps were brought to the stockade, and one spring day, probably in April, a man came up to me and introduced himself. He was a German Jew, and he had heard that I was a clergyman, and he began telling me one thing and another.

He said that he had been married to a non-Jewish German woman who was a leader of the Nazi women's movement in Germany, and that a lot of Nazis from the Grüne Polizei* came to her place, and they recounted what happened in Auschwitz, in Maidanek, in Treblinka. He told me in graphic detail how the gassing took place: that they were brought into so-called shower stalls and were given a towel and a piece of soap—but, instead of water, gas came out. At that time, we still didn't know what happened to people in Auschwitz, Sobibor, and so on, and when I heard that, I cried, "That is not true!" I couldn't believe it.

But, "Yes," he said, "alas, it is true." So, in the spring of '44, I, and together with me all the others, learned for the first time how diabolical the whole design of the Germans was. We could not believe that it could be so fiendish. But, as it turned out, it was true.

I stayed in the stockade for eight weeks, until I got notice from the commandant on May 4, 1944, that I could return to the normal camp. I was no longer allowed to do ecclesiastical work, but I was allowed to choose whatever other work I wanted. I asked to be detailed to the Aussendienst, outside duty: Each morning you got a shovel and you went to dig somewhere and I don't know what all, but I felt very good in the open air.

At the beginning of September 1944, as English forces entered Holland from Belgium and threw the German occupation authorities and their Dutch sympathizers into panic, the decision was made to evacuate Westerbork—where 4,000 were still interned—down to its last few hundred prisoners.

At that time, approximately 400 people were left in my group. The church had succeeded in effecting a certain protection, even in the camp, for those who belonged to the church. But the Germans had managed to make this group smaller at every turn; we had to look on each week as members of our group went, despite everything, on trans-

---

*Grüne Polizei: green police (German); nickname in Holland for the German Security Police, from the color of their uniforms.

port. I was recognized as having been baptized before 1941 and had the same advantages as all the others, but so many had been deported that, in the end, only a tiny core remained from the whole long list we had drawn up in The Hague.

On September 3—"the first time ever," notes David, "on a Sunday"—a large transport left for Auschwitz. The following day, a second transport left Westerbork, this one for the concentration camp at Theresienstadt, in what is now the Czech Republic. Included in this transport with David's Protestant group were the so-called Barnevelders, 660 prominent Jews who had been singled out for preferential treatment through the efforts of a pair of high-ranking Dutch civil servants.

Theresienstadt, where the transport arrived on September 6, was an old Bohemian walled town that the Nazis had turned into a ghetto and touted as "the city that Hitler has bestowed on the Jews." Those sent to Theresienstadt were considered privileged, but conditions there, while they may have been better than in many other concentration camps, were still inhuman: Nearly one-fourth of the 140,000 people who arrived in Theresienstadt died there. Chances for survival were further reduced by the high incidence of deportation; around 87,000 of those who at one point inhabited this "model settlement" were ultimately shipped to the extermination camps in Poland.

Three weeks after we arrived in Theresienstadt, the transports began for Auschwitz. There were, alas, around 3,000 Dutch Jews who went on those transports; only the Barnevelders and the so-called Protestant group, to which I belonged, stayed behind. With the transports that left Theresienstadt for Auschwitz in October '44, they again began to draw from our group, however. They said, "We are bound to the promise we made to the church in Holland. But here, as we are no longer in Holland, we will allow only the baptized Jews of Dutch nationality to stay behind. The baptized Jews who are not Dutch will be deported." As I had not yet been naturalized, I, and my family with me, were among the group that was to be deported on October 15.

The Thursday or Friday before the transport was to leave, people from our group were summoned to the commandant's office. A big shot from Berlin was there—I can still see him now, he had one eye—and we had to make a declaration to him. I was called before him with my wife and children. I told him who I was and what I did, that I was a curate in the Reformed church in the Netherlands.

He said, "Then, you are a Christian?"

I said yes.

"A Jew who becomes a Christian! How did you become a Christian?"

I said, "Aus Überzeugung"—out of conviction.

He began to laugh. "A Jew who becomes something out of conviction!" He couldn't believe it.

There was a typewriter there, and we had to go up to the typewriter, where our names were typed. Then, finally, we were allowed to leave. When I came out, Professor Simons, one of the leaders of the Barneveld group, was standing outside waiting for me, and there were other people standing around as well. "Kornbluth," he asked, "what happened in there? People are saying that they are questioning you today, but tomorrow they are going to question us." Very perceptive.

I told him what it was like: "I think that I will be going on transport with my family, because we had to go to the typewriter."

But he said, "Now you are lying, because the last time there was a transport, the only ones who stayed behind were the ones who went to the typewriter."

I said, "Yes, that is possible," because I too knew that. "But," I said, "there is one thing you must not forget: We are dealing here with the Germans. And they think they are smart enough to lead us up the garden path. This time, I say that we are going on transport precisely because we were at the typewriter, and I would therefore advise all of you who have been through the typewriter to do everything you can to stay behind."

Then I left with Professor Simons, and he asked me what had made me so certain that we would go on transport, whereas the last time the typewriter people did not go on transport. "Listen here," I said. "I had a good look around, and I observed who went through the typewriter and who didn't. Through the typewriter went I, with my wife and five children. Through the typewriter went old people. Through the typewriter went the infirm. And as for those who were young and strong, they did not go through the typewriter. What do *you* make of that?" I asked him.

"You may be right," he said.

Then I said to him, "Now *you* can do *me* a favor. What do I have to do to get out of it? You heard what I told the others: 'Do everything you can to get out of it.' What can *I* do?"

He said to me, "We do not want to believe it." Well, they could suit themselves, but I wanted to get out of it because I was going on transport.

Then he asked me, "What did you say inside?"

I told him.

"You know what?" he said. "You now have to get the use of a typewriter yourself. Write a letter to the man from Berlin and to the commandant of the camp, and whatever you told them, say it again. Make it short and to the point, but lay it on thick. Because," he said, "what you told him went in one ear and out the other. He has to see it in black and white."

I went to one of our group, a certain Dr. Eduard van Cleef, who worked in an employment office in the camp and who had a typewriter. I said, "Eduard, may I borrow the typewriter from you for a bit tomorrow morning?"

He said, "Fine, of course."

Instead of going to work the next day, I went to his old wreck of a typewriter and typed out a letter. But now that I had written the letter, whom should I give it to?

The elder of the Jews of Theresienstadt, Dr. Murmelstein, was the liaison officer between the commandant and the people in the camp. So you could give such a letter only to him. That Saturday, before the transport was to leave, I went very early in the morning to the barrack where he had his office. It was still dark—it had to be half past four in the morning—and there were already thousands of people standing there, people who wanted to speak to him. "He is a god," they thought, "and he can help us."

We stood until nine o'clock in the cold and the dark and the rain. Then, suddenly, there was a ripple among the hundreds, the thousands—yes, there really were several thousand Jews waiting there. A wave of excitement: "Murmelstein is coming!" All at once, as he came by on the way to his office, he looked over at me—we knew each other because I, as representative of our group, regularly came into contact with him. And he asked, "What are *you* doing here?"

So I took out the letter and said, "May I give you this letter for the commandant, because I am going on transport?" He snatched the letter out of my hand, threw it into his briefcase, and went on his way.

That day we did indeed receive the order to get ready for transport. At eleven o'clock, the barrack elder—himself a Jew, but you know how it is, he had to make sure he wasn't reprimanded—said, "Everyone who is going on transport: Out! Out! Out!" I left with my wife and children and went down to the so-called Schleuse, the entry gate to the train. We put down what we were carrying—everything all wrapped and packed, people always believed they were going to paradise, whereas they were going into a hell—and we waited for the train to pull out.

Around quarter to two, perhaps a quarter of an hour before the train left, my name was called. Someone came running up with a handful of little paper strips, shouting, "Kornbluth! Kornbluth!"

I say, "Here."

"Out of there!" he said. He gave me half a dozen of those slips, and with the slips we were able to return to the barracks.

It appears that Murmelstein had passed the letter on. And the one-eyed Mof* from Berlin who two days previous had laughed so in my face may have thought, now that he had it in black and white: "Ach, half a dozen Jews more, half a dozen Jews less, what difference does it make?" And he gave the order to rescind.

In February 1945, some 150 of the Protestant Jews reached freedom when they were transported to Switzerland, but David and his family stayed on with the majority until Theresienstadt was liberated and they were brought back to Holland in mid-May 1945.

There is a psalm that says, "When the Lord turned again the captivity of Zion, we were like them that dream." I also had that feeling. I dreamt. Back home, in spite of everything, with my wife and all five children. All my other family who had stayed in Poland were wiped out, down to one cousin and a niece. But we were spared.

If it had been only me personally, or only my family, who had come out of it alive, then I know what I would have done after the war: I would have hanged myself. But, thank God, it was not only me; we returned together with 400 others whose lives were saved through the efforts of the church. I belonged to this group—I didn't force my way in, nor did I become a Christian for fear of what Hitler might do to

---

*Mof: a derogatory Dutch term for "German," roughly equivalent to "Kraut" or "Hun."

me—so I have no pangs of conscience in that regard. I still went through the camps. That I was one of the very few to come out of it is a miracle; but there were others besides just me who came out of it, thank God, and they are not at all as I am.

So my religion was no special guarantee that I would be saved. Moreover, there were others here in Holland who were in the same position: All of the Barnevelders returned home, and there were 600 of them, more of them than there were of us. But, once again, if I had been the only one who could have said after the war, "Because I was thus-and-such, I came out of it alive," I would surely have hanged myself.

When the war was over, I felt, "I must shut off the past—it was an evil dream, a dangerous dream—and we have to build a new life here." It was easier for me than for the others inasmuch as I didn't have to set up a business or go looking for work; my work was waiting for me. The work I did after the war was, however, quite different from that I had done previously. I no longer did much missionary work; rather, I worked for the church in building up a dialogue, as that is called, between the church and Israel.

My vision begins with the principle of teaching Jewish thought to the Christians. It is something whose importance I have seen, and something in which I had a very great predecessor: namely, the apostle Paul, who in his letters says, "You who were earlier heathens, be incorporated into Israel." That was one of my favorite sermons, invoking the apostle Paul to show the Christians that they make an indissoluble whole with Israel, with the Jews—and that, for this reason, they must always stand on the side of the Jews, because the fate of the Jews is their fate as well. It will always be a joy to me that I have been able to do something to better understanding between Jews and Christians, between church and synagogue, and to foster goodwill toward each and every Jew and toward the state of Israel.

Understanding, however, was not always automatic. At the time of the interview, David had for many years been the spiritual leader of a small group of men and women of Jewish origin and Christian faith who often feel that they are kept at a distance by both sides. And David's ideas on the unity of Israel and Christendom do not resolve all ambiguities. On the one hand, there are some Jews who he says have told him, "If you believe that Jesus also has to be a part of it, that is your own business, but you think and speak and act like one of us"; on the other hand, he notes, "The 'regular' Jews have regarded me since the war just as they did before the war: My name is known among the Jews here in an unfavorable light."

He has preached to Christians, he says, "without introducing myself in any particular way—but you can't deny the background. And they have said, 'Here speaks a Jew'—it is precisely that which has so captivated them." Still, there have been non-Jews who have annoyed him by failing to give up the notion that "in becoming a Christian, one leaves off being a Jew."

David, however, has long been used to the position of the outsider.

I am an individualist. I didn't just swallow everything that was taught me—I thought it through. When I was at the yeshiva,* we were learning a passage from the Talmud, and I asked a question that the rebbe† didn't like. He got angry. "One day," he said, "you will have yourself gesjmad."‡ Later, when I was indeed gesjmad—because, strangely, it had come to pass—I was at the Christian yeshiva, the theological seminary. We were in a seminar, and I was asking questions, and the professor said the same thing: "If you continue with that sort of thinking, there is no place for you here at this school."

Millions of Jews, once they are brought up in Jewish traditionalism, simply go on with it. I don't condemn them for this, they are every bit as dear to me, for Israel is my people and they are my brothers and sisters. But I thought critically and have remained critical in respect to the church—I have said things in church that have led Christians to say, "He is a heretic," just as I am considered a heretic by the Jews.

Rev. David Kornbluth remained with the Dutch Reformed church until his retirement in 1967. In the postwar years, he made several extended visits to Israel, where he studied with such renowned Jewish philosophers as Gershom Scholem and David Flusser. His first wife died in the early 1960s, and at the time of the interview he was remarried to a Dutch Protestant woman, not of Jewish origin, with whom he lived in a small town not far from Amsterdam.

When the interview had ended, Mrs. Kornbluth suggested lunch; then, suddenly fretting, she said she hoped it wasn't imperative that the meal be kosher.

------

*yeshiva: Jewish institution of higher learning; in this case, the afternoon school in Lodz where David continued his Jewish education after he left the Jewish day school.
†rebbe: teacher in a yeshiva or other Jewish school.
‡gesjmad: baptized; see note p. 125.

"But what does 'kosher' mean, anyway?" David remarked. "It only means 'clean, pure.' The dietary laws were made many thousands of years ago, in a warm region, under particular sanitary conditions. Today, with modern methods of preparing food, we can consider that everything is actually clean"—and thus, he insisted, kosher.

You can see that my life has been a straight path. I didn't get where I am today by a circuitous route. When I say circuitous, I am thinking of those Jews—and I do not judge them, there are truly fine people among them—who, when Hitler came, went into hiding. And where did they go into hiding? Here in Holland there were, thank God, believing Christians who, putting their lives and the lives of their families in danger, took these people in. And those Jews who were in hiding with them saw a religious life that they felt drawn to, and in this way they themselves came to the faith.

But in my case it had nothing to do with that. I became a Christian in 1928, when no one had yet dreamt of any Hitler. Nor did I do it for the sake of assimilation, as a way of disappearing into the other nations—of having my nose fixed, as it were. A straight line led from my birth through my Jewish religious upbringing, my Zionist and socialist conviction, and my confrontation with Jesus—who touched me precisely because he stood up for the poor, for the oppressed, and for his people, for whom he ultimately gave his life.

There have been occasions when someone has said to me, "But now you are no longer a Jew, after all, you are a Christian."

That really gets my hackles up. "What did you just say?" I ask. "A 'converted Jew'? I never want to hear that again!" And they never did say it to me again.

Because I wonder when I was converted. Now that you have heard my life story: When was I converted? It hasn't happened at the expense of a deeply Jewish background—in fact, my religious convictions, my whole line of thought, are the pure consequence of my orthodox Jewish national upbringing.

I was raised as a purposeful Jew, and as a purposeful Jew I have lived, worked, and thought. You do not have to become anything else, you may not become anything else, you must not become anything else. But follow the path that God has laid out for each person. And be prepared to bear the consequences.

Hilda Dujardin

Hilda Dujardin's parents were born in the late 1870s in an area of the Austro-Hungarian Empire that today is part of the Czech Republic. Her father, the son of orthodox Jewish shopkeepers, seemed destined for an academic career until he quit secondary school to take a job with the railroad. Hilda's mother, a domestic from the age of fourteen, met the aspiring engineer while working at a hostelry in Moravia when she was twenty. Although Hilda's mother had no Jewish upbringing, she believed herself to be a Jew. "From everything I know about my mother's maternal grandparents, who were small farmers, I don't think they were Jewish," Hilda says. "But my mother's paternal grandmother was definitely a Jew, and my mother assumed her father was as well." Hilda's mother found in preparing to file marriage papers that "this 'father' was not her real father but a stepfather"; and Jewish law stipulates that Jewishness passes through the mother in any case. As a kindness to her fiancé's parents, Hilda's mother converted to Judaism. "This must have taken place before I was born," Hilda says, "because I have a birth certificate rather than a baptismal certificate."

Hilda was born in 1902. She spent her first ten years in the town of Oderfurt, which today is incorporated into Ostrava, then as now an important rail center and leading Czech industrial city. One of Hilda's earliest memories is of an episode that took place in the streets of Oderfurt before she had started school.

There were a few children chasing after a Jewish girl and shouting, "Zid! Zid!"—"Jew! Jew!" Where they got the Czech word I don't know, because among us there was hardly any Czech spoken; the countryside was Czech, but the town itself was German. I was tagging along in the group, as children do, when my mother, who was on her way home from shopping, spotted me. She took hold of me and snatched me away from there, saying, "You should be ashamed of yourself! Don't you know that your father is a Jew?"

Well, I didn't know it. My mother hadn't stayed long in the Jewish community, and it was at a time I don't remember myself and know about only from being told. She once said that she had tried to observe Jewish holidays, but she didn't know the practices so she'd dropped it again. And as my father had already resigned from membership in the Jewish community, my mother did as well.

In leaving the Jewish community, Hilda's parents had officially taken on the status of konfessionslos—without religious affiliation. Such a step, "comparatively rare" in pre–First World War Austria, was an earmark of the socialism that was the dominant belief in Hilda's household. Like their neighbors, the family celebrated on Christmas and Easter, but the festivities were entirely secular. "Religion itself," says Hilda, "was of no significance."

Still, Hilda was aware of her Jewish descent through her father's relatives, whom she loved dearly and with whom she was in close touch till her midteens. When she was fifteen, Hilda traveled to her grandparents' home in Bielitz—today the Polish city of Bielsko-Biala—to celebrate Passover for the first time. In 1918, after the Austro-Hungarian Empire had been carved up into nation-states, she sneaked across the Czech-Polish border to pay a final visit to her widowed grandfather.

In line with her parents' progressivism, Hilda tended to see herself more as a socialist than as a member of any other group; at the same time, in line with their broad-mindedness, she felt she "belonged everywhere" and paid little mind to profession, religion, politics, or mother tongue. "If children are on good terms with their parents," she comments, "they by and large follow their parents' lead. They don't seek out other paths."

When Hilda was ten, her family had moved a few miles up the Oder River to Neu Oderberg, largely at the urging of one of Hilda's uncles, who was disturbed that none of the secondary schools accessible from Oderfurt admitted girls. In Neu Oderberg, both she and her parents remained outside Jewish circles.

There were a few Jewish boys and girls in school, but I didn't know them. Still, when a Jewish Wanderbund* was established in 1919, I was

---

Wanderbund: hiking association. Hiking clubs were a popular form of social organization for young people in the German-speaking world at this time.

invited to attend its charter meeting. I was very hesitant, but my mother told me to go anyway and look it over. They all knew each other, while I didn't know anyone; but just as I was deciding to leave, a girl I had played with in Oderfurt called to me. So I had a foothold.

Shortly thereafter, the non-Jewish children from school founded a Wandervogel.* They came to me and said, "You don't belong in the Wanderbund, you belong with us. We need you to be a leader in our group, so forget the other nonsense and come along." I went to their meeting, and I believe that what influenced my decision was that they drank beer there; in the Wanderbund people were saying, "We don't want anything to do with alcohol," and that was more to my liking. So I stayed in the Wanderbund.

Nevertheless, it was quite interesting that I was the only member of the Wanderbund they approached. The explanation may be that my parents didn't belong to the Jewish community. How cohesive it was I can't say, but there must have been a rather sharp division between the Jewish community and the non-Jews, and our connections were with the non-Jewish part of town. This followed naturally from my father's profession: The people we went around with were railroad engineers, and we, of course, were the only Jewish family among them. As a child, I had taken this for granted; the children I had known were, in general, the children of engineers. It was probably through the Wanderbund that it first struck me that there was this division and that we belonged not to the Jews, but to the other side.

In 1921, Hilda began studies at the University of Vienna that were to lead to a Ph.D. in geography. Always on the left, she joined the Communist student organization; in 1923, the year of the Beer Hall Putsch, she took part in one of the earliest anti-Nazi demonstrations while on a visit to friends in Germany.

There were no Jewish geography students—the Jews, according to Hilda, were concentrated in medicine, law, and languages—"and thus," she says, "I ended up outside Jewish society through my field of study just as my father had through his profession." But her best friend in Vienna, the daughter of a large landholder from Bohemia, was Jewish—and Hilda recalls that she and Marianne had felt "very drawn to one another" even as each assumed, based on their fathers'

Wandervogel: hiking or social club. The term *Wandervogel,* as opposed to *Wanderbund,* is associated with the larger German youth movement of the time.

respective professions, that the other was not Jewish. Marianne, who was studying social work, was engaged to an art history student named Paul, who was also Jewish and with whom Hilda became fast friends as well.

By the time Hilda had received her doctorate in the late 1920s, she was living with her husband-to-be, a German national of Huguenot descent who ran the Communist bookstore in Vienna. With Europe in deep depression, jobs were scarce, so when Hilda heard, "quite by chance," that Vienna's Jewish school was looking for a geography teacher, she presented herself as a candidate.

The director of the school was enormously open-minded. At the end of the interview, when we had more or less come to terms, I said, stupidly enough, "Well, I really should tell you that I am a Communist." Hardly had I said it than I thought, "You could have kept that to yourself"—because it was certainly no recommendation at that time.

But he said, "That's just fine. I already have one of everything else in this school, that's all I was missing in my collection."

In the course of the two years Hilda spent at the school—which, she notes, were not particularly significant for the development of her connections to Judaism or the Jewish community—her husband lost his job. After remaining some time without work, he found a position managing a "bourgeois" bookstore in Cologne, and in 1931 the Dujardins moved to Germany. Almost immediately, they became deeply involved with the Communist Party, in which they enrolled under false names; "the Nazis were already rather strong," Hilda explains, and her husband, feeling it would be wise to conceal his political activity from his employer, had the idea of using the noms de guerre. "Aside from the Party leadership and our closest friends, hardly anyone knew our real names," says Hilda. "It would never have occurred to me to do this, but if we hadn't, we would probably have been arrested right away in 'thirty-three."

Not long after her arrival, Hilda contacted the Jewish community in Cologne.

Pregnant as I was—my daughter was born in June '32—I couldn't take on a permanent job, but I had my papers from the Jewish school in Vienna, and I went to the community and said that I wanted some kind of work. It was the worst moment of the depression, and they said, "We would like to organize courses for the unemployed Jewish youngsters we have here. Would you like to plan out and teach these courses?" That was, of course, just what I knew how to do, and I worked there up to my eighth month.

As the election for president of the Reich grew near, several gentlemen from the Jewish community came to speak to the young people. "Those of you who are old enough to vote ought to know this for yourselves," they said, "and those that aren't should tell your parents: You must vote for Hindenburg."

But I said, "Hindenburg means Hitler!"*

There was quite a commotion. They said, "What of it!"

"What of it?" I said. "Just imagine what it will mean if Hitler comes to power!" I couldn't really imagine it myself, but I still had a lot better idea than they did.

And then these gentlemen, these influential figures from the Jewish community, said, "Barking dogs don't bite. If Hitler comes to power, he'll find out which side his bread is buttered on when it comes to his Jews in Germany. We won't have a thing to fear."

I opposed them vehemently; there was a big debate, and they told me, "If you want to stir up our youth against Hindenburg . . ."

But I said, "Hindenburg, my foot! It's Hitler we have to fear!"

On January 30, 1933, nine months following his election victory, Hindenburg named Hitler chancellor at the head of a coalition government. Hilda felt the effects of Hitler's accession to power almost immediately.

When I was pregnant, I had arranged a half-time teaching appointment at a girls' high school not far from where we lived. I was to begin after the 1933 Easter vacations, so I went to see the director in February. By this time, of course, I would no longer have said that I was a Communist, but I had to tell her that I couldn't furnish the Ariernachweis† because my father was a Jew; so this fact began to play a role. "Now I can't hire you," she said, but she comforted me: "This specter will not last long. I believe that I will be able to take you on after the fall vacations. They won't hold out any longer than that."

Seven months after Hitler had come to power, and during a period in which she and her husband were exposed to extreme danger as members of the anti-Nazi underground, Hilda took an unusual step.

---

*Field Marshal Paul von Hindenburg, the erstwhile-monarchist incumbent, and Hitler were actually running against each other, with a Communist candidate the only alternative to right-wing extremist rule. However, it was evident to many that even if Hindenburg held Hitler off in the presidential election, he would not be able to keep the Nazis out of the government for long.

†*Ariernachweis:* a certificate documenting "Aryan" descent.

I believe that it was at the beginning of September 1933 that I said to my husband, "I am more or less ashamed at being considered an Aryan by these people here. And besides, I feel that I must now take my stand alongside my Jewish father and my Jewish grandparents—my father is a Jew, and now I also am a Jew, and I will never disavow it. I am going to join the Jewish community."

All I had to do was fill out a paper, nothing more. I had that birth certificate that I could show. I just didn't say that my mother was not Jewish or that my parents had left the Jewish community.

Everyone was terribly nice. "You are the first one to do this," they said, "and we value it very highly. But now you'll have to pay dues."

"I can't pay that much," I said, "but of course I will pay my dues if I belong to our community." Up to this point, not so much had happened to the Jews that people took this as something so special—it was just someone who was a Jew and who now said that she was a Jew, which she hadn't done before.

In fact, a nationwide boycott of Jewish-owned businesses had taken place on April 1, 1933, and by September Jews had been all but excluded from the civil service, the legal and medical professions, and the arts. Although she feels that her "wish to belong to the Jews" and her opposition to the Nazi regime "had nothing to do with one another"—and she notes that her Party comrades, hostile as they were to religion, ridiculed her action—Hilda attributes her decision in part to her general commitment to social justice, citing the newspaper motto she had adopted as her own: "Where there are stronger, always on the side of the weaker." But there were more specific motives as well.

There were practical, or quasi-practical grounds: I did it in order to shake off the Nazis. They were always coming around collecting for something or other, and I had no desire to give. We didn't come forward as Communists, of course, but now I could say to everyone who came, "Listen, I don't come into consideration, because I am a Jew."

But I didn't really do it just to have it in black and white. I was saying, "Now I'll show you: This is where I belong." Because even before I joined the Jewish community, I had pretty much felt myself to be a Jew. I believe this was through my grandfather, of whom I was very fond; and through my father, whom I found admirable in his way; and also through my father's youngest brother, the uncle who had insisted that I go on to secondary school and whom I loved passionately.

This uncle died in battle in 1915. He had been seriously wounded in the arm, and my grandmother had rejoiced over the wound, saying, "It doesn't even matter if they amputate your arm, because now you won't return to the front." His arm healed, however, and my uncle, a captain, went back to the front as a volunteer. His rationale was that there were so many Jewish draft dodgers:* "Although we Jews are guests in this country," he said, "they have treated us quite well and we belong here. So, since we are part of this land, it is our duty to defend it in time of war." I later saw this act as totally senseless because I missed my uncle very much; but this was another strong connection to Jewishness and an instance of taking one's stand as a Jew and having obligations as a Jew.

When I went home in the summer of '34 and told my parents, they said, "Well, all right, if you really think you have to do that just now."

And I said, "Yes, I think now is the time it has to be done." In fact, this sort of thing seemed to run in the family. My parents had done similar things, such as identifying themselves as Germans when it wasn't particularly advantageous to do so in Czechoslovakia. Now, just as I had had to tell the principal of the Jewish school in Vienna that I was a Communist—why, I don't know—I felt it was time to take my stand as a Jew.

As for my husband, I had talked it over with him at great length, and he had said, "Of course. If you want to do it, then do it." In his family as well there was nothing terribly unusual about standing up for what you were. My husband's forefathers had left France for Holland; they weren't obliged to emigrate, they could have become Catholics. My father-in-law, a professor at the polytechnic institute in Aachen, had always openly identified himself as a Huguenot in a Catholic region. Moreover, when we first moved to Cologne, he had put his arms around me and said, "Up to now, we've had no Jews in the family—it's high time for you to be bringing us some Jewish blood." So things weren't such that I had to feel inhibited on account of my Jewishness.

It is impossible to know how much of what later befell Hilda and her family can be attributed to her enrolling in the Jewish community in 1933 and how much might have occurred regardless.

---

*A widespread rumor that Jews were underrepresented in the German and Austrian armies was later refuted by a survey that proved embarrassing to the anti-Semites who had commissioned it.

Even without joining the community, I couldn't furnish the Arier-nachweis—this fact, which caused my husband problems professionally, would have remained a constant. Of course, if I had been able to foresee what was still to come, it is highly probable that I would not have done it. Once I had, however, I actually never regretted it, even with all the consequences it may ultimately have entailed.

One direct result of her decision to declare herself, and of the fact that she "made it known far and wide," was that Hilda became visible as a Jew in Buchforst, the Cologne suburb where she lived with her husband and daughter. Buchforst's Jewish population numbered two: a Jewish stationer who "spoke only Cologne dialect and was very popular in town" and Hilda. Hilda believes that, despite the fact that she did not qualify for the Ariernachweis, she might have remained "totally unnoticed" in her immediate surroundings. Still, she says, "Although I couldn't have known in advance, if I hadn't labeled myself as a Jew, I never would have experienced all the positive things that I then did experience."

Of our friends, only one turned his back on us. The Aryans we associated with were full of earnest warnings: "Don't go trumpeting around all the time that you're a Jew—that just isn't necessary." But I felt obliged to go trumpeting it around.

Once I had been reclassified as a Jew, there was one shop where I was so badly served—when I was served at all—that I stopped going back. But in others I was specially favored. And when people came by for the collections that regularly took place, I said, "I can't give you anything. I am a Jew, and certainly you don't want anything from a Jew."

Eventually a collector came by who replied, "Your husband is an Aryan, you know, and we have to cover everyone. But however little you give, it will be fine."

I told him that, in that case, I would give one mark per month. "Fifty pfennig will do just as well," he said.

Such things happened constantly, and I was always asking, "Where are the Nazis?" Because I ran up against so many people who weren't—except in our own building. First, the Gauwart* had moved in; we had seen even before 'thirty-three how terribly clever he was in recruiting people for the Nazis, how he sat down with the garbagemen and ex-

---

Gauwart: a Nazi Party regional official.

plained to them that Hitler was the greatest ever. Then, in 'thirty-four, a terribly energetic Nazi fanatic from somewhere in the Baltic moved in and declared right away: "Buchforst must be made Judenrein!"* She made short work of the poor Jewish stationer: When she was named Frauenschaftsleiterin,† she ordered a few women to stand guard in front of his shop to make sure that no one bought anything from him, and he couldn't hold out very long.

This Frau Schneider lived on the second floor, and we lived on the third. The first run-in I myself had with her took place because she was constantly saluting "Heil Hitler!" and I would answer "Good day." Once she started yelling at me, and I said, "I am a Jew"—you see, that seemed to me a good solution when up against such people. Then she spit at my daughter and called her "You bastard!" and Colette came upstairs and said, "What is a bastard?"

She was always peering down through her opera glasses to see who I was walking with. I had a friend who also had a child and who used to come by for me. Most of the time she rang and I went down, but once when I had heard the ring and gone out onto the balcony, she called out, "Frau Dr. Dujardin, are you coming now? I'm waiting for you."

Later, I said to her, "Listen, Frau Hauer, why did you do that? Schneider's up there, and she's always spying so."

"Do you want to know why?" she said. "It's because she came up to me on the street yesterday and told me I wasn't to have any contact with you."

My cleaning woman came once a week—she was also a Communist, by the way—and when she was doing the stairs, Frau Schneider stopped in the stairwell and said, "Frau Müller, you're not working for that Jew anymore! You know that Aryan women don't clean up the Jews' filth for them."

Frau Müller came up sobbing and said, "What am I going to do?"

"Frau Müller," I said, "you can't come anymore, that much is clear. You have four boys, and if you keep coming, you'll end up in *Der*

Judenrein: free from Jews; official Nazi terminology regarding expulsion of Jews.
†*Frauenschaftsleiterin:* a leader in the Nazi Party Women's Organization.

*Stürmer,** and your sons won't be allowed into the Hitler Youth. I'll wash the steps myself, that's no skin off my back."

Frau Müller said, "Then I'd like to do your laundry. My husband will come for it in the evenings, and you won't have to pay me anything."

Sometime later, Frau Voss, who had newly moved into the building, rang my bell; I hardly knew the family, but I had seen "Police Officer Voss" and I had my misgivings. "I heard the argument in the stairs," she said, rather coolly. "Won't you let me come in?" So, all right, I let her in, and Frau Voss said, "I'm taking over your stairs from now on."

I said, "Where do you get that?"

"It goes without saying," she answered. "What that Schneider is doing disgusts me so, and it's only normal that I do your stairs until you find someone who can come in spite of all this."

Not long afterward, the Gauwart's wife came up to me. "I hear that Frau Schneider is pestering and threatening you all the time," she said. "She mustn't be allowed to get away with that. If she keeps it up, you come to me." I never did go to her with it, but I was thunderstruck that this Nazi wife was taking my side.

Despite Hilda's surprisingly "strong following" in Buchforst, conditions rapidly became untenable for her family. Hilda could earn money only as a private tutor, and her husband was barred by his Jewish connection from the Nazi Party's literary association, the Reichsschriftumskammer. Although his employers covered this up to keep him on the job, they soon began to wonder aloud how long they would be able to do so; furthermore, they shied from requesting official permission to raise his salary, which had been cut substantially under an austerity program enacted before Hitler came to power. "The fact that I was a Jew," Hilda says, "weighed more and more heavily."

As pressures increased, Hilda and her husband talked about leaving Germany.

We had actually begun thinking about emigrating in 'thirty-three, but before we could make any definite plans, someone from the Com-

---

Der Stürmer: a Nazi newspaper known for its violent anti-Semitic propaganda. Its denunciations of those who maintained friendly relations with Jews often led to their ostracism.

munist leadership told us, "You can't even consider it, because we need your house." Cologne, which is near the borders of Belgium and Holland, was the place where people who were to be taken across the border spent one last night in Germany. As we had arrived only in 'thirty-one and hadn't been working under our real names in the Party, we were still virtually unknown, and they told us that we were "extremely important." So we had put aside thoughts of emigrating—Communists, you know, are disciplined. We were in constant danger, but we hid many people; most of those we saved were later killed in the Spanish Civil War.

Nevertheless, Hilda and her husband visited neighboring countries to prospect for a refuge. In 1934, they were told by the Dutch branch of the Dujardin family that the behavior of wealthy German-Jewish immigrants had soured Holland on receiving Jews; two years later, friends in Switzerland warned them that the Swiss were accepting only the wealthy and the famous. England demanded a deposit of 50 pounds sterling per person; "this seems a ridiculous sum today," Hilda comments, "but considering our tiny income, the 150 pounds we would have had to pay might just as well have been 50,000." And the United States, which had strict immigration quotas and long waiting lists, was "not at all in the picture."

As the years went by, the Dujardins' resistance activity tapered off.

We lost touch with the Communists, as almost all those we knew had disappeared: They had pulled back into other areas, or they were in concentration camps, or they were already dead. In the end, we were no longer part of an organization, so we didn't work anymore and were hardly in danger on that account.

But with their political motivation for staying in Germany diminished, the Dujardins found the arguments for emigration even more compelling. As the Nazis' regimentation of economic life mounted, Hilda's husband was less and less sure that his employers would keep him on. In addition, he had been called before the Gestapo twice, and the family's apartment had been searched. With Colette to start school in 1938, the Dujardins' dilemma came to a head. " 'What will happen when she is treated in school as a non-Aryan child?' we said. 'We can't go on like this. We have to get out.' " Over the objections of their Buchforst friends, who pledged to protect them, the Dujardins chose to leave for Czechoslovakia, where, owing to the presence of Hilda's parents and friends, they had a "base."

Hilda and her daughter went in the summer of 1937 to live with Hilda's parents. Finding no way of making money around Ostrava, Hilda soon left Colette with her parents and went to Prague, where her friends from student days, Marianne and Paul, put her up. Hilda held a German passport, and, as an ethnic German born before the founding of the Czechoslovak Republic, she had no claim to Czech citizenship. Nor did she have any hope of obtaining a residence permit: Under German pressure, the Czechoslovak government was interning new immigrants in camps. While refugees of means tried desperately to leave the country— "there wasn't a consulate in Prague," she recalls, "where people weren't standing in line day and night on the chance of getting a visa"—friends of Hilda's advised her to go into a camp. "You'll never be able to support yourself here," they told her. "In the camp you'll have food and shelter and be recognized as an immigrant, so you'll have no worries." But when Hilda paid a visit to one of the camps, she found the site filthy and desolate, and its residents' "nerves very much on edge" from waiting. "As it turned out, it was in a certain sense advantageous for them to have stayed there, because a large number were ultimately brought in groups out of the country," Hilda says. "But I thought, 'No. I'm not going to do that to myself, and I'm not going to do that to my child.'"

By late fall, Hilda had rented a modest apartment, using bribery to obtain a residence permit; using her name to convince the landlord, who like most Czechs at that time was violently anti-German, that she was in reality French; and using a gift from her Dutch in-laws to pay six months' rent in advance. Although she could not get a work permit, and thus might have been sent back to Germany if caught, Hilda gave language lessons—"there were enough Czechs who felt they should learn German"—and provided practical advice to department stores on a freelance basis, an activity she had initially tried in Ostrava. After arriving in Prague in 1938, her husband represented German publishers to booksellers around Czechoslovakia. He also taught German, and, "always trying to come up with new ideas," the Dujardins put out language primers.

In her first two years in Prague, Hilda never once made contact with the Jewish community. But after the Germans had marched into Bohemia and Moravia in 1939, she again—this time, she claims, unwittingly—took a step that ensured she would be regarded by Nazi authorities as a Jew.

I had to go renew my passport at the German embassy in Prague. The clerk wrote down "Volksdeutsche"* and said, "Are you Protestant or Catholic?"

---

*Volksdeutsche: ethnic German (feminine form); applied to ethnic Germans born or settled outside German territory.

"Well," I answered, "I belong to the Jewish religious community." Whereupon I got that big, red *J* stamped in my passport. And, with that, all roads were barred.

This was just idiocy, unqualified imbecility. In 1933, my husband and I had talked it over for quite a long time, and it was thus after considerable reflection that I had said, "Now I am going to stand by my father." That was deliberate; and, besides, you always had the excuse that you didn't know what the Nazis were capable of.

But by 'thirty-nine you already knew something about that, so this time it was an act of nonintelligence. Perhaps it was a kind of short circuit, a failure to make the connection quickly enough; or maybe it was being accustomed to always telling the truth; or simply a failure to anticipate fully what the consequences might be later on, which at the time you couldn't foresee. It's possible that if I'd had a little time to think about it, I would have said that I was a "believer in God" or whatever people said in those days rather than feeling I had been put before a choice: "To which religious community do you belong?" All the same, I don't remember that I reproached myself at all, although perhaps I said to myself that it was dumb, that I shouldn't have said it, that I could have said, "without religious affiliation," or something like that. And I don't remember my husband reproaching me on account of it either.

As in the case of her decision to join the Jewish community six years earlier in Cologne, Hilda can only guess at what effect her spontaneous disclosure to the German passport clerk had on subsequent events.

Perhaps they would have gotten to the bottom of things one way or the other, or perhaps they never would have—I don't know. In 'forty-three, when all mixed marriages were registered, they told me, "Of course, you joined the Jewish community in 'thirty-three," so they had that down very precisely. But I can't be sure that, had I said in 'thirty-nine that I was a Catholic, they would have found me out.

Even if Hilda had not exposed herself as a Jew, her inability to qualify for the Ariernachweis would again have become a factor, since the Germans brought with them to Czechoslovakia the very racial policies that had led the Dujardin family to flee Germany two years before. She did have one major advantage: As a spouse in a "privileged mixed marriage"—under the Nuremberg Laws, the marriage of a Jew and a non-Jew whose children were not members of a Jewish community—Hilda was exempted from many anti-Jewish measures, and her family was consequently under less pressure than the majority of the Jewish population around them. Still, the threat they were exposed to intensified steadily during the war years—despite which fact Hilda never explored what she felt to be the very real alternative of documenting her mother's "Aryan" ancestry. "Although my mother's personal documents had been destroyed by fire," she says, "from the few she still had, her origins had been recognized. So it wouldn't have been all that difficult for me to get myself papers that would have established me as a half-Jew." With a resulting change in her status from "Jew" to the less prejudicial "non-Aryan" would have come an added measure of security for the entire family.

In the first years of the war, the Dujardins' life grew more oppressive in a variety of ways. Hilda's consulting income, which had depended largely on Jewish-held department stores, vanished with the stores' owners, and her husband's activity was limited by both the number of publishers who dared to employ him and the number of booksellers he himself dared to call on. It was Hilda's language pupils, sympathizing with her plight and paying "even when they didn't show up," who kept the family afloat. Meanwhile, Colette, as a so-called Mischling—a child of mixed parentage—had been barred from entering secondary school. Hilda and her husband had previously been bullied by Nazi authorities, eager to emphasize the German-speaking presence in Prague, into transferring her from a Czech to a German-language school—despite her mixed origins, and, says Hilda, "much to my distress, because she then felt herself pretty much as a German child, with all the privileges German children had." Now, however, Colette was assigned to an institution spitefully named German Grammar School for Mischlinge and the Mentally Deficient.

These years were also marked by the loss of Hilda's friends Marianne and Paul and of Hilda's parents. Paul, the director of the Communist bookshop in Prague, was arrested soon after the arrival of the Nazis and died in Dachau. Marianne, deported to Theresienstadt, ultimately died with their son in Auschwitz.

In 1942, Hilda's father received notice that he was to be transported to a concentration camp. He had been on a transport once before: In October 1939, within weeks of the signing of the Hitler-Stalin Nonaggression Pact and the resulting partition of Poland, he had been among a large number of men shipped from Ostrava across the newly drawn border into the Soviet Union. Although welcomed "with open arms" by the Soviets, who needed railroad engineers, Hilda's father did not want to be separated from his family. He walked out of an internment camp, the only escapee, and was back in Ostrava within a week.

Once returned from this exile—which, had he accepted it, might in the end have saved his life—Hilda's father remained with his wife at home. Hilda says her parents were "a great help"—in particular her mother, who, because of her "Aryan" status, could move freely and drew larger food and clothing rations than her husband, daughter, or granddaughter. But as deportations of Jews accelerated, Hilda's father was again summoned for transport. Holding no illusions as to what awaited him at his destination, he chose not to report; and, judging his chance of escaping the Nazi net to be poor, he and his wife, after a marriage of more than forty years, together ended their lives.

In early 1943, when Hilda was registered along with other Jewish partners in mixed marriages, it became apparent that the Nazi authorities knew not only of her joining the Jewish community ten years earlier in Cologne but also of the specifics of her ancestry: Otherwise, they would not have designated her a Geltungsjüdin, the Nazi term that applied to a woman or girl of mixed parentage who had been affiliated with a Jewish religious community. Hilda more than embraced the label.

"So you are a Geltungsjüdin," they said, "and now you consider yourself to be a full Jew."

To which I said, "I have always done so." My God, in principle you didn't dare say a word there. You were viewed as a rebel if you said such things, and they hissed, "You! Shut up!"

Soon after this registration we were summoned to forced labor, and for the first time I found myself in the Jewish community in Prague, with which I hadn't had any contact up to then. The Nazis had founded a Jewish-run trust company to organize the forced labor; its first task was to clean out the many Jewish apartments that stood empty in Prague. There were fifty or so warehouses set up in the city—a furniture warehouse, a lamp warehouse, warehouses for paintings, carpets and tapestries, porcelain, beds—to which our men, who were known as gladiators, had to bring everything piece by piece. We quickly saw through this operation: As a rather large staff was needed to administer it, this was a way for a bunch of SS men to keep themselves comfortably in Prague at a time when there were already old men and young boys at the front.

In the beginning I worked in the apartments, which were to be made all bright and shiny for the SS. When these apartments had been completely emptied out, they were freshly painted and new stoves were put in—right in the middle of the war, when there was nothing to be had. They ordered furniture and carpets from the warehouses, and we got things ready right down to the washcloths in the bathrooms; we even made the beds. They were all Jewish beds with Jewish bedding—since they made that distinction between "Jewish" and "Aryan"—but everything had of course been disinfected and the houses fumigated because "all Jews have vermin."

I suffered terribly from this—these were Jewish apartments, and you knew where the people now were. I also suffered from how these Jewish women acted, and I had awful arguments with them because they did things that were totally unnecessary. When we were just about done and were waiting for the SS overseers, the women sat down and started clipping doilies out of paper to line the kitchen drawers. "Are you crazy?" I said. "You are doing this for the SS!"

"Yes," they said, "but they should see that what we Jews do, we do well."

Hilda notes that she had "continual clashes" with people from the Jewish community. One run-in took place following an incident in a streetcar.

Jews, who were normally barred from streetcars, were allowed to ride them to work. But we had to wear the star, which partners in mixed marriages had to wear only in connection with forced labor, and we were allowed only at the back.

One morning, a few rather young SS men riding up front blocked the exit when we came to our stop. As the next stop was on the other side of the river, we would have had a long walk back. And if you didn't get to work on time, the Jewish Gestapo—it was the Jewish Police, we called them Gestapo—were under orders to denounce you to the SS, in which case you'd be deported. What I did was to holler at the SS men, "Get away from that exit! These women have to get out now, and you're going to step back!"

Immediately, they stood aside. I hadn't thought it out—I'm always doing things without thinking, some of which have stood up all right, others of which haven't stood up well at all—but as it became clear to me afterwards, this was the tone they were used to. If I had asked them please to make way, they wouldn't have drawn back.

Hardly had we gotten off, however, than the women tore into me: "What did you think you were doing? We might have ended up in a concentration camp! After all, you can't shout at the SS!" But there we stood, and they had already crossed the Moldau.

Hilda's outspoken behavior was not the only thing that caused concern and anger within the Jewish community. By her own admission, she never stopped making illegal excursions, going to the movies, staying out after curfew—doing, in short, "all the forbidden things." Hilda realized that not sticking to the rules did constitute an additional danger, having witnessed the arrest of a co-worker who had been denounced for illegally possessing fresh fruit, but nothing seemed to curb her defiance. Finally, this penchant for disregarding anti-Jewish regulations prompted a co-worker to appeal to her better judgment.

One of our gladiators, Herr Herz, came up to me and said, "Frau Dr. Dujardin, you are putting all of us in danger with the antisocial things you do. I beg of you, please stay in line with the regulations."

Well, I could see that, and I said, "Herr Herz, maybe you are right. I will make an effort not to do such things anymore."

A few days later his wife came to us and said, "My husband has been arrested."

"How is that possible?" I asked. "He stays so meticulously within the rules."

Herr Herz had been among five Jewish forced laborers assigned to a factory where Czechs were working as well. One day, when two of the Jews were off making a delivery, inspectors came and found the three Jews who were still there sitting together with Czechs, whereas they were supposed to sit in separate areas. The Czech factory owner was arrested, and these Jews—who had had no say in the matter, they'd had to work where the owner put them—were sent straight to the Kleine Festung of Theresienstadt.* A week later, the death notice arrived.

At that point I said to myself, "Herr Herz held to the letter of the law, and now his wife is a widow and his son is an orphan. So it really doesn't make a bit of difference whether I respect the rules or not." From then on, I did just as I had done before.

Following a spat with one of the community's officials, Hilda was transferred out of the apartment detail and put to work splitting mica into hair-fine sheets. Once she learned that the mineral was to be used for the V-2 rocket, however,

---

*Kleine Festung: the "punishment" compound at the Theresienstadt concentration camp.

Hilda *"couldn't manage to produce a single piece." This made her supervisor angry—"justifiably" so, Hilda says—and she was transferred again, this time to a depot set up in a former synagogue to which books that had been owned by Jews were brought from all over Bohemia and Moravia. Some of these books were claimed by SS men, who had them delivered to their homes; a great number were sold for a nominal price to a large Prague bookstore.*

Throughout her period of forced labor, Hilda was out of the house from five-thirty in the morning to past seven at night; her husband, whose activities as a publishers' representative had dwindled almost to nothing, generally looked after their daughter. In early 1944, however, he was taken into the Wehrmacht, from which he was rapidly released as *"unfit for military service"* because of his mixed-married status—only to be sent to a labor camp with other *"Aryan"* husbands of Jewish women. This left Colette, who in the spring of 1944 had not yet turned twelve, alone in the house. The Dujardins' concierge saw to it that Colette ate at her place when no one else was around, but Hilda enlisted the help of her co-workers at the book depot, *"a very close-knit community,"* so that she might *"disappear"* for an hour or two most days to have lunch with Colette. Tied to the appointment with her mother—at which they discussed the daily shopping, which Colette had to do while Hilda was at work—the child *"couldn't spend the whole day just roaming around."*

Hilda's concierge was not the only Czech to help her and her family. Their cleaning lady disregarded two Gestapo warnings against working for them; claiming that she herself could get enough to eat through relatives in the country-side, she also brought them coupons to supplement their meager *"Jewish"* rations. And Hilda had been kept exceptionally well informed of developments both at home and abroad by two of her language pupils. One, the secretary to Czech President Emil Hácha, *"often played hooky, but always paid this Jewish woman for the lessons in advance"*; the other, a Dr. Jiri Halek, was a director of one of the largest Czech industrial firms. Halek obtained excellent information—from both sides. Frequently called to Berlin to discuss supply orders with the Wehrmacht High Command, he also worked with a resistance group that received newspapers, among other things, via parachute drops organized in England.

When Hilda's fellow forced laborers began, in November 1944, to be summoned for transport to Theresienstadt, Halek was deeply pessimistic about their chances. *"Whoever goes to Theresienstadt now is going there to be liquidated,"* he told Hilda. *"That they are still taking people away at this point means they don't want any survivors."*

Then I got my summons. They were always delivered on the job:
A man came up and gave you a slip of paper. This was a Monday, and
on Wednesday evening I was to report. But Jiri Halek said, "There is a
representative of our firm living in Brandenburg* whom I'll order back,
and you can live with Colette in the apartment he has there. The war
is going to last a few more months at the longest, and for those few
months you can hole up with regular documents as a representative of
the firm. I can take care of all that, but we'll have to get you false papers
without the *J.*"

Halek had, in fact, driven straight to police headquarters as soon
as I'd called to say that I'd received the transport order; then he'd driven
over to my place. "I have a friend," he said, "in the Czech section"—
police headquarters was divided into a German and a Czech section—
"who will be waiting for you. Tell him that you are a Volksdeutsche
refugee, that you come from Bielitz"—where my grandparents had
lived—"that you'd gone to Oderberg, and that when you'd heard that
the Russians were approaching"—the Russians had advanced quite a bit,
but no one knew exactly where they were—"you left with your child
for Prague. You wanted to continue on to relatives in Saxony"—Brandenburg was not to be mentioned—"but when you got to Prague this
morning on the train from Ostrava, someone snatched your purse with
all your papers in it, and now you need a duplicate identity card. You
have to be right on time, so go now. You will run into him as if by chance
in the hall, just at the stroke of eleven. He will take you into his office
and have you give him the particulars"—Jiri told me the questions his
friend would ask—"and he'll dictate it to his secretary and give you an
identity card."

It all went wonderfully up to the point when it was about to be
pulled out of the typewriter. Just then, a German Kripo† came into the
office looking for something and asked, "What does this woman here
want?"

Jiri's friend, who had been frightened enough during our whole
transaction, turned white as death. "That is a Volksdeutsche whose

---

Brandenburg: a German city west of Berlin.
†*Kripo:* an officer of the Kriminalpolizei, which dealt with common criminal rather than
political matters.

handbag was stolen this morning at the railroad station," he said. "She has to continue on to Saxony on the evening train, and I am issuing her a new ID."

The Kripo snarled at him, "You can take care of Czechs, that's your job, but you know that a Volksdeutsche belongs to us!" Then: "Madam, come with me."

Once in the hall, he said, "These Czechs—such an idiotic people! We never would have dreamt that they would be so stupid and ridiculous that they can't understand the simplest things!"

He brought me into his office, where a second officer asked me, "Would you like a glass of wine?"

"No," I said, "no."

"Drink. It will do you good after the shock you've been through this morning," the first Kripo said. Then he asked me where my husband was, and I said he was a first lieutenant and named the unit of an acquaintance who was at the front. "No!" He gasped. "A friend of mine is with that unit: Captain So-and-so, do you know him?"

"Yes," I said, "I've often heard the name."

"How small the world is," he said, "that we should run into each other like this! Of course we will help you!"

Then he recorded in the greatest detail what had happened. I thought to myself, "Now watch out that you don't make any mistakes"—but I made a mistake quickly enough. "I assume," he said, "that when you were in Oderberg, you reported there." There were very severe penalties for not registering, but smarter people would have said, "I was so upset that I didn't report." I, however, often slip up in such situations and, convinced that Oderberg was already in Russian hands, I told him that I had reported. Whereupon he said, "That's wonderful! I don't know whether the Russians have already reached Oderberg, but we can try telephoning there to establish the number of your old ID card, which would make this whole business a lot easier. I can't do it myself, though, as I don't have a line. You'll have to go to the SD;* I'll bring you over there."

At that point at least, I had the presence of mind to say, "Please,

---

*SD: Sicherheitsdienst; the Nazi Party intelligence organization, which worked in concert with the police.

don't trouble yourself. I need a bit of air, and I want to go by the station first to see my daughter, who's still sitting there with the baggage. I'll take the trolley that goes through St. Wenceslas Square; I know my way around in Prague."

"I'll call the SD right now," he said. "There's a very nice gentleman there who will probably already have made the call to Oderberg and will give you the papers." Then he gave me ration coupons—such stacks of them that if I had gotten them at any moment up to then, we would have been the happiest people alive.

"I rode the trolley to the museum," Hilda recounts. "There, the road branches off. On one side, it goes to the train station, across from which was the SD; on the other side, it goes up the hill to where we lived." Although she told herself at that moment that "the ID card without the J" was what she had "wanted all those years," Hilda did not feel she had much of a choice. "I stood there, thinking: 'Shall I now be cowardly and not go,'" she recalls, laughing, "'or shall I be cowardly and pass it up?'" Although concerned that she might put Halek's policeman friend on the spot if she failed to show, Hilda decided "in favor of being cowardly" and went home.

Jiri Halek was there still, and he praised me to the skies. "You did right," he said. "Going would have been a mistake because no one knows whether the Russians are there or not, and if he had gotten through to Oderberg, it would have come out that you hadn't reported there at all." Besides that, I had thought to myself, "The man at the SD won't be such an idiot as the one at police headquarters. He'll ask me questions I can't answer"—for instance, what time my train arrived, because all the trains were running wildly late.

Halek tried to persuade a doctor he knew to give Hilda a shot that would drive her temperature up and cause her to be taken off the transport list, as official policy exempted the sick from transport. But the doctor refused, pointing out that transports were leaving regularly and that forced labor and tiny rations had left Hilda too weak to withstand the strain of repeated fevers.

So now it was decided. And that was so much easier than sitting there at police headquarters, than making up stories, than knocking around all the time. Now I had let myself go. The Sabras in Israel reproach the older generation that they simply went, but I saw at that moment how much easier it was to give up, and to go.

Colette, who had never been registered with the Jewish community, was not summoned for transport. The concierge offered to take care of her in Prague, but through another of Hilda's former pupils, Colette was placed in a children's home in the countryside, where she spent the last months of the war more or less in hiding.

Then came the transport. In the middle of the night, after sleeping—or not sleeping—a few hours on straw somewhere, we had been put in blacked-out streetcars and taken to some totally unfamiliar freight depot on the outskirts of Prague. Next to me in the streetcar had been a man with a six-year-old boy. The boy was relatively small for his age, and the man had held him in his arms, pressed closely against him, because he was bawling so.

The mother had run alongside the streetcar, and I heard the scene outside the train when she said good-bye to them; the women were chased away twice, but they kept coming back until the men got on. I was sitting in the train, and the man was standing in front of me with the boy in his arms, and we were being tallied for the umpteenth time; an SS man was going through taking names and vital statistics and checking them against his list. Then, as the SS man moved a little farther on, I said, "My God! The boy has scarlet fever!"—loud enough for him to hear.

"What!" the SS man said. "The boy has scarlet fever?"

"It's plain to see," I said. "All you have to do is look at him." The boy really did have a face full of red blotches—from crying and sobbing.

"Are you a doctor?" he asked me. I said I was—but if he'd checked up, it would of course have come out that I was not a physician but a doctor of philosophy. The train was just about to leave when the SS man called to the engineer, "Stop! Stop!" Then: "Get that child out of here! Get him out!" The mothers were still standing there, so the man ran to the exit and handed the boy into his wife's arms.

When he came back, he said to me, "Does he have scarlet fever?"

"Come on!" I said. "And what if he did? The main thing is that he doesn't have to go."

The man found me in Theresienstadt and gave me a huge sausage he had brought with him; he later died in the camp of typhus. After the war, when we returned to Prague, his wife came to me and didn't know how to thank me. I hadn't done anything for her other than saying this one phrase: "He has scarlet fever!" But, in this way, the child survived.

On her second day in Theresienstadt, Hilda had what she considers a singular stroke of "luck." Recognized by a clerk at the inmate-run office where all had to report for work assignments, Hilda was brought before Leo Baeck, a famous liberal rabbi from Berlin who was in charge of the camp's educational system. In the presence of this "truly great man" the clerk made Hilda a proposition.

"We have quite a lot of children here," she said. "We had outstanding teachers, but they've all left on transport and we're in urgent need of new ones; we want the children to go to normal schools once the war comes to an end. But the people we need must have daring, for though we are allowed to give the children supervision, instruction is forbidden. Before you declare your willingness to take on this work, I have to tell you: It stands under the death penalty. Are you willing to teach?"

"Of course."

Then Leo Baeck brought it up again: "But the penalty of death . . ."

"What does that mean, 'penalty of death'?" I asked. "We're all on a first-name basis with death here." So I taught children up to the end, which was good fortune indeed.

Theresienstadt's 17,320 remaining inmates—after living, Hilda recalls, in the "deep suspicion that we could not come out alive"—were liberated in early May 1945. Hilda returned to Prague, where she was reunited with her husband and daughter, only to discover that "the long-pined-for freedom was a highly imperfect freedom." With her German passport and broken Czech, Hilda was persona non grata among the local population, and her daughter was sent home in tears from three Prague schools. "It was," recalls Hilda, "not at all a good thing to be a German in 1945."

The next year, the Dujardins left for Munich. As there was no housing in that bombed-out city, they were placed in a small town on its western outskirts whose inhabitants, they soon learned, had strong pro-Nazi sympathies. The family managed to make ends meet, complementing Hilda's income from a part-time teaching job at the town's public school by raising vegetables on a small plot whose use their openly anti-Semitic landlord granted them following the intervention of the police.

By 1948, however, Hilda's marriage had broken up and her husband had moved away. On top of that, with the progress of "denazification"—an administrative procedure that generally had the effect of clearing of the Nazi taint all but the most obvious war criminals—the school where Hilda taught was handed back to its former principal, a convinced National Socialist who went around whisper-

ing, "No Jew is to be tolerated at our school!" Hilda was dismissed on the ground that newly "denazified" teachers had to be given their old places back, but she carried a "bitter struggle" all the way to the Bavarian provincial parliament, winning reinstatement only to face "constant" harassment by the authorities and complaints from the parents of her pupils.

Upon her arrival in Germany, Hilda had joined the Jewish community in Munich; "as we lived in a particularly Nazi town," she says, "the Jewish community would have been more or less my home base." She was, however, put off by the reception she got—"not a soul took notice of me," she recalls, "and I just stood against the wall, listening"—as well as by the fact that the postwar membership consisted largely of Polish Jews, with whom she felt little in common and whose language she could not understand. Still, she would have remained in the community but for the fact that rival groups vying for administrative control woke up to her existence just in time to solicit her support on a crucial vote. "This was too much for me," she says, "and I wrote identical letters to both groups: 'I joined the Jewish community in 1933, and now it is 1952 and I am resigning from membership because what is going on in the community doesn't suit me at all.'"

At the time of the interview, Hilda Dujardin had lived in Vienna for many years. Her apartment was modest; her pension, based on her eight-hour-per-week teaching schedule, was paltry; and her reparations payments were well below what they might have been, since she had no written evidence of the job she was to have begun in the spring of 1933 and thus had been unable to prove that she had been hurt professionally by Nazi policies. Although Hilda was not a member of Vienna's Jewish community, she stayed "in touch," giving what she could when contributions were solicited for Israel.

Looking back, Hilda claims to have no second thoughts about her decision to "make a stand" on the side of the Jews, or about her unpremeditated affirmation of this position when she "might have had an opportunity" to hide her Jewish affiliation from the German bureaucracy in 1939.

As I said, once I had taken this step, I never regretted it; I always felt that I belonged. With my mother in Ostrava, I would probably have had a relatively easy time getting Aryan papers, and then I would have been unequivocally a half-Jew or not a Jew at all. But I believe that I would have suffered far more from that than from the fact that I embraced it and belonged to it. Because if I had had Aryan papers, we would of course have had to take the Nazi newspaper, we would have had to join certain organizations—maybe not the Party itself, but one or another of the ancillary organizations—and we would have had to move in Nazi circles. As a Jew, you always had a shield against this. You lived a charmed life.

The fact Hilda felt she suffered less as a Jew is, in her words, "a question of character," which she says is "probably determined by upbringing and heredity." To illustrate, she cites parallel incidents.

Engineers are very independent when it comes to their locomotives. Once there was a stationmaster in Cracow who wanted to ride in the cab with my father. My father said no. Even though the stationmaster outranked him considerably, my father said no. Both of them certainly became angry, and the stationmaster persisted. He was standing on the steps that lead up to the locomotive and trying to get on when my father, truly a hot-tempered man, dealt him a resounding slap. The stationmaster almost fell from the steps, and my father rode off. This landed my father in a disciplinary hearing, and my mother went to Vienna in advance to speak with the people at the main office of the railroad. My father was acquitted, but I believe there were two or three months when he was not allowed to work.

In Theresienstadt, I once did something that was awfully stupid and caused a big stir. In front of the commandant's office in Theresienstadt was a large square with an avenue around it where Jews were not allowed, but connecting to the avenue was a sidewalk Jews could use. The sidewalk was very crowded, and I was walking illegally in the street when I saw an SS man on horseback coming straight at me. The obvious and more sensible thing would of course have been to step aside, and if it hadn't been an SS man, I would certainly have done so without thinking about it. But I couldn't—I continued on a collision course with him.

People were looking down at me from the windows of the school building, and those in the street were watching as well. It was such a comic sight: A lone figure facing him there on his horse and not yielding a step. And I was convinced—God, was I ever convinced—"Now he'll just run right over me, probably trample me to death."

But what did he do? He made a curve around me and continued on. Those who fell upon me were my good Jewish coreligionists; they crowded around and reproached me most bitterly. Of course, I didn't accomplish anything with this. But sometimes one has to do something for one's own spiritual well-being and, for once, I couldn't make way.

IDENTITY
IMPOSED

In contrast to those who paid dearly for being separated from their fellow Jews—in contrast also to those whose choices suggest that separation, even in the face of a grave threat, was beyond their emotional means—stand others from whom it was belonging that exacted the higher price. Shared by many who fit this description was a conviction that whatever might make one feel Jewish was foreign to them as individuals, as well as a perception that being of Jewish origin had been of minor if any consequence in their lives before they became subject to persecution on account of it. Rather than hiding from the outside world a Jewishness they felt was theirs, such people viewed Jewishness as something the outside world had imposed upon them. They saw the conflicts with which they struggled as arising not from any personal sense of who they were but from the unsought, unaccustomed, and generally unwelcome position in which they had been placed: that of being regarded by others as a Jew.

What happens when two basic elements of identity—how one is seen by others, and how one experiences oneself—come into conflict? To what extent does each determine who one is and where one belongs? And is the identity one presents to others, or even to oneself, always consistent with inner reality?

Those whose Jewish origins were brought to the fore by persecution were anything but a uniform group.

In the early decades of this century, European Jews to whom the religion and tradition of their forebears meant less than their own place in the society around them sometimes went so far as to change their names or convert to Christianity—and those who did so might hide their Jewish roots not only from neighbors and associates but from their own children as well. When, however, Nazi rule prompted the tracing of "racial" affiliations that in some cases had long been effaced, members of the younger generation could be confronted at the selfsame moment with a Jewish background and the dangers connected with it.

Even when they were not in the dark as to their origins, those who had grown up without the Jewish religion might not necessarily look upon themselves as Jews. If, on the one hand, they equated being Jewish with practicing Judaism, they might feel that, not being religious, they were not part of the Jewish group. If, on the other hand, they had been brought up with the notion that they were in fact Jewish but with little idea of what Jewishness might signify in other than religious terms, they might be confused as to whether they were part of a Jewish group or not. Christians of Jewish origin, if they saw being Christian and being Jewish as mutually exclusive, might feel that it was their faith rather than their ancestry that defined them; if, however, they viewed the traditions as linked or saw a content to their Jewishness that was not strictly religious, they might be more inclined to view themselves in some way as Jewish.

Those who managed to outlast the Third Reich went in a variety of directions. Some, wishing to become invisible as Jews, changed their names, moved to new surroundings, or embraced Christianity. Others held to their original position; their ambivalence, perplexity, and degree of acceptance or rejection were largely unchanged by what they had lived. Still others felt closer to Jewishness—whether they moved toward it in some positive way or simply came to a realization that for better or worse being Jewish had always been, or had become through their experience of the Nazi years, an inalienable element of their condition.

Leonore Hoffmann, whose Jewish origins were unknown to her early in life and who grew up a German nationalist and a Lutheran, contemplated suicide in the 1930s, her self-destructive reflex perhaps mirroring her rejection by a society with which she identified but which had declared her a "foreign body." Leonore's time in concentration camps was spent in the most difficult of circumstances: She was able to draw to a far lesser degree than her fellows on the ties of family and community that for many constituted the most important source of both physical and emotional sustenance—partly because those ties were denied to her, partly because she herself was reluctant to build them. It is in her later years that Leonore seems to have developed a sense that she is a Jew—something she lacked during the persecution, which, she says, she "never lived . . . as a Jew, always as a Christian."

For Hélène Terlinden, in contrast, accepting the idea of being Jewish was never easier than during the Nazi occupation, when the generous reactions of some of her French fellow citizens led her to find "something . . . touching" in Jewishness for the first time. But Hélène's own fluctuating attitudes of acceptance and rejection seem to have had little to do with how important being Jewish is to her existence. In childhood she was at first confused about her Jewish origins, then repelled by them—but her confusion was acute and her repulsion passionate. Even at the time of the interview, when there was barely a hint of Jewish content to her daily life, the terms in which she chose to explain her relation to being Jewish equated it with a fact of the human condition that is basic and inescapable: mortality.

Unlike Hélène Terlinden's rejection, Etienne Lenoir's never wavered. But in his case as well one may question whether attitude and self-image reliably reflect centrality. For even as Etienne distances himself from what he calls "would-be Jewish identity"—which, he says, he rejects "not only for myself, but . . . for everyone"—the fact that he is of Jewish origin seems to shape both events in his life and his response to them. Why did he have to condemn the narrowness of the Polish Jews he met in the camp while finding charm in similar qualities of French farmers, whose values and habits were equally foreign to his own? How might his life have been different if the Jewish origin whose significance he so vehemently denies had not been such a preoccupation? Could his feelings toward Jewishness—others' and his own—parallel those of the healthier camp inmates toward the debilitated "Mussulmans" he so movingly describes: Confronted with proof of the precarious nature of the Jew's status in the West, did Etienne shun the pariah Jews of the East, and even blame them for the misfortunes to which they were subjected, in an attempt to avoid coming to grips with his own vulnerability?

Rev. Leonore Hoffmann

Leonore Hoffmann was born in 1916 in the German city of Hanover. Her physician-father, the son of a Jewish father and a non-Jewish mother, "did not want to be a Jew," according to Leonore. In fact, he insisted that Leonore's mother, both of whose parents were Jews, convert to Protestantism. Leonore's mother agreed, says Leonore, "for my father's sake," and the couple's two children were baptized in the Lutheran church. Leonore believes, however, that her mother "never became a Christian deep down" but remained "a Jew in her heart up to her dying day."

In line with her father's "rejecting" stance, Leonore and her older brother were raised as Protestants, and Leonore says that she "didn't know at all" during her early childhood that she might have "anything to do with the Jews." Her mother imparted nothing in the way of Jewish culture or tradition—"my father wouldn't have allowed that," she remarks—and Leonore "didn't know any more about Judaism" than what she learned gazing "with great interest" through the window of her Jewish neighbors on Sabbath evening. It did strike her as "odd" that her mother should have her substitute "God" for "Christ" in the children's prayer which, as her schoolmates recited it, went

> *Ich bin klein.*
> *Mein Herz sei rein.*
> *Soll niemand darin wohnen,*
> *Als Christus allein.**

---

*The prayer, literally translated, reads: "I am small. / Let my heart be pure. / No one is to dwell in it, / But Christ alone."

But her puzzlement faded, as "such things were never discussed" in her home.

If Jewishness was banned completely from the Hoffmann household, Lutheranism hardly played a greater role. Dr. Hoffmann's religious affiliation was purely nominal compared with his German nationalism, and Leonore's brother was equally indifferent to religion. Nonetheless, Leonore had spiritual yearnings "from childhood on," and these feelings—which were encouraged at the Protestant school she attended, as well as at the children's services to which she was introduced by a playmate—did receive some support at home. "My mother, who from what I can tell was religious, taught me to pray and made sure that I did it," Leonore recalls. In addition, she says, it was her mother's example that showed her that "piety is not just in words but implies consequences, in help for the poor and so on."

Leonore's religious bent—which, she stresses, was "in no way Jewish, but rather Christian"—remained undeflected by her chance discovery, at age nine, of her Jewish origins. During a visit to her mother's sisters in Breslau, where both of Leonore's parents had been raised, Leonore was suddenly "filled with excitement" as she walked with her mother through a cemetery.

"Look at this!" I said. "You can see from the letters where Jews are buried." My mother gave me a nudge; I was to keep quiet, and I didn't know why.

When we returned home, she said, "I had wanted to tell you that I am a Jew by birth and that all my relatives are Jews, but only after you had gotten to know Jews and had seen that they too are good people, just like all the others."

"From then on," says Leonore, she "knew"—if not about her father's background, at least about her mother's.

But it didn't make any further impression on me. Nothing was said about it at home, as it was considered taboo. We didn't live in accordance with it. And as my father didn't want to acknowledge it, it was natural that I wouldn't be occupied with it either.

Although she was later grateful that her mother, who died in 1930, had not lived to see the arrival of the Nazis in power, Leonore herself "wanted to be enthusiastic" when, shortly before her seventeenth birthday, Hitler was named to the chancellorship of Germany. Both her father and her brother were members of the Stahlhelm, the paramilitary wing of the rightist German National Party, and Leonore remembers that she had "never respected the black-red-gold," the colors of the democratic Weimar Republic. "That's the way I was brought up," she explains, "and here was something that went along those lines. I never even gave it a second thought—you just parroted what you heard."

Leonore adds that the "overall situation at the time in Germany" contributed to her initial warmth toward the Nazis. "There had simply been nothing to inspire us young people," she says, "and then, suddenly, there was something that made the hearts of us Germans beat faster. From one day to the next, flags were being hung out. We Germans are, after all, a people enthused by a smart step." Leonore was eager to share the feelings of her girlfriends, who "had been caught up by Hitler somewhere deep within," and while she found the nationwide boycott of Jewish shops on April 1, 1933, "very distasteful," she remembers that she "hadn't yet thought things over all that much."

Then I saw Hitler in a newsreel—the way he spoke, the whole way he held his mouth—and that's when it came over me: "This man is a criminal." And you heard people whispering behind their hands that there were concentration camps. Of course, you didn't know what was happening there, but you did know that it was gruesome and that innocent people were being brought there. Why didn't other people grasp it? I was seventeen or so at the time, a dumb young thing, and others could also see Hitler speak.

Leonore rebelled against her own perceptions—"I didn't want it to be so," she recalls. For a time, her understanding of her own position "was somehow split." But despite her attempts at enthusiasm, Leonore began to realize that she was "being rejected" by German society.

I had to leave school—that is, I left voluntarily but because I had seen that I would no longer be able to get my diploma. I would have liked to study medicine, but I saw that was finished. All my girlfriends joined BDM,* but I couldn't join. I couldn't do this, I couldn't do that; and so I did in fact know that I was a victim, and that there was much I wasn't allowed.

Facing an academic dead end and burdened at home by problems with her father's second wife—"an Aryan, by the way"—Leonore applied in 1935 to become a nurse trainee with a Protestant nursing order. She was accepted and allowed to live in the order's hospital—known as a Diakonissinnenhaus—despite her confession that she would be unable to furnish an Ariernachweis, the certificate attesting to "Aryan" descent that was required for most employment during the

---

BDM: Bund deutscher Mädchen (Confederation of German Girls); the female equivalent of the Hitler Youth.

Nazi period. "This was the only Diakonissinnenhaus that took you even if you didn't have an Ariernachweis," says Leonore. "In any other you would have needed it, and it would not have been possible for me to work at a municipal hospital or for the Red Cross either."

A few months after Leonore had left home, Dr. Hoffmann died—"right when the Nuremberg Laws were decreed," in September 1935. "They promised him at the Diakonissinnenhaus—where, in fact, he died—that they would take care of me and wouldn't put me out," says Leonore, noting that this was a "difficult" promise at a time when religious nursing orders "were also being persecuted" by a regime intent on closing them down. Her father was granted a funeral with military honors—"a salute was fired," she recalls—but by that time Leonore "was no longer part of it inside," and as time went on her disaffection with Nazi rule increased.

The young minister who gave us classes at the Diakonissinnenhaus pointed out quite a lot that was horrible, seen from the church's point of view, and at that point it really started to crumble for me. It was, however, not the fate of the Jews but the fate of the ministers who were put behind bars and sent to concentration camps that led me to renounce it totally.

After her father's death, Leonore sought to clear up all questions regarding her origins. "My mother had been a full Jew, that much I knew," she says, "but I had never been sure about my father." With the Nuremberg Laws in force, the point was a critical one: Those with two Jewish grandparents who, like Leonore, had never held membership in a Jewish community faced a reduced—though still significant—level of persecution; those with three Jewish grandparents were considered "full Jews" and, no matter what their religious affiliation, subjected to the entire range of anti-Jewish measures.

From my father, I had gotten the papers for his mother's side only, not for my grandfather. My mother's relatives said, "Your grandfather was a Jew," but since my father had never told me, I had never quite understood it. I still had some small hope that I would get out of it—that I would, in the end, come up with different information.

Her personal doubts notwithstanding, Leonore was officially classified as having three Jewish grandparents. Over the next thirty months she managed to lead an uneventful existence, living in the Diakonissinnenhaus and working as a student nurse. But in the spring of 1938, when the regime began moving toward confiscation of the personal holdings of German Jews, Leonore's bank account was blocked, and she was forced to sell off her valuables at nominal prices. "I was," she points out, "treated just as any other Jew."

By this time Leonore's brother had decided that, even though his friends were standing by him, it was best to leave Germany, and his wife's American relatives agreed to sponsor the couple's application for a U.S. visa. When he was incarcerated along with more than 25,000 other Jews in connection with Kristallnacht, the "Night of Broken Glass" that took place on November 9–10, 1938, the visa qualified him for release. With Leonore paying for the passage, her brother and sister-in-law left before the year was out.

Leonore convinced herself that she would be safe as long as she was at the Diakonissinnenhaus. But before the year was out, she had been summoned repeatedly by the Gestapo—something that was done "to keep you in a state of agitation," she says—and the appointment of a new Nazi Party district leader had alarmed those who ran the Diakonissinnenhaus into telling her they could not shield her any longer. In July 1939, she left the Diakonissinnenhaus and prepared to travel to Toronto, where she was to work at a mission school. But war broke out on September 1, before Leonore was able to sail. Prevented from leaving, she resumed her nursing duties at the Diakonissinnenhaus, telling herself, " 'It's war now, and everyone has to pitch in.' I was a German, you can't forget that. My father had been a very good German, and he had passed that along to me."

Leonore continued to look for a way out. She thought of Switzerland but found out the border was already closed. A message came via Sweden that a steamship ticket for North America was awaiting her in the Netherlands, but she had scarcely packed when, on May 10, 1940, Germany invaded the Low Countries. After a summer of uncertainty, Leonore decided she should try to finish her training and obtain her nursing certificate. In September, she applied to Hanover's Jewish hospital.

My father had placed his patients there at one time, and I remembered from my childhood that it had been a good hospital; the matron, who had been splendid, was long dead, but I knew a few of the nurses. I couldn't say that I was a Jew when I was not, of course, and I told them exactly how it was and that I was eager to do my nursing examination. They had a shortage of nurses, and—reluctantly—they took me on.

But then came the mad absurdity that, because I was a Christian, they didn't allow me to live at the Jewish hospital—while in November I was thrown out of the room I had rented because there they were disinclined to share a roof with a non-Aryan. At that point a Christian shelter, a home for what in those days were called fallen women, took me in.

Leonore, it turned out, had a "terribly difficult time" in her nine months at the Jewish hospital. The new matron was, she says, "somehow against me from the beginning and always trying, bit by bit, to run me down." Leonore's efforts at getting along with the other nurses also met with rebuff: "I really took a lot of pains, because I was used to working together and having good rapport, but it didn't ever click." Although she "never made a secret" of her Christian beliefs, Leonore stresses that she doesn't know whether religion affected her relations with the others. "Whenever they could somehow manage it, they saw to it that I had to work on Sunday so that I couldn't go to church," she observes, but she adds that her problems seemed to spring from the fact that, "at the time, the Jewish hospital was not a very nice place" in general.

On my very first day, the assistant chief of the medical staff came up to me and tried to get me to inform on the chief of staff and on some of the nurses. I wasn't used to such things at all, and it came as a horrible shock to me. The chief of staff was a good physician, but the backbiting was dreadful. And the matron was having a relationship with an assistant nurse, the head nurse was going with one of the other nurses—for me, a new world.

The nurses' lounge was over a patient's room, and for diversion in the evenings they would dance. "I can't do that," I said. "After all, the patients have to sleep." For me, it went without saying that the patient came first. It was an atrocious state of affairs: They did naked dances in front of the doctors, including the assistant chief of staff. Of course, it displeased them greatly that I never took part in these festivities—and, as I said openly why not, they felt my rejection in turn.

Professional jealousies also contributed to the ill feeling. Leonore's training in X-ray and lab work allowed her to fill in when needed for the assistant chief or head nurse, something the others found "hard to swallow."

Actually, many there hadn't wanted to become nurses at all but could no longer enter any other profession. That they didn't like being nurses was evident from the way they performed their duties. Now, I was a nurse heart and soul, which the patients could see as well; and because the patients liked me, the others became envious. People were saying, "The nurses at the Jewish hospital are worthless, and the only one that is any good isn't even a Jew"—which wasn't to my credit, it was simply that the others didn't have it. As everyone knew each other in Jewish circles, the others heard this also.

Nor did it please her colleagues that, when Leonore took her municipal certification exam in March 1941, she alone among four candidates—the three others were "Aryans," she notes—received the highest possible mark. As a full-fledged nurse, the matron told her, she would be allowed to continue working at the Jewish hospital, although she would not be paid. The abiding friction may ultimately have contributed to the death of a patient. Because it was she who was calling for help, Leonore believes, the rest of the staff responded nonchalantly to an emergency, and by the time they arrived it was too late.

Leonore had been able to continue living in the Christian shelter to which she had moved the previous November, but her freedom was becoming more and more limited.

At first I still made secret visits to the Diakonissinnenhaus, where I was let in through a back door, but then that was forbidden, and the friend I had there came to see me at my place. In the house where I lived, I was gradually being confined to my room. But even after I could no longer come downstairs to the common room, there were a few who remained loyal to me; they knew why I was leading such a solitary existence and continued visiting me. Then the problem of the air raids started: I was actually not allowed into the cellar. This was awkward for the housemother, who didn't really want to make me stay upstairs—but of course she had directives she had to hold to more or less. So I came down to the ground floor, and a few of the others came and sat with me there.

Between her personal isolation and her difficulties at work, Leonore's aliena-tion grew. "I was separated from my original friends and removed from familiar surroundings," she explains, "and placed into a new orbit where I was rejected—and which I also rejected, because I couldn't go along." Her "dander up" over the decision of the Jewish hospital not to pay her for her work, she approached the municipal health board's chief medical officer, whom she trusted as a "very decent man" for his "risky" decision to give her the highest grade on the certification exam. Incensed by her story, he vowed to help her find a post in an "Aryan" hospital, even though, as Leonore notes, "he almost landed in jail for standing up on my behalf." But by June, Leonore recalls, "all this agitation had managed to get me sick."

I went to a doctor, the father of a schoolmate, and he certified that

I was ill. The minister who had become my guardian when I was orphaned at eighteen then sent me to recuperate at the home of his daughter, who was married to a minister and lived in a village. But when her husband, who had been on the battlefield, came home on furlough, they explained to me that the Gestapo had been making inquiries and that I would "have to understand, but it wouldn't work out." He didn't want a non-Aryan in his house.

After I had been there a month, I left. I had a friend, also a nursing sister, who worked in a hospital in Celle, and she talked with the chief of staff there. He was furious: "That's not right," he said. "Let her come here." He went to the police and to the Arbeitsfront* and told them, "I need a trained nurse, and she can work in the quarantine wing; she doesn't have to circulate in the rest of the hospital at all." They put up a lot of resistance, but they finally did give him the authorization.

After I had worked there four weeks, the Gestapo appeared and arrested me right on the spot; unfortunately, it was on a Friday afternoon, just when the chief of staff was going to be away through Sunday. I landed in prison and was then transferred to Hanover, where the Gestapo claimed that I hadn't said who I was and had taken the work under false pretenses. He intervened as soon as he could, and after a few days I was released, although I was no longer permitted to work in an Aryan hospital. It was actually ridiculous when you consider what a helpless creature I was: I didn't stick my nose into anything, and they took as much trouble over me as time and money would allow.

Leonore's arrest took place in August 1941. Upon her release, the Diakonissinnenhaus took her back in, this time in secret. While she was there, Hanover's Jews were expelled from their homes and "squeezed" into a handful of buildings in town, including a funeral chapel. That Leonore did not join them was the result of an appeal by the pastor of the home for fallen women, who, "strangely enough," was able to persuade the Gestapo to let her return to his institution.

But this was the only exception made for Leonore. She was spared neither the yellow star, which had to be worn by Jews in Germany from September 1, 1941, nor forced labor in the "Jewish section" of a Hanover cardboard factory, to which

---

*Arbeitsfront: National Socialist Labor Front; a Nazi Party organization to which all employers and employees were required to belong.

she had been assigned at the conclusion of her brief stay in prison. Life in the factory was "far more pleasant" than life at the Jewish hospital, she says; her fellow laborers were "good comrades," by whom she was "accepted right away" and who appeared to disregard totally the question of her religious beliefs.

Of course they knew. I didn't have much reason to talk about it, but I never made a secret of it either; another nurse who had left the hospital was there with us, and I assume she told them some things as well. But I stumbled into splendid people at the factory, and I had much better contact with them than with the nurses in the hospital.

Outside working hours, Leonore was largely on her own. Her freedom of movement was dwindling as anti-Jewish measures intensified; "we were allowed to shop in only two stores in Hanover by then," she remembers. And home was hardly a refuge, as a mother and daughter had moved into her tiny room and virtually taken it over. "The staying alone," she says, "was getting even worse." During the fall of 1941, this burden was exacerbated by rumors of imminent deportation.

I saw it coming, and I said, "I'll never make it." You know, always being in an exceptional position—not really being at home anywhere—is a very difficult thing. Where one feels drawn, one is not allowed; and, on the other side, there were no ties. I was actually on the point of wanting to take my own life.

But on the very day I hit bottom, a minister I knew from Celle came to visit me saying, "I had the feeling you needed me." That was a very intense experience for me, and I told him everything. "You can't do it," he said. "A lot of people have their eyes on you, and you can't let them down." After that, I never again tried to kill myself—that is, I didn't try it then either, but I wanted to and all that remained was to ponder how I was going to do it. Now I had the feeling, "Aha! Right when you couldn't go on anymore, God took care of you. Someone came."

Complying with an order to hand over her radio and camera to the Gestapo in November, Leonore asked whether she was likely to be included in the deportations that were rumored to be approaching. "'That's out of the question,'" she was told. "'You're a long way from your turn, if it comes at all.'" But on December 10, 1941, she says, "they came to pick up those who were in mixed marriages or otherwise didn't live in one of the houses the Jews had been packed into." Thus, as it turned out, Leonore was among the first to be taken away.

A short time before, I had been speaking with the housemother, and I said to her, "I know full well that God can save me from going to the camp. But if He doesn't, then He has a mission for me there, and I'll go willingly." That's the way it was, too, from the first moment on—or perhaps I should say from the second moment on. Because I was alone in the police van for a bit—we were awakened very early and taken away by the Gestapo—and, sitting there, I wept; I figured I would never come out of this. But then we made another stop, and a young girl got in; she had been snatched away from her relatives and she was crying so! Well, then I no longer had any time for myself, I had to comfort her. A woman, seventy-one years of age and partially blind, got on at the next stop; she too had been torn from her family, which was not purely non-Aryan, it was "privileged."* So I had both hands full.

And that's how it was all through the camp period: From the moment the bars of the marshaling camp closed behind us, all oppression was gone. I had so much to do, so many to console. Of course, the fear kept coming back—it was a particular torment in the morning, when one saw the day ahead and didn't know what it would bring. But I never had time to dwell on that; at every turn, I needed my strength to comfort people. And, through this consolation, you yourself were consoled. That is an important experience, which, as a human being, one must go through again and again: As long as you are taken up with yourself, you cannot cope with life. Only by joining with others in shouldering their affliction does one gain strength.

At the marshaling camp, where she spent five days, Leonore found herself "completely cut off" from all those she knew—and, "for the first time, exclusively among Jews." On her last evening in the camp, she began what was to become a lifelong friendship with a kindergarten teacher who, like herself, had volunteered to pack small sacks with provisions for the next day's journey. Leonore also ran into an acquaintance of her brother whom she had helped treat at the Jewish hospital. During the subsequent five-day train ride toward a destination "no one knew," the two sat together, so she felt "not so totally among strangers."

Leonore was sent to the Riga ghetto, one of the main destinations for

---

*Privileged: refers to a particular category of mixed marriage under the Nuremberg Laws; this woman was presumably the Jewish wife of a non-Jewish husband.

transports of Reich Jews, which had begun in mid-October 1941. Her arrival, on December 20, followed by three weeks a bloodbath in which over 10,000 Jews had been gunned down by a detachment from Einsatzgruppe A, one of the SS mobile killing units active in Russia, the Ukraine, and the Baltic. Leonore and her fellow deportees got off the train in a ghost town: "There was food still on the stoves," she recalls. "Everything had been left standing." The only Jews Leonore remembers finding were "300 Latvian skilled workers, a few women who had hidden themselves, and some children who lived in a separate ghetto."

Upon her arrival in Riga, Leonore was put to work as a nurse. The job was a difficult one because, as she recalls, "in the beginning you had no medications, no food, nothing, so all you could do was go see people and console them." Moreover, a number of nurses from the Jewish hospital in Hanover had also been transported to Riga, and Leonore found herself back in their company. "This was no great delight," she says. "On the one hand, I was able to have good consultations with them, but on the other their rejection of me came along with them into the ghetto."

Leonore was obliged not only to work side by side with her former colleagues but also to share quarters with them on one of the small slum courtyards around which the ghetto was organized. Again, she found their outlook different from her own.

There was an awful lot of good clothing that had been thrown out into the court so that we would have someplace to put ourselves. While I was giving clothing to people who didn't have anything to put on, the others kept it to swap for food. That never occurred to me; I didn't have such a head for business. Besides, I thought that it was more important that people have something to wear.

The nurses' trading partners were friends and relatives who were assigned to work outside the ghetto, where they could scout up food, or who went prospecting in uninhabited sections within the ghetto's walls.

At first, I didn't notice that others had more to eat, and I made do with what was distributed to us, which was not all that much: one hundred grams per day of bread, which was often moldy anyway, and one hundred grams of other provisions every two weeks, which you can't do a great deal with either. So they had something to eat while I didn't, but it never crossed their minds to give me anything.

Snubbed by her fellow nurses, without relatives or other personal connections, and "too dumb, somehow, to get anything" on her own, Leonore lacked the resources that many of those in the ghetto called upon to supplement their rations. But former patients "showed their gratitude" for the treatment Leonore had given them by slipping her something to eat from time to time, while her factory comrades insisted on sharing their food with her—and in this way, she says, "more or less saved my life." Still, Leonore fell ill, and in March 1942 she became a patient in the ghetto infirmary.

Leonore was relieved upon her release several months later that she no longer had to live with the nurses, who had effectively "eaten up" her belongings during her hospitalization. Suffering from severe rheumatoid arthritis, she was unable to participate in a normal work detail, or kommando, so she darned socks and altered clothes in exchange for food. When she had regained her health and strength, Leonore was assigned to kommandos in which, cleaning, peeling potatoes, and performing similar manual tasks, she frequently enjoyed "good rapport" with her co-workers. "I got to know many fine people and had many lovely experiences of comradeship," she recalls. "I don't believe I would have held on otherwise; one is, after all, very dependent on that." In particular, she remembers the response of fellow kommando members and of another friend when she broke her arm and was once more unable to work.

The first time I broke it—I broke it again shortly before we left the ghetto—was precisely on the second day of Christmas* in 1942. I was in an external kommando in a hospital, and that was bliss: I was so utterly famished, and there I saw milk again for the very first time, and I planted myself on a crate into which old scraps of bread were thrown. But one day, on the way there, I fell and broke my arm, and that was the end of that.

I got my normal rations, but you couldn't live from that, and they were bringing me the soup from the hospital; you got a mess tin full of soup there. That was sweet of them, I must say, but they did it in the beginning, and then, obviously, it petered out. At that time I had been cooking together with a friend; she would bring something with her, and I would bring something with me. But when I broke my arm and could no longer contribute, I said to her, "I won't come anymore because I can't bring anything for the meal."

---

*In European countries, Christmas is a two-day holiday, celebrated on December 25 and 26.

"That's out of the question," she said. "It's precisely now that you need it."

Leonore's personal experiences, good and bad, took place amid dangers she had recognized "from the beginning": She and her fellow deportees "knew very well that frightful things were going on." It was shortly after her arrival in Riga that she had become aware of the systematic murder of ghetto inhabitants.

There was a report that older people were to go work in a fish factory in Pünemünde, where they would be better off. It was clear to me right away that that was impossible—they weren't as nice as all that. These older people were put into big, closed vehicles, and the word was that the inside filled up with gas. I thought, "That has to be a foul rumor"; you witnessed it, yet you still couldn't imagine it to be possible. But it was in fact the truth. There were quite a number who died. And some had reported so blissfully, even bringing along rocking chairs.

Later they brought people outside the ghetto and shot them, and we always heard about it. There was a column that had to go pour lime over the corpses and bury them. They didn't live with us, they lived in the central prison in Riga, but it reached our ears nonetheless; whoever was willing to listen knew about it. In addition, there were transports, generally of a thousand people or so, arriving constantly, but we had been the last transport to enter the ghetto in full strength. Since food and clothing would come into the ghetto—but no people—we knew that the people had been shot down right on the platform.

Among Leonore's most poignant memories of Riga are those of the role played by the deportees—herself included—in organizing and readying the transports that left the ghetto for the camps.

We all lived on different courts: the Hanoverians, the Westphalians, the Rhinelanders, the Berliners. The leaders of these courts were also the transport leaders; they had to name the names. And they did it, too—what were they to do? But it was horribly difficult. Just like when, as a nurse, you got people ready to go.

All the others would be ordered to stay in, and then I would go to the patients and prepare; I told myself, "Better that I do it than the SS." So I ran from one house to the next, weeping in between—because the patients weren't to see that either. There was nothing else we could do. But, of course, one isn't totally at peace with it.

During this period, the coexistence within herself of Jewish origin and

*Christian belief led Leonore to see herself as "always falling between two stools."
On the one hand, she "didn't have much time to reflect" on her membership in the
persecuted group: "I was simply obliged to feel part of it," she explains. "I was
thrown into it, and, beyond all question, I belonged." But "then again," she says,
"I didn't belong to it, because I could never really embrace Jewishness internally.
On the inside, I was far more strongly tied to the Christian faith than to anything
in the notion of a Jewish people; I was totally attached to it."*

Of course, I didn't have to go around debating and pondering to
know what my experience was, but I must say that I never lived it as a
Jew, always as a Christian. And I had the feeling, time and again, that
I was looked upon as a Christian and therefore had a big responsibility
to demonstrate that the Christian faith is also a source of strength. So to
that extent I couldn't really identify at all.

*On one occasion, Leonore's lack of affinity for the Jewish religion became a
formal barrier: Before her arthritis had abated to the point where she could do
physical work, she requested assignment to the ghetto kindergarten but was refused.
"They said it wouldn't work out because the children really were to be brought up
Jewish," she says. "I certainly wouldn't have been able to do this, and, of course,
I understood." But apart from this instance, Leonore found her own perception of
herself—as "a person among people," to whom "it was all the same whether
someone was a Jew or a Christian"—mirrored in the attitude of others toward
her. In the end, Leonore's acceptance of her circumstances seems, in combination
with the rigorous demands of everyday life, to have led to an identification of sorts.*

That was such a community of suffering that one was linked to
people; one can't cast that off. I said to myself, "You are here now, and
you simply have to come through this with the others." And while it
may sound a bit prideful today, along with this went pity for the people
who had to suffer so. Although I didn't identify directly, I certainly went
through the same things they did—but as I was needed by these people,
I didn't have much time at all to think about myself.

For example, when I was in the infirmary, there was a woman in
the bed next to mine, also a nurse, who was terribly afraid. Later, when
there were Aktionen* in the ghetto, she came to me to be comforted

---

Aktionen: could refer to various kinds of moves by the SS against the ghetto's inhabitants,
such as deportations and executions.

although I couldn't do anything other than give her a pep talk. At such times no one asked, "Are you a Christian? Are you a Jew?" Rather: "Can you help me or not?" Of course, you also experienced loathsome things—people let people they were sitting with at the same table literally starve to death. But that had nothing to do with Christians and Jews. It had to do with need.

In mid-1943, as the ghetto was gradually being dissolved, Leonore was transferred to the barracks of Kaiserwald, a concentration camp on the outskirts of Riga. There she spent the summer months doing "terribly heavy work"—clearing fields, carrying rails, sorting coal for the Luftwaffe—and going extremely hungry. Noticing that her arthritis was acting up with the approach of autumn, Leonore answered a call for volunteers to work in a nearby factory that had been taken over by the German manufacturer AEG and was connected to the Kaiserwald camp. "As a rule, I was not in favor of volunteering for things, because it might always have been something objectionable," she says. "But at that point I said to myself, 'It won't do me any good to keep working outside, and there you have shelter.'" Quartered across from the plant in an empty factory building that served as a barracks, Leonore worked making telephone cables until a flu epidemic hit and she was again pressed into service as a nurse.

Up to that point I had gotten along well with the Lagerleiterin* and the kitchen; they were all our people, of course. But the moment I became a nurse I saw the kinds of intrigues there were—that much of the food we were supposed to get was being prepared mornings in the kitchen for the camp's internal staff. I simply couldn't reconcile that with my conscience, and when I didn't join in, I ran into trouble once more. But I had good relations otherwise and was able to put up with it.

Strangely enough, we didn't have that many deaths when we were in Kaiserwald—thank God—but during the flu epidemic a woman died, and a big truck came for her. I had to be present while the truck was loaded, and I went up to it: nothing but smashed-in heads. I thought, "I'm not seeing right"—you see it and you can't grasp it. They had wrenched the gold out of their teeth and beaten their heads in. But I couldn't tell anyone—the people would have gone mad—and so I had

---

Lagerleiterin: camp leader (feminine form); the highest supervisory function in the prisoner hierarchy. The leaders were appointed by the SS administration of the camp.

to carry that around with me all those years. Still, there were some things one did manage to do as a nurse, and that, on the other hand, was really rewarding.

In July 1944, with the Red Army advancing, AEG began shifting operations toward the west. While being processed for transfer, Leonore was threatened with the loss of the Bible she had managed to keep with her since leaving Hanover.

We had to strip completely naked and, with only our shoes in our hand, walk past the SS—so I couldn't take the Bible with me. But I thought, "I can't live without a Bible," and asked my friend, "What am I to do?"

"Get rid of it," she said. Well . . . I thought, "No."

One of the SS there was named Hirsch, and—in all probability to prove that he wasn't a Jew*—he was raging, kicking the women and beating them. I went up to this raving man and said, "May I take my Bible with me?"

He gaped at me; then he said, "Bring it here!" I brought it to him. He leafed through it a bit and then, as if he wanted to give me a blessing, he said, "Take it with you." The next moment, he was again hitting and bellowing; and I was a wreck, that I can tell you. It was an enormous experience.

The transport's destination turned out to be an unused fort at Thorn, the present-day Polish city of Torun, that served as a subcamp for the Stutthof concentration camp near Danzig. The mortality rate at Stutthof has been estimated at 67 percent, higher than those of all but the six camps where deportees were gassed upon arrival. Housed in casemates belonging to the fort, the group from Kaiserwald was joined by a large contingent of Polish Jews sent from the main camp. Leonore, who continued working as a nurse, found the atmosphere at Thorn extremely tense.

She had gotten along well with the few Polish Jews she had treated as patients in Kaiserwald. "I had taken tremendous pains to understand Yiddish, which of course made them happy," she says. At Thorn, in contrast, acrimony was the rule: Petty annoyances could lead to insults and worse. After a spat over who should have the use of a hot plate, members of the kitchen staff denounced Leonore

---

*Since the last name *Hirsch* was common among both Jews and non-Jews in Germany, it might in some instances have led to speculation about the bearer's origins.

to an SS overseer, who let her off with a warning. Amid charges and counter-charges, it took Leonore a while to see that she was not the only object of the Polish Jews' animosity.

At first I thought they were doing this because I was a Christian, but then I noticed that they were simply in a terrible rage against everything that had to do with Western Jews. I had no notion of the difficulty that existed between Western and Eastern Jews—I thought, "A Jew is a Jew, after all!"—and I didn't understand it a bit. Oh, I did understand that the Western Jews were very assimilated and that the Eastern Jews very much held against us that we didn't speak Yiddish and had a totally different culture; but that they should go around trying to get people in trouble was beyond my powers of comprehension.

Besides cultural rivalry, starvation fueled the tension at Thorn, where much suspicion revolved around the distribution of food.

As an internal worker, I was allowed a double ration, because I got nothing from outside. There were five of us in a small room, one on top of the other; while the patients lay there, I doled out the food, then sat down at a table in front and ate. So I didn't do anything on the sly at all, but they squealed to the overseer that I kept too much food for myself, which of course was nonsense. Then I had a stomach ailment and couldn't digest the food—we got a kind of chicken feed, and it just lay there in the stomach—so I traded my soup ration to someone who had bread. The others didn't know, of course, that I hadn't eaten anything warm in weeks; they thought I was trading rations that were not rightfully mine, and they told.

Then there was a woman with a fifteen-year-old daughter, and growing children have an even bigger appetite. I got the bread already cut up from the kitchen, and I would always try to get the heel to her, because you had the feeling that it was a tiny bit more, perhaps five grams. She said I gave her the smallest piece every day. But that's the way it is. People looked into each other's plates and always had the feeling, "They have more"; and if you looked at someone cross-eyed, he took it wrong. But that's what hunger does, and from that standpoint I can understand it. You can't blame people who are starving.

Toward the end of the year the military took over the Thorn fort, causing Leonore and her fellow prisoners to be moved from the armored vaults into "very flimsy barracks." There, in the "miserably cold winter," a typhus epidemic broke out.

In November I got typhus, and there was the rheumatoid arthritis on top of that, so I just lay there. My friend took care of me faithfully—she fed me and tidied me up—and then she caught typhus from me. One evening, as I lay there with a high fever, the woman who had had the bunk underneath mine at Kaiserwald came in and brought me an apple that a worker in the factory had surreptitiously thrown into a crate for her. This woman would certainly have been delighted to eat the apple herself—it had been a long time since she'd seen an apple—but she peeled it for me and put the sections into my mouth. It was something I will never forget.

Leonore recalls the first day of Christmas in 1944 as a day the camp commandant toured the infirmary.

Others could keep it somewhat secret if they'd been sick for a long time, but he knew me because I had worked as a nurse, and he assured me that I'd be going into the gas in the coming days. He didn't say it in so many words, but a frightful number of people were being gassed at Stutthof, and of course they had no use for the sick.

Not long thereafter, the camp was evacuated.

The inspection came one afternoon from Stutthof and ran down a whole list of things that had to be done, and the next morning we already had orders to prepare to move out. At that point there was constant shelling from the Russians with no warning whatsoever, and we were hearing that they had broken through. It was really difficult for me in that I had had a high fever since November, and of course I couldn't walk. I kept thinking, "What is going to happen?" When you see freedom before your eyes like that and think, "Now freedom is coming and you won't live to see it," it's not very pretty.

At the end of January, with everything in total disorder, we finally left. We were supposed to march to Berlin—which was nonsense, of course. I was on a sled which the SS had rigged up to haul their provisions and whatever else they had managed to get their hands on, but on which they put three sick women because we could no longer walk. Five women had to pull the sled, and they were terribly angry at us because of it.

We were on the road three days and two nights. The sled broke down continually, and we were totally separated from the column, but we had a Hungarian SS guard who never let us out of his sight. I got frightful chills and told him that he should just leave me or shoot me because I couldn't go any farther. But he said no and supported me on his arm back onto the sled and traveled on with us. We were still following the column because he wanted to rejoin it, come what might—but it made no difference anyway because, as we heard later, the SS simply left everybody behind and ran off to save themselves.

Our guard called up the concentration camp in Bromberg* to ask whether he was to shoot us or let us go free, and they told him "neither": He was to bring us in. He intended to do it, but on the way we ran across Polish women who told us that we shouldn't go into Bromberg: The Russians were there already, the SS had left, everything was in flames, there was no more bread. They said we ought to go to a place they named where there was a gardener and to stay in his shed. Now this tension: Does he do it, or doesn't he? Because it was clear to us that, if he brought us to that shed, we'd be free.

He brought us there. People of ours were lying there sleeping, and they were terribly startled when an SS man awakened them. "Calm down," he said, "I am bringing you some more comrades." We lay there between the lines, with fire from the Russians and the Germans flying over us all the time, until the Russians came. When they arrived, our guard ran away, but the Poles no doubt cut him down; he should have left beforehand, and we were advising him to do it, but he wouldn't go.

Driven from the shed by hunger, Leonore and the others took refuge at a Russian camp. After four weeks of hospitalization, Leonore worked for the Poles as a nurse in Bromberg, receiving "a bit of food" as pay. While on the job she ran into one of the doctors with whom she had had a difficult time in Riga, as well as the Lagerleiterin from Thorn; both proved unexpectedly cooperative, and each suggested that she sign on to work with them, offers Leonore refused. In the meantime, she had been reunited with the friend who had nursed her at Thorn; in the late spring of 1945, with three others, they took to the road and made their way westward to Berlin.

Shortly after the war, Leonore managed to procure her paternal grandpar-

---

*Bromberg: the present-day Polish city of Bydgoszcz.

ents' marriage papers, which proved beyond doubt that her grandfather had been a Jew. "It was no longer of any importance," she says, an allusion to her failed efforts of a decade earlier to document her ancestry. "I just wanted to know for sure." The knowledge left Leonore unmoved: "It didn't affect me at all," she recalls.

With the passage of time, Leonore's faith had deepened. "It had been a very long development from childhood on," she says. "All I can say is that God never released me but drew me to Him again and again, even when I wanted to pull away." She adds that during the years of persecution she "experienced with particular intensity how one cannot live by one's own strength alone."

After the war, Leonore felt called upon to "do something out of gratitude" for having been liberated. "I had the feeling that I ought to help people who were in a similar position—people who were in prison." Although she started with neither a secondary school diploma nor money to finance her studies, she earned a degree in theology, was ordained a Lutheran minister, and became chaplain at the women's penitentiary in a large West German city. At the time of the interview, Leonore Hoffmann had been retired for several years, but she maintained contact with both former prisoners and some still on the inside. "With all that was difficult in this work," she says, "it has made me very happy."

That Leonore should pursue her faith along Christian lines, even though it was strengthened through her experience as a persecuted Jew, seems to her a matter of course. "I could never call myself a Hebrew-Christian," she says. "As far as I'm concerned, that's something that doesn't exist." Both during her years in the company of Jews and thereafter, she has found little in the Jewish religion to attract her.

I was quartered for a short time in the infirmary at Kaiserwald, and there was a young girl there who was very devout. As I love the Old Testament very much, and the prophets and psalms helped me enormously right at that very time, I hoped on that basis to have good rapport with the girl. But while I did get along well with her in a purely human way, and we talked a lot about religion, I was disappointed. She prayed every morning and kept the dietary laws to the extent she was able—you couldn't do it all the way in the camp, a woman with us died because she did—but she had nothing living from her faith, which consisted exclusively in complying with the law. She actually knew only the Torah;* she hadn't ever heard anything about the affirmation and

---

*Torah: the five books of Moses (the first five books of the Old Testament).

promise of God's love that is in the Old Testament. And that made me very sad.

I have also gone to Jewish services. As I can speak only about services in Germany, I don't know whether I am committing an injustice, but the Jewish services seemed empty to me. One must take into consideration that they're waiting for the Messiah, and as long as they're waiting actively, a certain vitality remains; but when it's all become somewhat schematic, then I'm not so sure. I have met rabbis and other Jews who were totally different; it was really a delight to speak with them about these things, and one was very close to them. But then again I have come upon so much legalistic piety.

Leonore still feels "nothing at all religiously" for Judaism and says her bond to the Christian faith continues to outstrip any sense of Jewish affinity. But she adds, "Today I have a totally different relation to Jewishness, of which I have become a lot more conscious. And I now somehow feel connected to the Jews."

This took time to develop, because you mustn't forget that it is difficult, with the kind of past I had, to identify with the Jews. In fact, I would have had to throw over everything I grew up with.

As a young person, I had pushed it away from me; it didn't interest me then, and it was a problem for me to take the position, in my heart, that I ought to belong to it. And when one is a victim, it is very hard to acknowledge belonging where one hadn't belonged before—particularly what with the various unpleasant things one went through on top of it.

Thus, I couldn't experience what others experienced, and at the time I found fault with myself for it. Precisely because they went through this, many became very proud to be Jews. I thought, "This isn't right: You too should be proud to be a Jew and to be persecuted." But at that time I couldn't manage it. I somehow lived in a certain resistance, for the reason that I was being forced into it.

Today, I can go further in embracing my Jewish past—although I never actually lived it as such—than I did formerly. Then, my attitude was one of rejection, because it had simply overtaken me; now I feel much more a participant in Jewishness and everything that appertains to it. It torments me terribly that there is no peace in Israel and that anti-Semitism in general is still so strong everywhere—and I experience that as something which has to do with me. So while I don't have any tie to the religious aspect—something I lament—I do feel myself linked to the destiny of the Jewish people. Nor, in any case, can I separate myself from it because, precisely through the experience I have had, that's where my entire sympathy lies.

So there has indeed been a change as opposed to before: Before it was simply that I had to, and today it is my will.

Leonore's heightened interest in Jewish matters has not, however, led her to any formal Jewish affiliation. Told shortly after the war that she could qualify for the food packets passed out by Jewish organizations only by taking membership in the Jewish community, she balked. "I was still hungry," she recalls, "but I said, 'I can't do that,'" adding that the experience left her with a feeling of "rejection." But that she has remained outside Jewish circles despite the subsequent evolution of her feelings has mainly to do with the way she has lived. "I was so busy behind bars that I hardly have touch with anyone," she says. "It was not my intention to reject Jewish connections—I haven't been able to keep up strong ties to either Christians or Jews." In fact, her most direct contact with Jews has come during three visits to Israel, where she has been warmly received and has "gotten to know good comradeship."

A sign that, as Leonore says, she may "identify more strongly with Jews today than formerly" is to be seen in feelings arising from her prison work.

It was always a very intense experience for me when we got Jews in the institution—it hurt me personally. At times, I thought to myself, "After all the trials they have lived through, it is out of the question that they should be subject to punishment." I felt especially linked to them.

But this link remains, for Leonore, a mysterious one.

It is purely an emotional affair. One can't do much of anything about it: All at once, it's just there. I didn't feel myself connected this way in the camp. Rather, that was simply a community of suffering: I felt needed, and I didn't ask whether someone was a Jew or a Mohammedan or a Christian or anything else. I can't explain at all where it comes from; and when it really began in earnest, I can't say. But it is just that my heart beats a little faster, somehow, when I meet a Jew.

In summing up her experience of persecution, Leonore explains that—in contrast to "those poor people who afterwards could only learn to curse"—she was brought into deeper touch with herself, and with "the purpose for which we are here on earth."

One saying stayed with me the whole time in the camps and

helped me again and again. It is what Joseph told his brothers: "You meant it for evil, but God intended it for good."*

I have had frightful experiences with many who were there together with me. I lost a friend—after we had stuck together faithfully the whole time, and on the way back—who can't stand that I am not embittered, who simply can't see any meaning to her own life. But for me it has an enormous meaning: The very fact that it brought me to the prison here, which is something positive; and the fact that one grows as a person, which is what it all comes down to, after all.

So I can say of the time in the camps: It was the high point of my life. It sounds strange, but it is so. Of course, I lost my entire youth, if you want to look at it that way, and a lot of my health, and I don't know what all. But that doesn't outweigh what I gained. I had experiences there that one can never have in a bourgeois life, because one is too swaddled in comfort. In the same way, the people Israel lived in the desert, from hand to mouth, but it was also the high point of the people Israel. And that is an experience I would not want to miss.

I still dream about the camp sometimes. I would not like to go back. But it was simply that time which—I hope—made me as a human being.

———

*Upon revealing himself to his brothers, who had sold him into slavery in Egypt, Joseph says, "Now therefore be not grieved, nor angry with yourselves, that ye sold me hither: for God did send me before you to preserve life" (Genesis 45:5).

Hélène Terlinden

My father was born in a village near Moscow. Around 1910, he traveled on foot from Russia to France, finding work in the cities and towns he passed through and earning a little money so that he could continue his journey. After returning to Russia for his mother and bringing her to Paris, he met my mother, who came from Cracow, and they married. My father didn't have any particular profession but worked at whatever he could find. I don't believe my mother was working; my sisters were born in 1913 and 1914, and she took care of them.

When war was declared, my father enlisted in the Foreign Legion. I don't know what could have been going through his mind: He was leaving my mother alone with two daughters, and my mother was very unhappy because she spoke little French at the time. But, albeit it without any great enthusiasm, my father went off to fight. The fact that he had two children permitted him to come home on occasion; still, he was often at the front. He was wounded and in the hospital for a while, but before the war ended he went back to his unit.

As life in Paris had been hard, Samuel Bialystock decided, once the war was over and he had been discharged, to follow the lead of a neighbor lady who was moving to the area of Hirson, a small town near France's border with Belgium. He and his wife, Esther, sold clothing at open markets in the region, eventually saving enough money to buy a shop in Hirson itself. In 1920, the family was naturalized with little ado thanks to Samuel's status as a war veteran. And it grew: Michel, the oldest son, was born in 1922; Hélène, near the close of 1925; and Jacques, in 1928.

Following the birth of their last child, the Bialystocks moved to Roubaix, an industrial city not far from Lille, where Samuel's mother lived. They bought a milliner's shop and, working the markets on the side, were soon able to take over a larger business and to bring a brother and a sister of Samuel's to live in the region as well.

When Hélène was six, an event shook her family: eighteen-year-old Monique, the Bialystocks' second daughter, eloped with a man twenty years her senior.

This fellow was a friend of my father, and my father had a kind of admiration for him. He was of Norman descent and a cultivated man, a man whose level of learning I think my father may subconsciously have envied. I myself liked him very much. He was kind to us, and he paid a lot of attention to me; it was he who taught me to tell time. The departure of my sister with this man, whom she loved very much, made a big impression on me because I saw how my parents suffered.

I think that what made them suffer in the beginning was that an unmarried daughter's taking off like that with a man is a difficult burden to shoulder in provincial circles, especially when one is in business in town. Everything was put in order very quickly in the sense that they were married and my father helped them start a business, at which both my sister and brother-in-law worked very hard. Since it was, after all, his daughter, my father tried to keep up almost normal relations with his son-in-law, and things worked themselves out, though very much on the surface. I was very young, but I sensed that something between my father and his son-in-law didn't click at all.

My brother-in-law turned out afterwards to be a pronounced anti-Semite. I don't think my father was aware of this when he was friendly with this fellow, but I do think he felt certain things intuitively that were confirmed later. When my sister and brother-in-law started their business, their commercial relations were exclusively with Jews, and it sickened my brother-in-law to think that he was dependent on Jews for his livelihood. I remember conversations at the house during which my father complained that his son-in-law didn't like Jews, and there was a terrible ambiguity that remained in contacts between the two of them. It was a great sorrow for my father that his daughter had left abruptly; and, secondly, that it was with one of his friends; and, finally, that he wasn't a Jew, but, to top it all off, an anti-Semite.

It seemed to Hélène, however, that her father went out of his way to seek the company of non-Jews and even to acquaint himself with anti-Semitic thought.

As he often said in discussions at home, my father believed that the only means of eliminating the Jewish problem was to assimilate completely, that the only solution was to take on the customs and the culture of a country: to become, to use the relevant example, totally French. My father read enormously—he had a huge library, and he used to irritate everyone by reading at the dinner table, by reading everywhere—and at that time he read authors who were considered to be anti-Semites, well-known reactionaries who wrote for *L'Action Française.** He was revolted by those people, and he read them with what I would now interpret as a form of masochism. I can't say for certain why he read them—was it his aim to be informed?—but I believe that he was searching for something in them.

There were hardly any Jews in Roubaix, but my parents were friendly with Jewish families, and I remember that when we received Jewish friends, there were intense discussions of assimilation and of the way in which one could be Jewish in France. These friends were people who put a lot of emphasis on being Jewish and didn't understand my father; they were opposed to what he was and reproached him for his assimilation. That struck me. They always told my father he would one day regret what he had left behind—although that is not to say his religion, because my parents were not at all religious and the people we knew were not religious either.

While her father was struggling with the meaning of his Jewishness, Hélène, though still quite young, was going through a related struggle of her own.

It was hard for me to understand what Judaism was, and with good reason: In that we didn't have any Jewish religion, it was complex. At home I never learned about keeping the Shabbes† or anything like that, and I never knew about the holidays, not even the Day of Atonement.‡ My parents never went to the synagogue nor in fact did they have even the slightest inclination to practice, something for which they were frowned upon by the Jews in Roubaix. I heard things about race, but at that time there were no blacks or Asians in Roubaix—just white people, and a few Jews—and I couldn't figure out what a race might be. Even

---

L'Action Française: a French fascist periodical with a pronounced anti-Semitic stance.
†*Shabbes:* the Yiddish word for "Sabbath."
‡Yom Kippur, Judaism's most solemn holiday.

the question of who was Jewish and who was not Jewish was not very clear in my mind. The only meaning that I attributed to this word *Jew*—which otherwise didn't have any meaning for me—was that it was something that differentiated me from the others. To be Jewish in a provincial city was, simply, not to be like the rest.

I went to other children's homes, I spent time there, I slept over. And when I took stock of my own home, I realized that the customs and the culture and the atmosphere of the household were very different from what I found elsewhere. For one thing, my parents spoke Yiddish; they spoke it together when they didn't want us to understand, because otherwise we always spoke French together at home, none of the children learned Yiddish.

Not knowing Yiddish left the Bialystock children somewhat estranged from their Russian-born grandmother, who impressed Hélène as "not like the others" in several respects: her language, her habits, even the apartment in which she lived.

My grandmother adored us, but as she had never learned French and spoke only Yiddish, we had no contact with her other than culinary contact. She made things for us which were typically Russian-Jewish, and which we were wild about because there were a lot of sweet things—things with honey, with almonds—and as children we loved sweets. When we went to visit her in Lille, there was a very distinctive cooking odor that I ran into in all the Jewish homes I went to at that time. It was a mixture of onions and I'm not sure anymore what else, but it was in all the buildings she lived in because, wherever she lived, there were only Jews.

I also had a name that was not like the others, because, until I was twelve or so, our name was still Bialystock. This was enough to provoke a reaction on the part of schoolmates, and on the part of the teachers as well. As soon as you said your name, people seemed to react automatically: "Say! What a strange name! It's foreign. Where does it come from?" And so on and so forth.

And then I was not like the others in that the others went to catechism and I didn't go, the others had their communion and I did not. I spent my vacations with a Catholic family that had girls my age, and when they went to mass, I went with them. I enjoyed it once or twice, but that's all, because I found it a bore. Even so, it was very curious that I didn't want to go on with it—because I might have wanted to be like my friends, and I certainly could have said so to my parents. In fact, my father brought up the question with us himself: "If you want to become Catholic, that would bother me," he said, "but, well, it's your business." He left us our freedom of opinion on that point, but I remember that I was never tempted.

So I did know that I was not a Catholic, but being Jewish still wasn't clear in my mind. It was always connected to something strange, something out of the ordinary—and something terribly threatening to my security, which robbed me of security in my contacts with others and which prevented me from being totally integrated with the others. Being Jewish troubled me in my daily life—although not constantly, from time to time—and I know that I suffered greatly because of it. It gave me a royal pain.

Hélène believes the "problems that resulted from not being like the others" to have been "connected to what happened at home" rather than caused by hostility from the outside world. She has "absolutely no memory" of being insulted or of encountering other forms of overt anti-Semitism during her early childhood. "My playmates had absolutely no idea what Judaism was," she observes, "and I don't remember any reactions toward us on the part of either children or their parents."

Nevertheless, Hélène recalls that, at times, her feelings led her to "rebel against being Jewish" in public.

We lived on a square, and at the corner of this square was a little basement where a shoemaker worked. As all children like basements and craftsmen, I loved to sit on the steps that went down to his place. My little brother and I sat there and talked with this shoemaker from morning to night; it was as if we were his own children.

Right next door to the shoemaker's shop was a big clothing store that was owned by Jews. The shoemaker—who was a man I liked very much, his personality really appealed to me—said one day, "Those people there, the ones next door, are Jews like you." He said it as he would have said "hello" or "good-bye"—it was simply a statement of fact that he was making. But I started to cry, and I ran away from his shop, howling, "No! It isn't true! I'm not Jewish, I'm not Jewish, I'm not Jewish!" I don't remember that there was anything aggressive in the way he said it, but it hurt me very much, and I remember that I had a hard time going back to see him after that.

I had these difficulties when I was between ten and twelve years old—I remember this anti-Jewishness mostly at that age—because I was still named Bialystock. But when my father changed his name to Bialy, making it sound more French, there was, without a doubt, something that changed. Even though this name says pretty clearly what it has to say when you come right down to it, it must have soothed me to be known by the name Bialy at school. I remember going through much calmer years after the name change as far as Jewishness was concerned; I don't remember disturbances in my life that were as intense as before. I led the calm life of a little girl from the provinces whose girlfriends were all from the working class and who didn't have too many problems.

Still, I don't believe that I actually accepted the fact that I was Jewish. The only thing I remember is that, when I was thirteen or so, I detested my father. At that time there were people who said that the Jews had horns and hooked noses and frizzy hair. My mother did not look typically Jewish; she had a rather fine nose. But my father was very much a Jewish type with a very prominent nose, and my grandmother in particular had a typically Jewish appearance according to what I imagined Jews to be like at the time and according to what I had read surreptitiously in books. My father's nose bothered me, and my grandmother's nose bothered me, and I didn't like being with my father and my grandmother because they had appearances that were not like the others'.

I myself have a nose that is somewhat pronounced, and my own nose bothered me enormously. I used to put a rubber band around the tip of my nose at night to lift it—but in the morning, to my great disappointment, my nose would fall back down at the end of five minutes. It was a horrible thing, because I said to myself that I would never have a cute little turned-up nose like everybody else, and this nose reminded me of my Jewishness. And of my father. And of my grandmother, who spoke only Yiddish—which singled me out with respect to the others, who had grandmothers who spoke like everyone else.

By the time Hélène turned thirteen, Europe had again made its way to the brink of war. Although the "Jewish question" had always been a topic of discussion in the Bialy household, she can recall no mention at home of events in Germany or of the plight of the German Jews. Still, Hélène was quite apprehensive.

I well remember having a horrible fear of war throughout my entire childhood. This had nothing to do with my Jewishness but came from my so-called godmother, the lady who had brought my parents to Hirson and had given me my first name. We were very close, I went to her house for vacation, and she showed me horrible photos of the First World War; I had heard a lot about the war as well. So when war almost broke out in 'thirty-eight, I was in absolute panic; and when war finally was declared, I wept the entire night.

My father was a little panicked as well because I think that he was in fact aware of what had been happening to the Jews in Germany and in Austria. Jews began arriving from those countries, and we had them sleeping all over the house because my father said, "This could happen to us one day. And if we are in the same position, we too will be happy to find a place where we can take refuge."

In May 1940, German troops marched into France. Joining the "exodus," a stream of millions fleeing southward before the German advance, the Bialy family left Roubaix and, crossing Normandy, found shelter in the Vendée, a rural region just to the south of Brittany on France's Atlantic coast. They stayed about two months, working as farmhands in a remote village. "We actually had some relatively happy moments there," recalls Hélène. "It was a little like a vacation."

I heard the people of this totally backward village—who lived in these kinds of huts, and didn't have electricity or anything like that, and had never washed in their lives—talking about Jews as if they were monstrous creatures, devils. I must have changed, because it made me laugh a little to hear this, and I said to myself, "These people are really crazy." We didn't say we were Jews, though. In the first place, I don't think they would have understood. And, secondly, I don't think it was necessary: We were refugees like everyone else.

By midsummer the Bialys had returned to Roubaix, which had been grouped with Lille in a zone that was subject to the laws of France's Vichy government but was administered by the office of the German military commander in Brussels. The family found their store intact and managed to live free from harassment for about a year, but in mid-1941 an "administrator" appointed under the Germans' "Aryanization" program pushed them out of their business; as their apartment adjoined the store, they were forced at the same time to move, taking up residence in a house on the outskirts of town. In the spring of 1942, Hélène's paternal uncle, who had remained a Russian national, was among the hostages taken from what the authorities described as "Judeo-Bolshevik circles" in reprisal for the murder of a German woman soldier in Belgium. Although pardoned on the eve of their scheduled execution when it turned out that the killing had not been political, the hostages were not released, and, following an act of violent resistance in Lille several days thereafter, they were put before a firing squad.

This was a big revelation for my father. I had never seen him in such a state. Because he had been directly affected, my father realized the fury of the Germans. Up to that point he had said, "I am a Frenchman above all else. I fought in the First World War. They will never bother me, and they will never bother my family." He repeated that to us so often that we believed it. But at that moment he realized that it wasn't quite so simple and that he had to open his eyes.

Around the same time, an event of another sort provided a second shock for Samuel Bialy.

My older brother, Michel, was a very good-looking guy who had a lot of success with girls. There were girls of all social classes, but there was in particular one girl who was from a very wealthy background, the daughter of an industrialist. My brother was very much in love with this girl, but her family would not receive him because they knew that he was a Jew. He was deeply affected by this, and I think he saw only one way to fight against it: converting to Catholicism.

I remember very well my father's suffering. I saw my father weep, but really weep, when my brother came to tell him: "I am leaving for a seminar with the Catholics because I want to convert to the Catholic faith." I also remember conversations in the family in which my father said, "Michel has doubtless been infected with mysticism." I don't think my father had a very good understanding of what was taking place in his son's mind. And while I myself understood it better as I grew older, at the time I too was very shocked by his conversion. I was deeply nonreligious, and seeing my brother convert to Catholicism was a blow to me as well.

It was, in fact, a blow to us all—but in particular to my father, much more than to my mother. I can still see him crying and saying, "This is terrible! If he had to do something like that, the least he could have done was become a rabbi." I think my father would have accepted much more easily that his son, in his "mysticism," convert to Judaism— well, not convert, but in any case become Jewish—than become Catholic. I realized then that, despite everything, my father had deep roots in Judaism, even if he did all he could to deny them in front of others.

In the meantime, anti-Jewish measures had accelerated. In the late spring of 1942, Jews were required to sew the yellow star onto their outer garments. Shortly thereafter, large-scale roundups of Jews began in Paris and the French provinces alike, and a transit camp for Jewish deportees from Belgium was set up at Malines, near Brussels. But Jews of French nationality were still generally exempt from mass arrest and deportation. Although over 40,000 Jews had been deported from France by the end of 1942, most of them were foreign or stateless Jews offered up by French authorities in Vichy, who were attempting to protect French nationals while satisfying German deportation quotas for Jews.

Actually, as I was then beginning to realize, there were three classes of individuals among the Jews: There were Jews who had been living in France for several generations; there were people like us, who were naturalized citizens but who had been in France for quite some time; and there were foreign Jews, who for one reason or another had not been naturalized, or who were refugees from Austria or elsewhere, even Belgium. While we were in the middle, we were the only ones among our family in France who had been naturalized, and all our friends were foreign Jews, who in any case made up a large proportion of the Jews living in Roubaix.

Although things were less dangerous for French Jews according to what we heard at the time, our life followed the same rhythm as the foreign Jews'. There were people in the resistance who were specifically involved with Jews, and they passed on signals to us that apparently came from Lille, where there were many more Jews than in Roubaix. My father made us follow these alerts just as if we had been foreign Jews; if the alert went out, for example, that there were to be mass arrests the next night, we hid. Often nothing happened, but there was a feeling of being threatened.

Although they lived in the same house, Hélène was unaware that her oldest sister, Annette, had been active for some time in a resistance network that specialized in providing false identity papers and ration coupons to Jews. "I had heard about this business with the papers," recalls Hélène, "but that kind of thing was beyond me at that time." As the atmosphere in the region became more and more charged, Annette helped Michel, who had by then turned twenty, leave for a training camp of the French armed resistance, or maquis, near the town of Tulle in the mountains of central France.

It was my father who had more or less forced Michel to go, telling him, "You are young, and the Germans will get you one way or the other, so you have to get out of here." At the same time, all our friends were trying to convince my father that, as a Jew and not too old a man, he also should go into hiding. He finally left for Normandy, but he was a man who was totally incapable of living outside his family, and he couldn't bear being separated from us, so he came back. We chased him away again, but he returned a second time.

It was during this period, says Hélène, that her Jewishness "began to exist."

I became aware of the fact that I was a Jew, which was something that up to then I had rejected. The thing that impressed me most of all is what happened the first time I wore the Jewish star. When I got to school with my star, all the children in my class wept, but really wept. And that moved me deeply. I said to myself, "There is something in Jewishness that must be touching." From that moment on, something was changed in my state of mind.

Hélène says she cannot remember any unpleasant experiences arising from wearing the yellow star, nor any display of hostility toward herself or members of her family. In fact, her experience was just the opposite.

When I took the streetcar, older people got up to give me their seat. Things like this impressed me: I realized that there was a kind of solidarity surrounding us Jews, that there were people who were taking our side. And whereas up to that point being Jewish had been, for me, something that threatened my security, I now realized that it was not something totally negative. It remained an awful threat, but I got the feeling that there were after all people for whom the Jews were not the enemy, for whom the Jews were not the devil, for whom the Jews did not have horns—but for whom they were normal people. And I got the feeling that I could take my place as part of this race of normal people.

I also began associating with Jews who taught me that being Jewish was not in itself something totally reprehensible. There was in particular a family of Austrian Jews whom I saw all the time because I was in love with one of the sons. From them, I learned a lot of things that I didn't know at all about Judaism. The parents were practicing Jews, although the children were not, and I learned bits and pieces about the religion— little things about certain holidays they celebrated, for example.

My boyfriend was both Jewish and a Communist at the same time, and I liked that. As I was rather impressionable, I followed his lead in everything automatically. He told me about Marxism, which I didn't know anything about at the time, and about socialism generally, and he made me read books by Léon Blum. He loved Léon Blum. There were Zionists among the Jews I knew, but I didn't subscribe to Zionism on account of my boyfriend. So this Judaism that imbued me was, in the end, a very secular Judaism, because I was deeply nonreligious and I didn't subscribe to Zionism.

Through her meeting with the family of Austrian Jews, her experience wearing the yellow star, and the shock of her brother's conversion, Hélène was, she believes, "forced to be a Jew." And, feeling herself part of a Jewish "consensus," she "accepted being Jewish much better" under the stress of the occupation than she had before the war.

In fact, I can't say that I felt my life to be unhappy. I don't have unhappy memories of the period up to the moment we went into hiding, which was in mid-1943. After all, I went to school, I had a bunch of friends—non-Jewish friends in general, but Jewish friends as well—and I had a normal romantic life. My romantic life was terribly important to me at that time, and I can say that I had moments of enormous happiness—enormous. I wore the Jewish star, but I didn't consider myself to be so abnormal compared with the others. In fact, I had the impression of being more or less a typical teenager.

This period, associated by Hélène with the feeling of being well adjusted, was nonetheless marred by what she calls "the first tragic event in our lives": the arrest, late in 1942, of her father.

My father was a very athletic man who did a lot of hiking and who loved to swim. As he wanted to go to the swimming pool, and as Jews were not allowed there—we had been forbidden from going to the movies, to the pool, and so on—he had taken off his star. But there were so few Jews in Roubaix that the Germans knew my father with his star, and he was apprehended on the street by a German who recognized him and asked, "Where is it?" He was taken to the station, and we never saw him again. He was brought to Malines, and, from there, he was deported.

Because Mr. Bialy had been arrested for a specific infraction of anti-Jewish laws, French nationality was not likely to prevent his deportation. Still, Hélène's sister Annette made an official approach to the French head of state, Marshal Philippe Pétain.

She wrote to Pétain with all the background, saying that Papa was a naturalized Frenchman and a decorated veteran who had been wounded in the First World War. Since French Jews in general were not then being arrested, she petitioned for his release. We received a letter signed by Marshal Pétain saying that, because my father was born in Russia, he was a Russian Jew, and that it was a matter of course that he be deported. Everything that had happened in between had no meaning—the whole rest of his life did not count.

For a time following Mr. Bialy's arrest, life was without serious incident for Hélène, her mother, Annette, and her little brother Jacques, who remained together on the outskirts of Roubaix. Hélène's second sister, Monique, who lived in nearby Tourcoing, was also being left in peace by authorities, presumably because of her status as the spouse of a non-Jew. But when Hélène's mother accepted flowers from her children for Mother's Day in May 1943, it was with foreboding. "Mama had a superstition connected with flowers," says Hélène. "It was silly, of course, but she always said, 'Each time someone has given me flowers, a misfortune has befallen me.' "

The very next day, Mama said to Annette, "A fellow came to see you while you were out. He spoke Yiddish, and he said he needs papers to leave to fight with the maquis, something like that."

My sister said, "I'll take care of it. Is he coming back?"

"He's coming tomorrow," said Mama, but she told Annette, "I don't like this guy's looks. He doesn't seem trustworthy to me, and I ask you not to receive him."

"You're too jumpy," Annette told her. "You're blowing everything out of proportion. If he speaks Yiddish, there can't be any problem."

The same man did come back the next day, and it turned out that he was a Gestapo agent—so there apparently were Germans who learned Yiddish in order to catch resistance people. Perhaps there was something in his Yiddish that bothered Mama a little, or maybe it was the overall impression he made that unsettled her, but in any case her intuition was completely right.

When I came home from school that day, I saw a Feldgendarm in front of the house. I was with a friend who lived nearby, and she told me not to go home. I debated with myself whether or not I should go in, but, knowing that Mama was there, I went. The Gestapo had searched the entire house looking for documents that we knew nothing about, and Mama was in a terrible state.

My mother and I were dreaming of one thing only: that my sister not come home. While we waited in the house with the Gestapo, the fellow who had been stationed outside moved away a bit. Finally, a little later than expected, Annette came in. She saw right away what was up and turned pale. They told her, "Get some things together and follow us."

She asked, "For how long?"

"I don't know. It's an interrogation, but take a suitcase with you in any event."

She got her things together and left. She was put in the prison near Lille where resistance people were automatically sent, and which was used more for them than for Jews, but then she was sent to Malines and deported.

When the Germans came for Annette, they told us that they had intercepted a letter from Michel in which Annette was incriminated for her resistance activities. After the war we found out that Michel, along with some resistance comrades, had been picked up in a train with a shipment of arms. The others had been brought to Bordeaux and exe-cuted, but my brother, because he was a Jew, was held, tortured, and then deported.

Even though we didn't know this at the time, we said to ourselves that if they had obtained this letter, it meant that Michel was in danger as well. On top of that, neighbors we were friendly with told us, "After all that has happened, the last thing you should do is stay here. You are already off to a bad start, and there's no reason this episode will stop here—they will come for you, too. You have to find a way out as fast as you can."

But when they arrested my sister, the Germans told Mama, "We're only interested in your oldest daughter, because she is in the resistance and has been making false papers. We have nothing against you. It is therefore our urgent request that you and your two children not move but stay in this house, because we must know that you are there." As we were semi-French Jews and so on, he told us, "Nothing will happen to you."

The Germans used this trick all the time, but we didn't know it then. Besides, up to the arrest of my sister, I can't say that we had had the impression of living under a very significant threat. We had not been singled out for persecution, and you can't say what might have happened if my father had not committed that foolish act. Also, it always impressed me that my second sister continued to live in her own house and that neither she nor her three children ever had any problems although she was, after all, registered with the Germans as a Jew. So, despite everything, my mother and my little brother and I stayed in the house.

But after a while Hélène and her mother reconsidered and began looking for places to hide. While Hélène's brother-in-law was asking around among his friends and the family's Jewish acquaintances were proposing that Jacques at least be sent to a cloister or a farm, Hélène's mother contacted a trusted non-Jewish friend, who immediately offered to take her in. Jacques's terror at the prospect of being separated from his mother—"he was young," explains Hélène, "and really quite traumatized by this war which he barely understood"—led Esther Bialy to ask her friend whether there would be room for her son as well.

With unmatched generosity, she said, "I am prepared to take both of you." This lady, who was my mother's age, was a laborer; she worked sewing potato sacks from jute cloth, a very modest trade. She lived in workers' housing, which was far from the center of town and very complicated in that all the units were mixed up in one another. The Germans would really have had to think hard before it would have occurred to them to go looking for someone in such an out-of-the-way place, so this was a great comfort to my mother.

In the meantime, Hélène's brother-in-law had procured an offer from an industrialist with thirteen children aged between one and sixteen to hide Hélène in his house in Tourcoing.

These people lived in a château and, the way they were dressed, I think they must have had a large fortune. They had had a number of domestics, but, at the time I arrived, you could no longer find people to work as servants. They told their friends and neighbors that I was a refugee from Dunkerque, that my family had been killed during the events there, and that, as I had no work and no family, they had taken me in and given me a job out of generosity. In fact, I feel that they totally exploited me, because you don't make anyone work the way they made me work. I got up at five in the morning and never went to bed before half past ten at night. I tutored the older children and washed the little ones, and it was a very hard life for me.

The father was in the resistance, and as a matter of principle he wouldn't tolerate black-market dealings in his household; so there was nothing to eat, and all of us were more or less on the verge of starving. By the end of the war food rations had been reduced to the barest minimum, so that only the two youngest were entitled to a real ration. The others had coupons and got the normal rations for their age, but those were extremely small. As I was hidden, I had no coupons, and in the last days of the occupation I had to exist on one plum—one plum!—per day.

There was a sumptuous wine cellar, and the older children drank at night to forget their hunger. This was actually my only distraction: staying with them, drinking, and talking. The things that counted for me were the work, which kept me very, very busy; and this war, which went on forever; and the separation from my family and from the Jewish boy from Austria whom I'd fallen in love with before it all started.

In general I didn't go out, but that wasn't much of a problem, because the house was very pleasant; and in any event, I was always a little anxious when I had to leave the house. I did go once to see this boy I adored, who was not far from where I was. It was madness to do it, but I could think of only one thing, which was this love that had overrun me. I left on a bicycle to look for him and did see him briefly. Later, I found out that he was a member of a resistance group and that he was living in terrible conditions himself.

During the year she spent hiding in Tourcoing, Hélène was able to see her sister Monique only twice, but it was Monique who convinced her to attempt the French high school finishing exam, the baccalauréat.

The principal of the secondary school I had gone to, a Communist whose attitude toward me during the war had been remarkable and who had protected me in many ways, sent me the course materials. I ended up working around the clock because, in the little free time I had at night, I studied for the exam.

To take the exams in the different subjects, I would go by bicycle to the house of a very good friend who was also taking the bac, sleep there, take the exam, and then go back to where I was in hiding. I didn't know it at the time, but the house where I stayed overnight was right next door to the place where the Gestapo conducted its interrogations. So I took my bac right under the nose of the Germans, without incident, and, to top it off, in my own name. After the war, I found out that I had passed.

When the north of France was liberated in the summer of 1944, the Bialys' life was a shambles. Annette and Michel, both of whom were to return from the concentration camps to which they had been deported, were still missing. The family home had been searched—"the Germans had come around with my photo and asked the neighbors whether they had seen me," says Hélène, "so they were looking for us"—and all their possessions had been stolen. While their business was still there, reclaiming it required lengthy administrative procedures. But after a while the family got settled again, and Hélène began university studies at Lille. There, she joined the Jewish Students of France.

Right after the war, I spent a lot of time in Jewish circles. I went through a period when most of the people I associated with were Jews, when I belonged to Jewish organizations, when the boys I was in love with were Jews. I wanted to know a little bit about everything, to know what it was like in all respects, so I joined Jewish political groups and Jewish religious groups, I was in all the Jewish camps. I even went to a Talmudic camp.

It was a kind of necessity. After the war I found out everything that had happened in France—the horrible things the Milice* had done, how disgusting the French had been toward the Jews—and I reacted against it. We had some good friends who were not Jewish, but at that point I realized that, in the end, anti-Semitism was a part of the French temperament. And I myself posed the questions that had haunted my father: How does one fight anti-Semitism? Through assimilation? Or through Zionism?

I was too young to have discussed all those things with my father, but after the war my sister Annette made me aware of what he was: a liberal whose attitudes were rather exceptional for a Jew of his time. My sister had a limitless admiration for my father, and she tried to transfer this admiration to me. Although there had been that whole period during which I had profoundly hated my father in certain respects, she succeeded rather well.

Still, for me there were only two answers: either become a Zionist,

---

Milice: militia; a paramilitary force organized by the Vichy authorities to combat the maquis, the Milice was both tireless and brutal in hunting down Jews.

which I couldn't do, or a socialist, which I could. Just after the war I saw this boyfriend again, and I joined socialist groups, saying to myself, "It is to socialism that you must look, to internationalism." In the end, however, I lived this socialism, and this internationalism, among young Jews: Jews with socialist ideas, but Jews all the same.

I did associate with non-Jews. There were some non-Jews who were part of this socialist group; and I went to the university, and there were a lot of non-Jews there. We talked about the problems of the war, and I felt very tough because I had lived through this war as a Jew. I liked to talk about it then—in fact, I took an almost unwholesome pleasure in it. I realized that it was totally stupid and ridiculous, and I am not proud today of the way I acted after the war. But, at that time, that's how it was.

Hélène transferred to the University of Paris, where she met Motti, an engineering student, at a Jewish student association party. "What was marvelous," she recalls, "was that he was a Sabra—born in Israel!—and totally vivacious; he sang wonderful Israeli songs." Soon the two were living together, but when Israel's war of independence broke out in 1948, Motti was called home to serve in the army. Once the war was over, he wrote asking Hélène to join him, and she decided to immigrate to Israel. "So here I was," she says, "leaving on aliyah* despite my anti-Zionist ideas."

Upon her arrival, Hélène found Motti still in the service and went to live in Jerusalem at the home of his parents, extremely observant Jews whose own parents had emigrated from Persia. Motti's parents were happy to have Hélène in their home, even though they lived "eight or ten in two rooms," but they didn't want her to work and expected her to live in accordance with their own religious practices, which were utterly foreign to her. Hélène liked Motti's siblings, but although they were university educated, she says, "there was something in their way of looking at life that escaped me."

Seeing that Hélène had reached her limit, Motti told her that as the wife of a soldier she would be given an apartment and suggested that they be married. Opposed to marriage on ideological grounds, Hélène "died a thousand deaths" before deciding to go ahead with it. She had found work and was beginning to feel more at home when another blow struck.

I met an uncle of mine who had been a Zionist from the earliest

---

**aliyah:* immigration to Israel (Hebrew).

days and had come to Palestine in the first Russian aliyah. "What?" he said. "You're marrying a Sephardi?"

That infuriated me, and I said to him, "So, there's racism here also? How can you say such things?" This racism toward the "blacks"—they called the Sephardim *shachor*, for "black"—shocked and upset me. It also made me feel a bond with those people although, at the same time, I couldn't really manage to relate to them for other reasons.

Around this time, things were going very badly between me and my husband. We had been unable to have children, but there were disagreements nevertheless. I wanted secular children and circumcising a child was something that didn't even cross my mind, but Motti said, "If we do have children, they will be raised in the Jewish religion." There literally were fights over such things.

Besides, I had seen in Israel a world which was totally different from my own and which I was unable to assimilate, unable to understand. My first reaction to Israel had been to say to myself, "My, but what a lot of Jews there are here! Nothing but Jews!" And I never really became a part of it. It was a country that charmed me in certain ways, but, all the same, I rejected it. Perhaps I was not there in the best conditions—and it may have had a lot to do with the family in which I had been living, where I really did suffer—but Israel was not a beneficial experience.

In 1951, Motti and Hélène decided to return to France. A victim of anti-Sephardic prejudice, Motti had had trouble finding work; and, in any case, he wished to resume his studies. At the same time, Hélène, greatly weakened by a serious case of hepatitis, was advised by her doctors that she would recover more easily in an environment where material conditions were not so hard. Upon returning to Paris, Hélène found a job as a scientific researcher, and Motti, in addition to his schoolwork, took a job with a Jewish welfare agency. The change of scene did not, however, save the marriage, which some years later ended in divorce.

The war, the immediate postwar period, and my passage in Israel had left their mark on me, of course. But, little by little, my Jewishness was attenuated. At my job, I found myself in surroundings where there were very few Jews; I had the classic life of people who work in France, and I became part of things. Outside work I had Jewish friends, and Motti associated exclusively with Jews, but we nonetheless had friends whom I knew from work and who were not Jewish, so it was a mixture. Very slowly, very gradually, came my integration into a non-Jewish environment—and it was not so much the integration of a Jew.

When I began working, I didn't feel free to speak about my Jewishness and spoke of it only with a certain reticence. In fact, I didn't really say that I had been in Israel, where I had, after all, lived for two and a half years. Our last name had been gallicized when Motti was naturalized French, but there were people who had known me from before. I explained that the name was of Israeli origin, and that we were Israelis; "Israel" and "Jewish" were two different things for people, and in my mind being married to an Israeli was better. A whole calculation took place that wasn't totally honest. And when someone attacked the Jews—not that they actually attacked, but there are dumb comments, like "Oh, that guy is greedy like a Jew"—I didn't speak out. I had a kind of cowardice with regard to Jewishness that I kept for a long time.

When the interview took place, Hélène was living in a Paris suburb and working as a researcher. She was remarried, to a non-Jewish Frenchman of Belgian extraction. The couple had two teenage daughters, the younger of whom was planning a summer visit to Israel. Hélène had stayed in contact with Motti and introduced him to her children, who liked him a great deal.

It is only very recently that I have begun to work my way clear of this cowardice in regard to being Jewish—and of other forms of coward-ice as well, because it is an overall cowardice. I am, I believe, rather cowardly by temperament with regard to certain fundamental things. Is it a question of upbringing? Is it something in my character? Both, I believe.

But things have improved, and this change, I think, goes with getting older—when you get older, you demystify many things. I have fewer anxieties in my professional life. I am able to lay out my ideas for scrutiny, I manage to disagree openly with my superiors, I can do things I could never do before—although I have always taken part in the strikes where I work, and they have always known that my political ideas are on the left. But there are things that I now get through more easily, that I see more philosophically.

And when the occasion presents itself now and I say that I am a Jew, I do it a little more naturally, with less cowardice, with less appre-hension. But I wouldn't say that it's totally normal—in fact, I'm sure it is not. I still haven't gotten to the point of being able to do it in a truly free way—I still have a lot of trouble, there are still these calculations in my mind. I know that it's there, and I am trying to free myself as thoroughly as possible; but, at bottom, there is something which, in spite of everything, has remained.

On occasion, events reinforce Hélène's fears. A popular figure at the country club where she has long been a member, Hélène was the leading vote getter in an election for the club's board of directors that was held shortly before the interview. When the day of the interview came and Hélène had to leave her regular doubles tennis match early, she decided to reveal to her partners—who, like most others at the club, were unaware that she was Jewish—the subject she was to discuss. "I had to force myself a bit," she says, "but I was curious to see if there would be a reaction."

The reaction was immediate. One of her partners, a young business executive who had also been elected to the board—although less resoundingly—remarked, "Oh, so first the lady gets all the votes, and the next thing you know she's being interviewed about her origins!" In later weeks, when Hélène disputed a point on the court, he muttered about her "typical carpet trader's mentality"—a classic anti-Semitic insult.

Still, Hélène says it is not so much today's environment as her background that accounts for her lingering hesitancy.

Even after the war, I was never able to get off my mind the fact that I had suffered as a Jew during my childhood; it's something that stayed with me for a long time. During the war was the period when I felt the most Jewish, certainly—although what do you call feeling Jewish? I don't think that what I felt was anything enormous. But, well, I knew I was Jewish—that, yes. It was a given, I wore the Jewish star, it was marked—not on the tip of my nose, maybe, but it was marked. And because it obligated me to a whole bunch of unpleasant things, it gave me a royal pain. But circumstances shaped me in that way, and, if you will, I became Jewish. I was forced to become it.

I have long suffered from a fear of death that is extremely profound—that overwhelms me, and increasingly so as I grow older. I have had psychotherapeutic treatment for this fear, and there was a relation drawn with the fact that I am Jewish—that, as a Jew, I had lived this fear of death much more than someone else and that it left much more of a mark on me. I believe it is linked in part to that. And I believe that, as a Jew, I am still not at ease.

Of course, I push out of my mind the idea that there could be a rebirth of an anti-Semitic movement as vast as that which existed during the war. But at the same time that I tell myself such a thing is not possible, I sense a latent anti-Semitism that I have felt even in the comments of intelligent people. And so there remains this deep insecurity, which means that if I am identified as a Jew for the outside world, it troubles me. It troubles me for me, and it troubles me for my children. It has traumatized me deeply, and it continues to leave its stamp on me as something that is a threat to my security. As something of death.

I believe that, for me, to be a Jew is death. And it is something that comes from far off; so, for that reason, I reject it.

Etienne Lenoir

I am speaking as myself: that is to say, as a French sculptor who has what are referred to as Jewish origins, a term I reject. I was born in 1918, during the shelling of Paris by Big Bertha, and I am the son of a humanist man of letters who gave his children a perfectly secular education and of a painter-mother who transmitted to me her love of art. My father had been wounded at Verdun; he was still at the front a short time before my birth. My mother, to earn a living, made drawings that appeared in the newspapers.

Ours is a French family. We have been in France since the remote past and are, on my father's side, a military family. My grandfather was a colonel in the Imperial Guard, my great-grandfather played in a band in the army of Napoleon, and my great-great-grandfather was a music teacher. It is an old family that comes from Lorraine. My mother's family traces back to a Swiss gardener who was in the service of the count of Provence and who bore my mother's maiden name. I am less certain whether that family was from Lorraine or Alsace.

It is difficult for me to speak of a connection with Judaism, because none has ever existed for me. There was no Jewish religion practiced in our family; in fact, there was no religion of any sort. My mother was very spiritualistic; she had a religious temperament, but not in the formal sense. We knew that we were of Jewish origin, we never denied our origins—since the subject is "origins"—but Judaism never played any role in our family.

I think that my father's parents or grandparents practiced this religion, and then the way military people might practice it. There may have been more religious practice in my mother's family. But while I had ancestors who practiced the Jewish religion, to what extent they practiced, and whether there weren't ancestors before them who practiced other religions, who can say? As with everyone—as with the most observant Jews, for that matter—no one can know who his ancestors were.

So it was something we were cognizant of, and that's all. It was something that didn't matter, and there was no particular reason to talk about it. We did have occasion to talk about it at the time when there were anti-Semitic campaigns—then, of course, yes. But it was far from being an obsession. It was like having a distant Berber lineage, or Alsatian, or Burgundian, or whatever else. And my father, in fact, was the very image of the poilu* of Verdun, which is to say that his appearance was as typically French as one could possibly imagine.

I myself have always felt perfectly French. It is a question that doesn't even come up for me, just as it never came up for my father or for any member of my family whatever. We didn't have to ask ourselves whether we had a desire to belong to the society in which we lived. It was not a matter of having a desire—we simply did belong.

The proof is that as soon as I had religious aspirations, I went to the Catholic church, since the church was the most familiar and prevalent religious structure. It was in adolescence, at the time when all young people have their religious crisis; I wanted to get to know those things a little more intimately and to experience an atmosphere that was in keeping with my yearnings. Above all, I was attracted as an artist to the form that the church gave to religion. But Judaism counted so little that I turned to the church without ever reflecting on it or making a choice. Nothing else ever came to mind.

Etienne says his father passed on a deep reverence, shared among progressive intellectuals of the time, for the order, austerity, and love of country that France's first republicans upheld in the face of what they saw as the moral laxity and internationalism of ancien régime aristocrats. Another important influence, both artistic and intellectual, was what Etienne refers to as the "spirituality of Lorraine," after the French region in which his family has its roots. He speaks of

---

*poilu: French foot soldier of World War I; French equivalent of "doughboy."

an affinity that links both his own artistic style and his father's literary style to the Lorraine engravers, whom he admires as "France's greatest."

In engraving, the needle cuts directly into the copper, so there is no compromise possible. There is only one line that is the right one, there cannot be two. For my father, there was only one word that was the right word, there could not be two, either.

Etienne was in his fifteenth year in 1933, when the Nazis came to power in Germany. From the very first, his family was without illusions as to the nature of Nazism: While they "certainly did not imagine that France would be invaded," he recalls, they realized that "Hitler would put into practice the ultimate racist policy." Anti-Jewish feeling was in evidence in France as well, and Etienne ended up in fistfights with classmates in secondary school—something he attributes to the fact that he was known at the time by his family's Jewish-sounding last name.

Such things happened very rarely. I believe that there were only two or three times when I had altercations during my entire school career—on account of my name, of course, there was no other possible reason that anti-Semitism would have been directed at me. We fought, and it was never mentioned again. I even became friends with one of those adversaries when it was over, which often happens once you've really mixed it up.

If its Jewish background played any role in the life of Etienne's family, he says, it was when Jews began leaving lands under Nazi control.

We took in and aided refugees from Germany and elsewhere, and thus made the acquaintance not of Judaism but of Jewish refugees. We followed developments very closely and fought this anti-Semitism as we fought all forms of racism and fascism. My father served on antifascist committees and struggled with all his might in his writings and other endeavors against the rise of fascism. I myself was constantly being alerted to these problems as a member of the Socialist Students and the Socialist Youth, which were antifascist organizations. I participated in their demonstrations—that is to say, we battled fascist organizations in the Latin Quarter.

In 1939 I was drafted. Contrary to what has been said, the morale of the French army was extraordinary. Had we been able to fight right away, we would have fought with unyielding fervor and patriotic feeling; and there was perfect solidarity, totally without distinction of class, or of profession, or of education, or of anything at all. In the end, what is called the Phony War little by little demolished this morale, as it was calculated to do.

I was in a regiment of officer candidates, and when the Germans finally attacked, we were still in training camps. Some of us sent a letter to our commanding officer asking to leave to fight at the front, but the answer was that if we persisted in sending letters of that kind, we would be placed under arrest.

Etienne's regiment made for Bordeaux but could not realize its hopes of sailing for North Africa. When the German army arrived in the region, the regiment crossed what later became the Line of Demarcation separating the occupied and "free" zones of France. Reaching Vichy, it was the first regiment reviewed by Marshal Pétain.

By January 1941 we were no longer doing anything whatever, and I'd had enough; two of us went to the officer responsible for discharges and succeeded in convincing him that there was no reason to keep us in uniform. I left with my discharge, while my class remained on active service—well, but who were they serving?—until the end of the year.

Though it may seem surprising for an artist, I loved military discipline. Unfortunately, I had no deeds of glory to my credit—unlike my brother, an extraordinary resistance fighter who, by the way, saved many people of Jewish origin by helping them slip into Switzerland. He was a magnificent soldier in whom the family tradition shone through. Still, military discipline and the life of the infantry—out in nature, in the open air, with marches at dawn—aroused my enthusiasm. If I hadn't been an artist, it might not have displeased me to continue as a soldier.

I would also like to say that from the moment I was called up I felt in perfect harmony with all my fellow soldiers and that I never witnessed the slightest trace of anti-Semitism. Never. Neither on the part of my fellows nor on the part of my superiors. There was total understanding and excellent solidarity up to the end, and I was perfectly happy among my comrades in arms.

After being discharged at Grenoble, Etienne rejoined the Ecole des Beaux-Arts, the fine arts school in which he had been enrolled before the declaration of war and which had been moved from Paris to Marseilles. As the winter of 1940–41 neared its end, he went with a number of painters, architects, and sculptors to live and work in a village in the region, where he remained until the spring of 1942. During this time, he often bicycled from the village to Aix-en-

Provence to visit his parents, bringing them whatever supplies were available from the countryside.

It was when Etienne joined the artists' group that he assumed the nom d'artiste that he was never to cast off: Etienne Lenoir.

Before the war, I had already signed a certain number of things with this name. My brother chose the name one day, and I simply adopted it because my brother had a lot of influence on me in my youth; he was very important to me from the intellectual point of view. I don't know at what moment I had papers in this name, although it was rather early, but my friends in the group knew very well who my family was.

I left the group to live on a farm in one of the wildest and harshest regions of France, where I worked for something more than a year and from where I could continue bringing my parents sacks loaded with food. The farmers are marvelous people with whom I got along perfectly and whom I still see from time to time. They are very devout Protestants and were quite unhappy that I didn't embrace their religion. Theirs is the country of the religious wars, where a Catholic would never set foot in view of a Protestant farm or vice versa. During elections rifles are at the ready, and the deputies are elected not for political reasons, which interest no one, but as the Catholic or the Protestant. All the villages there are completely Catholic or completely Protestant, which led me to play the role I always play: that is to say, to want not to be labeled. I would go to the Catholic village and chat with the priest, but the locals themselves didn't cross the line.

I did my job as a farmhand with delight. In the beginning the farmers were very skeptical of the work of the Parisian, but afterwards they were in despair that I was leaving because I really did help them a great deal. And I remain enormously grateful to them. They knew exactly why I had come and what they were doing in sheltering me.

I left the farm in September 1943 to join my brother-in-law, who directed a resistance network in Vichy, but I was arrested almost immediately. I had arrived only days before and was on the eve of a departure for Paris—I was supposed to carry some document—when a meeting at the house of my sister and brother-in-law was raided. The Gestapo had apparently been staking out the apartment; everyone there was picked up.

I was taken to the jailhouse of the Gestapo, which was in the basement of a charming little villa in Vichy. The first thing I saw in the cell was a mattress—well, a straw mat—but I quickly realized that it contained a lot more bedbugs than straw. It was impossible to lie down; you had to stay on your feet, completely naked, in order not to be eaten alive by the bugs.

After several days, a blowhard who claimed to be a leader of the maquis* arrived in the cell and started telling all kinds of stories. It was written all over his face that he was a plant, that in reality he was there to try to get the others to talk. At that point they brought my brother-in-law into the next cell, which was linked to mine by a little peephole. Each time we talked, this windbag came up to listen to what we were saying. Obviously, we weren't taken in, and we spent days on end reciting Alfred Jarry's *Ubu Roi,* which we both liked equally and which we knew almost by heart. What he passed on to the Gestapo must have plunged them into the most absolute perplexity.

It is not worth dwelling on the interrogations; one can imagine what that might be like. One day, they took me out of the cell, and I crossed my brother-in-law on the stairs. I didn't recognize him right then, because his face had tripled in size; only later did I realize that it was he. That is the last memory I have of him. I myself must surely have been in about the same condition.

Afterwards they brought me to the barracks in Clermont-Ferrand, which had been transformed into a prison. There were twenty of us there who had been arrested for resistance and other things, and I found a solidarity and a spirit comparable to that of the regiment. One day the order came to depart, and at the gate of the prison I met up with my mother and my sister—which, of course, was a shock.

Etienne and his sister had been arrested in the same raid. The Gestapo had had little difficulty establishing that they were brother and sister, and, as his sister did not have false papers, Etienne's origins were easily pinned down. His mother, who was living in a village near Aix-en-Provence, had become upset at not hearing from her children and had come looking for them. She was arrested, and the arrest of her husband was ordered as well.

They didn't arrest my father because he was at the barber's when

---

*Maquis: French armed resistance; partisans.

they came. He wanted to give himself up to the Gestapo afterwards so that he could be reunited with his wife. But he arrived after six o'clock, the offices were closed, and he was told to come back in the morning. It was at that point that friends managed to convince him of his folly and stop him from returning.

My mother, my sister, and I were put on the train for Paris, all three of us in a compartment with a military policeman. I often thought about escaping—which would not have been very difficult, since there was only the lone MP with us and by opening the window you could jump out quickly enough when the train slowed up. But the MP wasn't worried about it, he left the compartment unconcerned; and he was right, because it was unthinkable that I would leave my mother and sister.

The three were brought to the transit camp at Drancy, a suburb of Paris, where Jews were held for deportation. Soon afterward they were placed in a transport for Auschwitz.

In the family, we had known for a very long time that there were camps. All antifascists knew that there were camps and that all the opponents of Hitler's regime had disappeared into them, Communists and socialists as well as Jews. But, without a doubt, no one imagined what they might be like—no one. We were convinced that it would be in our interest to stay together in order to help each other, that we were going to labor camps which would be very harsh, but, well, where one could live. That's what they had led us to believe.

On the ramp at Auschwitz, completely dazed by the week's voyage in cattle cars, you get off the train, the SS are there with the dogs, they send some to the right and others to the left, you don't know why. They sent me to one side, my mother and sister to the other. Perhaps I was naïve, but I didn't think at all about what that might mean. Of course, I never saw them again.

After only a few days in the main camp, Etienne was sent to Fürstengrube, a subcamp which was under construction near a coal mine and to which a small number of inmates had been assigned for "punishment." Having deduced that his resistance affiliation was behind the transfer—"no one told me so, but it seems logical"—he observes: "This shows to what lengths the Gestapo had gone in marking me." Etienne estimates that, at Fürstengrube, "maximum life expectancy was two weeks"; he himself remained there around fourteen months.

Fürstengrube was a harsh camp, certainly one of the toughest in the whole universe of German concentration camps. I saw entire populations of Hungarians, for example, disappear within a few days. The Hungarian Jews were almost all farmers, and when they arrived they were strong, well-fed, and stocky, which made an extraordinary impression on us. But within a week or two they were depleted, and not one of them survived.

The work was terribly hard. I remember painting with red lead astride the beams of a factory that was under construction, dozens of meters in the air. I worked building barracks out of bricks, and I worked in the mines as well. The work at the bottom of the mine was the best there was because, when you were at the bottom of the mine, you escaped the SS. You were with German civilians, who weren't so nice themselves—but, well, they weren't the SS. And you were warm in the mine.

The problem was that they were old mines that had been abandoned before the war, which is to say they weren't particularly solid. One day I had to push off against a wall to move a wagon full of coal because the rails were clogged with coal debris. A comrade came to help me, and finally, with a lot of effort, we got it rolling. Scarcely was it moving when the whole mine caved in right where we had been—all the supports, which were in bad shape, gave way. But other jobs were much worse: those that were outside. Carrying rails was particularly murderous because it was always in arctic cold, and if the rail fell, it crushed your hands or your feet.

Then there was the food, if you can call it that. There was soup, which was water with some cabbage stems and bits of kohlrabi, plus a chunk of horrible bread accompanied by a little piece of artificial sausage. Its quality was such that the body no longer had any resistance. The majority of the comrades had boils—boils is not saying enough; they had these craters that dug all the way to the bone and that wore them down. But the main cause of death was dysentery, constant dysentery, which little by little emptied you totally of your vital substances.

There was a rather strange phenomenon that I would like to describe because the camps are, in the end, microcosms that enable one to see more clearly what in reality happens everywhere. I observed that when a comrade began to weaken, you saw him gradually losing his grip until he became what was called a "Mussulman"; I don't know where this term came from, but it was used, I believe, in all the camps. Well, at that point he was repellent to everyone. You didn't have any desire to help him—rather, you had to hold yourself back from pushing him further in that direction. It's a startling thing, but it brought me to the realization that the same is true in everyday life: One always has more of a desire to help the rich than the poor. It is remarkable how want and misery attract misery, how misery grows on itself.

This microcosm also enabled one to see that social position made no difference to the ability to stand up to an ordeal. I saw people who had had very high positions in prewar life conducting themselves in a frightful manner, ready to grovel before anyone to get anything. On the other hand, there were fellows from perfectly modest social backgrounds who behaved marvelously: That is to say, their conduct was worthy of a human being, and they never forgot the necessity of helping others and of moral resistance. Those who held up best were, without a doubt, those who had an ideal—whatever it was—while those who died most rapidly were those who were obsessed with food. Most of the prisoners passed their time describing meals to one another. It was all they talked about, and it literally became an obsession.

I am going to pass over the massacres and all that; that's been told dozens of times and there's no point going into it. I was, however, witness to rather extraordinary things in this regard. The SS had a big celebration in honor of Wodan. At the end of their feast, as they were all dead drunk, they surged through the camp with their submachine guns—massacring quite a few people—and they unleashed their dogs and so on. Of many such instances, I also particularly remember a roll call that lasted all night. There had been an escape attempt during the day, and we stood there all night dressed only in our uniforms—and one must realize that that night it was minus thirty. There were many who fell. In the wee hours, the SS commandant arrived with his submachine gun and began shooting randomly at everyone there.

I myself never left off thinking about escape from the first day to the last, and I managed to put aside a pocketknife, some civilian clothing, and other things that might have helped me if I had tried it. But I never did—and I think I was right not to—because as a Frenchman in Poland I would have been denounced immediately. On top of that, there were five or six rings of SS guards deployed deep into the countryside.

Soon after he had arrived at Fürstengrube, Etienne faced one of the frequent "selections" in which inmates—particularly, but not exclusively, those who were ill or otherwise unfit for work—were singled out for the gas chamber at Auschwitz.

I owe my survival to an architect of Lithuanian origin who had convinced the German prisoner in charge of the camp architectural office that I should not leave with the selection. During the roll call, I saw the finger of the head SS man of the camp point at a number of prisoners, then point at me. But this SS man—one of the most fearsome, Moll, whose reputation has become a matter of record since—was accompanied by the German architect, who deflected his arm, saying, "No, not that one. Another." So I wasn't selected that day.

If I managed to hold up after that, it was thanks to the way my parents had raised me—thanks to the perfect physical equilibrium they had given me and to the attachment to artistic, political, and spiritual values that transcend everyday life. On the one hand, I showed great physical resistance: In particular due to my training as a farmer, I knew how to handle a pick and shovel, how to go about hard, physical labor without wearing myself out any more than necessary. And, on the other hand, I thought about other things.

Something else that enabled me to keep going was my profession. Outside of working hours in the mine or at the outdoor work sites, I never stopped drawing. I did a lot of portraits and was paid in food. From time to time I was able to escape a day or two of work to do the portrait of one kapo* or another. I remember in particular a kapo who was a German common criminal. I took fantastic pleasure in drawing him, because he was an extraordinary beast. In civilian life he had been a kind of Bluebeard, and he was very good-looking—he really had the face for the job. He was decent as a prisoner, and I had good relations with him, as one often did with the common criminals there.

Besides common criminals, the classifications at Fürstengrube included political prisoners, Jews, homosexuals, and Jehovah's Witnesses. As was generally

---

*kapo: in the concentration camps, a trusty prisoner. Kapos were often put in charge of work details and were sometimes given authority over fellow prisoners in other contexts as well.

true in the camps, each inmate was made to wear a triangular badge whose color identified him as a member of a group. "There were no 'Jewish resistance fighters,' " Etienne remarks. "I was there as a Jew."

I was never conscious of any Jewish solidarity or other Jewish ties. We grouped ourselves exclusively by nationality: as Poles, Germans, Frenchmen, Czechs, whether Jewish or not. Only the Poles of Jewish origin stayed among themselves, not mixing with the non-Jewish Poles because there was too much of a tradition of hatred between them.

The non-Jewish Poles were not really congenial; although it's always wrong to generalize, they were not very good comrades with the others. But among themselves they stuck together in an extraordinary manner and exhibited courage and patriotism beyond compare. It was the Poles who made the few escape attempts that there were—which is understandable, because it was in Poland—and I remember Poles who, the noose around their neck, sang patriotic songs as they were about to be hanged.

And the Czechs stayed together, and the French, although the French formed less of an island, less of a community. One might say that the French were the most cosmopolitan. But there were very few.

We arrived in a group of 100 or 150 Frenchmen. Immediately, a little group organized itself to share tasks and to help one another, each according to his abilities. As we saw right away that the problem would be food, each would try to arrange his activities—some of the French comrades were interpreters, for example, and I did portraits—so that they would be able to provide for the needs of the others. As long as the group existed, we pooled our food, sharing, of course, with others who had no possibility of procuring any extra.

But selections and transfers had soon thinned the ranks of Etienne's French comrades, and he found himself reassigned to a block populated by Polish Jews.

I must say that, at that moment, I had one of the most painful sensations I have ever had: I truly had the impression that I was with people from another planet.

Being in the camp was something in itself. I had arrived from France to find myself in a landscape that one could only conceive of as lunar or Venusian: As if one had made an abrupt landing on the planet Mars, it was indescribable, totally aberrant, in total defiance of logic.

But the unpleasantness caused by this forced cohabitation with these people who were so foreign to me—by finding myself suddenly confronted with this group to which I was supposed to belong but to which I did not belong, with which I had no link, no affinity—is something that unquestionably left its mark. The camp itself was almost spectral in its horror. But being immersed in this totally foreign community was an extra burden, and not an insignificant burden, that added to the otherworldliness.

These people had habits that truly were totally different from everything I had known. One thing that struck me—it horrified me a little in the beginning, although I got used to it later—was that they never went to sleep without wailing. It was a kind of plaintive chant—well, not a chant, no, it was literally wailing, a kind of lamentation. It was very, very curious. I don't know whether it was a custom, or a prayer, or what it might have been, but I heard that wailing every night, and it exasperated me.

Another factor was that, at the time of our arrival, a majority of the kapos were of Polish-Jewish origin. Some of them had been there for three, four, five years, the wretches. As, sadly, they had been in the camps for so long, they had gradually taken over certain jobs that they couldn't have kept if they hadn't carried them out with the utmost cruelty. That would have been the same for everybody: Those who were not violent and brutal didn't stay in place. They made terror reign; and so, obviously, one had no great fellow feeling towards them.

Speaking generally, Etienne says, the Polish Jews "may have been a thousand times my superior—that's not at all the question—but a wall was there that could not be scaled."

There were several reasons for this wall. First, everyone from Central Europe detested the French, and rightly so. They felt that France had betrayed them, which was true—not for Poland, but for Czechoslovakia and so on. I observed a profound rancor against France on the part of all these people from Central Europe; the Jewish question didn't make any difference on that score, it was a question of nationality. This rancor unleashed a hostile reflex, and there was nothing you could say against it, for it was in part justified.

Then there was the problem of rancor among those people from Poland who had lived in a state of persecution well before Hitler and who may have begrudged to those who were from Western Europe and who were full-fledged citizens that they hadn't known this persecution. The Poles of Jewish origin, above all, had suffered abominable anti-Semitism on the part of the non-Jews. These Poles told of how, when they had been arrested by the Nazis and were leaving for the camps, there was a crowd on either side of their convoys that shouted insults at them: Encircled by the SS, on the way to their deaths, they were being cursed by the non-Jewish population. So they felt a hatred that was easily explicable, if not justifiable, toward the entire non-Jewish world—a world from which I did not feel separate at all.

Finally, I think this sequestered life in what had been ghettos—and were ghettos still, for all intents and purposes—had literally withdrawn them from the world. They had traveled very little, and there had been as yet no contact with the Western world as we know it in the life they led. Of their civic customs, if I can put it that way, they held on to the habits of staying together and of helping one another a great deal. So communication was difficult, since they were accustomed to living completely unto themselves and they weren't used to communicating with other human groups.

I never ran into these problems in dealing with Czechs, Germans, Austrians, and so on, where there was a kind of openness that existed as among any Europeans. But in comparison to us—or to the Belgians or the Lithuanians whom I met there and who were fantastic people—they were really apart, completely different from anyone I'd associated with up to that time. They were totally outside normal European society. It wasn't the same civilization. It was another world.

I was unable to get a totally clear picture of how they lived. They were not peasants, since there were no peasants among the Polish Jews—among the Hungarians, yes, but not among the Poles. But they were on a different cultural plane. Again, I am not speaking of superiority or inferiority; rather, I mean to say that the cultural concerns of a Frenchman or an Englishman or an American were totally absent for them. If it was painful for me to be isolated suddenly in the midst of this mass that was totally foreign to me and that considered me as foreign, there was a cultural side to it: It was a little as if a student had been plunged overnight into a community of common criminals.

And then there was this language that they spoke among themselves and that is not very pleasant to the ear. Well, one always finds the language of the other unpleasant, that's no criterion. I believe that most of the Germans, Lithuanians, Czechs, Poles, and so on knew Yiddish, but I had never heard Yiddish spoken, and I don't speak German or Polish. So I had no way of communicating with these people who, themselves, did not speak French and did not understand French.

I will always remember the day when a detachment of Italian prisoners of war arrived in the camp. Seeing on those faces a more human expression, I could have hugged them: All of a sudden I was again among brothers. I didn't share a language with the Italians, either—well, of course, you can understand Italian better than Polish if you are French—but you could always communicate with gestures, you always managed to put together some sort of gibberish to make yourself more or less understood. It was a geographic community, nothing more, but it made for a certain immediate solidarity.

"The problem," Etienne concludes, "was that I had been placed with so-called brothers who were not my brothers."

I had been taken from my family and put into a family that was not my own. I had no contact of any kind with the Polish Jews, not even a feeling of solidarity. Whereas Judaism is something that doesn't exist for me, they, after all, lived within this Judaism as if it were a nationality; there was no common ground. I had the feeling that they realized perfectly that I was not one of their own; there was no doubt about that. Although I have no proof of it, I wonder whether they didn't hold that against me.

And on every occasion that anyone tried to decree me to be a Jew, I rejected it internally. One was forced to accept it materially, but it was not a revelation of any identity whatsoever, it was a coercion imposed by the enemy. I wanted to struggle as a Frenchman: I was French as far as my comrades were concerned, and it was painful for me not to be regarded as French in the sense that I was fighting against the Germans, struggling to survive. But I was considered neither as a Frenchman, nor as a resistance fighter, nor as whatever else, I was considered as a Jew—whereas for myself I was not a Jew and I never felt myself to be a Jew in any way. Never.

It was a very heavy burden to be bound to people with whom I had no bonds when the bonds I did have were to others from whom I had been separated. If I had not been recognized and deported as a Jew, I would have been sent to another camp, where I would have found my normal and natural ties of affinity, at once national and political. I would at least have been able to spend this time with people I understood and who shared my concerns, rather than with these strangers whose language I didn't speak and who didn't understand mine, and whose habits were totally different from every point of view. I would have been able to struggle on my own terms—and it would have been easier for me to struggle for what I was than for what I was not.

In January 1945, as the Red Army approached, the SS evacuated the camp, leaving behind only those too weak to be moved. Etienne had planned a quick escape, but the man he chose to team up with proved unreliable once outside the camp gates. Reluctant to strike out alone in the vicious cold, he stayed on the march.

In the month of January, I marched through the snows of Upper Silesia. It wasn't the march that frightened me, because I was, thank God, still hearty enough; but the slightest pause meant death. That is to say that the SS shot all those who stopped and all those who fell. It went on like that for days and nights, and there were marches through the forest during which I was certainly no longer conscious.

At the end of several days we came to a camp where prisoners from other camps had been brought as well. They put us all together and made us get into open cattle cars to continue on. There again, at the moment we got into those cars, there were separations. I will always live with the memory of a French comrade who was calling to me in a heartrending fashion. I was blocked in the midst of a huge number of comrades standing in these cars, and I didn't know where he was going, and I couldn't get to him. I never saw him again.

There followed what was surely one of the worst voyages in the history of the camps. We were ten days in those open cars without water. After that I can say from experience that hunger is nothing, but that thirst is something which is unbearable in the literal sense of the word. The thirst was such that, when we stopped after several days and bread was passed out, no one was able to eat. We had mouths like boiled leather, and it was literally impossible to swallow anything at all. A good number of comrades became delirious, and some of them went stark-raving mad. What saved us was that a few had the idea of letting the tin cans that served the prisoners as mess tins trail through the snow at the end of a string. We were able to get a little moisture from the snow, and in that way we managed to hold out.

So numerous were we in this open car that we couldn't stretch, and if you happened to leave the place where you were crouched, it was taken immediately—even if unwittingly—by the mass of the others. If you succeeded in putting a foot in the place where you had been, your foot was stuck there, but you yourself couldn't get into the place. This meant that you were doomed to stiff joints and unbearable cramps; or, if you got up, you couldn't find another place and were doomed to wander all night long above the mass of bodies in the bitter cold, without being able to care for yourself in any way and without ever finding a place.

We wandered randomly: through Czechoslovakia; and to Mauthausen, where there was no place for us; and I think we passed through Munich as well. There was a short stop at a little station in Germany to clear out the corpses. Half of those in the cars, if not two-thirds, were already dead, and within a few minutes the platform was covered with a heap of bodies, all along the train. On another platform in the station was a young, middle-class woman—German certainly, or at least I think so—who was looking at that sea of corpses that had been taken off the train. I studied her face, and I didn't see the slightest trace of human feeling. Let me be quick to say that I am antiracist and therefore opposed to all notions of collective responsibility. I have returned to Germany, and I don't hold the young Germans responsible for what their fathers did, which would be absurd. But the face of this middle-class German woman has remained stamped in my memory.

The convoy continued on to the town of Nordhausen. When we got off the train, the first thing we did—all of us—was to throw ourselves into the snow that lay on the ground and to eat as much of it as we could. It was gold for us, that snow. We came to a camp, we were brought to the showers, and the first thing we did was to rush into the water. Trading started up right away, and we exchanged the bread that we had been unable to eat for water. We missed the bread later, but at that moment anything else would have been out of the question. I must say that for at least fifteen years afterwards I could not drink water without thinking of the extraordinary feeling I had in drinking that first water. I don't know how to describe it. It was prodigious.

The camp, it turned out, was Mittelbau Dora, a subcamp of Buchenwald. There, the members of Etienne's transport were put to work building V-2 rockets in a huge tunnel cut into the side of a mountain. The work site, designed to be hidden from Allied view, was unventilated, and the prisoners, most of whom had arrived in a depleted state, rarely survived the long hours and inhuman conditions for more than a few weeks. Still, Etienne says, they found the energy for sabotage; the reward for their efforts was seeing parts upon which they had made identifying marks returned.

Things were very difficult for me at Dora, not so much because of the work but because this trip of ten days or so without water had used up all the physical and mental resistance I had managed to hold on to. I have a strong constitution, and I was very robust when I was arrested. I had held up for fourteen months or thereabouts. But the voyage, the fasting, the thirst, had gotten the better of my reserves. By my arrival at Dora, my resistance was gone.

Whereas I had escaped the dysentery and the boils at Fürsten-grube, at Dora the two began. I had those sores on my legs, those enormous, gangrenous craters that never closed and that had killed so many of my comrades. I found myself on the downward slope leading to the state that was referred to as "Mussulman"; I was not a Mussulman, but I was more or less on the way to becoming one.

At Dora I had been reunited with some of the French comrades who had been so great for so long and who had organized mutual aid among themselves, as I mentioned. I can't say that they turned away from me, but I did see that in my physical state I did not, perhaps, inspire the same sympathy in them that I would have if I had been healthy. So I ran into what I had observed before: the phenomenon of rejection by the collectivity of elements that are felt to be on the road to perdition and beyond recall.

To show to what point I had weakened, one day after work, when the SS had come to take us from the tunnel back to the camp and we were standing for the roll call before leaving, a terrible spasm ran through me. I just couldn't hold it, and I left for the toilets, letting the detail go on. I was nearly unconscious; I wouldn't have done this otherwise because it was idiotic, I should have gone in my pants. When they noticed that I wasn't there, the SS came back to look for the prisoner who was trying to escape. An SS man brought me back, thrashing me with his fists and feet, but what is amazing is that he didn't machine-gun me right on the spot as he had done to dozens of others. So I had again escaped death, and I really don't know why.

Etienne was not in Dora "long enough for the phenomenon of degeneration to run its course," he explains; with the Allies approaching, he and his fellow prisoners were loaded onto a new transport "in time to interrupt the process." The train was strafed: "They were shooting right at us," he recalls, "but they were Allied planes, so it felt great to be getting it." The SS decided to abandon the train, and the transport continued on foot.

After all these months, I had managed to pick up some German. I never uttered a word, always saying I didn't understand, and that was precisely what saved my life—because I understood full well at a certain point that the SS was going to liquidate us. We were marching along in the forest, and the SS man in front could no longer see us because he'd turned a corner, while the one behind us was looking at an Allied plane overhead. Just at that instant I signaled to three of my comrades that the moment had come and plunged into the forest.

And something extraordinary happened. I saw that the second you take the step, you are free. At that second, that very second, you are no longer a prisoner. The fourteen, sixteen, eighteen months are erased in one stroke, and you are a free man.

As Etienne and his companions crawled through the woods, the SS guards, apparently most concerned about the planes, sprayed a few bullets in their direction and marched on. Etienne's hunch proved right: The rest of his detachment died when the SS loaded them into a shed for the night, then set the shed on fire and gunned down those who tried to get out. Others in the transport reached Hamburg and were put onto barges that were then sunk, although Etienne no longer remembers whether by the Germans themselves or by Allied bombers.

The four escapees traveled at night, nourishing themselves on raw potatoes they dug up. They tore off the swatches of striped cloth that had been sewn onto the backs of their otherwise civilian clothing to mark them as concentration camp inmates, and they filled sacks they found with potatoes so that they would look like farmers—"although I wonder," remarks Etienne, "what kind of curious farmers we must have seemed." Having caught sight of German soldiers retreating in panic, the group determined it must be close to the Allies and decided to travel by day but to split into pairs to attract less attention. At length, Etienne and his partner ran into a squad of American shock troops who gave them medical treatment and ordered German peasants to lodge and feed them.

Etienne recovered his strength as the weeks went by, but he had great difficulty establishing the fact that he had been in a concentration camp and melted into the mass of civilians wandering around in the rubble of 1945 Germany. Even when he managed to convince Allied repatriation officials of who he was, their promises to send him home proved empty. His frustration growing, he walked away from one refugee camp after another until he came to one that was next to a prisoner of war camp from which airplanes were leaving regularly for Paris. A French POW agreed to sneak Etienne and other former concentration camp inmates onto a plane. Finally back in Paris, he contacted his father's publisher, who helped him locate the surviving members of his family.

When I returned from the camps, my mind was made up that I should rid myself of this Jewish cloak that they had stuck on me and that I detested—not because it was Jewish, but because it was not mine. I didn't want it, I did everything I could to get rid of it completely, and I would have preferred never hearing about it again.

In the late 1940s, Etienne legally adopted his nom d'artiste. His original surname is "considered Jewish internationally," although in France, he says, it is more common among Christians than Jews despite its Old Testament ring. As it entered his family when a clerk erred in recording the name of one of his forebears, Etienne considers his own change of name in line with "family tradition."

Furthermore, it was a request which my mother made before she disappeared and in which I was encouraged by my father, whose initial reaction during the occupation had been to write, "Try as they might to decree me a Jew, there is no wise in which I am." Also, it came at the moment of my marriage, and it was my own wish to spare my descendants this label. Because it *is* a label; and the experiences I had—which are not at all out of the ordinary—have led me to believe that one of the principal causes of hatred in the world is what I call "the label."

All you have to do is stick someone with a big label—on which is written "Jew," "Catholic," "Protestant," "Moslem," "Communist," "Socialist," "Fascist," "Englishman," "American," "Frenchman," "German," or whatever, so that you no longer see that there is a human being behind—and you can have at him without a qualm in the world. Since I've been back from the camps, I have refused these labels relentlessly and with all the means at my disposal, and I have torn them off each time I had the chance.

I believe that a large part of the so-called Jewish problem would be resolved if it weren't for these names that act as labels. Each one would then be free, not having the label-name, to practice the Jewish religion if he so wished. I am convinced that no one would see the slightest wrong in this, and that anti-Semitism would vanish to a great degree. But after all that has happened, it is certain—and I have seen so myself, at close range—that it can start up again. Since in my case there was neither religion nor inheritance in the social sense of the term, there was no reason for my children also to put on this cloak that is not theirs. We are not of the Jewish religion, so there's no use our suffering that. I would rather choose my own occasions to fight—and there is no lack of such occasions—than fight for something that has been imposed on me.

Tracking down ex-Nazis and French collaborators is one of Etienne's chosen battles. Prudence demands that he keep the nature of those efforts secret: "There are still a few of us doing it" is all he will say. But when it comes to his own background, Etienne stresses that, now that the name change has made him less readily identifiable, he takes no further measures to cover it up.

Not only do I not deny these so-called Jewish origins, but I make them known each time I judge it necessary, so that everything will be clear. I do this when there is an expression of anti-Semitism of any kind or a discussion along those lines. And since one way or another I come into contact with people of social importance, I reveal my origins precisely so that I don't seem to be hiding them—although I must say I do this reluctantly, because I think it absurd.

My situation is a thousand times worse than if I had a Jewish name. Because, obviously, it is far more painful when you are forced to declare your origins—whereas nothing would lead anyone to believe that they were yours—than if it were written in the form of a star, or the name, or something of that sort. But that is the price I pay for my posterity, and I believe that it is well worth it; I regret nothing. My children, too, reveal the origins of my family when it is necessary, but I have enabled them no longer to have anything whatsoever that might prevent their full participation in the community to which they belong.

That is not to say that I believe anti-Semitism to be in the hearts of the French population. But that there is a part of the population who become anti-Semitic as soon as it is demanded of them, no one would think of denying. That Pétain and the faction he represented, which was fundamentally fascistic and anti-Semitic, made use of the German occupation to take power is true beyond a shadow of a doubt. And that someone might succeed in sowing it again—that, yes.

Because, unfortunately, it is much easier to sow a feeling of hate than a feeling of love, one has to be very careful. I am convinced that Zionism is one of the things responsible for the rebirth of anti-Semitism—I don't say that it started it in motion, but it provides it with fertile soil. Zionism is an a posteriori justification of Hitler, because Hitler said that the Jews were foreigners whom it was necessary to expel. Now it is the Zionists who are saying that the Jews are not of the country they live in, that they ought to leave for Israel. They are putting themselves in the position of foreigners, and if they are foreigners, the others will tend to want to chase them out. This is a gamble that places in an aberrant position many of my compatriots who claim Zionism as their own. One cannot be of two countries at the same time, that is not possible. One must choose in life.

Moreover, Zionism itself is necessarily racist, because it is based on blood, and it is based on blood because he is recognized as a Jew who is born of a Jewish mother. The term *of Jewish origin* is a racist term for the same reason. What does it mean? One could say "of religious origin," meaning that the ancestors practiced the Jewish religion. That, yes. And what is Jewish identity? There are religions that might be practiced from father to son for centuries; in that case, where there is a religious tradition, one could talk of a Jewish identity. But if it is not a question of religion, what is it? A racist question, nothing else.

I had occasion to talk with someone who is otherwise extremely charming and of whom I have a high opinion, who lives in France but who was Egyptian before. But his Egyptian family came from Morocco. And before Morocco it was Spain. So in the end, as he told me himself, he is from nowhere. If, then, he can't claim this so-called Jewish identity, what roots remain to him? That is the tragedy: Man cannot live without roots. So if he has none, he invents them himself. But the reality is the nation; the rest is a delusion that adversity rapidly dispels. As long as there was a Jewish nation, there was a Jewish people; when there is a dispersion, there is no more people. As of 2,000 years ago, it was finished.

Now, it is certain that anyone who is obliged to live with the same people for centuries, I mean absolutely any human group, will acquire, whether they want to or not, certain common traits: a manner of expressing themselves, a way of dressing, a common way of thinking. And there are minorities who continue to practice a religion and who, having been prevented from associating with those around them and from exercising the same professions, are forced to acquire common characteristics. That is what makes up what one might refer to as an ethnic group.

But such common characteristics will disappear as soon as the limits disappear, which is what happened with the Frenchmen of Jewish origin who, once the Revolution had wiped out their social inequality, very rapidly blended into the mass. And of whom no one would ever have heard again if they hadn't kept distinctive names on the one hand and if, on the other, it hadn't been for the Nazi wave. It is something that was no longer talked about in France, and it would certainly be better if no one talked about it anywhere. I don't mean the religion, but everything that has to do with people, race, and anything else that might become a source of enmity, of hatred, and of difference.

I myself have always felt as perfectly French as . . . well, as all the others. I have a perfect love for my country, in which I feel all my roots embedded. And I love my country not in a nationalistic way, because I don't believe it to be superior to the others, but in a patriotic way, which is to say, because it is my country. Other ties do not exist for me and have never existed for me. I saw that during the ordeal and have always felt it thereafter. I feel no connection of any sort that might be laid claim to by a would-be Jewish identity, which I expressly reject—not only for myself, but, in fact, for everyone.

The passage through the camps was, for me, a tribute paid to this Judaism that is nothing to me. I consider that I have paid my tribute, and I feel that we are now quits, that it has no more claims to lay on me. I have rid myself of the Jewish cloak, and I have no desire whatsoever to put it back on. Nor do I have any reason to wear it, because it is the cloak of someone else who is a stranger to me; it does not correspond to anything in myself—neither in spirit, nor in sensibility, nor in the family, nor by way of atavism, nor in anything at all. And I think that it is the fact of having lived through this period which gives me a little bit of protection from Zionists and other Jewish militants who would be very happy to crush me—insofar as they know me—but who are held back a little because of it.

Man's honor is in his freedom of choice. It is not because Hitler decreed that I was a Jew that I am obliged to lay claim to this Jewish identity, for that would really be making a present to Hitler. It was precisely for all those reasons that I fought against him: I refused to accept what Hitler had decreed. I choose what I want, and it isn't because someone tells me that an ancestor did some particular thing that I myself am obliged to do it. I feel no obligation in this regard, to the extent that I am a free man.

I am in the first place an artist, and after that a Frenchman. For the rest: No.

BETWEEN
COMPETING POLES

While Leonore Hoffmann, Hélène Terlinden, and Etienne Lenoir felt they had been trapped in a Jewish identity against their will, people who were officially recognized as being of mixed Jewish and non-Jewish origin often found themselves in a similar position—except that they appear, at first blush, to have had a way out. In general, they were not marked with the yellow star, nor were they pushed out of the mainstream of society or threatened to the same degree as those whom Nazi law considered "full Jews." And their parentage may have provided some with an emotional escape hatch as well: The pressures of holding a Jewish identity expressionless within or the demands of repulsing the imposition of a Jewish identity from without could be less intense when there was a non-Jewish identity already in place. But what such people's lot offered in flexibility it gave away in clarity, since oftentimes neither they themselves nor the society around them knew precisely where they belonged.

Both legally and emotionally, the position of those whose origin was mixed tended to be more complex within the German Reich—Germany, Austria, and annexed portions of Czechoslovakia and Poland—than in the rest of the territory under German control. The Nazi racial laws, which drew a distinction between "full Jews" and other categories that represented lesser degrees of Jewish ancestry, were enforced far more assiduously inside the Reich: While the Nazis had qualms about spilling blood that was part "Aryan," the fate of the Mediterranean or Slavic blood that presumably helped fill the veins of those regions' Jews troubled them little or not at all.

But if this heightened legal complexity at least promised to work in the favor of those in Germany, a heightened emotional complexity was potentially burdensome. In most of the countries they occupied, the Germans were alien not only to Jews but to the majorities among whom the Jews made their homes; thus, people with Jewish roots did not necessarily have a reason to distance themselves from the society in which they had lived, and they almost certainly had no basis for identifying with the force that was oppressing them. But in Germany, so sharply divided between Jews and non-Jews, an individual with ties to both sides was caught between forces whose opposition to one another was absolute: The state, with the support of most Germans, was humiliating the Jews and seeking to wipe them out, while German Jews generally needed to reject state authority in order to preserve their self-worth, and to resist it in order to preserve their lives.

The conflict that had rent society could therefore be mirrored in the persons of those who had a foot in each camp—although it is not easy to know, for a given individual, whether this conflict was created, supplied with content, or simply sharpened by historic events. Ostensibly, several paths to resolution of this dilemma lay open to those confronted with it: identifying with one side to the exclusion of the other, identifying with both sides, and identifying with neither. But, considering what was going on around them, how could they know which alternative was authentic? What might be the basis for choice? And did they in fact have the inner freedom to choose?

In the case of Ernst Franz, historical and personal reality are entwined to an extraordinary degree. Growing up in the strained household of his non-Jewish, German father and Jewish mother, Ernst reacted against what he saw as his mother's insecurity by rejecting his own "Jewish part"—to the point of backing the Nazis. "I identified with this aggressive tendency against the Jewish people," Ernst observes as he recalls taking part in a Hitler Youth demonstration. "But for the other part I felt, 'I am related somewhat to these Jewish people who are to be killed.'" Although Ernst's intellectual appraisal of Nazi ideology changed with age, he is left struggling with the anti-Jewish prejudice which lives on in his heart—and which he directs most fiercely against himself.

Ariel Levi grew up outside the Reich, but the Zagreb of his youth, as capital of a breakaway Croatian state that had aligned itself with Germany, was full of Nazi sympathizers. The Croatians had their own equivalent of the Hitler Youth, and Ariel, whose mother was Jewish and whose father's identity he never knew, became a member—although, unlike Ernst, he joined not out of identification but for purposes of disguise. It may be impossible to tell whether Ariel's passage through an assortment of affiliations—in a few brief years, he went from hunted Jew to Croatian "fascist" to Communist youth leader to Zionist immigrant— is the cause or the reflection of what he calls a mistrust of "grown-up society." But in his most spontaneous declaration of who he is, the adult Ariel invokes an identity that is purely personal: "I am a painter," he says, and, as for the rest, "I've got nothing to do with it."

While Ariel Levi can't quite say what being a Jew means to him, Walter Roth answers the same question unequivocally: It means moral responsibility. Walter never thought of himself as anything other than Jewish, but it was only when he was offered a chance to renounce his Jewishness—and supposedly to improve the odds of his and his father's survival by doing so—that he seemed to make it his own. Perhaps he equates being Jewish with taking responsibility because it was through a considered and purposeful choice to "become a Jew" that he transformed his identification from grudging to affirmative. But what made him choose the course he took? Why did he reject the majority society when there might have been so many advantages to joining it? Why refuse, as he disdainfully puts it, to "take refuge in the ordinary"?

Ernst Franz

Ernst Franz was born in Berlin in 1929. His father was an advertising salesman for a magazine publisher; his paternal grandfather, well known as a former national sports champion, was a prominent figure in the German publishing world. On his father's side, all were Protestants and longtime Berliners; it was what Ernst calls "the 'Aryan' part of the family." Ernst's mother was a Jew born in the Rumania of the Austro-Hungarian Empire. Her family had moved to Vienna, then to Berlin, where her father had set up a small factory.

In the late 1920s, Ernst's parents had both been employed by the same firm. At the instigation of a co-worker who thought they would make a good couple, each was told that the other was interested. This scheming led to a marriage that soon ran into difficulties.

My father had originally been in love with a young woman who was going with his cousin. When the cousin and this girl broke up a couple of years later, right around the time of my birth, my father met up with her again. All of a sudden he felt, "This is *the* woman of my life," and they continued seeing each other.

In 1933, the year Hitler was named chancellor of Germany, Ernst's father was on the verge of leaving his wife. While the political climate, Ernst believes, had in no way inspired his father's personal desires, it all but dictated his decision not to act on them: A divorce, it was feared, would remove any protection the marriage might afford his wife and son against the Nazis.

My father's family, which had not been in favor of his marriage to a Jewish girl, now told him out of a feeling of loyalty, "This is a very difficult situation for the Jewish people. You can't leave her." So my father, who was very susceptible to such influence, changed his mind and stayed with my mother and with me.

My mother, however, being insecure in general and particularly insecure emotionally, became basically peevish from that time on. She clung to my father while at the same time grumbling and yelling at him, weeping, and showing an increasing lack of tenderness toward him. And, especially in 1933, when I was four, she clung to me as well. Youngsters of that age begin to react against this kind of overprotection; I must have sensed my freedom was being restricted and had begun to feel hatred toward my mother. When my father came home, I ran up to him and tattled on her: "Mummy has done this, Mummy has done that." So I had troubles with my mother before I knew that she was Jewish and I was half-Jewish.

Ernst was in the dark as to his mother's Jewish origins throughout his early childhood. There were no religious clues, as the family's sole observance was attending Protestant services at Christmas.

My mother never mentioned the Jewish religion, and she had no religious books. She was not brought up orthodox to begin with and had loosened whatever ties her parents might have had after she came to Berlin, and especially after she married my father. I think this had something to do with the social prominence of my grandfather, a typically German, authoritarian paterfamilias who was very much respected by my father. When my mother had finally won my grandfather over, she felt that this family had accepted her because she had shown a great deal of un-Jewishness, and in the process of overadjusting my mother began to believe that she was not Jewish anymore. I may be exaggerating a bit, but I think she was on her way to forgetting it.

During the Nazi period, my mother did whatever she could to disguise her Jewish belonging. Because she was unquestionably identifiable as Jewish from her facial characteristics, she had her nose operated on in 1934 or 1935. The operation was very successful as far as her own conception of herself was concerned, and perhaps also for the way others perceived her. At the time, I didn't understand why she had done it. But I remember wondering about it, so there was obviously a suspicion on my part that there was something going on or that something was different with us.

The hostile atmosphere of prewar Berlin made life increasingly tense, something that seems only to have magnified Mrs. Franz's insecurities and, with them, the conflicts in the family. But Ernst's understanding of his mother's origins, and of the threat they carried, remained vague. His parents avoided bringing the matter up—his mother for reasons of personal reluctance, his father out of prudence.

Although Ernst's father had, in the years leading up to 1933, shared his own father's right-wing nationalism, he was no believer in Nazi racial ideology and had never supported Hitler. He shied, however, from providing his son any political or moral direction, "knowing," as Ernst says, "that a youngster of that age could involuntarily let the cat out of the bag." Such a danger might have arisen on one occasion, when Ernst referred to Germany's form of government as "dictatorship" in answer to a question from his history teacher. "I did this in the naïve conviction that what I had heard my parents say was in line with the official language," he recalls. "We were fortunate that this teacher wasn't a fanatical Nazi who would have informed the authorities."

Spending his early years in a neighborhood where there lived "a number of liberal if not to say anti-Nazi families," Ernst was as sheltered in his immediate surroundings as he was at home.

I don't remember being discriminated against by friends or in school before 1937 or so. The beginning came when the primary school teacher asked the class "Who's part Jewish?" or "Who's mixed?" or something like that. I'm not sure whether I answered "I am" or whether he already knew from investigations the school had made, but he said my name. I felt as if something had happened to me: I went pale, and others looked at me, and all of a sudden I was a special person, somebody who had a kind of stigma. After class, the teacher—who was relatively German and authoritarian and strict, just as all the teachers were—came up to me and said some kind words that did quite a bit to help me overcome the situation. Because, before that, I had had the feeling, "Now I'm no good at all."

Ernst had turned nine by November 9–10, 1938, Kristallnacht, or the "Night of Broken Glass," when Jews throughout Germany were murdered or arrested, synagogues were destroyed, and businesses owned by Jews were sacked.

The next day, together with a couple of friends from school, I ran along the streets in the direction of a synagogue that had been set on fire by the SA* during the night. We went in and saw the ashes; I still

---

*SA: Sturmabteilung; the Storm Troopers, a Nazi Party paramilitary organization also known in English as the Brownshirts.

remember the postcards, half burnt, with stamps from all over the world. And I remember a Jewish woman—I must already have had a notion of Jewishness—whom I experienced as ugly, and her son, whom I experienced as ugly in turn. The woman yelled at some of the people standing there, "You will regret what you have done!" I looked at her, and I heard people snicker, at least some of the people. At that moment I knew, not that I belonged with her, but that there was a relationship between her, the son, and myself—and I didn't like that at all. So that was the beginning of my inner resistance against this part of myself.

In this synagogue I was approached by an SA man, or perhaps he was a policeman. These people had developed a specific sensitivity to Jewish facial characteristics that had to do with the hatred and all that, and obviously seeing in me a little bit of Jewishness, he wondered whether I was Jewish. When he came up to me, though, he saw a pin I had gotten from the Winterhilfe* or somewhere; and he must not have been that highly sensitive or that sharp intellectually, because he said, "He can't be Jewish, he's wearing that pin." I was so relieved that he said this, because to my mind he was saying, "No, you are not Jewish. You don't belong with these people here, you belong with us."

What he had seen at the synagogue, along with the whispered conversations of his parents and relatives at home, awakened in Ernst a feeling of impending danger. But it was not until the war had begun in late 1939 that Ernst's father found reason to offer explanation.

My father had a talk with me, and the solemn face he displayed made me feel very uneasy and anticipate that something extraordinary might be at stake. He said, "You probably don't know it or haven't fully realized it, but your mother is different from other people. She is nichtarisch."† He didn't say "Jewish"; that word was taboo for him, at least in his relations with me, as it was to remain for me in the decades to come. I can see myself standing there doubly stunned: Here is my father confirming what I have heard in school—and then doing so at this late moment, when he should have told me a year or two before.

Winterhilfe: a Nazi Party–run "charity" that collected obligatory "donations," purportedly to aid those suffering from hardship during cold weather.

Although Ernst spoke English during most of the interview, he often left Nazi terms and names of organizations in German.

†*nichtarisch(e):* non-Aryan (adjective); *arisch(e):* Aryan (adjective); *Arier:* Aryan (noun).

Partly because my father wasn't explicit enough about the whole thing—although also because I had a friend whose mother was half-Jewish and I wanted to be like him—I believed then and for several years thereafter that I was only one-quarter Jewish, or three-quarters Arier. The way my father informed me was so cautious, in fact, that the question of which side he might have been on politically remained open as well.

I actually think my father told me when he did because he was forced to. At the age of ten, all arische youngsters were enlisted in the Jungvolk* unless prevented on specific grounds, and quite a few of my schoolmates and friends had more or less automatically been made members. Though I already had a suspicion of why I couldn't go in myself, I saw people my age in uniform, and you want to belong. *I* wanted to belong. It was probably because he had sensed this that my father finally told me.

Around half a year later, when I was eleven, my father managed to get me into the Jungvolk. I don't know whether he saw that I was having this problem with my mother, but he felt—and quite rightly so, I believe—that as I was an only child, I should be given the feeling that I wasn't different, that I belonged among the others. My father usually told the truth, feeling it was less risky, so I imagine he said, "My wife is thus-and-such, and my boy is a good boy who wants to be like the others." People were not as rigid in those days as they were later, and apparently there was a relatively tolerant and good-natured fellow at the headquarters of the Hitlerjugend who said, "I understand" and "Your boy should be educated to become a German boy."

At this point, a very complicated process began: I started—under the influence not only of the Jungvolk but also of school, and the teachers, and of the news on the radio and in the papers—to identify with Nazism and with the cause for which Hitler claimed to be fighting the war. We all had maps and map tacks with little German flags attached; with mine, I followed the progress of the German army in the countries Hitler occupied just as enthusiastically as my arische friends.

---

*Jungvolk: the junior division of the Hitler Youth (Hitlerjugend), for boys aged ten through fourteen.

When I was eleven or twelve, I prayed. Before I fell asleep, I said, "Dear God, let us gain victory." Let *us*—meaning, "I belong."

And although my relationship to my mother was, of course, negative not only because of her being Jewish, this was just the time when I was furnished with arguments against the Jewish people. As soon as I had learned that my mother was Jewish, I had begun to rationalize the aggression I felt in terms of "She is responsible for the fact that I am being discriminated against in school and among my friends," and so on. There were enough unpleasant occurrences for a boy to nourish bad feelings toward his mother if he held her responsible in this way. Under different circumstances, I would probably have found something else: that she was short, or that she was tall, or whatnot. As things were, it had to be that she was Jewish.

But out of the image Ernst had of his own physical appearance grew a double-edged relationship to Nazi ideology.

When I was ten or eleven and already had some knowledge—or at least an idea—of my situation, I came across a bunch of old copies of *Der Stürmer.** In them I saw these cartoons: the typical short, fat man with a watch chain on his fat belly and, of course, the nose, the Jewish nose that was a specially emphasized detail in Nazi propaganda. I had an uncle who looked like these caricatures, or at least bore some resemblance to them, and I felt it was true, Jewish people looked like that. Then, when I saw my own nose in the mirror, I thought, "Oh, God! I have this nose, and now I'm ugly!"

From my present point of view, I think this was off-base, although I realize that the self-perception I had did make me unattractive to a certain extent because it had a psychological impact on my looks. Fortunately, however, I was tall. It was very, very important—crucial—that I could say to myself, "You may not look like those Germanic blond giants, but at least you are tall." Had I been short and fat, I'm sure you would find a different person here today.

Another part of the anti-Jewish propaganda held that Jews were the enemies of working people, and there is a story from 1940 or '41 that shows I must have accepted that part. I had a friend who came from a

---

Der Stürmer: a Nazi newspaper known for its violent anti-Semitic propaganda.

not very pro-Nazi background but who, of course, had also been influenced by the propaganda. One day, when we were talking about a workman who hadn't done a good job in the apartment, my mother said, "Ach, you know those workers . . ." My friend and I must have had some agreement beforehand about Jewish people being no good, because when my mother said this, my friend winked at me, giving me a look that I took to mean, "Jews are always wealthy and don't want to have anything to do with working people." I remember that I blushed, or went pale, because of course I didn't want my mother to say things like that and to be looked down upon by my friend as typically Jewish.

Ernst's friendship with this fellow—whom he describes as "blond, and a physically strong guy, although not taller"—was warm and lasting despite what he remembers as "an undercurrent of competition." The friend, who was from a Catholic family, invited Ernst to a monastery where Catholic schoolchildren went for vacation; after the boy's father had spoken with the prior, Ernst was admitted. During his stay, another subtle yet significant event occurred.

I had been given some candy by one of the fellows there. A package then came from my parents, and either I myself felt, or I was reminded by my friend, that I should give the fellow something in return. When we were already in bed—there were five or more boys to a room—I threw two candies over to him. At that very moment I felt it was a mistake, because it was not the equivalent of what he had given me, which was perhaps half a chocolate bar. It was just an impulsive reaction, but I had already seen the critical look of my friend and I couldn't change it anymore.

My friend then mentioned—or I myself felt—that "this Jewish part of you makes you stingy." That was a shock. Looking back, I understand why I was stingy: It didn't have much, if anything, to do with Jewishness, but with the position of someone who did not feel part of things and who thus wanted to have more for himself. But again, this was the propaganda: "The Jews take but don't give." And I identified.

Ernst kept his Jewish descent secret from his Jungvolk comrades, but even this could lead to what he describes as "a very difficult situation."

I remember marching in a large demonstration of Jungvolk and Hitlerjugend. We were singing a typical German anti-Jewish song that the SA or SS had composed:

Die Juden ziehen dahin, daher.
Sie ziehen zum Roten Meer.
Die Wellen schlagen zu.
Die Welt hat Ruh'! *

With one part of myself I was against the Jews, and thus I identified with this aggressive tendency against the Jewish people; but for the other part I felt, "I am related somewhat to these Jewish people who are to be killed by drowning." Then came the very clear feeling: "How good that nobody knows I am half"—or "quarter," or whatever—"Jewish!" And "How *come* nobody has any sort of suspicion?"

Later on, I voluntarily joined a Fanfarenzug, a music unit made up of trumpets and drums that played fanfares at large meetings and rallies. I was the only one in this unit who also had a bugle, which I had bought with my pocket money in order to outdo the others—my interpretation today being that because I felt I was not as good as they were, I wanted to be better. So I had a trumpet in my hand and my bugle around my neck, and on certain occasions—for instance, when we were collecting scrap metal for the military—I gave a signal so that people would open their windows and look out. Some, of course, yelled at us—"Shut up and go away!"—while others didn't dare. But I felt great. I was somebody.

Partly through his membership in the Fanfarenzug, Ernst had become a standout in his Jungvolk unit by the time he was thirteen, in 1942. Impressed by his intelligence and dedication, the boys who acted as "Führer," or leaders, of his Jungschaft and Jungzug—rough equivalents of the Cub Scout den and pack—invited Ernst to a social evening attended by leaders like themselves and by members of the girls' organizations corresponding to the Jungvolk and Hitler Youth. Ernst recalls feeling "very insecure" during the outing, which took place in a large, wooded park; "all these guys were Führer," he explains, "plus they were a couple of years older and much more aggressive toward the girls."

After a while, my Jungzugführer asked me whether I wouldn't like to become a Führer myself. That was a difficult predicament for me—it was, as we say, the moment of truth. I told him, "No, it is not possible,

---

*Literally: "The Jews wander here and there. / They march to the Red Sea. / The waves crash together. / The world has peace!"

because I am thus-and-such." I think I said "a quarter"—again a quarter. I was close to trembling; there we were in the woods, only two or three meters from the comrades, and I just hoped nobody would hear.

I felt I needed to tell my leader very frankly why I couldn't, because I knew that, the moment he applied, they would automatically check my background. It would then be a question of only a few weeks before they found out about me anyway, and waiting this out would have been far worse than coming out with the truth right off. By making him my confidant, I tried to force my leader not to tell the others—and I think this was the right strategy, because it seems he respected the matter as something between him and me and didn't talk about it. If, on the other hand, I had said yes and let him find out for himself, it could have been much worse. He might have come and asked, "Why didn't you tell me?"—and then when there might be a hundred people around.

But there was a further reason: Everyone yearned to be a leader. At least that's the way I looked at it, although maybe it was only because I knew I myself could not be that I believed this. I had the intellectual qualifications; and although I was too fearful to be very good in sports, I was tall. So I felt that, as somebody who was considered a potential Führer, I should have an explanation.

About six months later, however, I conceived an urgent need to be looked upon as a leader. I went to shops that sold badges and braids and what have you for the Jungvolk and Hitlerjugend, and I said, "I have just become Jungschaftsführer, and I would like to buy the braid"—there was a red-and-white braid that the Jungschaftsführer wore.

I went from one shop to the other, and most people said, "I'm sorry, I'll have to see your commission."

I said, "Well, I don't have it yet. I'll come back"—although I knew I wouldn't.

After all these refusals I was feeling pretty bad. But, finally, I came to the shop of an old man who probably didn't give a good goddamn about the whole thing anyway, and he gave me the braid.

Around that time, I was invited to spend a two-week vacation with a branch of my Aryan family in Hildesheim. I decided to travel in full uniform, which wasn't exactly unusual, but not entirely typical unless you were along with a group. And I felt particularly conspicuous: Number one, I had the special shoulder straps of the music unit; number two,

I had the Jungschaftsführer's braid; and, number three, I did not have a patch denoting even the lowest rank in the Jungvolk, whereas there was hardly a leader who didn't have a rank. In the train, I was under constant stress, because from the beginning of the trip I anticipated that people might be asking me questions.

I became more nervous once I saw some youngsters from a unit that was on its way to Hanover. They noticed me, and perhaps some of them even recognized me, because with our horns the Fanfarenzug stood out at the rallies. I of course was saluted first, which was what I had wanted to enjoy the whole time: the almost sexual, or at least sensual pleasure of being a leader and being looked upon as such. So I was this little half-Jewish boy who wanted not only to feel that he belonged, but to make certain he belonged; and a Führer, as the one who must be saluted first, has to belong.

While he was saluting me, one of the guys looked at me very, very closely—interested, and a little suspicious and questioning. I still re-member the guy: not a very tall fellow, a little older, husky, with a kind of piercing gaze. Either he knew me and knew that I was not a Führer or he had become suspicious because I had the braid but no patch on my arm; he may have been a Jungschaftsführer himself, I'm no longer sure. I just trembled and wondered, "What will happen? Will he approach me? Will he ask me?" But he didn't, and I began to feel relief.

In my nervousness, however, I envisioned exactly what a couple of weeks later came to pass. My father and I were summoned by a very high official to the headquarters of the Jungvolk in Berlin. "People have reported seeing you wearing a braid in the train to Hanover," he said.

I went pale, of course, but I said, "That's not true," and I insisted. It's a funny thing, but it was probably more on account of my father than on account of that official. I don't think I wanted to confess to my father that I had done such a thing—because I felt it was wrong, that it was silly, to admit that you needed to be looked up to by people in that way.

So we went home, and I was still stunned, but my father said, "That's strange. How could anyone say this? Because, as you told me, it's not true."

And I said, "Yeah."

But I couldn't stand it much longer than two hours. My anxiety over lying to that fellow grew; it was 'forty-two by then, and I was more mature and knew more about what was going on. I felt I had to tell him the truth before he checked and summoned us again, at which time I wouldn't be able to lie; but I felt I had to tell him in the absence of my father. I excused myself, saying I was going to play with my friends, and I went to the nearest telephone booth and called the man.

I said, "Heil Hitler, Thus-and-such-führer! I lied to you, because I didn't want my father to know. But it's true, I did it." Then I told him the whole story: that I had done it because I couldn't become a leader owing to my being Jewish—half-Jewish or quarter-Jewish, I don't know whether I knew the full truth at that time—which is, in turn, the reason I wanted to have the feeling of being a leader.

And he understood; I mean, that was odd. He said, "All right, don't worry. Heil Hitler!"

Slowly, Ernst's understanding of his position in Nazi society evolved— partly through the results of his attempts to be included, partly through "little situations of a discriminatory character" which arose in everyday life and which, he says, "had a great impact on my consciousness and my feeling of security."

What I remember as a very, very unpleasant incident, and one of the first in which I got a clearer picture of my situation, took place in 1941 or 1942. I wanted to go to a movie based on a story by my favorite writer at the time, Karl May, a famous German author who had written about a hundred books of adventure tales. I was standing there in joyful anticipation about to go in when one of these Nazifrauen,* who was sitting outside the theater, asked me, "Are you arisch?"

Stubbornly, I said, "Yes, of course." What could I say? I was not able to stand my own reality and identity in the situation, and especially because there's always the group thing: There were others waiting in line, and they looked at me. She gave me the ticket and I went in, but I didn't see the film for half an hour. Going to the movies became a risky thing for me, psychologically speaking, until a couple of years had passed without this happening again and I relaxed.

Although nothing much happened in school, discrimination did take place in the sense that I had to get up at the beginning of each new school year when the teacher checked the books—not to see who was

---

Nazifrauen: Nazi women.

Jewish, because Jewish children were no longer in school, but to see who was mixed and to what degree.* Until 1943, I kept saying I was only one-quarter Jewish, so I stood up when the teacher asked, "Who is three-quarters Aryan?" The new classmates turned toward me, and of course I interpreted their looks as more severe than they were probably meant to be. Then, when the teacher asked, "Who is half?" two others stood up, and I sometimes looked down upon them. It was that bad.

About six months after being caught for wearing the braid, Ernst received a form letter telling him that he had been excluded from the Jungvolk.

That was 1943, a time of stricter interpretation and enforcement of the Nuremberg Laws. The war was already more or less lost, but instead of realizing this and figuring out the consequences, some people became more aggressive toward those they supposed potentially dangerous to the regime—which the Jews in actual fact were not. So what they did to me, they did to everyone who was half-Jewish; and they didn't say I had been booted out in disgrace or anything like that. I, however, connected this with my guilt and ascribed being excluded to having pretended to be a leader: "This is the sanction you deserve after what you have done."

––––––

*Because he was descended from two Jewish grandparents and had never been a member of a Jewish religious community, Ernst was one of 65,000 in the German Reich whom the Nuremberg Laws classified as Mischling ersten Grades, "half-breed of the first degree"; a second category, Mischling zweiten Grades, or "half-breed of the second degree," applied to those descended from one Jewish grandparent. Mischlinge, while they were "non-Aryans," were not considered "Jews," and Ernst's status brought some protection to his mother, whose marriage was regarded as a privilegierte Mischehe, "privileged mixed marriage," because she had a child by an "Aryan" husband. A Mischling ersten Grades and his or her Jewish parent were generally exempted from the harshest anti-Jewish measures, including being forced to wear the yellow star and being deported to concentration camps, but they were systematically excluded from many schools and professions, from the military, and from the Nazi Party organizations that were an all-pervasive force in Germany's economic and social as well as political life. In addition, Jewish partners in mixed marriages were often assigned to forced labor, as was the case with Ernst's mother. Mischlinge zweiten Grades were subject to fewer restrictions but still suffered discrimination. And for "non-Aryans," as for Jews, the slightest legal infraction—proven or merely suspected—could have fatal consequences. The lives of mixed families were thus fraught with extreme uncertainty and anxiety, particularly during the war years.

Of course, my guilt feelings were probably quite complex. At the beginning of 1941, I had visited my Jewish grandma and aunt, who were still in Berlin, in full uniform. I loved my grandma on one level, but I wanted to demonstrate: "I'm different. I've made it on the other side of the fence. I do not belong with you." My grandma didn't say anything about it, and I don't know how she felt, but she must have felt very bad—although perhaps she was so good that she told herself, "As long as the boy is happy . . ." In July or so of '41 my grandma was deported to Auschwitz or one of the other extermination camps, and we had received the information that she was dead; the same went for my uncle and aunt. Most likely, the guilt I felt was related not only to the authorities but to these other things as well.

Meanwhile, I was beginning to exert a kind of reality control. I think that as early as 1942 it had begun to dawn on me that I was half-Jewish, even if I didn't accept it, at least not fully. The deportation of my grandma was big knowledge, and since I somehow knew or had heard that my grandfather had also been Jewish, I was in a position to figure out that I couldn't be a quarter, I had to be half. Then, as I gradually became more and more involved in the talks of my parents and relatives—about the situation, about Hitler, and about what had happened to my grandma and to my uncle, whom I liked very much—I began the very difficult emotional process of identifying with the Jewish part in myself. Or, to put it more precisely, I began to see the regime in a different light: I didn't pray anymore; I saw things critically; and I saw that it could mean my death, as well as the death of my parents—or at least of my mother—if it lasted more than another year or two.

Ernst's change of direction more or less coincided with the return in 1943 of his father, who since 1940 had seen his wife and son only while on leave from Germany's air-raid police. When command of that unit was shifted from Göring to Himmler, those with Jewish connections were rooted out—and although he held several decorations, Ernst's father was discharged upon declaring himself unwilling to divorce his wife. Back in Berlin, he found work in an auto parts warehouse, preferring that in any case to fighting fires.

When the family was together, we centered around my mother. There was a mixture of solidarity and concern, although I think the solidarity was with my mother's role as Jewish rather than with her person. She didn't discuss her feelings about being Jewish. I don't think she even mentioned the word *Jewish* when she showed her grief that her mother and brother were in concentration camps. And I can't recall her talking about what was happening to the Jewish people; she just said, "It's terrible," or she cried. But our concern was not just what they were doing or might do to the wife or mother, it was more a role thing; while we stuck together and would have done everything to protect my mother, the feelings toward the person herself were mixed. There was not much going on in the marriage, so I think there was some covert aggression on my father's part—he was brought up not to show his feelings, at least not feelings of discontent or displeasure. I, on the other hand, released my aggression in criticism, in teasing, and by not understanding when she was afraid.

Still, there were days when we laughed together; such is life. My father did his duty: He brought my mother to the S-Bahn* station early each morning so she could go to the factory where she did compulsory labor mending army uniforms, and he went every month to the Jewish section of the ration bureau to pick up her coupon books because she was ashamed to go herself. The presence of friends or relatives who sometimes lived with us had a neutralizing effect on the aggressive undercurrent toward my mother. And the fact that my parents treated me as an equal—"You belong to our group, and we have to stick together and see how we can survive"—made me grow. The growth, however, was probably more intellectual than emotional, because there was still this kind of ambivalence toward my mother.

Ernst continued moving gradually away from his earlier identification with the Nazi regime. He points to a pair of events whose contrast, he says, "shows that I was making progress toward accepting my mother and identifying with her as being Jewish and being threatened, as I was myself."

The first took place in 1943, shortly before I was excluded from the Jungvolk, during a bad air raid on our district. Our air-raid warden was a Nazi—not a longtime Nazi but a former Communist, one of those who changed affiliations the way you'd change your shirt. He knew that my mother was Jewish and my father was not, and while he couldn't do much against my mother, he managed to show his hatred, or disrespect, or whatever.

My mother and I were in the cellar, and when the warden saw me,

---

*S-Bahn: Stadtbahn; one of two rapid transit lines in Berlin.

he grabbed me and said, "Let's go, Hitlerjunge! Come with me and put out the fires!" He wanted me to go out with him onto the roof of our building to search for duds, as firebombs occasionally hit without going off right away. It was a risky business, but I'd had experience, and I was probably no more frightened than he himself was. Besides, although I didn't like the guy, I took this as another confirmation of my belonging: I was almost fourteen, I was a German boy, I was courageous. I wanted to go.

But then my mother interfered. In a sense, it took courage—although I think that, in her anxiety that I might be killed, she even forgot that this guy was a Nazi and that he knew she was Jewish. She grabbed him, or at least touched him, and said, "No! My son shall not go up with you!" He made a big fuss about it: "A Jew stuck her hands on me," and so on. This was ridiculous, but I was in conflict. I "hated" my mother when she showed so much apprehension in public because Aryan women, at least those my mother's age, didn't show that much. And at that moment I didn't want to be identified with my mother, not so much because of her being Jewish, but because of her behavior, which I found silly and which debased me in a way. I wanted to show that I had courage—or, at the very least, I did not want my mother to interfere. In the end I went up with the guy, but it was a very bad situation.

The second event took place in 1944. We had another bad air raid, and the light was flickering, and my mother, as usual, was whimpering. This I still hated; Jewishness meant cowardice, one of the Nazi stereotypes with which I had identified completely. But while I wanted my mother to show courage, on the other hand I felt I should protect her. So, with all sorts of inhibitions—it was very difficult—I kind of put my arm around her and said, "Take it easy, it's not that bad." That was an important step forward.

As the bombings intensified toward mid-1944, the school Ernst attended was moved to the countryside. In many ways a sheltered child, Ernst had felt ill at ease during a similar move four years earlier; in addition, he now doubted that he could continue claiming to be one-quarter Jewish and thus suspected that he might not be permitted along in any case. With his father's consent, Ernst notified the authorities that he wished to leave school, and he immediately received orders from the labor office to work in a munitions plant. He had, however, already begun working unofficially in the auto parts firm that employed his father, which was

*classed as essential to the war effort; thanks to the intercession of the firm's
attorney, he was allowed to continue there in an official capacity.*

*That summer, the German army, in desperate need of officer candidates, held
a series of recruitment rallies. Through an apparent oversight, Ernst was ordered
to report to barracks in suburban Berlin.*

Even though I knew this couldn't apply to me anymore, there was
no way of not going. A sort of foster brother of mine—a friend we'd
taken in because his mother was in Bavaria for some reason and his
father was at the Eastern Front—had been to such a rally a couple of
days before, and he played a joke on me. "If you don't volunteer," he
said, "they'll put you into a tank and throw dummy grenades at you."
With this lie in my mind, I went. I was anticipating great humiliation,
which I had experienced in school and elsewhere and which I thus
feared more than physical risk.

After they had shown us some films, a captain decorated with the
Ritterkreuz came in and said, "Who among you is willing to volunteer
for the German army?" I got up. What I thought was "First, adjust to the
situation, don't stay seated; then, when questioned, say, 'Yes, but I can't,
because I'm half-Jewish'; and, from the others, 'You bloody Jew' "—
although practically nobody had ever said that to me in all those years.
But what happened was that the others—the Aryans—said, "I have to
ask my mother," or "I'll think about it," while the half-Jew got up and
said, "Yes, I will."

Now I couldn't retreat. The captain said, "Oh, wonderful!" and
clapped me on the shoulder. I was taken—along with only one other in
our group of fifteen, a boy who was not part Jewish—to a special room
where you could inspect antitank weapons and such. One of the fellows
set off a bazooka, not realizing it was loaded; a jet of flame came out the
back and, as I was standing nearby, I took the whole thing right in the
ass. I, who was there only out of a desire not to be discriminated against,
was the most seriously injured of anyone.

*Ernst spent six weeks in military hospitals. During his convalescence, a
series of ironic incidents brought home to him the fact that his outlook was shifting.
The first occurred in Berlin on July 20, 1944, the day after he was wounded and
a date famed as that of an unsuccessful attempt on Hitler's life. The second took
place after he had been moved to Karlsbad.*

In Berlin I was in a room with German soldiers who were saying,

"Those bloody officers! Those bastards who wanted to kill our Führer!" Then, as I lay there, I was visited by high officials of the Hitlerjugend, because I was "Hitlerjunge Ernst Franz"; either they didn't check my file, or there was no indication that I was half-Jewish. They shook my hand and called me "brave boy"—while my mother, my Jewish mother, sat pale and shy at my bedside and had her hand shaken as well. I did not clarify the situation—how could I, or should I?—but I had reached a state in which I found it almost amusing.

Later, in Karlsbad, I had an experience that brought me back to the time when I was marching and singing that the Jews should be drowned in the Red Sea. A couple of fellows and I went to the movies, and they were showing *Jud Süss*—it would have to be *Jud Süss*.* Afterwards, we discussed the movie, and they obviously didn't take me for Jewish, or half-Jewish. "Oh, those Jews," they said. "And what that Jew bastard did to that poor blond girl! Don't you agree, Ernst?"

I said, "Yeah," but this time only because I needed to adjust, to pretend to be as critical as they were. I must confess that I didn't see the film as I would today—simply as propaganda against the Jews—but I saw it with the uneasy feeling, "Ach, the Jews," and "I would rather not belong to them." I had identified because I'd had to—because it was reality—and this was another acknowledgment of the stereotype I still held and would keep for many, many more years. But I was now at the point where I could take it with a grain of salt.

Back home, life continued for Ernst as a series of paradoxes. Among his duties at the auto parts warehouse was handling correspondence with offices of the SS. As tension increased in the war's final months, Ernst carried, in lieu of an ID, a form letter stamped with the signature of Adolf Hitler that he had received after volunteering for the army. This document helped him through one particularly tense identity check, conducted by a patrol of Hitler Youth that stopped him as he accompanied his mother home from work.

Ernst and his father kept the warehouse in business as late as April 28, 1945—when they sold a truck part to an SS man who came in bleeding from a shrapnel wound—but they spent most of the war's final days in a basement hiding from the German military police, who were rounding up all able-bodied men and

---

*Jud Süss: Jew Süss; a renowned anti-Semitic film produced in Germany in 1940.

*putting them into uniform. It was only on the eve of Berlin's fall that, figuring there
was finally more to fear from the Russians than from his countrymen, Ernst burned
the letter bearing Hitler's signature.*

*Ernst's parents stayed together after the war, but their marriage remained
affectionless, and Ernst's father stepped up relations with the "other woman," whom
he had been allowed to see once a year since agreeing not to leave his wife in the
early 1930s. From 1949, when a daughter was born to the couple, Ernst found
himself continually involved in disputes over the frequency and manner of his
father's visits to the lover and child. Despite everything, Ernst's mother calmed
down to a certain extent, "drawing gratification from her housewifely activities,"
which, Ernst says, "she performed splendidly, winning praise from guests and from
my father, who was always polite."*

*Ernst did not move out of his parents' house until 1961, when he was
thirty-three years old. But he spent 1951–52 at a university in the U.S. Midwest,
where he studied the sociology of racism, was active in the campus chapter of the
NAACP, and, to his discomfort, often found his Jewish origins a topic of discussion. "After the war, Germans were afraid to disclose their attitude toward Jews,"
he recalls, "and nobody would have dared ask me, 'Are you Jewish?' But in the
States I had to face quite a few situations in which people did ask me."*

*Feeling more secure in "a country which, for this reason among others, had
fought Hitler," Ernst was able on certain occasions to muster a forthright reaction:
He either repulsed unwelcome inquiries with a brusque "mind your own business"
or "stood up a little bit" for his background. And when a German roommate
bragged that he had been in the SS, Ernst was outspoken in his disapproval—
although he believes he "would have acted the same" in Germany, because it was
a "personal situation" rather than a fleeting encounter.*

It was different, though, in an incident in Florida, where I had gone
with a German student who was obviously anti-Semitic. He had mentioned his feelings, but he nevertheless had picked me—or I had picked
him, or we had picked each other—as company for a trip to Fort
Lauderdale. We spent New Year's Eve in a tavern, and at our table were
a bunch of sailors. As I was coming back from the lavatory, my friend
Kurt and one of the sailors were talking and looking at me, and all of
a sudden the sailor asked, "Are you Jewish?"

He didn't say it the way a Nazi might have said it during the Nazi
period—"Are you Jewish? Get out of here!"—but I was startled because
I didn't know what to make of it. There was something in his face; I

sensed an undertone if not of hostility, then of contempt. I concede that my perceptions may have been biased, but that there is anti-Semitism in the States is well known, is it not? On top of everything, he was a sailor, and my image of a sailor was that of a person who would rather beat you up than discuss things. And while there were a number of sailors, I was alone; my friend was a former boxing champion, but as he was anti-Semitic himself, I wasn't sure he would have defended me.

I was afraid of provoking this sailor with defiant answers, so I sort of talked around the question, saying, "No, I'm only half-Jewish," or something like that. Although it's true that I'm not Jewish in the sense of being totally Jewish and not even in terms of religion, when I said no, it was a lie. I was trying to present my non-Jewish half to him as OK, as like he was—just like when I got up in school and said, "I'm only one-quarter Jewish."

In Florida, we stayed with the parents of a Jewish fellow student from college, and when I mentioned to them that I was half-Jewish, they invited me to services. So for the second time in my life I was in a synagogue—but this time it was a functioning synagogue, not a burning one—and there I was greeted and bidden good-bye with "Shalom." I think I mentioned this to my friend, never expecting him to make use of it later on.

One day, he was on the beach with an American student, one of those muscular Superman types. When I approached them, Kurt told him, "He's half-Jewish," or "He was addressed with 'Shalom.' " I had the feeling that they were making fun of me. That made me feel insecure, as all the feelings that the Nazis had so deeply ingrained in me were being stirred up. And especially if this tall, good-looking, blond-haired, physically superior, American He-man—this Real Man—thinks that Jewishness is no good, there must be something to his point of view.

Back in Germany, Ernst often found himself in the "closed circles" where he says most anti-Semitic remarks were to be heard. At the home of a girlfriend, the "joking" observation of a fellow guest that "the last Jew managed to escape the roast" gave him "a shock"—"especially," he says, "because I didn't say anything like, 'Not in my presence, Mister, please,' since I didn't dare disclose my Jewishness."

I had quite a few such experiences in those years. It made me angry at myself, and ashamed, that I couldn't stand up and say, very casually,

"By the way, it would be better if you didn't say this or that." What I usually did was pretend not to have been an interested party. I pretended to be an Aryan who was trying to reason things out.

Politically—from the point of view of behavior modification or attitude change—this may have been wise. But I didn't do it because it was wise, of course; rather, I did it because my feelings didn't allow me to show how I felt about it. I was always in conflict: I felt aggression, but at the same time I felt a kind of anxiety at being discovered as belonging to these people. Psychologically speaking, it was the same as ten or fifteen years earlier, when being discovered was connected with real danger.

I started psychotherapy in 1959. I already knew that the neurotic structures I had to work through went back to the general background with my mother and to the conflict field in which I was reared. Having more distance, I had also realized that my mother was not responsible for what had happened to me; but the feelings were still there, a remainder of that mixture of aggression and love I felt toward her. I had a relatively long treatment, during which the main subject was my mother, and of course this Jewishness, and my self-hatred. We worked through all these complicated structures, and it helped tremendously.

A second line of change came through friendships in a student group I was in. My friends were the children of anti-Nazis, or at least of people who had not been sympathizers but who had adjusted overtly, as many had in those times. This was very important, because I did not have the feeling, as I'd had with some of my German friends in the States, that they were suspicious of me or just waiting to get me where they wanted me in order to show me that Jewish people were no good. In fact, they were very supportive, although in most cases I couldn't speak with them as frankly as I could with my therapist. I didn't want to confess, for instance, that I had had such a bitter desire to become a leader. For a long time I felt ashamed, especially because my friends had been against the Nazis even during the Nazi period—or at least they hadn't had much interest in being in the Jungvolk—and they wouldn't have understood my motivation. So I refrained from telling them.

Finally, there was in public and in the mass media some permanent commemoration, even if it was not extensive, of the concentration camps and so on, and most official German leaders seemed to believe in it. Well, I'm not so sure about Mr. Kiesinger, but Willy Brandt was an antifascist, as was Adenauer to a certain extent, and they represented a novel, peaceful, progressive development that was important for my feeling of security. Meanwhile, the German people were living a good life with a high standard of living, and that probably had an impact on their attitude toward the Nazi period. Former Nazis wanted to rationalize what had happened, but the people who talked to me were moderately anti-Nazi. This helped me formulate my position more clearly; I had had an anti position since 1944, but on the gut level I was still ambivalent.

In trying to work himself free from the past, Ernst has had to grapple with a nagging belief "that there might have been a nucleus of truth in the propaganda" and to "rephrase," as he puts it, "my own doubts about Jewishness." Despite this effort, there are still instances in which, he admits, "I'm probably trapped by the amount of Nazi propaganda in myself"; a "slight negative undertone" emanating from long-held stereotypes has never quite left his mind. "When I feel I've been stingy," he explains, "there is, even today, a connection between this stinginess and Jewishness." And he says he "cannot be completely happy" with his ease of expression "because there's still this connotation of communicative competence's being combined with bad character: According to Nazi propaganda, the Jews talk a lot because they want to persuade." He has, however, made progress.

One day, around 1965, I was able to say the words *Jewish* and *Jew* without, or—I should be careful here—practically without irritation, negative connotation, anxiety, or taboo. For a long time, even after the war, it gave me a start when someone used those words; and I myself circumscribed them, or, when I did say them, I said them hesitantly. For example: "What they did to the—ahem!—to the Jews." But now I can say this very quickly: "What they did to the Jews." For me, this is an important point.

And until 1973 or so, I always tried to sit in a corner so that nobody could see my profile. From the front I felt that I did not look that Jewish—that unattractive—but I didn't want them to see my nose. Since then, however, I have noticed with relief that I can sit right in the middle of a group with relatively few uneasy feelings, although a little of the uneasiness remains.

But it's been a long, long process. In photos taken when I was seventeen or so, I looked really unattractive due to something in my expression, in my posture; because I expected others to see me as unattractive, I became so, to a certain extent at least. The inhibition in my gestures that probably goes right back to the thirties and forties is still there in home movies we make now, but I've seen that what I thought about myself is not true: I'm not ugly.

Another important stereotype fell when Ernst, a professor at a German university, developed with some Israeli students the first warm relations he'd had with Jews outside his mother's family.

This experience was so important because among my prejudices, of course, belong "You cannot be warm with Jewish people, you cannot love Jewish people, because they are distant, calculating, stingy," and all that bullshit. Even when I myself experienced difficulties in expressing my feelings with girlfriends, I ascribed this to Jewishness as a matter of course. And although I had found out in the meantime that I could have more warmth, I suppose I may have rationalized that either in terms of "That is my Christian half," or "I have overcome the Jewish distance."

This brings us much closer to the present and to another important point: my relationship to Israel. I have long postponed going to Israel, even though I'd like to see the country and visit some of my relatives. I used to think the main reason was that I did not want to be confronted with the grief which, in a sense, is cultivated there in all those monuments and in the old people. As I break into tears when I see television documentaries on Auschwitz, this must be true; but now I'm sure it is only half the truth.

Another part, which has become a little clearer to me now, is that I have been afraid of a confrontation with so many Jewish people—among whom there are surely some who are unattractive, no matter whether from an objective viewpoint or by Nazi standards. What would my feelings be in that situation? Would all the old prejudices be stirred up again, on the gut level at least: "Aha! Here you see it," and "That's how they act," and all that? Which would, of course, have something to do with my own identity.

And, finally, the question for me has been, How shall I present myself to them? What am I? I was not brought up Jewish, so it would be a lie to say, "I am Jewish" or "I believe in the God of the Old Testament." But I have been afraid that I might stress this not being

Jewish in the formal sense of religion to a point where I would show them the remnants of the anti-Jewishness in myself.

Ernst ascribes the "sympathy" he has come to feel for Jews to "shared experience."

It is this shared experience that has brought me—originally, against my will—closer to the Jewish people, and especially to those who have been persecuted. But then a second question arises: whether I, in addition to my having been involved in the same history of discrimination, identify with, in quotation marks, the "blood." Although in saying "blood" I am merely symbolizing the possibility of tracing oneself back to members of the Jewish ethnic group, it is not unimportant that I put it this way. Again, this is something I have internalized on the basis of Nazi propaganda: that there is something in myself which is "the Jewish part"—that, as we joked after the war, "one leg is Jewish and one is Christian." Whether I do identify in this way I am not sure, although possibly I have accepted that I am a little different from those who cannot trace their ancestors back to Jewish people.

And maybe now I am beginning to believe that this can be a positive part of myself: not so much in terms of blood—I mean, blood as such is really nonsense—but in terms of the experience that I have had of mankind and of prejudice. I don't know if it necessarily would have taken losing my grandma in a concentration camp and being discriminated against. But once this had happened, it probably contributed something to my maturity—to my insight into human beings and into the deeper reaches of their structure.

This, perhaps, is reason to be glad. Perhaps—I don't know.

Ariel Levi

I don't know anything at all about my father, so I can talk only about my mother and her family. My grandfather came from Hungary. During the time of the Austro-Hungarian Empire, the family was more or less wandering Jews who moved around Vojvodina, an area belonging to Hungary where people were bilingual, speaking Serbo-Croatian and Hungarian. When the empire was split up following the First World War, they found themselves to be Hungarian-speaking Jews in a country which, all of a sudden, had become Yugoslavia.

I have a kind of special pride in my grandfather because he was probably the only Jewish farmer in all of the Balkans. Though he tried very hard to make it as a farmer, his two sons and eight daughters never had enough to eat, so he decided to become a businessman. But, here again, he wasn't the typical Jew: He wasn't clever enough for business, and he didn't have the patience. The story I always heard was that he arrived at the market with a horse and cart carrying bolts of cloth he was trying to sell. But one of the tricks of the market is that people bargain, and my grandfather wasn't able to play around with the price. After a couple of such discussions, he got so furious that he threw all the merchandise into the mud, trampled it with his feet, and led his horse back home. So he was a failure as a businessman.

Then my grandfather did another extraordinary thing. One winter night he got angry again—I think he was the irritable type—and he said, "I've had it with feeding you, buying you clothes, working so hard. Now get out of my house and find your own means to live." Then he opened the door of his cottage—there was deep snow outside—and he threw his children out. Only my mother and an aunt of mine, who were kind of clever, managed to remain with him; the rest of the family was dispersed.

My mother was a very funny kind of human being. It seems that she was a big adventurer, but I know very little about her because she was taken to a concentration camp in 1942, when I was eight and a half years old and too young to know the details of her life. Later on I asked an aunt about her, but she didn't tell me much, either because she was afraid of disclosing some unpleasant secrets about my mother or because the sisters actually didn't know much about each other.

I have never known exactly what my mother did to earn a living. I know that for long stretches she lived with the gypsies, moving from one place to another, finding strange jobs of all kinds, smuggling things, sometimes stealing in order to live. According to one of the stories I heard, there was a period of my mother's life when she was trying to be a kind of crooked businesswoman. She and another sister were selling paprika, but this paprika was a powder they made that combined a little bit of paprika with a lot of rust and dried red paint. They would go from one village to another selling packages of it to the peasants, and they were very careful not to come to the same village twice. Once, though, they made a mistake; they were chased by angry farmers and barely escaped with their lives.

I was told another very surprising story about my mother: that she had been caught by the Yugoslav Royal Police carrying arms under her skirt for the Communist Party. I thought for a while that this might be the key to who my father was, because one of the ways the Communists rebelled against bourgeois institutions before the Second World War was to conceive children and not to get married; it was their kind of leftish protest against society as such. My mother was tortured; they pulled all the nails from her fingers because, obviously, they wanted her to tell them names of people who were involved. I don't know the details, but I feel that nobody can stand up to such torture, that it's only a fairy tale that "a very important member of the Communist Party was tortured and didn't disclose any secrets." So I think that the antiheroic element in the story is that she probably did tell the names, because her life afterwards was much less idealistic. She didn't believe in parties anymore; she no longer had any interest in it.

I was born in 1933. I lived with my mother in a house in Zagreb, in a neighborhood where there were no Jews whatsoever; we were very poor, and even the poorest Jews were better off than we were. I had no Jewish education, although I did go to a Jewish kindergarten until the outbreak of the war, and there I was taught some Hebrew prayers. Mainly because my name was Levi—my mother's name was Levi, and her father was Levi, too—I knew, vaguely, that I was a Jew.

My mother and I had very little contact with Jews in general, and my family wasn't a normal, warm Jewish family where people care for one another. Each one lived his own life, and the different parts of the family helped each other very little, even in time of great need. Being thrown out of the house at a young age and having to find their own means of existence made them, I think, turn away from the Jewish part in themselves. They didn't like my grandfather, they didn't like what he represented, and as among other things he was a Jew, they tried to escape the fact that they were Jewish. All of them married non-Jews except for my mother, who never married, and one of her brothers, a baker who was killed in a concentration camp during the war. So it happened that I became the last Jewish survivor of that family.

Although Yugoslavia had abandoned its neutrality and concluded an alliance with the Axis powers two weeks earlier, German troops crossed into the country from Hungary, Bulgaria, and Rumania on April 6, 1941. Four days thereafter, the Germans were in control of Zagreb, and by April 16 they had created the Independent State of Croatia and placed at its head the Croatian fascist leader Ante Pavelic and his Ustase Party.

The Croats had bitterly resented their domination by the Serbs in the Yugoslav kingdom, and many welcomed the Nazis as the agents of Croatian independence. While the Croatian fascists reserved their wildest fury for the Serbs, whom they slaughtered with unbridled savagery, their treatment of the 30,000 Jews under their jurisdiction reflected their sympathy with German aims. Before the month of April was out, the new state had promulgated its first anti-Jewish law—under which eight-year-old Leo Levi, as the child of an unmarried Jewish mother, was defined as a Jew.

At the time, he had only a dim understanding of the fact that he was Jewish; and, like most others marked for persecution, he had not yet recognized the threat facing him. But Levi—who was not known as Ariel until years later—soon began to feel repercussions of the anti-Semitic climate in his daily life.

I was probably the only Jew on the street where I lived, and the neighbors knew that I was a Jew. They used to get rough with me from time to time, sometimes beating me up a little bit in the street. But I really understood that I was a Jew one day when I went with my mother, quite innocently, to see the film *Jew Süss*. This was a Nazi film about the Jews, and as the film ended—it is said that this happened every time *Jew Süss* was shown—the audience started to shout, "Death to all the Jews!" It was at that moment that I realized I was something really special—so special, in fact, that people wanted to kill me. It was quite a shocking discovery.

The Pavelic government rapidly applied a series of anti-Jewish measures patterned on those enacted in other lands under Nazi domination, and by October 1941 Jews were being moved to forced labor camps in Croatian territory. When deportations began in the summer of 1942, Leo's mother was among the first arrested.

My mother had gone into the city to buy some things for me, and I was waiting for her at home, but she was caught in a roundup on the street and she never came back. From the day she was taken, everything was changed in my life. I literally had to struggle for my own existence; I was no longer the child who was taken care of, but, from that moment, I took care of myself.

When his mother failed to return, Leo, who "did not know many people," sought refuge with one of his aunts.

There, they didn't tell me that my mother had been arrested, or where she had been taken; they simply said, "Maybe she'll come back, maybe she won't." There was a kind of atmosphere of fear in the house, because Jews were being arrested everywhere and my aunts were afraid for themselves. After some time, though, they saw that they wouldn't be taken; they had become Catholics, and their children were fully Catholic, and the only converted Jews taken to concentration camps were those who had no children. But all I myself knew—since my aunts didn't tell me anything—was that something very strange was happening, that something was going wrong with the Jews. And I had a kind of general feeling of fear without knowing exactly what it was all about.

Then, about a month after my mother was taken, I was arrested too. In the middle of the night I felt a strong beam of light in my face. There were two police inspectors in the room. They told me to get dressed, and I dressed completely mixed up because I was still asleep and at that time I slept so deeply that, even when I had been awakened, I didn't know what was going on. They had guns in their hands because they thought they were coming to arrest somebody grown up. And they asked me if my name was "Mr. Levi," but I was a child of eight, and in Yugoslavia you don't call somebody that age "Mister." So it was all very funny—I mean, getting flashlights pointed in your face, and two guns; it was a very weird kind of experience.

They took me to the police station. A sergeant gave me his coat to sleep in, and I slept another two hours. Some other Jews were brought in, and we were taken to a big school where Jews were being concentrated; there were a lot of Jewish families there. After two or three days, my aunt came to claim me—and, to my surprise, they let me go.

I was arrested again a couple of months later. This arrest was very different because by then we knew something about the concentration camps. The first morning, when we got up, I discovered that there were ten people or so lying with their blankets over their heads: They were the Jews who had committed suicide during the night. So we had been sleeping together with these corpses, and, when we got up in the morning, quite a few people didn't get up, because they knew what it was all about and they preferred to kill themselves. Two people were released, I and another kid.

Leo was arrested three times in all, but each time he was released for reasons that have never become entirely clear.

It seems there was somebody who took a kind of personal interest and wanted to release me. Ten years after the end of the war, a cousin of mine received a letter from a man who wrote, "My name is So-and-so and when I was a police officer during the war, I saved the lives of two Jews: your life and the life of Leo Levi." He didn't know there was any connection between us; he had simply saved two Jews. He was writing because he wanted to be accepted as a member of the Communist Party and he needed a letter of recommendation saying that he had behaved well in the war.

So apparently it was this guy who had succeeded in releasing me. But it wasn't that easy, and I think it happened in part because I knew what was going on and I kept insisting that I was not a Jew at all and that it was a mistake. I don't remember exactly what I told them, but I made up complicated stories about having a Catholic uncle and aunt. I had very light-colored hair at the time and very blue eyes, so I didn't look Jewish—and, somehow, they believed me. Or maybe they were looking for an excuse to let me go and I kind of helped them by making up this story. In any case, I think the officer who had been releasing me was the same one charged with arresting me, and he finally scratched my name off the list.

Sometime after his third arrest, which took place toward the end of 1942, Leo began attending an elementary school that had been set up for the few Jewish children still in Zagreb, most of whom had been left behind by chance when their families were arrested. The school served as a base for organizing transports of children to Palestine, and an initial transport, comprising several hundred young Jews from various Balkan states, was actually allowed through. Further transports were blocked, and Leo, who was scheduled to be in the third transport, remained behind. The school was closed down in mid-1943, after which he led an inconspicuous, if free-floating, existence.

There were many children who didn't go to school during the war, so I wasn't a special case and no one noticed. I had also taken off the star. At that time if a Jew had been seen in the street with a star, he would have been arrested immediately. And as officially there were no Jews left to wear the star—most of them having been taken and the rest being in hiding—there was no point at all in not taking it off.

But there were people from the neighborhood who knew I was Jewish anyway, and one day, when I was walking in the street, three kids began chasing me and shouting, "Dirty Jew." I picked up a rock and threw it at them; I hit one of them and hurt him badly, and I ran away. But these kids were on the lookout for me, and I waited on one particular corner for hours hoping to make it home without being beaten up.

While I was standing there, a small battalion of Nazi youth passed by, marching along and singing. I thought it would be a good idea to hide among them: Then I could reach my house and run quickly into my doorway. I told them that there were these three bad guys who wanted to beat me up—but not that I was hiding in order not to be beaten up as a Jew, or that I had hit one of the kids with a rock. They took it in a very sporting way, giving me shelter to my doorstep, and at the last moment I jumped into the doorway and disappeared.

Having come through the episode unharmed, Leo decided "it wouldn't be a bad idea" to become a member of a Nazi youth group as a way of avoiding further scrapes. He reported to the headquarters of the Croatian fascist youth movement, the Ustas Kamladis.

I met one of the leaders of the group, who was very friendly, and I asked him if I could be accepted as a member. He looked me squarely in the eye and he said, "Why not?" He asked me my name, and I said my name was Levovic—I invented a name on the spot that finished with -*ic* to make it sound more Yugoslavian. When I said my name, this leader gave me a very faint smile, which I didn't understand until the war was over. I got a beautiful uniform—khaki, with a blue cap—and an air gun, and I was a member of this Hitler Youth group for the last two years of the war.

In the group, we collected warm clothes and ammunition for the soldiers at the front as well as copper and other odds and ends that might be useful to the war industry. We heard speeches by real tough Nazis, some of whom were notorious for killing Serbians or whatever; they gave patriotic talks about Greater Croatia; and about Germany, the big ally; and about their experiences in the war. We also trained like soldiers, marching and shooting, and when we were in uniform, we had to greet all officers from corporal on up with a kind of Hitler salute when we passed them in the street. Every Sunday we marched—very orderly, in formation—to mass. We would fold our caps and put them under the strap on the left shoulder of our uniforms and leave our rifles at the entrance of the church. I was with the group whenever it was necessary, playing games, listening to speeches, going to church, training, marching, and doing whatever else they thought we should do.

Although he stayed somewhat on his guard with his fellow members of the youth group, Leo says he "didn't worry all that much" about keeping up appearances.

I had been more or less accepted as a person, and my relations with the guys in the group were normal; some I liked, some I liked less. I was very small, but my nose was not especially Jewish, and since I hadn't been brought up as a Jew at all, I didn't talk with my hands or have other such mannerisms. My Serbo-Croatian was accented because my mother had wanted to give me a kind of cosmopolitan education, and the first language I had spoken was German. But at the time this was a welcome accent; it would have been wrong to have a Hungarian accent, but not a German accent. I was like the other kids—or, if I was slightly different, it was not in ways which might have suggested that I was Jewish. The only problem was not to undress, because then they would have seen that I'm circumcised.

Actually, there were a couple of guys who may have known that I was a Jew, because from time to time they asked me to recite a prayer for them in Hebrew. These guys found it funny that I spoke a language none of them had heard, so I would show off a little by saying one of the prayers I had learned in kindergarten. I don't think they knew that knowing Hebrew means one is a Jew—or perhaps they just didn't make the connection, because the people in the area of Zagreb where I grew up were very simple people. Besides, from going to church I could recite whole prayers in Latin as well. So, at the same time, there were some for whom I was a kind of a Jew and others for whom I was not.

I made an enormous effort not to think about all this—it didn't exist, I put it out of my mind. But, within myself, a kind of total fear was developing. As a kid, you don't know what death is, you hardly know what a concentration camp is, and you don't know what it all implies for you; but I knew, somehow, that I was a Jew, and I knew, somehow, that I was in danger. I didn't understand the whole complexity of the war, but I had been arrested three times and I had seen people committing suicide, so I understood that it's not a game, it's something real. Remaining alone, and knowing that something was happening around me that could be the end of me, I felt enormous danger and I understood that I had to look out for my own life.

I also realized that, in order to overcome this fear, I had to develop an enormous lie and not dare to admit it even to myself. I had to become something else completely and to repress that part of me which was Jewish so deeply that I wouldn't be bothered all the time thinking about the duality—"Am I a Jew or not a Jew?"—but would believe in only one plane. It was not a case of my listening to Nazis talk and saying to myself, "I am a Jew—what am I doing here?" No. I was kind of freezing myself to the idea that "I'm not a Jew, I'm a member of the Nazis." While I didn't listen to their speeches with sympathy, I listened passively, saying, "It's not my business, any of this. My business is to stay alive." And I didn't give a second thought to playing my double. I simply became my double.

Ariel views his capacity for "carrying all these games so far" as the consequence of living in a nightmare.

This nightmare didn't start with the Nazi youth, it started with my mother disappearing. Up to the age of eight and a half, to be myself was, in a way, to be with my mother—that's the way I knew myself; it was a kind of complete being myself. But when my mother was taken, my life changed so much that I was no longer my former self; a big part of me was missing. When she disappeared, I somehow knew: "I'm in the nightmare." And the rest was easy.

When you are in the nightmare, you are no longer troubled by things changing, you don't have to struggle with each change. In the daytime, all kinds of things may seem strange to you. But if you dream that you are flying in a yellow submarine with blue wings, you don't wake up within the dream and say, "It's strange—I've got wings!" Because wings are not the only change, the whole setup is so changed that you have no problems with the details. It is a totally different world, another kind of existence, which has so many levels that you accept all changes and you don't think so much about them—although, of course, I knew that this fear existed in me, and there's no doubt that I was afraid all the time.

The fascist youth group met, on the average, twice a week. In his spare time, Leo read a great deal and otherwise simply lived as a member of his aunt's household.

Although in the family people generally didn't help one another, they made a kind of special exception in my case. They gave me shelter, and they gave it to me gladly; there was no tension over it, just the normal family tensions over other things. The only problem they had with me was feeding an additional mouth, and it was quite a big problem because everything was rationed and there was very little food around. But I took care of myself physically; sometimes you had to steal in order to survive, and I, too, stole from time to time. As they saw that I was helping them—being a Hitler Youth member, managing on my own—I don't think they had any special fears about harboring a Jew at home.

From the time Leo joined the Ustas Kamladis, his life was largely without incident. Zagreb, solidly in the hands of the Croatian fascists, was never a frequent target of partisan activity, nor was the city bombed from the air. The main "evidence of war" was, for Leo, the scarcity of food and the American planes that passed overhead on their way to strike oil fields near the Rumanian city of Ploiesti in the spring of 1944. But his circle of acquaintances did include two young men—one a member of the partisan underground, the other "an officer of the local Nazis"—who were killed in connection with their wartime activities.

Still, it was not until the final months that we really felt the presence of the war, because then the Nazis and the partisans were killing each other like dogs whenever they ran into each other. I was living about a hundred meters from a big river, the Sava, and in the last month of the war the river was full of bodies. I mean there were tens of thousands of bodies floating, one after another. You couldn't swim in the water.

When the war was over, the Ustase were being arrested and executed one by one, including all the leaders of the Hitler Youth, who were shot down without even a trial. To my surprise, I saw the leader who had taken me into the group; he hadn't been arrested, and he was wearing a partisan uniform. I couldn't understand how he was still alive, so I asked him, "What is this all about?"

He said he had been the partisans' operative in the Hitler Youth. "When I accepted you," he told me, "I knew that you were a Jew in hiding and that your name was Levi. You couldn't fool me with Levovic!"

By April 1945 all of Yugoslav territory had been liberated from Axis domination, and Marshal Tito, the leader of the partisan forces, quickly established himself at the head of a reunified Yugoslavia.

If you were to ask someone who went through the war as a grown-up and who was in hiding, he would tell you that when the war was over and the Nazis had fled or been killed, he felt enormous relief, enormous change. That he found a new beginning, a new life. But as a child you look for stability, and when stability is absent—even if it's in the most pleasant of ways—you still miss whatever order you have been used to. Even in that nightmare as a kid without parents, you look for a kind of solid, organized life. I mean, people even got used to living in Auschwitz—until they were killed, of course—and I had become used to this nightmare.

So, after everything that had happened to me—having to hide, and making up this very big lie, and trying myself to believe in this big lie, and taking on a kind of second identity—at the same time that I did feel relief, I saw that I was again being forced to start another kind of life. And as I had been for so long in that lie, the change was somehow not completely welcome. To me, it was still a nightmare—what had gone before, but also what came afterwards. Because my nightmare was a personal thing: It was a kind of lost paradise. When the partisans came in, I immediately felt that a new kind of freedom was on its way. The partisans seemed to me to be a different kind of people—very simple people, but good people, less rough—and everything was freer. But when the political situation changed, it did not mean that my lost childhood, or my mother, or my time with her was returned to me. A change of regime doesn't bring a lost paradise back.

In the end, I think I carried this nightmare with me for many years. Since, in a nightmare, you all of a sudden have to assume that everything happening to you is a new reality and adapt yourself to that reality, after some time it becomes your skin. Then the nightmare slowly seeps out. But it takes a long time before you can wake up and say, "Well, it's over now. The sun is shining, and everything is OK."

Following the liberation, as Jews emerged from hiding and returned from the camps, the Zagreb Jewish community set up a residence for children who, like Leo, had been orphaned. Although material circumstances were good—thanks to the relief agencies, the children were far better fed and clothed than the general population—Leo did not feel at ease.

In the beginning I wasn't very comfortable with these Jewish kids. On the contrary, I didn't like them. First of all, they came from 100,000 different places—from Belgrade, from Zagreb, from Sarajevo—and they spoke with funny accents, and they came from various backgrounds. Then, some of them had fought in the war; they were very rough types and not easy to get along with.

While I found myself, all of a sudden, among Jewish children, I can't say that I discovered Judaism. In fact, very few of these kids had a Jewish education. They all came from semiassimilated families and weren't a very good example of what Jewish children actually are.

And because the Jews had been fully accepted as citizens—or as partisan fighters, or whatever—the subject of the Jews as such didn't really come up in Yugoslavia. There were Jews among the leaders of the country: The president of the parliament was a Jew, as were some very well known members of the Communist movement and a couple of the teachers at the school I went to, which was the most Communist school in Zagreb. I myself was, by my own choice, a very active participant in the Jewish youth movement and the Communist youth movement—which were really the same thing, as there was no way not to be a Communist at that time. So the Jews had become a part of the whole.

The school I went to was a very privileged school. It had been set up specifically so that the children who had suffered during the war—some were the children of partisans or had themselves fought with the partisans—could finish two grades in one year and in this way get their diplomas. Some of the kids in my class were years older than I was—there were former partisan officers and heroes of the underground—and sometimes the teachers had problems with these pupils. They wore all sorts of souvenirs on them, including guns and small, round Italian bombs, which looked like something you would wear around your neck but which could go off and kill the whole class. "Please don't bring the bombs with you into the classroom," the teachers would tell them. "Hang them outside."

By the time I was fifteen, I was president of my class and one of the leaders of the Communist youth. There was heavy indoctrination at this school, and we had a well-known Communist system of managing things: If someone was a bad student, he was forced to make a self-analysis. There was a girl in the class who was famous for killing ten German paratroopers with a bazooka and who held one of the highest decorations in Yugoslavia, but she was a bad student and it was my duty as class president to stand her up in the middle of the class and make her tell everybody honestly why she was so lousy in school. She was eighteen at the time, but she was like a little child being taken aside and made to say how naughty she was, and how untrustworthy; it was a damned difficult moment for her, she was practically crying. I felt that I was doing something wrong, but according to the doctrine we had at that time, it had to be done. Still, that was the beginning of my problems with Communism.

Another incident occurring around the same time reminded Leo of the anomaly of his position and contributed to his ambivalence toward ideological imperatives.

One day, a child approached me on the street and told me that there was a guy who wanted to see me. I was very curious to know who it was, so we went to a park outside the city, and there I found one of the ex-leaders of the Nazis. He said, "Levovic, I know you also were in the Hitler Youth. I want to start a small Nazi underground against the Communists. What about your taking part?" I could have done something about it: I could have turned him in. But then I caught myself.

It was a very funny kind of dilemma. Being a Communist—and a Jew—I should have given his name and the names of the others involved to the authorities. But if I did that, a lot of my friends from the group would be arrested, too. I couldn't have these guys arrested; not all of them were mean, some of them were nice guys. And in the case of this leader, it wouldn't have been just an arrest. He was in hiding, and if they had caught him, he would have been shot. So, on the one hand I was a Jew, and on the other hand there was somebody trying to recruit me into the Nazi movement after the war. Of course, I wouldn't have joined them, that was out of the question; but there was no point in turning them over to the police either. I really didn't know what to do. I just let things go, I didn't meet with them again, and that was that.

It was a minor dispute at school that finally tipped the scales.

Two kids were arguing over the score of a soccer match. Right in the middle of the argument, a son of the president of the republic got up—as it was a very special school, we had well-connected kids in our class—and he said, "What is this bloody discussion, anyway? Of course the score is 4–0 and not 4–2, because I read it yesterday in the *Borba*."

Borba was the official organ of the Communist Party. And I felt, "There's something rotten here. You can't even discuss the score of a football game without somebody coming up and saying, 'I believe that newspaper because it is the newspaper of the Party.' " That, for me, was the break with Communist ideas.

When Israel declared its independence in May 1948, Leo began to follow the news of the war between the fledgling state and its Arab neighbors.

There was a huge photo hanging in the Jewish community center showing a dead body stretched out and someone crouched behind it firing a rifle. The title read: "The Haganah soldier takes cover behind the body of his fallen friend and continues the struggle." They were asking young people to come, either to join the Israeli army or to work.

I didn't know anything about Israel or about what Zionism meant, and I was too young to fight. But I was told that Israel was something Jewish, that it was a country we had had before, and somehow that started to work on me. At that time, we thought it would be only a matter of hours before Israel was overrun, and we had the feeling that we would be going to save Israel, to help Israel not to disappear. On top of that, all my Jewish friends were leaving, and I didn't want to be left behind, so I decided to go with them.

But, as with every change, there came the question of whether it was welcome. I arrived in Israel in winter. It was terribly cold, and I was put to work picking onions in a frozen field. I must say I didn't like it—I didn't welcome this experience in any way. After one hour of picking onions, I took the first bus and went off. But then I came back, because I had no place to go.

Had he remained in Yugoslavia, Ariel says, his status as a victim of Nazi persecution would have assured him a scholarship in his chosen field of study. He was even offered an appointment to military school, which implied a bright future as a "cultural commissar."

In Israel, I had to put in six hours a day of very hard physical labor on a kibbutz and could study only three or four hours. And since it was a very left-wing kibbutz, we didn't get a normal education: We studied Marxism and Zionism and agricultural theory. I couldn't find much use for any of that stuff. It was really a kind of brainwashing thing, and by then I was fed up with Communism anyway and I wanted to be a painter.

In the early 1950s, Ariel Levi—his name now Hebraicized—served in the Israeli army as a member of the military theater, his job being to show the soldiers how to decorate the mess halls and other public spaces in their camps. One of his stops was a camp in the south of Israel that adjoined the training camp of an elite paratroop commando unit that "later on," Ariel says, "became very famous in Israel for their actions across the border in Arab territories."

As part of their training, they were to penetrate a well-guarded Israeli military camp and, to prove they had made it, bring back someone from that camp. One evening I was taking a walk when all of a sudden I felt a hand grab me; then a sack went over my head. I didn't know whether it was terrorists attacking, or a kind of joke, or somebody simply wanting to beat me up. But my first reaction, the first thing that came to my mind, was to say, "I am a painter, and I've got nothing to do with it." They began laughing their heads off; they got a big kick out of my remark.

Ariel was married upon leaving the military, went to live on his wife's kibbutz, and continued his studies of art. After he had established himself as both an artist and a teacher, he was offered a European sabbatical; he traveled with his wife and children to the Netherlands and decided to settle there. At the time of the interview, he had been divorced for some years, but his former wife and his children had also remained in Holland.

Ariel says that, in the intervening years, "the nightmare has disappeared very gradually."

Some people get sick from it; I didn't, but you can't get rid of it all. There's the feeling that you can't disclose yourself completely, the urge never to tell everything but to keep certain things private. People ask me, "Why didn't you tell us this, or that?" and I sometimes get furious.

"I have a right to keep a couple of things for myself," I say. "I don't have to tell everything."

I also retain a deep mistrust for the motives of all political systems, and I don't take them seriously. From the moment my mother was arrested, I lost not only the stability I had known as a child but also my belief in grown-up society. So, while I didn't swallow what they were saying during the war, I somehow didn't believe in the change that came afterwards, either—even though I have freely accepted all sorts of changes in my life, and even though I was an enthusiastic Communist for a time. I think I carried this disbelief into the kibbutz movement, because I didn't believe in that either, and I continued to be suspicious thereafter. You remain armed, in a sense, for any nightmare that might come your way.

The experience that led him to reject the adult world has left him, Ariel says, to cope with "two very different things in my character."

If I want to be an artist, I can't be suspicious, I can't be sophisticated, I can't go on disbelieving things. In order to be creative, I really have to believe, I have to hold on to my naïveté. But, on the other hand, I have lost my childish credulity and I can be very mistrustful—even though I don't want to be, because that works against me as an artist.

But the fact of his being a Jew, which was so connected to this experience, seemed not to have been a source of such tension for Ariel in recent years.

How do I feel about it today? Well, I like some of the traditions. Chanukah is nice: candles. I like Jewish girls. I have Jewish kids. It was in Israel that I actually discovered Jewish culture and Jewish tradition, but I didn't have a particularly good experience in Israel—I didn't dig the country and I still don't. I don't go to Jewish meetings, or to the Israeli Independence Day celebration, or to the Chanukah service at the Jewish community. My friends are not necessarily Jews—in fact, there's something in Jews I don't like—but I don't necessarily prefer goyim [gentiles]. The friends I have are my own kind of people; some of them, by chance, are Jews, and some, also by chance, are not.

In fact, I myself am a Jew just by chance. I could have been born Mongolian or Italian, I could have been born anything. The fact that I was born a Jew—well, it may be a funny way of putting it, but it's a little like a soccer player who thought he would play for PSV-Eindhoven but ended up, just by chance, playing for Ajax.* It's not that the club is any less good, it's just that it is another club.

As long as you are going to play for Ajax, there are things you can enjoy about it. The club has a long history. There were all those prophets. They wrote a bible. There have been famous Jews, and Jews are regarded to be clever people. But I feel it would be abnormal discrimination on my part to be proud of it. How can I be proud? My mother didn't have to be a Levi, she could have been a Rastrapovic—or she could even have been a Nazi.

But I do think the whole fact that I am Jewish has a value somewhere. Symbolically, magically—it's written somewhere in the sky. Or perhaps, before I die, I will get a kind of magic illumination showing me: "You need it, because it was your destiny to be a Jew." And because of that—all the star combinations involved in being a Jew—something will happen.

At the moment, however, I simply feel that I am a member of this particular football team. The fact that I have been born among the Chosen People is just a way of saying that I am playing not for PSV but for Ajax. I don't see it as any particular privilege to be a Jew; and, as I said, I am not proud of it. But I also feel that if I am going to be a member of this football team, I shouldn't be ashamed of it either. I just have to be a good sport and say that my club was passing through hard days— the Second World War, wearing stars. It was a very uncomfortable football team, let me tell you.

PSV-Eindhoven, Ajax: teams in Holland's professional soccer league.

Walter Roth

Walter Roth was born in Vienna in 1925 and grew up in a working-class section of the city. He, his parents, and his older brother lived with Walter's widowed paternal grandmother in the apartment she had occupied since moving to the Austrian capital from Slovakia in 1902. Walter's father, a quiet man, made a modest living as a tailor. In 1936 he opened his own shop, and Walter's mother, a strong-willed woman with a head for business, came to work with him.

Living in a largely non-Jewish district of a city where, according to Walter, "it was, at that time, exceedingly tempting to conform," the family was still moderately observant. Although he was not religious, Walter's father was "traditionally Jewish," going to services on the High Holidays. Walter became Bar Mitzvah in July of 1938, several months following Germany's annexation of Austria, in one of the last Jewish ceremonies the Nazis were to permit in Vienna. Walter's mother kept a strictly kosher home until the death of her mother-in-law in 1934; it was only when the family opened its business and the household chores were left to a non-Jewish cleaning woman that observance of the dietary laws ceased altogether.

A foundling raised by Christian foster parents, Walter's mother had converted to Judaism for her marriage in 1921. The union met with initial opposition from the Roth family; however, several of Walter's first cousins, who came of age not long after Walter's parents wed, subsequently married non-Jewish women as well.

As the whole family was in a rather weak economic position, my father and his nephews weren't well enough off to make the good shidduchim* that appealed to them. Considering their circumstances

---

shidduchim: plural of *shidduch,* arranged marriage (Yiddish and Hebrew).

and the strong assimilation in the Vienna of that time, there was actually a greater likelihood of their marrying Christian girls than Jewish girls.

When I was a child, I didn't really know the circumstances of my parents' marriage, nor whether my mother had been brought up Christian or Jewish. I did know my mother's second foster parents, whom we went to see rather often when we were little, and I knew that Auntie Marie—the spinster sister of the foster father, whom we regarded as an aunt—was a Catholic. In fact, you couldn't miss it: There was Jesus, and the cross, and so on. But there was no question of Jewish or not Jewish; my mother was a Jew. She lit candles on Friday night, she koshered the meat, her friends were all Jewish women the same age, and their children, whom we played with, were Jews. It was a totally normal situation for me; I didn't see any conflict whatever in all this.

While the fact that he came from a Jewish family was self-evident to Walter, "being Jewish itself" was something he says he "understood, in any conscious way, relatively late."

Although I knew that I was of another religion than most of the people around me, for me that wasn't anything out of the ordinary. My family had almost exclusively Jewish friends, but I myself grew up among all the children in the neighborhood without the slightest distinction. I knew, of course, that our household was kosher, but I didn't know exactly what that meant, other than that you weren't supposed to eat Schmalzbrot*—which is what I got at the house of a boy my age who lived in the building. It was pork fat, naturally, but it tasted good; so I ate it, I just didn't talk about it.

Even singing in the temple choir—which I did as a nine- and ten-year-old—was, for me, something on the order of an extracurricular activity. There, I did behave differently; there, I put on a hat, and I played the role that was expected of me. But my life was this wide river of getting up, going to school, playing, doing my homework—no conflicts—and, on top of that, there was an extra activity, which was going to temple to sing.

So it's only in retrospect that I can say that there came a point when I consciously felt my Jewishness as something that set me apart—a

---

*Schmalzbrot: bread spread with rendered fat, a popular snack in Austria.

feeling that then slowly grew. This consciousness certainly did not arise from someone initiating me into Judaism, but I was simply confronted with it in the usual unpleasant way: People swore at me or made fun of me, or I ran up against some barrier all of a sudden.

This happened from the time I was four, five, six years old. I can't remember anything anti-Semitic happening in school, but—and this struck me—people recognized me, when I walked down the street, as a Jewish child. You couldn't tell from my speech that I came from a different household; we spoke High German at home, but I had a facility for speaking like the others and I picked the dialect up. So why did these confrontations take place? How did people know?

We lived in a working-class neighborhood. Times were very bad. We weren't well off, and the neighbors in the building were no better off than we were, but we were better dressed despite our equally poor financial situation. Jewish children had nicer clothes. We spent what little money we had differently from the rest, and it showed.

And if I came by my Jewish consciousness in a negative way, that had also to do, in part, with the somewhat negative feelings I had when I had to put out any extra effort. For example, the High Holidays were a disturbance to me, because on those days singing in the temple choir was connected with a big strain that didn't go along with this wide river of life but was something else. These same feelings were there the next day, when I went back to school—either with an explanation for my schoolmates, or without—and found myself in the special position of someone who had other holidays. At that point there was a confrontation that on other occasions did not take place; and it always felt like a confrontation, because children try—or at least I myself tried, in the beginning—not to be different.

As being different was, so to speak, forced on me by circumstance, I experienced Jewishness more or less as an obligation. It was, well, not a disease, but like having red hair:* You have it, the possibility does exist to dye it, but you don't do it. Doing it would have gone counter to my whole upbringing, and it would have hurt my parents. And, really, this

---

*red hair: In certain European countries where red hair is uncommon, redheaded children are often subjected to taunting and ridicule.

didn't weigh on me so much—although it was no pleasure in and of itself to be a Jew, which is something I have always plainly felt.

When he was ten or eleven years old, Walter joined the local Zionist youth group, which was much like a scouting organization. There, he was popular with his playmates, and he received a distinctive nickname that bolstered his self-esteem. "I must confess that I connected my being Jewish with this Zionist organization in only the most muddled way," Walter recalls. "Still, this group actually brought me closer to Jewishness, although in a way that had nothing to do with the Jewishness I had known up to then. If such a thing exists, it was the second root of my Jewish development."

During the mid-1930s, however, Walter's main allegiance was to the Austrian state. In February 1934, he followed intently the four days of civil war in which forces allied to the rightist Christian Socialist Party of dictator Engelbert Dollfuss suppressed opposition from the country's Social Democrats. His patriotism grew under the regime of Dollfuss's successor, Kurt von Schuschnigg, whose National Front opposed Austria's absorption into the German Reich but itself practiced authoritarian rule—and a measure of anti-Semitism besides.

I was, above all, an Austrian. In school we had to stand at attention all the time, and we had to sing, and I remember with absolute clarity my feeling of awe—the shiver that would run down my spine—when we sang the national anthem. The sympathies of my father and my relatives and the friends of my family lay with the Social Democrats—because they were not anti-Semitic, or were less anti-Semitic—but that didn't stop me from being a stouthearted little Austrian in those years under the Austrofascist government.

On March 12, 1938, the eve of a plebiscite Schuschnigg had called in the hope of showcasing Austria's insistence on independence, German troops—accompanied by Hitler himself—marched into the country. Austria's Nazis, outlawed under Schuschnigg, surged through Vienna's streets in the ensuing days, corralling those they recognized as Jews and forcing them to scour National Front slogans from walls and pavement or to paint the Star of David and the word Jew on the windows of Jewish-owned businesses. "I was an eyewitness to these persecutions, these humiliations," Walter recalls, "and I felt very deeply, and very distinctly, that a misfortune had befallen us."

The consequences of this misfortune were not long in coming for the family. "Customers of ours who owed money—the Christian customers, the 'Aryans'—stopped paying," says Walter, "with the exception of the whores, who continued to pay." Sometime later, the Roths' shop was assigned "Aryan" administrators, and

they "grabbed off whatever was left" of the assets. At around the same time, the
family was forced to leave their apartment. "We were the only Jews out of perhaps
forty or fifty tenants, and the family had lived there for decades," says Walter.
"But, within days after Hitler came, the tenants' association drafted a petition to
make the building 'Judenrein'"—free from Jews. Two months later, in May, the
Roths moved to an apartment house owned by a Jew.

I was going to a rather posh high school at the time of the German
takeover, and among my schoolmates there were some who had quite
well articulated anti-Semitic opinions. I was absolutely astonished that
anyone could think such things, but they stated them with conviction:
that the Jews were exploiters and so forth.

There was no school for around six weeks after the Germans
arrived. When school reopened, the physical education teacher, who
also taught English, had replaced the Jewish teacher of German and
Latin as dean of our class. As our first homework assignment, this PE
teacher gave us a composition with the title "What Has Impressed Me
Most Since the Events." I can still remember very clearly my shock
when a vituperative anti-Semitic essay written by one of the boys—the
nephew of an Austrian bishop, whom I had always thought of as a
Christian Socialist, National Front sort of fellow—was read aloud to the
class.

The gist of his composition was that, just after the German takeover, he had gone back out onto the street for the first time and seen how
many Jewish businesses had been closed down. So the implication was
that the Jews had owned all the businesses. I felt deeply affected by that:
first of all, that this fellow in particular would write such a thing; and,
secondly, that people took the fact that Jews had owned businesses as a
pretext to discriminate, as if it were a bad thing in and of itself. Perhaps
for the very reason that we, too, had a business, it really hit me.

I didn't understand enough about politics to grasp this politically;
I had friends the same age who were confirmed Marxists, for example,
and who saw things differently. But although I was very naïve in this
respect, I felt that I was being discriminated against wrongfully, that
they were doing something that wasn't right—even if it was the authorities, even if it was the government, even if it came from the police. I felt
it to be unjust, and, as for the group that was doing this to me, I rejected
it. I felt this very deeply, and I was terribly unhappy.

In line with one of the first official steps taken by the Nazis' anti-Jewish apparatus, all eligible Austrians were required to apply for the Ariernachweis, an attestation that the bearer was "Aryan" as defined by the Nuremberg racial laws.

As my mother was of unknown origin, the problem of Aryan and non-Aryan—of Jewish and Aryan—arose in my family for the first time. In one sense this wasn't anything new for me. By the time my grandmother had died in 1934 I had known—without, however, really being conscious of it or bringing it into any connection with religion or descent—that my mother was not a born Jew, that she had some other origin. But until Hitler came, no one had ever thought of investigating who people's parents or grandparents were and inferring from that whether someone was good or bad.

Walter's mother appears to have been the illegitimate child of Austrian aristocrats. Under an old law designed to protect the highborn from embarrassment while providing a decent start in life for the issue of their moral lapses, she had been designated a "discreet birth." As such, she was assigned a name and furnished with a large sum of money; neither of her parents was identified, and her papers provided no hint of her ancestry. "She had a torn certificate documenting the sum that had been paid out for her: It was a yellowed paper with red printing, and there were figures written in black with a quill pen," Walter says. "She really waited her whole life for someone to show up and tell her what her origins were and who she was."

The future Mrs. Roth spent most of her first ten years on a farm. "Other children were there as well," recounts Walter, "but she was a bit of an outsider because she was being paid for. She didn't feel that she totally belonged, and she demanded special treatment." In particular, he says, she refused to eat what the others ate and insisted on sweets, as a result of which she gained weight and got stuck with a nickname that emphasized her outsider status: Fat Viennese. When her money was gone, she was put into an orphanage, spending a couple of years there before being taken in by a second set of foster parents at the age of thirteen.

My mother was of the persuasion that she was a born Christian who had converted to Judaism, but what she felt had nothing to do with what the authorities wanted to know. They didn't care whether somebody felt Jewish or not-Jewish, only whether they had four "Aryan"—Christian—grandparents. Since my mother couldn't complete the Ariernachweis in the usual way, she had to send her papers to the competent "scientific," in quotes, body in Berlin, which was to determine whether she was an Aryan. With the papers, she had to send photos—of her head and of her ear, which was specially photo-graphed—as well as certain measurements of the height and width and depth of her skull.

Stamped on the birth certificate she had, however, was that she had left the Catholic faith and been received into the Jewish religious com-munity. This birth certificate, had she sent it in, would have put her at a disadvantage, because in their imbecility they said that an Aryan would be repelled by everything Jewish. Since an Aryan would never voluntarily—without, so to speak, being ensnared—feel drawn to a Jew, this would have been a sign that she was not an Aryan.

So she had to get a birth certificate which wasn't marked that she had converted to Judaism. She went to the Catholic priest at the church in whose birth registry she was inscribed, and he made out a duplicate certificate which didn't have that on it. My mother was extremely grateful to him for taking that risk; it was clear that it truly was a dangerous thing to do, because in not including these emendations he had in reality forged the document.

When my mother came back from the church with these new papers, she left the Jewish community and was stricken from the regis-ter. For me, this was all a necessary act of deception: In order to protect herself and us, and possibly to save whatever there was to save, my mother was pulling the wool over their eyes. But it was nothing that affected our relationship, because her ties to us had not changed at all, and there was no change in my feelings. Even after the war, when my mother felt she couldn't return to Judaism out of gratitude for the fact that this priest had exposed himself to danger—and, without going to church or anything like that, she became a Catholic again—it was no problem as far as I was concerned. For me, my mother was my mother: She was no more a Jew before and no less a Jew afterward, she was the same as always.

Walter's mother sent the necessary documents to Berlin, not mentioning that she was married to a Jew. The question never came up—"they must just have assumed that she wasn't," says Walter, "as it would have been noted in the papers"—and in June 1938 the authorities announced their determination that Mrs. Roth was an Aryan under the Nuremberg Laws. In consequence, Walter and his brother, who was to die in 1940 after a lifetime of chronic illness, were assigned the status of Geltungsjude.

The term Geltungsjude—meaning "counting as a Jew"—was applied to those descended from two Jewish grandparents and registered as members of a Jewish religious community on September 15, 1935, the day the Nuremberg Laws were enacted. Under the racial laws, Geltungsjuden* fell between two much larger groups: the Volljuden, or "full Jews," who were descended from three or four Jewish grandparents and classed as Jews no matter what their religious affiliation; and the Mischlinge ersten Grades, or "half-breeds of the first degree," who were descended from two Jewish grandparents but had no Jewish religious affiliation. The latter escaped the category of Jew for the somewhat less disadvantageous category of non-Aryan, and in cases where they had one "full-Jewish" parent, a degree of protection was extended to that parent in turn.

Although they were classed as "Jews" and subjected to most anti-Jewish measures, the Geltungsjuden—unlike the Volljuden—were never deported wholesale to concentration camps. As in the Roths' case, the presence of an "Aryan" spouse generally spared the Jewish parent from deportation as well. Walter and his father were thus to find themselves in an exceptional position: Although classified as "Jews," they were able to live openly in Vienna through most of the Second World War.

As one of the first anti-Jewish measures to be implemented barred Jews from attending school with "Aryans," Walter was forced in mid-1938 to transfer to a school set up by the state exclusively for Jewish children.

I had never been a terribly successful student, and in this new school I wasn't particularly successful either, but there were no demands placed on you anyway. From the beginning of 1939, however, I went to a Jewish afternoon school that was started by the Zionist organizations after it was no longer possible for Jews to learn skills through study or apprenticeship. About 1,200 to 1,400 adolescents went to this school, which was officially called the Youth Aliyah School† and which was recognized by the authorities as a preparatory school for Jewish emigration to Palestine.

The school was under the authority of the Gestapo. For example, the school had to provide children to harvest asparagus during the

---

*Geltungsjuden: plural of *Geltungsjude; Volljuden:* plural of *Volljude; Mischlinge:* plural of *Mischling.*

†*Aliyah:* immigration to Palestine (today, to Israel; Hebrew).

military campaign of 1939, so we went to Northern Germany for five or six weeks, then returned. Another time, we were all called in to the Gestapo and had to stand for hours in the courtyard. But this was not a problem for the kids there—these incidents aside, the atmosphere was extraordinarily positive. It was a pleasure to go.

I was very good with my hands, and I learned the trades of electrician, locksmith, and plumber one after another. When I was fourteen, I no longer went to the state school—school was compulsory only to the age of fourteen—so, besides this practical instruction, I had academic subjects in the mornings at the Youth Aliyah School. There, I was confronted with Jewish lore really for the first time. We had courses in Jewish history and philosophy, in the Bible, and in Yiddish literature, and the teachers were outstanding. In addition, the school, which for the outside world was a school for emigrants, was internally divided into Zionist factions—left, center, and right—and I was the leader of one of the small groups.

As I got more and more deeply involved in the Youth Aliyah School, I severed my connections to the non-Jewish world. For two years I more or less lived there, coming home only to sleep. I was confronted with Jewish thought, with Jewish tradition, with the Zionist worldview, and I accepted it all. We had a really good teacher who brought us closer to German culture but who also showed us very clearly the Jewish influence; and the contrast was presented—deliberately, I assume—between the Jewish spirit that was at work in German culture in a positive way and the rejection that the positive side of German culture had suffered at the hands of these criminals. There were, so to speak, the good and the bad, and the Jews belonged to the good. Some Germans also belonged to the good, but the Nazis were the ones who had rejected or abused the best parts of their tradition.

Thus, I actually did experience a positive Jewish consciousness at that time. I identified fully. We had a common enemy, and it wasn't we who were the Untermenschen,* but *they* were the Untermenschen. I developed at this Youth Aliyah School. I was successful there, and it

---

Untermenschen: subhumans; a term applied by Nazis to Jews, Slavs, and others they considered inferior to the "Aryan race."

affected me emotionally, perhaps, that I became something among the Jews.

In the meantime, anti-Jewish measures had been stepped up. The Roths requested permission to leave Austria but, as was typical, were refused a visa. Toward the end of 1940, with Europe plunged deeply into war and the possibility of emigration virtually nil, the Youth Aliyah School was closed by the authorities. Shortly thereafter, Walter and his father were assigned to forced labor. Alongside other Geltungsjuden and Jewish partners in mixed marriages—"and under Aryan supervision, of course"—they crafted uniforms for the German military.

Walter and his father were paid almost nothing, and the family was at a disadvantage under the rationing system, but, thanks to the great energy and resourcefulness of his mother, Walter says, "things were never that hard." During the entire war, Mrs. Roth kept food on the table through black-market dealings, some of which went via the Roths' original landlord, a grocer who was sympathetic toward the family. Mrs. Roth also used her wits to bring the family through several scrapes with the authorities.

Our house was searched two or three times. Somebody who wanted our apartment denounced us, and the police came; once, my mother was arrested because someone said that she had threatened him with a knife. Incidents like that were terribly dangerous for us, and there were also regular moves of one sort or another against the Jews, but my mother always managed to fend these things off. She went to the Gestapo, she argued, and, as an Aryan, she prevailed.

One result of Mrs. Roth's efforts was that the family was able to stay at the same address from 1939 to 1945—a rare feat, especially considering the size of the apartment.

We had two bedrooms, a toilet, a kitchen with a bath, and a sitting room; Jews generally lived several families to one apartment, so by Jewish standards that was downright palatial. We had to post the yellow star on the door of the apartment, but in contrast to the house where we had originally lived and where they threw us out immediately, the neighbors were friendly toward us. Within a short time after we'd moved in, the members of the one other Jewish family in the building had all either emigrated or been deported. So Christians lived all around us, but we were not considered foreign bodies there.

As we were among the few Jews who had a relatively large apartment, and as our neighbors not only accepted us but were apparently also willing to accept lots of people coming to our place, we had a very hospitable household. Two of the nephews of my father who had married Christian women still lived in Vienna and came to see us, and other mixed couples came over as well. We played cards, and listened to foreign broadcasts, and all manner of astounding things took place. There was never any trouble on account of this, something that actually was totally unbelievable in this police state.

Walter saw few friends other than the guests who came to the family's apartment. Beginning in 1941, however, he met on Sunday afternoons with a dozen or so former classmates from the defunct Youth Aliyah School at the apartment of a Jewish former army officer who had lost both legs fighting for Austria in World War I. There, the youths—some of whom, like Walter, were still living officially in Vienna, others of whom had gone into hiding—received tips on how to handle themselves in combat.

If circumstances had been a bit different—had we known, for instance, that things were heading toward a complete extermination of the Jews—I think we would have begun to organize ourselves into combat units. But, as it was, everything remained rather theoretical and nothing came out of it. As a highly decorated disabled veteran, this man was privileged to a certain extent; he thought he would remain under protection, and some others in the group were in a similar situation.

The psychology of it was interesting: People believed that authority and justice were linked—and that, no matter what kinds of things those in power were spouting, injustice could never take over completely. You didn't want to acknowledge—you couldn't acknowledge—that this might be possible. You held on to whatever small measure of justice had been accorded you; you avoided putting that into jeopardy. So this man thought he had something to lose—he just didn't know that he had lost it long before.

Of course, if we ever had been caught, they would have brought us to trial and beheaded us or I don't know what, even though everything was absolutely harmless. But at the end of 1942, the man was deported—deported and killed—and the group dissolved. We had no goal other than waiting, and it was simpler to wait on your own.

Beginning in September 1941, Jews in the Reich were required to wear a yellow star on the left breast of their outer garments. Walter rarely complied and, passing as an "Aryan," he silently defied many anti-Jewish restrictions: He rode the streetcar, went swimming, and in general enjoyed a freedom of movement that would have been impossible otherwise. This freedom was bought at the price of great risk, for, had he been caught, Walter would have become a prime candidate for deportation.

He developed a number of strategies to protect himself. He always rode the outside platform of the streetcar, which allowed him to see who was getting on and to jump off quickly if he spotted someone who knew him. He avoided enclosed spaces such as movie theaters, where there was a possibility that military patrols might come looking for AWOL soldiers. Walter's caution paid off: Not once was he stopped for an ID check while moving without the star.

The reason I didn't wear the star was, to be completely honest, that I was ashamed. Not that I was a Jew—well, that too, perhaps—but that I was forced to be marked. And then, it was very simply not opportune to be a Jew in those days. If I had worn the star, I would have had anxieties all the same: Only in that case it would not have been because the police might have arrested me for not wearing the star, it would have been because I wouldn't have been able to do all those things—going swimming, going for a walk—and because I could have been beaten up. Jews were outside the protection of the law, so anyone could do whatever he wanted to you, and I was fifteen, sixteen, seventeen years old then and the Hitler Youth was around. The risk was there either way; and if I didn't have to advertise that I was a Jew, it was a good thing for me, so I avoided it. But the main reason I didn't wear the star was that being marked disturbed me enormously, and I didn't want it.

I had a windbreaker with the star on it and, as the windbreaker was yellow, even if someone had been looking for the star, he might not have seen it right away. I also had a briefcase, which I carried in such a way that I could cover the star with it; that was one of the normal methods, it wasn't my invention. I had to leave the house with the star, but as I went around the corner, I let the windbreaker fall open—as if it had happened just then, by chance—so that the flap fell over the star and hid it. If I had seen someone from the neighborhood, he would have figured that it was accidental, and it wasn't as if everyone looked. Then I had to find someplace where I could take off the jacket and put it into the briefcase. I had a similar problem at work: I had to come in with the star and wear it in the workshops because people knew me there, but I had to leave without it.

When I had taken off this jacket, I behaved as if I were not a Jew. Playing the role of an Aryan was limited to passing circumstances; it was only a question of bridging a short time, the way somewhere. I was never in the embarrassing position of having to present myself as an Aryan or of having to say "Heil Hitler" or anything like that.

Whatever happened, I managed not to make myself conspicuous. It was a kind of mimicry. I always had a sensible appearance; that is, if I was eighteen and not in uniform, I tried to look younger, made myself into a schoolboy, because people would have expected an eighteen-year-old to be in a uniform of some sort. Although I didn't have much contact with people as an Aryan, one example comes to mind: I went swimming and boating on a tributary of the Danube with a girl I'd met. There, I told all kinds of untrue stories. In a bathing suit I had it easy, because everyone was in bathing suits; young men my age were sitting around in bathing suits exactly as I was, so I didn't need a uniform. But most of the time I remained aloof.

I was very conscious of playing a role when I was in the role of a non-Jew. Maybe I was also playing a role when I wore the star, because that also involved a certain change in my natural demeanor. I was called in by the police—which didn't happen just once, I was summoned or brought in ten or fifteen times in the course of these years—and whether at the labor office, the Gestapo, or wherever, if I did in fact play a role, I played the Jew. I was reserved, I didn't act outspoken, I didn't hold myself erect. Rather, I fulfilled the expectations they had of a Jew in the Third Reich: I acted depressed, behaving in such a way as not to provoke aggression.

The other contacts I had as a Jew were almost exclusively at work, where I didn't function as a Jew, but rather as a worker—we were all equals, so to speak. It was hard to keep up relations outside work, because you could go without the star when you were alone, but in groups you couldn't. On the other hand, people who didn't have to wear the star would have felt encumbered if someone like me, who was supposed to wear the star, had exposed them to danger. So it wasn't without its problems, and, in general, you were on your own.

Despite all his precautions, Walter was recognized as a Jew on several occasions. Once he was followed by the former classmate whose anti-Semitic essay had so shocked him. Walter believes the young man was trying to check whether he was in fact wearing the star; at length, the boy appeared to give up, but Walter "was frightened for days that the police would come." Another time, Walter was surprised in the stairwell of a deserted office building as he was changing out of his windbreaker and had to think and talk quickly to allay the curiosity of the building's superintendent.

There were "positive" instances as well. When a shouting match broke out on a streetcar he was riding, Walter was warned by a fellow passenger he guesses "must have known" that he was a Jew to "scram" before the police showed up. During another streetcar ride, a lady handed Walter a bag of grapes—a rare commodity in those days—with the words, "You must not have had any of these in a long time." Saying it "was perfectly clear that she had recognized me as a Jew," Walter admits to mixed emotions: "I was frightened to death—but, on the other hand, I had the grapes." In an atmosphere where even a kind gesture could be a reminder of the "unremitting" danger he faced, "there was," Walter declares, "never a peaceful moment."

Still, he and his father continued making uniforms, and, although his family was occasionally threatened by the police, life went on without serious incident. Walter had become convinced as early as 1942 or '43 that the Allies would win the war; by 1944, believing that "it was a question of weeks" before Germany collapsed, he had developed what he describes as a "devil-may-care" attitude. Although it was a capital offense, Walter and a Jewish co-worker regularly went out on the town with a supervisor from the factory, an "Aryan" girl whose fiancé, an SS man, appeared to be missing in Russia. At the same time, however, Walter felt that the danger to himself and his family was greatly increasing. "In those days," he says, "harassments not organized from above—someone or other just coming along and shooting us down, or I don't know what—became more of a possibility."

And it was perfectly obvious that the net was being drawn tighter and tighter. Even though I didn't know any Geltungsjuden who had been deported, we all kept deportation in mind as a very real possibility. As early as 1942, we had known exactly how dangerous it was to be deported. We had spoken with people who had fled to Vienna from the occupied territories—we supported them, we gave them black-market food or food we had left over—and they told us that everything there was far more dangerous, far more life-threatening, than it was here. We didn't know anything about Auschwitz or the gas chambers, but we knew of the enormous incidence of deaths in the ghettos and about this forced labor that was not at all comparable to the forced labor in the Reich itself.

At the beginning of 1944, the first Hungarian Jews had arrived as deportees assigned to forced labor in Vienna. We met them on the street and brought them to our apartment, and they told us how people had been shot down along the way. Still, at this point the extent of the genocide was not clear to us—although it could have been clear, because we were relatively well informed.

In the spring of 1944, word was spreading that Geltungsjuden could request the more favorable Mischling status if they were prepared to renounce their membership in the Jewish community and make application to the same office that had declared Mrs. Roth to be an "Aryan."

This got around at first exclusively through the grapevine: People heard that someone had tried it and been successful. In the summer of '44, they announced it, making the rumors official. We couldn't find out why they were doing this, but apparently they were trying to mobilize the last possible reserves, and in order to do that they wanted to "entjuden"* them, so to speak.

So, one day, this question arose for me. My father was sitting in the living room that evening—my mother, my father, and I—and he said to me, "Look, now there's this possibility. And we don't know how much longer it will go on, even though we believe that the end is near." He actually tried to persuade me to consider it, to consider leaving Judaism, and he said this was not something to be judged negatively on moral grounds, because when it's a question of life and death, and so forth. . . . And I felt acutely that I might have a duty to do such a thing in order to give my parents and myself a better chance to survive, as it was clear that things had become extremely dangerous.

My father asked me, "Do you want to remain a Jew, or do you want to leave Judaism?" Now, it may sound extremely silly, but when the question was put to me—and I remember exactly, there is no doubt about it—the story of Hercules came to my mind.

There is a story I knew—a fable, a fairy tale, a legend—in which Hercules was going down a road and suddenly came to a fork in the

---

*entjuden: to purge of Jews or Jewish influence, to "dejewify" (Nazi terminology).

road. One path would have led him the way of the comfortable life—the other, the way of heroism and all that goes with it. It was that second road that he chose. I saw this story right before my eyes and I said, "No." I refused. I said, "I will not leave the Jewish religion, and I will not make this request." And I saw myself as someone who had made that choice: the choice to walk the hard, the uncomfortable, but the honorable road.

Certainly, the question is to be posed: What moved me to act in this way? I believe that the strongest impulse, emotionally, was without a doubt that after everything I had gone through, I despised the others. Although compared with what I heard afterwards—what people suffered, how they died—I of course went through very little, in my own eyes I had had to endure a whole lot of humiliations and terrors, and I despised the non-Jews around me. Compared to me they were swine, and I didn't want to belong to them, not on any account. I didn't want to identify with them in any way; that would have been to take refuge in the ordinary, and I didn't want that.

I should say, so that it doesn't sound so heroic—because it wasn't—that it was much more certain in my mind than it was in my father's that it could be a question of only days or weeks: that the danger to us could be doped out, and that we would survive. But whatever the other reasons were, whatever the motivation—and certainly there were also a large number of things in my upbringing and background—at that point I consciously chose: I will become a Jew. I made a decision that wasn't based on knowledge of what Jewishness was and what not being Jewish was, I couldn't gauge that; but at that point I allowed myself to be guided, probably not by Jewish thought, but by the thought of the ancients. These concepts of honor, and that it is more meritorious to take the hard road than the easy road, had a decisive influence on me. A choice was then thrust upon me: There was a fork in the road, and I made a conscious choice, even though I didn't know what it truly involved.

In September or October 1944, Walter and his father received an order to report to the offices of the Jewish community, which had long since been integrated into the Nazi administrative apparatus.

We were brought in and had to line up; there were a few hundred people who had to come before these two SS men. Each of them had a narrow little office with a door at the head of it, and a window behind, and a desk placed crosswise near the door where you came in. At this desk sat the SS man. On the right, behind him, was a small table with a telephone on it, and before him was our file. In front of the desk, against the wall, stood a Jupo, a Jewish policeman.

I remember the name: Girtschik. He was a well-known SS man from the Jewish section. As we came in, he said our names, loudly—"Moritz Israel, Walter Israel Roth"—and he opened the file and looked in. He kept his head down; he didn't look at us, never once. He said, "Has he left?"—whether I had left Judaism. And my father answered, very depressed, dejected, very hesitant, "No, but—"

He interrupted, saying, "Einziehen!" Einziehen. *Einziehen* meant "arrest them."

We had talked about it beforehand, and it is a decision we had made at the time: "We'll go, because if we don't go, they'll come looking for us. And if they come looking for us, then the situation is bad." But at that moment I saw everything before my eyes and I regretted I had come, I regretted we hadn't gone into hiding. I felt a bead of sweat trickle down my damned face from the agitation. All this happened in an instant.

But at that same instant the telephone rang. He moved to the side, turning his back, and he picked up the phone and said, "Yes?" He snapped to attention—it must have been some high official calling, it was almost comical—and he gave his full attention to the conversation.

Then this Jupo, who did not have a very good name among the Jews—there were two of them, and this one was the worse of the two—did something absolutely extraordinary. He took the file, he closed it, he stuck it away somewhere, he said to us, "Beat it! Out!"—and he sent us away. We went through the door and down the stairs, and we were free.

Of the group of Geltungsjuden and other exempted Jews who were there at that point, those they arrested were sent to build fortifications. They went to the Ostwall* construction at the border of Austria and Hungary, and they were with the Hungarian Jews on the death march

---

Ostwall: East Wall, a line of fortifications intended to stop the westward march of the Red Army.

to Mauthausen, and a number of them died. The others went into the Organisation Todt.* I actually came out of it the best I possibly could: I neither went into the Organisation Todt nor was I arrested, but I went home.

Although they continued to show up for work, figuring that not going would bring the police straight to their door, Walter and his father decided it would be best not to sleep at their own apartment for a while. They accepted an offer of overnight accommodations from a non-Jewish family they had known for years, to whom Walter remains grateful but whom he nonetheless calls "opportunists": "They saw that there would be no particular danger to them and that we would have to show a large measure of gratitude, which we did: They got money for it at the time, and the wife took some jewelry from my mother." Once three weeks had passed without word from the authorities, Walter and his father resumed sleeping at home, and they stayed there until the end of the war.

We had no difficulties; nothing happened to us for five months. But the tension was constant; it was much worse than between 1941 and 1944.

On the one hand, there was no doubt that the collapse was near; I was almost sure that if something happened to me now, I would nevertheless survive, because time was on my side. As far as we knew, around 2,000 Jews were still in Vienna for one reason or another, including the "U-boats," the people in hiding. I knew about cases of people who had been in hiding for years—years!—and now there were only weeks left, months left. Besides, I had long been living under the illusion that the German military might get rid of this Hitler band, and I was certain that I would run into friends—well, not friends exactly, but people who wouldn't do me any harm because they also expected this.

So I was more self-confident, and I didn't feel so isolated. I thought, "I'll keep going, I'll struggle through"—totally false, as I realize today. My number might have come up. There were, even in the final days, the last hours, friends of mine who were killed. But I was not yet thirteen when Hitler came, and I was twenty when Hitler left. These are forma-

---

*The others were those who agreed to renounce their membership in the Jewish community and seek Mischling status. The *Organisation Todt* was the Reich agency in charge of construction.

tive years, and I had suffered all that time because I couldn't throw off this oppression. Then, in a swing to the other side, I became overconfident—totally without foundation. But that was my state of mind then.

There was also a feeling of exultation because we knew that we were in the right. I thought, "I belong to the victors"; and, although we certainly didn't think about it in such terms, we knew that even if we weren't around to see it, those beasts were going to pay. We had made it, even though we hadn't made it yet. So there was a question of revenge and of rage, and in this sense we were expectant.

At the same time, it was clear that the danger was more immediate than ever because there was not a man between the ages of sixteen and sixty who was not in uniform—except for foreign workers, and the foreign workers were very easy to pick out, we couldn't be mistaken for them. I acted out dramas in my mind sometimes: what would happen in this situation or that. I saw much more clearly than in all the years before how dangerous it was. Until then, I had been afraid of being locked up, but at that point I was afraid of being killed. I knew that it was no longer a question of being slapped around or given too little to eat but of being faced with death.

But another reason I felt it was far more dangerous was that it was now up to me to act, and that weighed heavily on me. As I said, I regretted, at that moment when he said "einziehen," that I had come. After that experience, we were sure that if such a situation came up again, we would flee. There was no longer this possibility of letting things happen to you: You had to act.

But this pressure to act is an uneasy feeling, because, you know, a person tends to prefer to do nothing. Not to be active. Not to take his fate into his own hands, and to challenge that fate. I felt that we'd done everything wrong up to then—all the Jews—because we hadn't acted. But now we felt that we could no longer sit still and wait for it to be over. And the fear was all the greater because when you act, you bear the responsibility, the full responsibility.

Despite being "a lot more careful" than ever, Walter had been through another close shave or two by the time the Red Army reached Vienna in April 1945. Its arrival set off fierce street fighting.

Houses burned all around us, and bombs fell, and we were shot at. My family was well integrated in the building where we lived, and the closer it came to the fall of Hitler, the better we were treated. I was the only younger man there, along with a Dutch forced laborer, and I ended up playing a leading role. In the days of the collapse, I actually identified with this neighborhood, with my immediate surroundings, and I did everything imaginable, everything I could: I helped put out fires, protect children, bandage the wounded—not soldiers, civilians. It was a very heroic time. And just as the people there didn't regard me first and foremost as a Jew, I didn't regard them first and foremost as fascists.

In the next two or three months we came to understand the overall extent of the persecution that had taken place. The whole horrible body of facts was becoming known. We heard about the concentration camps. You saw photos of the emaciated corpses, the mountains of them. And I reported for duty with the Austrian police.

I spent four months with the police, locking up Nazis. I was in the department that worked with the dossiers, and I requisitioned documents, examined them, annotated them, passed them along. But after a moment of elation, when I went around embracing everyone, I saw that there just was a difference between myself and the rest. I was always on one side and they were always on the other. I could rejoice unreservedly that the Allies had won the war; the others couldn't. For me the Russians were liberators, for them they were occupiers. I cooperated with them because we had a common goal; they cooperated with them because they had to. And there was an overwhelming number of my police colleagues who actually had a guilty conscience; they looked for every possible excuse, but not one said, "Mea culpa." I wasn't very happy there, so I left.

After that I was never again happy with Austria, either. I had seen that it simply wouldn't work—it was too difficult, there was too little in common. I was happy as all hell that I belonged to the Jews and not to the others, a feeling that was growing stronger. But it still was not so that I saw the Jews, or Judaism, as a positive force. It was a question of antifascists and fascists, of victims and perpetrators; it wasn't a question of Jews and non-Jews. As far as I was concerned, the Americans and the Russians—the opponents of Hitler—were the positive forces; and they, naturally, were not Jews.

In the months following the end of the war, a great many Jewish displaced persons were brought to Vienna, which became an organizing center for illegal *immigration to Palestine. Walter was reunited with a number of friends from the Youth Aliyah School, and the group got in touch with the Zionist organizations. "We heard about the heroic deeds that were taking place in this illegal immigration, and stories about the war, and about the Jewish Legion,* and we wanted to emigrate to Palestine," he recalls. Walter himself smuggled convoys of Jews from Austria to Germany, where they boarded ships for Palestine.*

But, influenced by family concerns, Walter never did emigrate to Israel; instead, he spent a few years in the United States in the early 1950s. He then returned to settle in Vienna, where, at the time of the interview, he lived with his Israeli wife and their children and ran a small business. A highly active member of the Jewish community, Walter claims to be "always ready to take up whatever cause"—and to do so "publicly identified as a Jew" in a city where it still "doesn't do any good to show it off"—in line with his belief that to live as a Jew is to live "in an exemplary way."

Maybe I'm crazy, maybe I'm a nut, but I feel responsible if Jews do things—as Jews—that I disapprove of, or fail to do things I think they should do. I try to cut in, I try to rectify it, I try to put things in order again. For I am of the opinion that I have to live as a Jew and only as a Jew, that anything else would be a denial of the circumstances. So I live as a Jew in Austria; as an Austrian Jew, but as a Jew, not as a Jewish Austrian. This represents a great change from my childhood.

Walter places the beginning of this change—the beginning of what he calls "my positive connection to Jewishness, my identity with Jewishness"—in his days in the illegal immigration movement.

If you were to go over this again, you'd see that I actually never said that I ever felt Jewish, so to speak. Even when I was in the temple choir, it didn't have any great significance for me. I was always made into a Jew from outside. People swore at me. They said:

Jud', Jud',
Spuck' in Hut.
Sagt die Mama,
"Das ist gut."†

---

*The Jewish Legion fought in Palestine during World War II.
†A classic anti-Semitic rhyme. In literal translation: Jew, Jew, / Spit in the hat. / Mama says, / "That is good."

I got into fights over it, but it wasn't any choice of mine that they said that to me.

That I arrived at a positive relationship to being Jewish was a mental process of self-affirmation. It certainly could have gone the other way: I might also have said that I wanted to push it away so that I had nothing to do with it. The reason this did not happen may well have been that when Hitler arrived in 1938, I felt I had been pushed in an altogether unfair way into a situation in which I was being persecuted. Even up to 1944, I had a completely unbalanced relationship to my environment and to my own identity. My identity was still determined at that point not by me, not by my feelings about Jewishness, but through circumstances, from outside.

For this reason, says Walter, his refusal to renounce membership in the Jewish community was a decision not to remain but, as he phrased it, "to become" a Jew.

What was determinant was that I had decided to walk the hard road. Though I said that I looked down on the others, perhaps that isn't completely true: I refused to belong to the mass. But I was still a part of it, I hadn't yet distinguished myself—I had been distinguished from it, excluded, but that was nothing for which I myself could claim credit. I feel that I began, at that moment, to want to achieve something.

Thereafter, I would have had to make a conscious effort not to be a Jew, or not to identify, or to reject it. Before that, it was possible. Before that, it would have been a choice: here, or there. Afterwards, it would have been a repudiation.

Although at that moment I didn't really know what it involved, it was obvious to me that I had a lot yet to accomplish.

TRANSMISSION
and BELONGING

Having observed some of the ways in which Jewish identity manifests itself in individuals' perceptions, feelings, and actions, and having considered what it does in various instances to shape their lives, we might not be out of place returning for a last, explicit look at a question that applies to all the life histories: What makes people feel that they are Jews at all?

In the case of those who were raised with the Jewish religion or who grew up in a Jewish cultural environment, the answer seems obvious. Taken for granted in almost the same way is identification on the part of those who shared the experience of persecution. But there are people whose upbringing left little mark on them, just as there are people whose treatment at the hands of the Nazis failed to deepen their bonds with fellow Jews. What makes an upbringing or a shared experience take hold? Why does identification work?

These questions find answers in the lives of all those who identify as Jews—and of all those who, while they may have a reason to, do not. But perhaps they are most vividly illustrated by the stories of individuals who are drawn to Jewishness even though the weight of their experience would seem to pull them in another direction.

Taken from her orthodox household as the Jews were being rounded up in Amsterdam, Dvora Goldenberg was brought to live with a family of devout Protestants in the Dutch countryside. But, even though this change took place before her fifth birthday, Dvora never felt at one with her new environment. She rejected its manners and values, and if for a time she shared her foster parents' religion—a brand of Christianity that in some ways recalls orthodox Judaism—she had a crisis similar to the one Isaäk Feldman experienced at Auschwitz: Seeing herself comfortable in heaven while the Jews suffered in hell, Dvora was ready to give up eternal salvation if that was what it took to belong. Did Dvora's first four years matter so much that the following fourteen mattered little? Why did she cling so firmly to her beginnings, and what part did Jewishness play in her wish or ability to hold on?

"I believe, very strongly, that there is a way of behaving, of thinking, of feeling, that is culturally determined," states Pavel Balázs. "But that can't be the whole story," he observes, "or I wouldn't be a good Jew." The youngest member of his family, Pavel was the only one ignorant of the Jewish origins they were hiding. But something told him that the family had a secret—and at the same time provided him with the clues and the drive he needed to get to the bottom of it. Had his parents' silence regarding the persecution taking place around them made an impression on Pavel without his knowing it? If what his brother took from his parents was their overt strategy of concealment, had Pavel inherited their unknowing tendency to allow their most important choices to be determined by the Jewishness that they concealed?

Mina Landau has no memory of her parents and, as a young child in the years immediately following the war, had no idea that they had been Jewish. Her discovery of her origins became a source of fantasy, of anger, and of a feeling of specialness that was the foundation of much of her self-worth; it is as if she identified with something to which she was never consciously exposed, something that existed only in her imaginings. But, wherever her Jewishness came from, she felt deeply obligated to it, and it was not until she had paid her debt—by marrying a Jew and raising Jewish children—that she seems to have been able to detach a bit and look at it in other than a highly idealized light. Is it only in rebuilding the ancestral link, in taking her place in the continuity of a Jewish life she personally never knew, that she can find the freedom to be her individual self?

Dvora Goldenberg

At the beginning of 1943, I was four years old. We lived in the east of Amsterdam. I remember going to a park nearby, but then it was not allowed anymore. I remember that the parks were closed to Jews, the non-Jewish shops were closed to Jews, the schools were closed to Jews, the trams and buses were closed to Jews. I didn't need to wear a star because I wasn't yet six years old, but I remember my mother sewing stars on the clothes. I found that beautiful. I was very proud of the stars, but my parents were obviously very scared.

My father taught Jewish religion. He was also a mohel, and a bit of a chazzan, and he blew the shofar on Rosh Hashanah, and he studied for shochet—he did all those little jobs in shul.* I used to go with my father to shul, but what happened in shul I don't remember, I only remember the fact that I went.

My mother had a big family. They all used to come to our house on Friday nights, and there was all this singing and such that went on. During the war the Jews didn't have much work, and my father didn't have much money, but he brought home one chicken to be divided amongst the whole family. This continued till he was picked up and till the other people had to go into hiding.

We also had a lady living at our place; I don't know where she

---

mohel: man qualified to perform ritual circumcision; *chazzan:* cantor; *shofar:* ram's horn; *Rosh Hashanah:* Jewish New Year; *shochet:* ritual butcher for kosher meat (all Hebrew); *shul:* synagogue (Yiddish).

came from, but she was a Jewish lady called Mrs. De Vries. The Germans wanted this lady—why, I don't know—and I remember that once when they came for her, my father said, "Quick! Put her into a bed, put the blankets over her: She's ill." So they pretended that she was ill, but the Germans still wanted the lady, and they came to fetch her. My father said, "I'll go instead." I heard about this from a Jew who was living in hiding next door, but I also remember seeing the Germans coming to our house at night with their boots and everything and taking my father away.

Then, for half a year, my mother was alone with three children. I was the eldest, and she had a little girl a year and a half younger than me and a baby. Obviously, she didn't know what to do. She had no money for food or anything and she was all on her own. People were already hidden at that time, and nobody dared come out. She herself hardly dared to go outside, and she didn't dare to let me go outside because she was scared the Germans would pick me up off the street. Very often the alarm was up in town, and then you had to be hidden. We hid behind the stairs, and my mother's fear was passed to me, and I felt it.

I understood more than is usual for my age because my mother had only me to talk to. As the eldest one, I could speak; the younger ones couldn't speak properly yet. I remember that my mother had absolutely no idea what was going to happen with us if we were picked up, but she was scared stiff. The only thing I myself knew was that this was because we were Jewish—that was the answer I always got. Why are the shops closed, why are the parks closed to us? "We are Jewish." How could she give another answer to a child like that? I took it as a fact—like I took it as a fact that my father had been picked up, and, later on, that I had to go to people I didn't know at all—and I tried to shut my feelings to the whole thing.

In June 1943 people from the underground movement came, and they told my mother that she could give her children to the underground and that we would be brought to non-Jewish families to be saved during the war. She first gave my sister, and then a week after that she gave me—that was the twelfth of June or so—and the next day she was to go with the baby. But just the next day there was a big roundup, so it was too late for her.

Having thus left on the eve of the final large-scale roundups of Amsterdam Jews, four-and-a-half-year-old Deborah Voorzanger was brought to the town of Dokkum in the northern Dutch province of Friesland, where she was taken in by a Protestant family named Kuiper.

They had children of their own: one child who was eighteen years older than me, and another one who was sixteen years older, and another ten years older. They told me I had to say that I was sent away from Rotterdam because of the bombing, that I was the child of a cousin—eppes azoy*—and that my name was a different name than I really had. I was never allowed to say that I came from Amsterdam, or what my real name was—Voorzanger means "cantor" in Dutch and is known as a typical Amsterdam Jewish name—or that I was Jewish, of course. I knew why not; I understood a great deal for my age.

Some of the people in the town knew what the real story was, but I didn't know who did and who didn't; so I couldn't tell anybody, because that would have been too dangerous. People were suspicious, because the family was tall and blond but I was small and dark. Besides, they were too old to have a small child like that, it didn't look natural. I remember that people always used to ask me if they saw me in the tram or somewhere, "And where do you come from?"

"From Rotterdam. I am Margriet Voorhoeve."

And then they asked me, "Well, you've been to Artis, haven't you?"

But I said, "No, to Blijdorp."†

Because of the fear—they had told me, "You have to say that, it's dangerous if you don't"—I never made a mistake. But it always disturbed me.

My foster father was a baker. When he wanted to have me written into his passport, he baked a nice cake and he went to the town hall, which was just opposite where we lived. He said, "Here you have something to go with your coffee, but write this child's name into my passport." He knew exactly who was to be trusted and who wasn't, because you couldn't do things like that with someone you doubted.

---

*eppes azoy: something like that (Yiddish).
†Artis: Amsterdam's zoo; Blijdorp: the zoo in Rotterdam.

So I was written into his passport, but since they couldn't register me officially, I didn't have ration coupons, which you needed for clothes and food. In the beginning when my dress was washed, I had to stay indoors till it was dry. Shoes were no problem: They chopped down trees in the middle of the night, and my foster father went with a cake to the man who made wooden shoes, and he took my measure and made me shoes. And, in Friesland, you could always get a bit of food from the farms and from people you knew.

My foster father used to deliver bread on his bike—he put the bread into a big basket on the front—and he used to take me around on the bike with him. There were also non-Jews in hiding who had been ordered to work in Germany and who didn't want to go, and he used to wave and point at me to give them a bit of courage. I knew exactly where the people were hidden, and under which sewing machine people had hidden the radio, and where there were bikes hidden in the closets. And, as my foster parents' future son-in-law was one of the main people in the underground there, I heard about weapons drops and so on. I saw and knew and heard more than they thought, but I never talked about it, and they knew I wouldn't say anything.

A few times a week Queen Wilhelmina used to speak on the radio, and people who were in hiding came together in the cellar of the bakery to listen to the BBC. There was a peat-fired oven, and my foster father had a cellar full of peat; you took one block out, then another, and the radio was hidden behind, because you weren't allowed to have a radio. Everyone who was in hiding was there sitting on crates listening, and I always listened with them, I remember this clearly. It was really quite convivial.

Life in hiding was nonetheless a life of constant danger. A woman living a few doors up the street once wrote to the Landwacht, a police organization founded by the Dutch fascist movement but placed under the command of the SS, to report the presence of a Jewish child at the Kuipers' address.

I don't know how they did it, but the underground intercepted the letter. My foster father had a big piece of marble on the counter in the bakery shop, and he hid this letter under the marble, saying, "You'll see, I want to do something with this after the war"—he was so angry with this lady! My foster parents thought it was not safe enough for me to stay there at that moment; they wanted me out of the way for a few months so that they wouldn't have to think about it, and they brought me on the back of the bike to a very small village a bit to the north of Dokkum.

I don't think the village is even on the map; there are just a few farms and a church. My foster father had a sister there who was married, and they had a small farm, and that's where I was brought. It was very interesting for me on the farm, I quite liked it. Then, after a few months or after I don't know how long, they thought it would be safe again and I returned to Dokkum. To tell the truth, I saw the Germans making house searches and all that—and they saw me, even. But I don't think they were after me, really; they were more interested in getting the names of people in the underground than they were in a little Jewish child.

Subsequently the Kuiper family did run afoul of the authorities, although for a different reason.

One of the local people was in the Landwacht, and he knew everyone in the town by name. Once he came into the bakery all of a sudden when the family was eating—we used to eat in the bakery—and he saw my foster father's future son-in-law sitting there. I was there too, and I was trying to hide, but he had seen.

The son-in-law left quickly, as soon as the man had gone. But the next morning the Germans came to look through the house, and they said to my foster father, "We're taking you in"—for knowing too many people in the resistance, and knowing exactly what was going on.

I was nearby, hiding behind some clothes. This Landwacht man was there with a big gun, and he said to my foster father, "Hands up or I'll shoot!"

My foster father hated this man who betrayed his own people; he found that absolutely abhorrent. So he said, "For you"—he was sitting on a crate, peeling potatoes—"For you, my hands up? Never!" And he spit in his face and went on peeling potatoes. The man just stood there with the gun.

They took my foster father away and brought him to the prison in Leeuwarden, where they put people from the underground. The whole time he was in prison, my foster mother rode twenty-five kilometers up and back to Leeuwarden on a bike without inflatable tires to bring him food—which he never got. The underground made a raid on the prison, and it was a fantastic coup: They lost some lives, but they freed all the prisoners. So around a month before the end of the war my foster father was out.

Then the war ended, and the Americans and the English came, and we were freed. I still remember very vividly the moment of liberation. What was for me the most marvelous thing—the thing that made the most impression on me—was that I could tell everybody who I was. That I could tell the truth. I had a little friend, and I wasn't allowed to tell her where I came from, and when the war was over I ran to my friend's—I can see myself running, you know, I was running!—and I told her parents: "Look! I am not Margriet Voorhoeve, I am Deborah Voorzanger! And I am Jewish!"

I had learned to lie, which I disliked intensely. Though I was old enough to know why I had to do it—I didn't understand all the larger questions, but I knew it was dangerous—in a way it disturbed me that I could never tell the truth. And then—ooof!—I didn't need to lie anymore. That was fantastic!

But I didn't know at that point how many more years I would still have to lie and to hide my real identity—which I did, all the time. I felt much more unhappy after the war than I had during it; there was no comparison. The war wasn't such an unhappy time, really, except maybe for the separation from your parents. But you don't realize that straight away, either; you think you're going back to them.

Later on it was much worse, and it lasted much longer. Far too long in fact—it was like fourteen years in Siberia. The pressure on you becomes so great that you could easily snap. And I can't say I came out of it completely unscarred: I had to fight very hard afterwards to become myself again, to regain my own nature, which I had suppressed.

Deborah's parents did not survive the war, but one of her mother's sisters was still alive.

She and her husband had been hiding in Amsterdam—in the same house as Anne Frank, by the way, on the other side—and they had come through the war there. The underground still had the addresses where the children were hidden, and my uncle came to visit me. He also got the address of my sister, who was ten kilometers from Dokkum, near Ameland on the sea. They took me there, and I said, "Oh, yes, that is my sister, she was born the second of May, and she is so-and-so old, and this is her name." I knew it straight away, I still remember that. But she said in Frisian, "Who is this girl? I don't know her." She didn't remember anything.

My sister was hidden by a couple who had no children, and the wife wanted her as her own child. When she heard that an uncle was coming, she was hysterical that he would take the child away. But my uncle and aunt had a daughter who had been born during the war, and they had to build up a new existence, so they were too busy and they didn't want us.

Now, my father had a second cousin whose name was the same as his. This man was married and had no children, but he loved children; he was always active with youth groups and so on. When he heard that we were alive, he wanted to adopt us both, and he brought a court case. There was a social worker from the Jewish organization for child care who once a year visited the children who were in non-Jewish families, and this social worker was very much against bringing the children back to Jewish families. She testified that the children had been moved around too much, that it would not be good for them to be off again somewhere else, and since they were just getting used to being where they were, there was no point in it. The judge was against it as well—a non-Jewish judge. Although the cousin tried very hard, he didn't get us, and we were left where we were. We didn't know anything about this at the time, of course.

Although she was never officially adopted by her foster parents, Deborah called herself Riet Kuiper, a combination of her wartime pseudonym and her foster parents' last name, to avoid "complicated" explanations. "I did not feel I was this person," she recalls. "In my mind, my name was my real name, not my adopted name, which I did not feel was me." She lived under this name as long as she stayed with the Kuipers, which was until the age of eighteen.

My foster parents didn't have much education, but that wasn't their fault. My foster father was in fact quite an intelligent man—he had a natural intelligence, he could have done mathematics or something—but at the age of eleven he had had to become a baker's apprentice and to work day and night. My foster mother was good-hearted, though not very intelligent. But they were very honest and decent, simple, and very good. Which is why I had so many difficulties later: because they were so good.

I couldn't accept them as my parents. In my mind, I had parents.

I didn't know then that they wouldn't come back—and nobody told me, either; the subject was taboo. If you haven't seen them die, you think, as a child, that they will come back. You think you don't know that it's really true, because you haven't definitely seen it. And if you don't want them not to be there, you try to believe that they are alive.

I didn't want another pair of parents, so I never let my foster parents really be parents to me. I always kept them at a distance; I didn't even want them to touch me. I didn't call them Mother and Father, I called them Auntie and Uncle. They didn't want to force me in the beginning, and I never wanted it differently. I didn't mind being there, but in my mind I couldn't have a substitute for my parents.

The Kuipers, members of the Dutch Reformed church, were "orthodox Protestants" who observed the Sabbath assiduously—"twice every Sunday to church, and on Sundays no money was touched and there was no going on buses or sewing"—and who brought up their foster daughter in their faith. Deborah, herself deeply interested in religion from an early age, was shaken by the way in which the Jews were portrayed in church.

I always heard that only the people who believe in Jesus go to heaven—that the Jews have been cut off, that the people who believe in Jesus have replaced the Jewish people, all this kind of stuff. I thought, "And I'm Jewish!" So the only solution for me was to become a missionary in Israel, to save the Jews. It sounds strange, but the only thing I wanted was to save the Jews. For me, that was the only logical course.

Then, when I got a bit older, I started thinking a bit more on my own; when you're about eight or ten you want what the group wants, but when you get a bit older, you start thinking your own thoughts. I was still quite young, but I had a good imagination. As I had always heard that people who don't believe in Jesus don't go to heaven, I saw myself sitting comfortably in heaven and all the Jews uncomfortable there in hell. And I thought, "I am a Jew—I can't do that."

So I said to the minister, "I don't want to go to heaven." I didn't say why.

I remember that he answered, "You are stupid. If you were going along a canal and you couldn't swim and you saw somebody drowning, would you jump in?"

"Never mind," I said. "I don't want to go to heaven."

Then I started doubting, and I couldn't really believe all this with

Jesus. I had to sing those psalms—well, the psalms weren't so bad, but the songs about Jesus . . . I said to myself, "If there is a God and He hears what I am singing, then I am a hypocrite. I don't believe it, and I don't want to do it." But I was sitting in church next to my foster parents, who would have been very, very hurt if they had known that I didn't believe, because then I wouldn't go to heaven. So I couldn't show it at all, but I thought, "I can't be a hypocrite like this." It disturbed me terribly. So in confirmation class I learned to play piano and organ, and I said, "OK, I'll play the organ," and I didn't need to sing with it.

There were areas besides religion in which Deborah's outlook seemed to diverge fundamentally from that of her foster family. Even though she had grown up in their house, she felt she had little in common with them.

My sense of humor was completely different, for instance, and their style of humor I couldn't take. It wasn't witty, it wasn't clever, it was just coarse. If something is witty and a bit like that, OK—as long as it's clever, I can appreciate it. But not if it's just crude.

Something else I absolutely hated was the drinking. They drank a lot—far too much—and I overreacted against it by never touching anything. Later on, it was even difficult for me at first to drink kiddush* because of this.

And while there were still class distinctions in the small towns at that time, that kind of thing didn't matter to me at all. I had a friend whose father was a farm laborer and another whose father was a solicitor. My foster parents considered a solicitor to be somebody above their social circle and a farm laborer to be somebody below, but I had no respect for those things. Nor did I ever suffer from them: I helped in the bakery, and I had to deliver cake to my teachers, and I didn't give two hoots whether they saw that I was helping.

Contributing to her uneasiness was the fact that Deborah was "given things all the time" by her foster parents.

They paid for me to go to gymnasium,† so that nobody could say

---

kiddush: the Jewish blessing of the wine, said on the Sabbath and on holidays. The wine is sipped after it has been blessed.

†The gymnasium has the highest academic standards of secondary schools in the Dutch educational system.

that they hadn't given me the best education possible. We used to be members of school clubs—debating clubs and so on—and it all cost money, and they weren't rich, so sometimes I just didn't become a member because I felt it was too expensive. I didn't tell them anything, but if they heard about it later on, they would be very angry: "We want to give it to you, and you don't want it . . ."

But after I got something, my foster parents would say, "We give you so many things. We give you this, and we give you that—more than our own children." This hurt me, and I just didn't want it. Sometimes when they gave me a new dress, I would say, "I don't want the dress. I don't want to be given everything."

I was—I am—very proud. I hated being given things, yet all my life I had to take things from people. Maybe I didn't want to become too dependent on them so that I couldn't break loose later, but that was not conscious. They thought I was terribly ungrateful, of course, so this was doubly insulting; and I again felt the difference.

Later on, when I had become a bit difficult, they said, "Now you can still see that she's Jewish." There was nothing that hurt me more than that, and I would say, "Maybe *I* am no good, but you can't say that the Jews are like that." They didn't mean it that way, really. There was an expression for a person who is not honest: They would say, "Oh, it's like a real Jew." This would hurt me terribly, but they didn't mean anything by it. They weren't really anti-Semitic, and they knew very little about it—it's just part of the language—but it got me very angry.

Deborah had chosen to go to a gymnasium because classical languages were taught there, and she wanted to learn Hebrew.

In this gymnasium you had two years of Hebrew—not compulsory, but for the students who studied theology and needed to know it. It was a small school that had just started up, and our teachers were ministers who earned extra money, I suppose, teaching Greek, Latin, New Testament in Greek, Old Testament in Hebrew. The teachers knew I was Jewish, and they also knew I was interested in religion, and some of them tried very hard to win me over. Extra hard, I think, because they knew I was Jewish.

As I dreamt of going to Israel, I got some Modern Hebrew books and taught myself to write it. I had the books open on the table instead of Greek, but my foster parents couldn't tell the difference anyway; they knew I had a course in Hebrew, but not that I did anything extra. About Judaism, however, I knew nothing—I didn't even know that there was Yom Kippur.* I had forgotten everything, and I hadn't known much to begin with.

I started reading books about Mohammedanism and Buddhism; I searched, but I couldn't find anything I could really believe in. I felt everything was relative: What one says is good the other says is bad— there is nothing fixed, so one is floating. I felt terribly unhappy, because if you are floating, how can you know what is really good?

This sensation of floating disturbed Deborah from the age of fourteen or fifteen, and a "block" began to inhibit her studies in school as well.

I had been able to learn normally before, and then it all stopped. I had always liked drawing and painting, but at a certain moment I couldn't do it anymore: All I could produce was one big mix-up. I was so mixed up in myself I didn't know where to get things from.

A teenager always has a difficult time, but for me the gap was bigger, much bigger. My foster parents knew only about one-third of me, and they didn't think there was anything more, because I kept two-thirds back. It was too deep in me for me to be able to speak about it. In any case, we thought in completely different ways; with their own children they could speak, but we couldn't reach each other at all.

I had nobody else to speak to, either. I was the only Jewish girl in the school, and I didn't know any Jewish families. I had non-Jewish friends I could relate to very easily on the surface, but for the rest we were not on the same wavelength, not at all. And though I was there till I was eighteen or nineteen, I never wanted much contact with non-Jewish boys. I felt so different from them that I just couldn't. My foster parents found this very strange; they thought it was not natural. "All your friends are normal," they said, "but you will never get married."

So they thought I was a bit different from the others, and I was made to feel it. I didn't want to be an outsider; I wanted badly to be accepted somewhere. If you are always alone and don't belong any-where, it's hard. So I tried to have a character that would be such that they could understand me and I could understand them. I tried to

---

Yom Kippur: the Day of Atonement, Judaism's most solemn holiday.

behave like they behaved—and I tried to think like they thought, because I always felt like a hypocrite if I acted differently than I felt. I felt I had to suppress the Jewish side of my character, and I hated myself for it, I absolutely hated myself for it. I really tried hard, but I couldn't do it, it just didn't work.

Then I myself began to think that maybe I was not normal—because I was the only one, and when you see all the others being different, you think you are the one who is not normal. I got a very bad complex from this. Also, I was much smaller than the rest, and I had a complex because of that, too; that might not have been the worst thing, but it wasn't normal, either.

It was because of the difference between myself and the others that I became difficult and hurt my foster parents. But they didn't deserve to be hurt. They only did it to save me, and they had me all those years, and they gave me the best things they could give, and it was very hard for them. It disturbed me that I hurt them, and that made me even more difficult, and that disturbed me even more. It was a vicious circle.

For choosing not to adapt to my foster parents, and not to take them as parents, and not to take their religion, I had to pay a big price. It meant that I was completely separate, that I had nobody to speak to, that I was completely alone. I was thinking all the time and becoming absolutely crazy, and I didn't know anymore what to do. Then I read about the war, and I suffered terribly with it. I had sleepless nights, thinking and thinking; it went around and around in me. I couldn't find any solution to the problem: Why did it happen? Why the Jews? Why all those innocent people killed who hadn't done anybody any harm, ever? What have we done to deserve this? It touched me personally. It was as if I myself had been killed, really, and I did not want to be alive anymore.

When she was eighteen, Deborah returned for the first time to Amsterdam. While there, she made her first visit to a synagogue since she had left the city in 1943.

When I went to shul for the first time and everybody could see me going to shul—I didn't need to hide it—it was an enormous relief.

It was fourteen years after the war was over, but I had still been in hiding all that time, and I had felt it every moment. I had felt as if I were going through a dark tunnel: I couldn't see the end of it, and I didn't know how to get out, and I thought it would last forever. I had felt terribly unhappy and really believed that I was going crazy. Then I felt totally relieved, as if I had come out of a very tight harness that had been constricting me completely. And the relief was that I didn't need to hide anymore, that I could be myself. That, for me, was the end of the war.

Wishing to continue her education after graduating from the gymnasium, Deborah enrolled at the school of social welfare in Amsterdam. Upon her arrival, she dropped the name Riet Kuiper and took back her original name, using Dvora, the Hebrew form of Deborah and the name under which she had been registered at birth with the Jewish community. She set about trying to acquaint herself with the religious aspects of Jewish life, but she found the response of the main Jewish organization with which she dealt to be less than enthusiastic.

I got into a Jewish circle, but I had to fight for it. In Amsterdam, the first thing I had thought was "I am Jewish, but I don't know anything about it. I should at least know about it, being a Jewish person." I had a study grant from the Jewish welfare organization, which had money to provide grants to all the children who didn't have parents. But when I asked them for a room in a Jewish family so I could see what it was like—I had never seen it in my life—they didn't want to give it to me at first. I had to go back again, and again, and again, and again, till they were so fed up that they found me one.

I came to the house of an Israeli who had been sent to Holland for a few years to help with youth movements. The family spoke Hebrew at home and Yiddish, and they were more or less observant, they kept Shabbes* and everything. Frisians are very restrained and not so easygoing, and here people were friendly and open—it was something I wasn't used to at all, and I liked it very much. Coming from Friesland to a home where there was Israeli food, and it was always open house, and only Hebrew was spoken, was a 180-degree turn, really. I found it very interesting.

In Amsterdam, when I met Jews—even nonreligious Jews—I felt, "Ahhh, I am amongst people who are 'not normal,' just like me"; and I felt more normal because of it. I never knew that such a group existed,

---

Shabbes: the Sabbath (Yiddish).

and I never knew there was such a thing as being on the same wavelength with people until I was in Jewish surroundings. I felt so relieved to be out of the tunnel that I became a completely different person. I had been quiet and moody—not when I was very young, but in those years later on—and that wasn't really my nature at all. In Amsterdam, I felt that I could be myself, that I could open up. I no longer needed to hide.

I took private lessons in Hebrew, which I picked up very rapidly, and in other Jewish subjects. All of a sudden, school itself became much easier. I didn't need to do anything: I read things over once and passed my examinations just like that. I was on the board of the Jewish students' organization, I had boyfriends, I went out, I felt more at ease. I was active all over, and I felt happy for the first time in so long, just happy I was alive.

When she had first started looking into religious Judaism, Dvora had been guided to the offices of the Liberal Jewish Community, where she was received by Rabbi Jacob Soetendorp, who was well known in Holland for his learning in Jewish matters.

Ohhh, he was nice! He had been orthodox before he became liberal, and he said, "Come in! I was at the seminary with your father, we were in class together." I saw his shul, and he said, "Come here and be a member of my youth club."

But I also wanted to see the orthodox shul. So I told him, "No. I want to see all sides before I choose."

He said, "Do you want a siddour?* Which do you want, an orthodox siddour, or one of my siddorim?"

I said, "An orthodox one," because I didn't want the liberal one, I wanted the authentic. He went upstairs and looked in the rubbish for an orthodox siddour. I've still got it.

I used to go to the liberal shul quite often, but I found it inconsistent. They did certain things and not certain other things; it was not one line, and I didn't like the inconsistency of it. When I was searching like that, I didn't have a clear picture in my mind of what it should be, but I always knew what it was not.

As time went on, Dvora found herself keeping more and more of the Mitzvoth, the 613 commandments prescribed in the Jewish religion.

-----

*siddour: prayer book; the plural is *siddorim* (Hebrew).

At first, before I kept things, I wanted to know why. Then, in the end, I felt: This is me. So I started keeping more things, and I started eating kosher, and so on. But this didn't happen straight away—it is a process, you have to let it become you. It was hard in the beginning when I went to visit my foster parents, because all those years I had been eating there and all of a sudden I couldn't anymore. I found it very difficult to do that. But I felt that, in Judaism, there was a way that a Jew can live, and I felt happy doing it, more happy doing it than not.

We believe, in Judaism, that the Torah* is given by God, and that it is fixed. I saw that at least something was fixed in the world. I didn't need to be worried that one person thought this and one that—there is a fixed truth that nobody, no human being, can touch. So at least you have standards, you're not floating; and that makes a person much quieter, because if you keep the Torah and the Mitzvoth, then you don't need to worry, "Am I doing the right thing or not?" You know you are doing the right thing, and you have your energy left over for something else. Of course, you have to work yourself up to the standards; it's still possible to do things better or less well against these standards. But it was a big relief to me to see that there is a truth you can't change.

So I had to learn the technical things, which I did, slowly but surely. But when I learned the philosophy of the Jewish sages, there was a kind of recognition. The more I heard about it, the more I said, "Yes, that's what I knew all the time." Not that I could have produced it myself, but when I read it, I said, "Yes, I knew this." It was a kind of coming home.

When she felt she had taken Judaism as far as she would be able to take it in Holland, Dvora began looking elsewhere.

I felt that the way people practiced here was not the way it should be done; I was searching for something different. I had heard that there were many more Jews in England than here, and I thought that if there were a bigger Jewish community, I would have a better chance to find what I was looking for. I also thought, "I lack a basic Jewish education." I had learned Hebrew, and I had had lessons here and lessons there, but I wanted a proper, stable basis on which to build.

Torah: the five books of Moses (the first five books of the Old Testament).

Dvora set her sights on attending the Jewish Teachers' Training College at Gateshead, England. Her request for a scholarship was turned down by the Jewish welfare organization in Amsterdam—"I could have had the money," she claims, "if I had wanted to become a dancer or to go to a kibbutz"—and the headmaster at Gateshead tried to discourage her on the ground that she was several years older than most of his pupils. "I don't accept your 'no,'" Dvora wrote him. "I want the best, and I am going to get it."

Dvora went to London, where she took a job as an au pair girl with a family of Chasidic Jews from Hungary and continued her study of Judaism. While in London, she was introduced to the headmaster, who reversed his decision upon meeting her. After a year at Gateshead, which she greatly enjoyed, Dvora left Great Britain for Israel. There she worked, studied, and, after six months, met her husband, a rabbinical student named Saul Goldenberg. "I only wanted one who wanted to study Jewish matters," says Dvora. "So I got what I wanted, and I was happy."

After a number of years in Israel, the Goldenbergs moved to Amsterdam. The return to Holland put Dvora back into closer touch with her foster mother—her foster father had died in the meantime—and the two exchanged occasional visits up to the time of her foster mother's death. "I also phoned her every second day or so," Dvora says, "and we had a nice chat. But, of course, I lived in a different world."

The Goldenberg family leads a life in the service of religious Judaism. At the time of the interview, Rabbi Saul Goldenberg worked in an organization that promotes Jewish religious education in the Netherlands, while Dvora kept a strictly kosher household for the couple's six children. In addition, the Goldenbergs devoted considerable energy to "bringing back" nonreligious Jews to orthodox practice, an activity in which Dvora could draw on her own difficult experience of returning to what she considered her true, but suppressed, nature.

I've had to fight with myself a lot, because after so many years of keeping oneself back and not showing one's real nature, it's difficult to build up proper relations again. You put your defenses up automatically, it becomes your second nature, and it's very hard to get them down. You have to learn to face your human feelings again. It is like learning, if you have been in a hospital bed for many years, to walk again. You learn step by step. It has taken me years to work on this task.

For instance, I had never known the feeling of homesickness; after I was separated from my mother, I cut that off, because I didn't want to be hurt. I didn't want anything inside me to be touched—it was hurting too much. And I didn't want anyone to see that I was hurt. I was too proud to show people who were not my parents that I would ever cry or anything like that.

So I put up a barrier of coldness: a big barrier, all the time. In Friesland everybody always thought that I was not a feeling person, that I was cold, that I was indifferent, that I was nearly inhuman. I believed it, and that also gave me a very bad inferiority complex: I was worse than all of them. When I entered the school of social welfare in Amsterdam, you had to take a psychological test and then discuss it with a psychiatrist before you could be accepted. The psychiatrist told me that what had come out in my test was that I was very, very sensitive. For me, that was a big surprise. I thought he was just joking. It was the first time in my life that I had heard this, and I honestly couldn't believe it.

Then I had some very good friends, and when I was away from them was the first time I learned to be a bit homesick for somebody—I dared to do it again. Slowly but surely I made more real friends, and that gave me self-confidence, because if you see that a person accepts you as you are, it gives self-confidence. I got married and had children. From children you also learn a lot, and in any case you can't keep so much to yourself in a marriage, so I was forced.

But I can still be very withdrawn sometimes. I can still smile while I am in fact crying, and nobody can see. I am still not self-confident enough. I feel secure only in my own house: When I have to go out with my husband to public things, I still feel terribly shy. I wouldn't dare to phone this person, or that person, maybe it's the wrong time, maybe she doesn't want me to. Perhaps I don't want to be rejected, or rebuffed. It's a pity, because I could do more if I would dare more.

So it has been a long struggle indeed. And I'm still fighting on many fronts. I believe that it was just by a hair's breadth that it didn't go wrong psychologically—that close. But, Baruch HaShem,* it worked.

Being Jewish, on the other hand, has been a source of strength for Dvora and something about which she has "absolutely no complexes."

My mother's sister and her husband—the uncle and auntie who

Baruch HaShem: Blessed be The Name, Bless the Lord (Hebrew).

came back after the war and who didn't want us—used to invite my sister and me every year to come stay with them for the holidays, which was the only time of the year that my sister and I were together. After the war my uncle absolutely hated being Jewish, and he didn't want people to think he was Jewish. He was also very atheistic. All that disturbed me, because I was not inclined to be atheistic at all, and because I thought, "If you are Jewish and you can show it, why not show it? Why hide it?"

Sometimes, if we wanted to eat something Jewish, like matzo, the door had to be locked in case the neighbor came in and saw that they were eating something Jewish and might think they were Jewish. We were not even allowed to look at the family photo album. I wanted very much to see it, because there were pictures of my mother and my aunties in it, but they didn't want it out: too Jewish. They moved from Amsterdam to Nijmegen, which is a Catholic town, so that nobody would know they were Jewish. They didn't want what had happened to them in the war to happen to their daughter, and they thought that if they brought her up in such a way that she thought she was not Jewish, it would help. I couldn't take this, either.

Then, when I came to Amsterdam, I used to see that on Yom Kippur people would go to shul in leather shoes and carry sneakers with them that they put on in shul—because on Yom Kippur one doesn't wear leather, but they didn't want the goyim* to see them walking in sneakers like that. That I didn't understand, either. I went up to them and I said, "Why don't you walk with your tallis† around your shoulders to shul? Why don't you put those sneakers on in the street? What does it matter if the goyim see it?"

There are many Yiddin,‡ even religious Jews, who have this complex still. But I didn't have this complex at all.

I was too happy to be openly Jewish.

---

goyim: gentiles, literally, "the nations" (Yiddish, Hebrew).
†*tallis:* prayer shawl (Yiddish, Hebrew).
‡*Yiddin:* Jews (Yiddish).

Pavel Balázs

I must tell you what I know about my parents and their background. I underline this—what *I* know—because my parents have always been rather reluctant to tell me. That is to say, my father is less reluctant, but it's difficult to get information from my mother, she simply doesn't like to say anything at all.

Now, what I know is that my father's father was a baker from Galicia—from Polish Galicia, not Spanish Galicia, of course. My father's mother was a woman of Hungarian culture but from Rumania, from Timisoara in Transylvania. My father was born in 1897. His parents were divorced very early, and his father disappeared, so he himself doesn't know anything about his father. My grandmother lived with us for a few years in Budapest. She survived the war and died, at the age of ninety-eight, in Israel.

My father grew up with his mother in a little village called Hodosz. It was a village typical of all those Balkan countries, so rustic that my father and his brother went barefoot. My father's brother stepped on a nail and died very young, of tetanus.

Then there is a blank in my knowledge, but I know that at the time of the First World War my father was around eighteen years old, and he became a volunteer in the army of the Austro-Hungarian Empire. He fought in Italy and got a number of medals. Then he went to the university in Vienna, as all well-to-do Hungarians were supposed to do at that time. How he, or his mother, became well-to-do—or well enough off that he could go to the university—I have no idea.

My mother was born in Sarajevo, but she and her family came

from a region close to the Hungarian border which geopolitically speaking was Yugoslavia but which was of Hungarian culture. She had one sister and four brothers, and her family was totally assimilated: All my mother's brothers married Catholic women. Her father was a photographer and a very successful one—a ladies' man as well, apparently—who died in Jerusalem. My cousin showed me the house in which he died. My mother's mother was a very sweet person, whom I remember vaguely in my dreams because I spent some time as a very, very small child on some land she owned. She died in Auschwitz.

In the 1920s, Pavel's mother was living in a small village in Serbia, near the Hungarian border. There she met her first husband, a Hungarian-Jewish journalist who was an active antifascist and who, as a result of his stand against the Horthy regime in Hungary, had fled to Yugoslavia as a political refugee.

They had a son, who is my brother. And my mother, wanting to leave this little village, said, "I've had enough of this life, I'm going to Paris." Today, this would be considered, I believe, a "feminist attitude." So they moved to Paris, where they met my father, who already lived there, having moved there to do some kind of business after he'd quit his studies in economics.

They became good friends. They were all Hungarians, after all, and they were politically involved, particularly the first husband of my mother. My father was a Social Democrat at that time. Knowing him, I assume he never believed so strongly—but maybe he did, at that time he was young. They were friends of Léon Blum and saw each other at his house.

Then the first husband of my mother died, and the best friend of the family was my father, and my father married my mother. I was born in 1932 in Pecs, a town in Hungary. My brother, who is seven years older, told me that my parents returned to Hungary after they had tried to earn money in different little businesses and it hadn't worked out. I myself can say very little about this, because I know nothing and was not told anything. I grew up in Budapest with my mother, my father, my brother, and my father's mother, who didn't get along with my mother at all, but that's another story.

My father's name is Bloch—was Bloch. I presume that his father's name was Bloch as well. When I was born, I was born as Pavel Bloch. However, my parents had a very good friend whose name was Levoy—

which is Hungarian for Levi—who was always telling them, "You don't know what will happen, you don't *know* what will happen, *we* don't know what will happen. You must change your name, you must have yourselves baptized," and so on and so forth. In 1934, my parents changed the family's name to Balázs.

As a child, I didn't know that I had been born as Pavel Bloch. I was Pavel Balázs, we were Hungarians, my parents said that we were Catholics—and, for me, that was all there was to it. My brother is circumcised; he had even gone to a Jewish school. And my father's mother wore one of those old, awful reddish wigs, so I assume she must have been religious. But I didn't know it was a wig until much later. At that time I was three or four years old. To me, it was this strange reddish hair that I always felt to be a bit unnatural—but she looked so old to me then, anyway. I myself have never been circumcised, I didn't grow up in the Jewish tradition at all, and I was the only one in the family who didn't know we were Jews.

In the mid-1930s, Pavel's father worked in a travel agency in Budapest, assisted by his wife. In 1938, he was offered an attractive post in the tourism industry in Rome—"apparently he was very good," says Pavel, "otherwise he would not have received this offer"—and, in June of that year, the family left for Italy. The move greatly troubled Pavel, as he "had a big problem with Italians" and deeply regretted that his grandmother, whose tensions with her daughter-in-law had never been resolved, was staying behind.

Around the time that his family settled in Rome, Pavel began studying music.

I had had a very great affinity for music from a very, very early age. I didn't know it then, of course, but I have discovered since that a good Jewish boy must play violin. So, when I was six: "You shall play violin." Had I been a girl, it would have been the piano.

During the war years, the Balázs family was protected by their Hungarian nationality, as Pavel's parents kept their Jewish background successfully hidden from Nazi authorities. They also concealed it throughout the war from Pavel—a measure that, practically speaking, reduced the risk of a slip that might give the family away. The Balázses, regarded as citizens of an Axis-aligned state, initially enjoyed rights identical to those of Italians. And when Germany occupied Italy in 1943, an official document was posted on the front door of their apartment certifying the family's Hungarian citizenship. As nationals of a country friendly to the occupier, they were better off than the Italians, who had passed from the German camp to the ranks of Germany's subject peoples.

This Hungarian nationality saved us—or, at the very least, I would say that it helped us a lot. I don't remember any specific privileges, but I think it was a question of time. Because eventually the suspicion came, but by then it was too late for them. Thank God.

One morning there was a knock at the door. Who are they? Two SS. They want to speak with Mr. Balázs, my father. About what? They don't know, but they have orders to accompany him to Mr. Dollmann, who was the head of the SS in Rome. If you speak to Romans of a certain age, they know that this is a terrible name.

So, he went. And Mr. Dollmann asked my father to document all his movements for his entire life and those of my mother as well: where they were born, what they had done, where they had been. Names, and—well, everything. Of course, the German secret services had a suspicion, otherwise Dollmann would not have called my father. But apparently they were not quite sure because, if they had been, they would not have had this attitude. They would have just come and taken us, and that's all.

As it was, they were very polite. I remember my father saying that Dollmann was very correct: "Just tell me thus-and-such," in a very polite way. My father, who spoke German well, told him, "Well, you know, it's a big job to put this together. So give me forty-eight hours; I mean, two days at least"—because Dollmann wanted it immediately. And Dollmann said OK. This was a Saturday.

I didn't know what questions Dollmann had asked at that time, of course, but I remember exactly what happened. I myself slept, but I shall never forget my brother standing there; he couldn't sleep. And for two days my parents couldn't sleep, trying to decide what to do. And there was little they could do, by the way.

I shall never forget that Sunday evening. I woke up in the night because I heard something—you know, you hear things even when you are a child. So I woke up, and everyone—my mother, my father, my brother—was there, and they were looking through the blinds. And I went to look also.

We lived off the Via Salaria, one of the national highways that runs through Rome, and we saw German cars, troops, and everything, leaving the city. Just heading out. "What the hell is happening now?" And, "Tomorrow morning . . ." And all that. The appointment was for nine or ten Monday morning. He was supposed to go back there with this paper, saying, "Thus-and-such is my father's name, my grandfather's name"—the usual things—and, "I've been here, I was born there, I studied there . . ." I didn't know all this then. I just saw.

Well, to make a long story short, the next morning at five or so the Allied troops came into Rome. It was a few hours before the appointment. So my father didn't have to go back to Dollmann, and we were saved.

Even after the war had ended, Pavel remained in the dark as to the cause of the commotion in his household. He was still not told of the family's Jewish origins, and he was barely conscious of the fate of the Jews under Nazi dominion in any event.

If I knew absolutely nothing about what was happening to the Jews during the war, it was, first of all, that I was eleven or twelve years old—at that time that was young, although it is much less young today. And then there was the fact that my family had washed out its Jewishness. They never spoke about it—never, never, never. Well, maybe my mother and my father spoke with each other, but I didn't know anything about it, anything at all.

Around the age of thirteen—"I'm not sure exactly when," he says, "but during puberty"—Pavel went through a religious awakening.

I had had a little bit of Catholic religious training, but I didn't really grow up as a Catholic. My parents didn't insist very much, I must say. I went to mass one year when I was seven or eight, and there was a period when I was ten or eleven—a period of a couple of weeks, or maybe a month—when I was a fervent Catholic. But then, at thirteen, I had, in quotes, a "big mystical problem": Where is God? What is God? Which religion . . . ?

I went through all the different churches in Rome: the Anglican church, the different Protestant churches, the American church, the Presbyterian church—I mean all. I went just to have a look—it was superficial, of course—just to have a taste of what it was like: "Maybe I like this shop, this could be my thing." I also went to the Roman synagogue.

Now, the synagogue in Rome is the most Roman of the Roman of the Roman places in the world, and the Roman Jews—even today, those who are left after the Germans—are the most ancient Jews in Europe. And it was such a mess during the service! Everybody was saying, "Ah, Giovanni! Allora, ci telefoniamo domani, eh?"—"Hey, Giovanni! So, we'll talk on the phone tomorrow, huh?" And there was a sacristan—but no, this is a Catholic word—a shammes going between the benches and saying, "Hey, Giova', calm down! C'mon, Armando, be quiet! Shush!" And I thought, "This is a religious place? Of course, it cannot be! I mean, it is such a mess." Because everyone was, well, they weren't shouting, but everyone was speaking loudly during the service.

At the same time, I felt so much at home—but *so* much—that I was amazed. This was a Friday evening, and then I knew that there were services the next morning also, and I went back the next morning. It was the same scene, of course. And then the next Friday again. . . . I was absolutely fascinated by this amusingly awful place. I didn't know anything, because, from my birth, I had never known that we were Jews—that was a secret, you know—but I felt, I really felt, that there was something there that had to do with me.

Pavel became a regular at the synagogue. As the days lengthened toward summer, Friday night services let out later and later, and one evening he failed to make it home in time for dinner.

They asked me, "How is it that you are late?"—because, in those days, it was considered impolite for a kid to be late. "Where have you been?"

"I have been to the synagogue."

My mother immediately said, "To the synagogue! Are you crazy!" I shall never forget this. It was at dinner. I can even see the room, the table, everything.

I answered, "Yes. Why 'crazy'?" Well, I always had problems with my mother. Now I know why—because *she* had problems—but at the time I didn't know.

She said, "But you are crazy! If you go there, everybody will think that you are Jewish!"

And I said, "And then what?"

"[Gasp!] This kid"—to my father—"but this kid is completely crazy!" In such a typically Jewish way, as I remember it now—I didn't know it at that time, of course. So they warned me that it was better not to go there.

I went back. I went every Friday, and every Saturday. And another Friday I was late. "Where have you been?"

"To the syn——"

"What have we *told* you!" And so on. But it was always my mother, never my father. "You are not to go there," and so on and so forth. But I went back. I went back.

In the end, Pavel's obsession with the synagogue forced his parents' hand.

One day, my father said, "My son, I have to speak to you." And then he said, "I see that you are going back to the synagogue. I don't understand why, but there must be something." My father felt from me that I was being driven unconsciously toward Judaism. And so he said, "We are all Jews."

Then I knew the whole story. My father told me everything from the time I was born, about the name change—everything. My first reaction was "Now I understand." But he said, "But, you know, we keep it a secret," and he told me, "Be careful, never tell anybody—my God!—because, you know, we have hidden it."

"But, why?" I said.

"Because we are Jews! Don't you understand what that *means?*"

"And so what?"

Of course, I was happy to understand why I was going to the synagogue—back, back, back, back, every Friday evening, every Saturday morning, even though I didn't understand a single thing of what went on there. Because when you understand what has been incomprehensible for you, well, you are happy of course, even if you are a child. But I was fourteen, and I thought I was a Communist—I was a kid, you know—and I was not conscious of having identity problems of any kind. So I couldn't care less, and it was in that sense that, when he whispered, "Because we are Jews!" I answered, "And so what?"

I was also taken to a Hungarian church in Rome for big Hungarian celebrations once or twice a year. If somebody had told me, "They were typical Hungarians, and you remembered your childhood," and so on, I would have said, "Maybe." But the Hungarian church was like anywhere else for me, whereas I had never been to a synagogue in my life! What was there? How come I felt at home in spite of what I didn't like?—which is the most important point, I would say. Was it because I saw the ladies in the Roman synagogue—they were sitting separately, up high—and I recognized my grandmother with the wig? No! I just saw women there and that's all, so it's not that. Something in you tells you, "You belong there"—even if you don't like it, you belong. But what was it? Nothing. Nothing a young kid, thirteen or fourteen years old, could grasp.

Since his father's confession, Pavel's attempt to come to grips with his Jewish origin is a theme that has run through his life, although the intensity of his interest has varied.

During some periods, I was very much involved with Jewish identity, and at others I would leave it for other things; sometimes it would mean something one week, and I would deal with it, and then the next week I was busy and would leave it aside.

You see, I am a musician—thus, an artist. Although there are different worlds, of course, for all artists there is a world that is an abstract world. In this abstract world, there is no place, I believe, for Jewishness, for not-Jewishness, for Catholicism, for being French, for being this or that. It is a godly world. You lose a part of your identity to enter this world and work. And so, when I lost interest now and then in the particular problem of being Jewish, it was because I was so much taken up by my work.

Partly through his ex-wife, an Italian Jew, and partly through a German-Jewish psychoanalyst he met in Rome, says Pavel, "I realized much more that I am a Jew."

This psychoanalyst was my psychoanalyst for a few months only, but we met for dinner, we discussed things, we saw each other. We liked each other very much, and other people in Rome who knew him thought, oddly enough, that we were alike. I didn't know why at that time—because I said, "But you are crazy, we are not similar at all." They didn't know either. But *he* knew it was simply because we were Jews—non-Italian Jews, which makes a big difference, because Italian Jews, in spite of everything, have been so assimilated that they are really Italian.

This Berlin Jew got to know me, because to a psychiatrist you say things, of course. One thing which amazed me at that time involved an enormous problem I had at railroad stations: I'd panic. I still have this, but much less. I remember we worked on it, as they say, and he said, with marvelous intuition, "But, of course—you are afraid to be recognized as a Jew." There, in a railroad station, which is a melting pot after all.

"Oh, my God!" I said. "But this might be true." Then I thought about this, and I dreamt about it, and I checked with my mother and father. And they had it, too.

This man taught me that I was a Jew—in spite of my upbringing, in spite of my personal history, in spite of everything—and that left an extremely important mark on me. At that time, the fact that I am Jewish still didn't mean very much, or I didn't realize what it meant, but I think I owe to him the rebirth of the Jewish part of myself.

It has been more in recent years that Pavel has begun to "feel extremely involved" in the question of being Jewish. He attributes this in large measure to his first visit to Israel, an "overwhelming experience" that took place a year or so before the interview.

This was a marvelous trip, because psychologically speaking it brought up a lot of forgotten things and an enormous amount of emotion that I didn't even know existed. You must have heard this a hundred times—we read it in the papers, I know—but it's so, so true: It was in Jerusalem that I felt, for the very first time since childhood, at home.

While there, Pavel made the acquaintance of two uncles—brothers of his mother who had seen him only as an infant—and their children.

I have some cousins—my parents always said not to tell anyone— so I belong to a family! Remember, I grew up with a brother, mother, father, and that's all. And I had everybody asking me, "But, do you have children?"—in the good old family manner.

Now, for the first time in my life, I feel that I would like to have a child. I never felt this, I always avoided it. But—and I hope you will excuse me for saying it in such a silly way—I feel that we should put little Jews into the world. In other words, we must try to perpetuate this universal belief in the best side of humankind that I believe— from the little I know—to be one of the main characteristics of Jewishness.

The more I grow, the more I am interested in my Jewishness. Now that I feel at peace with myself, more or less, I plan to learn all about the Jewish tradition—in fact, I feel like a little child in this respect. I have a book like the kind little kids have, which shows what Rosh Hashanah is. Is that the name?—I never knew the name. I have Jewish friends, but I have always forgotten to ask why, during the service at the Roman synagogue, an old gentleman put his hand on me, as I saw others do. I didn't understand what was happening, but I was very moved, deeply moved. I want to know what that is, when the older puts his hand on the younger.*

So now I am facing the problem of being a Jew without being it in one way, which is not having been brought up as a Jew. But I would say that the Jerusalem trip made me perfectly conscious that, even though I'm not circumcised, I really am a Jew. Everybody told me so: not only because of my face, but my gestures, even my way of thinking. I'm very happy about that—I've always been like this without knowing it. I believe, very strongly, that there is a way of behaving, of thinking, of feeling, that is culturally determined. But that can't be the whole story, or I wouldn't be a good Jew.

Although Pavel retains the impulse to avoid mentioning his Jewishness—to non-Jews, but also to Jews—he has overcome this hesitation to some extent. "I so inherited this fear that I didn't even tell good friends when an occasion arose to do so," he admits. "But today I take my risks, and, more and more, I present myself as a Jew." His move with his Danish companion, Ariana, from Rome to Germany not long before the interview seems to have furthered the process.

In Italy, everybody who knows me knows my life story. But here I was—I am—afraid. A little frightened at bottom, just a little bit. Because, first of all, Germany, you must admit, does not have the best reputation from this point of view. And, secondly, I've heard since childhood: "You do not say it, you must not say it, when you go to a new country you mustn't say it." So, OK, I didn't say it. Then, little by little, I told this one, I told that one—but slightly, a little bit, a hint, you know. Gradually, I understood that they all knew, or had figured it out. Because of my face, because of my attitude? I don't know why, nobody said.

Once, when we went to dinner at the home of friends here, there was a professor from Jerusalem, and Ariana happened to be seated next to him. She told him that I am a Jew. I had never told him—well, I just never happened to tell him, because it's complicated, and because I myself, I must confess, have another problem: If I say I'm Jewish, and yet I don't know anything about Jewish tradition, I feel a little bit uneasy.

Then we came home, and Ariana told me about this, and I was upset. I told her, "But you are crazy—you do things that I don't want

---

*A reference to the practice of adults blessing children during a service.

you to do." And, "My privacy . . ." And, "My personal problems . . ." And so on. But I'm very happy that she did it, because later I understood—a month or two later—that this was still my psychological inheritance from my parents: "You must not tell anybody, you will lose your job, you will lose this, you will lose that . . ." This fear. So I'm very grateful to Ariana, because I would like very much to get rid of this problem. And when she said, "He is a Jew," everyone knew, so the problem was solved.

In contrast, the other members of the Balázs family still go to great lengths to obscure their Jewish origins. Pavel's parents moved to Switzerland after the war and have hidden the family history from neighbors there. "I think they now feel safe," says Pavel, citing the "little myth" of Switzerland as the haven of Europe, but he adds, "They are still frightened, so nobody who knows them knows that they are Jewish."

I remember the first time I told my parents that I had told someone I was a Jew. They were terribly upset: Why did I say this? Because I was not a Jew—I was baptized, so I was a Catholic. They were trying to convince me.

Actually, there are two attitudes: my mother's, and my father's. My mother thinks that I am absolutely insane to say that I am a Jew, that it's bad for her and bad for me. My father thinks that it is bad for me and bad for him, but he still likes it, because he feels Jewish. Although he never told me so, I know—knowing him as I do now—that he never liked the fact of becoming Catholic. He concealed his Jewishness because my mother pushed and because they had decided to do so, to survive. I see my father as a real Marrano, who, at the first opportunity, will say, "Yes, after all, this is me." Every time it is possible, he is very happy to tell me, "We are Jews"—but he doesn't tell the others, because, at eighty-three, he is still afraid.

My mother, on the other hand, has closed all this off. She is one of those "anti-Semitic Jews"—in quotes, of course. She was the one to tell me, "You know, Jewish people are awful," and so on and so forth. At the same time, it is very funny that every time there is a question regarding Israel—"Israel and the Arab World"—my mother is as irrationally pro-Israel as she was, in quotes, "anti-Jewish."

When I was younger, I went through a period of very strong criticism of them for hiding the Jewishness of the family. I told them openly, and I fought with them. But the last years I have come to understand all the fears, which must have been really terrible, and I can now imagine what they must have gone through. I don't criticize them anymore, I accept them as they are. I don't think anyone can say, "You are to blame for giving up your Jewishness." Of course, if you are a real believer, you don't give it up: "I will die." All right. But if one is not a real believer, then it's a different problem as far as I'm concerned.

Pavel's brother, "also raised with this fear of revealing his identity," continues to guard the family secret with similar care.

He moved to Canada, he married, he has grown children, and nobody—his wife nor his children—knows that he is a Jew. His wife is not Jewish—of *course* not—she's a real Catholic, she went to Vatican City and cried because she was in front of St. Peter's. I imagine he has told them very little about his background—that he's Hungarian, and that's all.

Now he is fifty-three, and I think this could be a time for certain persons to open up again, but he does not. He is not able to speak about this kind of thing with me, his younger brother, although he loves me—and I am not a stranger, of course. Every time I try to speak with him, he begins a little bit, he tells me a few little things—but nothing about himself, nothing at all—and then he closes up.

I asked him, "Tell me about our Jewish history," and I told him, "I know you went to a Jewish school," and so on.

"No, I don't have to speak about that." And this is today, last year, two years ago, five years ago.

My brother is a very unhappy person—but, if he is a terrible neurotic, I understand. It must have been an enormous shock for my brother to be told, as a child of ten or eleven, to forget that he went to a Jewish school, to deny his entire past. Because of this extreme shock— "If you tell anybody, ever, what you are, we are all dead"—my brother is nobody. He is a successful businessman, but, at the same time, he has lost his personality and he is no one. When you impose this depersonalization, it is the same as killing somebody. Psychologically speaking, it is a different type of Auschwitz.

It was during his visit to Jerusalem that Pavel was, for the first time in his memory, moved to tears. "This fact," he claims, "explains my whole life."

Now, if you said, and rightly so, that I didn't know anything of being a Jew, that I just happened to discover it . . . well, the way I happened to discover it is, I think, rather peculiar. It means that something in myself—and I am not theorizing at all, I am speaking about my own experience—that somewhere in myself, I was so much a Jew. Otherwise, I would have run away, because I didn't like it at all in the Roman synagogue, I found it vulgar and so on. What kept me there, and fascinated me? What told me, "I don't like it, but I feel at home"—without knowing anything, and being in a synagogue for the first time in my life? Why?

On a certain level, this is a problem of belonging to a group. On a different level, which is a more personal level I would say, this means that if you as an individual want to know what your life is, what you have done, what you may be doing in the future, what the problems are which confront you, what the meaning is of being alive, then this problem of belonging—which seems to be a very minor, ordinary, understandable problem—becomes very important. In my case, as in many other cases, there are individual problems, but this comes in to amplify our knowledge of ourselves—what we are, why we act like this and not like that. And it's important to know.

Now that I am forty-six—and a little bit successful in different fields, so that I cannot complain about life—I am involved in the question of Jewishness in particular. It is not a solution to my problems, but it is something that confronts me, and concerns me—in the depth of myself, my ancestors, and even a part of my psychology, my way of behaving, and so on. Now I can deal with this problem. And I think that if somebody does not feel this as part of himself and doesn't want, as I'm beginning to try to do, to know more about it, and to recognize himself in a tradition—if one cuts all this out—then I think one cuts out a part of his own personality. In this way, I think that my parents cut out a great deal of themselves, and my brother—to the extent that I know him—has always lived as if in prison.

"Under the Nazi occupation," recalls Pavel, *"I was a child, and I didn't know what was happening to the Jews. Then I knew. And I was shocked."* But for a long time, Pavel says, he was unable truly to face up to it. *"It is only now—I will repeat it, this is important—it is* only now, *since my trip to Jerusalem, that I am able to cry. And I do sometimes cry, by the way."*

I was in Rome recently, and I went to the Jewish library there. I was looking for some books I couldn't find, so I picked up a book about the destruction of the Jews during the last war. I was at a table in this little hall with the books, and somebody who seemed to be the director of this little documentation center looked over, and he noticed me. I went through the book, and I must say I was inclined to be depressed about all this. I looked at the photographs, and there were many pages in particular on Hungary, Budapest—Hungarian Jews—so I became even more depressed.

I closed the book, I put it back, and I was leaving. And he said to me, "Eh! Why are you so depressed?" It was very kind of him, because I was just another visitor, and he said it in a very friendly way.

"Well, lucky you," I told him, "who can sing."

Then he said a marvelous thing, this little man with his Roman face—he was not a rabbi, just the director of this center. He told me, "Have faith, and study." Which is so typical, of course.

I could have hugged him immediately—though I did not, because I didn't think he would accept it. And I left, and I was moved, moved, moved, moved.

Mina Landau

*Mina Landau was born in Amsterdam in 1942. Although her legal identity has
never been definitively established, there is evidence that her parents were Joseph
and Rachel Elzasser, a couple who ran a bakery in a Jewish working-class section
of Amsterdam and died in concentration camps. When she was only months old,
Mina was smuggled by a Dutch resistance operative out of an Amsterdam theater
used as a collection point for Jews who had been taken in roundups and were
destined for deportation. She was brought to the province of Limburg in the
southeast of the Netherlands, where she continued life as Mina Heemstra, the
daughter of a Protestant couple living in the city of Valkenburg.*

*Paul Heemstra, who took Mina in, was a workman employed by Holland's
state coal concern. Around the time Mina was two, Heemstra's wife fell ill and
died; several months later he married Mina's "third mother," a widow with sons
aged ten and twelve. "They threw the whole caboodle together," Mina relates, "so
it was a family again. All at once, I had two brothers, and they had a little sister."*

*But to keep their brood together, Mr. and Mrs. Heemstra had to struggle.
During legal hearings that were held shortly after the war and that were later
described to Mina by Mrs. Heemstra, a man presenting himself as Mina's kin
demanded that she be removed from the household and placed in a Jewish
orphanage. According to Mrs. Heemstra's account, the man appeared willing to go
"to any lengths" to forestall the possibility of the child's being raised as a Christian:
He first offered Mrs. Heemstra a fur coat on the condition that she and her
husband give up custody, then, when rebuffed, told them to name their price. At that
point a teenage girl who maintained she was Mina's cousin—and whom Mina
herself considers her only blood relative—urged Mina's guardians to stand their
ground. "Everyone told them, 'You have to fight, because after all a child is a lot*

happier and grows up more normally in a family atmosphere than in an institu-
tion,' " Mina says, adding, "Besides, they were attached to me and regarded me
really as their own."

> *Mr. and Mrs. Heemstra won the custody fight. Not long afterward a decree*
> *was issued allowing the Heemstras to give the child their own last name in the*
> *absence of anyone claiming to be Mina's parents or even of any "real proof" as*
> *to who her parents were. "My cousin had said I was Elzasser," Mina comments,*
> *"but I don't know whether the testimony of a child counts." Once it had "become*
> *evident" that neither Mina's parents nor any other relations would turn up, Paul*
> *Heemstra declared, "We will raise her totally in accordance with what we think*
> *right," and had her baptized in the Dutch Reformed church. Although she "had*
> *no say in it" and learned of the circumstances much later on, Mina has memories*
> *of the baptismal ceremony itself, which took place when she was five.*

> *Mina characterizes herself as having been a "hypernervous, oversensitive,*
> *and very insecure" child.*

I don't know whether that had to do with the war—which I hadn't
experienced consciously, of course—but I had been born in a very
nervous time, and a baby must notice something unconsciously. My
parents didn't always have it easy with me. I had problems with a rash,
a sort of eczema, which appears to have come of my nervousness. I
wasn't allowed to go to the movies much because if there was some
calamity, a death or the like, I would get so wrapped up in it that I
couldn't sleep for nights. And because my parents wanted to protect me
too much from everything, I was rather dependent. I was one of these
children who say, "My mother says that, so that's how it is." If my
parents said it, I had no doubts. I accepted everything without questioning.

> *This tendency to take over her parents' attitudes, combined with the tenor*
> *of the religious instruction she received, helped make Mina a believing Christian*
> *at an early age.*

My mother, though not fanatical, was truly religious, so I thought
it was all wonderful. As far as I was concerned, anyone whose thinking
differed from my mother's just had things the wrong way around. Besides, I hadn't really ever heard anything different and simply assumed
that's how things were; it's taught to you with such conviction that you
don't doubt. In any case, in Christianity you have to believe without
questioning—you have to believe whether you want to or not—because

EMBATTLED SELVES [337

otherwise there's the big stick: If you don't believe and accept all that
about God and Jesus as true, then there's the threat that later, after your
death . . .

*Growing up at a time when the Catholic majority and Protestant minority
in Limburg were still openly "intolerant of one another," Mina found herself the
object of religious slurs.*

Other people are called names for being Jewish, but I was often
called "dumb Protestant" and things like that.

*Protestantse apen
Liggen in bed te gapen,**

they used to say. I certainly felt that was aimed at me, but I never took
it much to heart. Children simply give it back and then forget about it,
and I went at it just as hard as anyone. Since I was in a Protestant school,
I didn't run into it there; rather, those were the squabbles you had
playing outside in the street.

*Being Protestant was not the only thing that marked the Heemstras off from
their neighbors. Unlike most of those around them, Mina's parents were not
natives of Limburg; her father worked in a shop at ground level rather than down
in the mines; and Mina felt that, whereas "in those days things tended to get a
little crude in a true miner's family," her household was "more refined." "Not that
I had any big illusions," she recalls, "but I always saw our family as rising a bit
above the others in some way."*

*At the same time that Mina noticed a contrast between her family and the
world around, something within the family itself struck her as "peculiar."*

I couldn't put my finger on it, but at times you had the feeling that
there were mysteries. My brothers had a different last name from mine,
and my grandfather had written "Wilhelmina Elzasser" on the calendar
beside my presumed birthday. "I do know that I'm named Wilhelmina,
but Elzasser seems so odd. My name is not really Elzasser, is it,
Grandpa?" I once asked him.

"Well, I'm telling you," he said, "you're Elzasser." My grandpa had
actually gone too far right there, because he wasn't really supposed to
talk about it. But it stuck in my memory nevertheless.

---

*"Protestant monkeys lie yawning in bed."

Then there was a lady from a Jewish organization who wanted to speak with my parents; she came again and again, and she was always asking after me. My mother was so afraid I would be picked up and taken off that she notified the police, asking them to keep an eye on me when school let out. Meanwhile, my brother was going with a girl who, when she was visiting at our place, once called me "little Jewish girl." The word *Jew* had been dropped from time to time, and my ears were primed for it. I didn't say anything back, nor to my mother, because I felt intuitively, "It's better not to ask anything about that yet." But I never forgot it, it always stayed with me.

Thus when, at around age nine, Mina was told the truth about her origins, "it wasn't that unexpected."

My mother told me the story. It didn't seem to come out smoothly. "Listen," she said, "I have to talk to you a minute. You have, perhaps, I don't know whether, whether you've already thought about it, or whether you've heard it at some point, because otherwise I have to, I really think I ought to tell you now: You are actually a Jewish child, you are not our own child. As a result of the war . . ."

She told the whole story, in a very childlike way. It gave me a start—for a second, of course, I was surprised—but, still, I'd already suspected it myself. My reaction was "Well, then, I'm just glad that I landed with you." I said it spontaneously—at such a young age a child does not yet say such things with ulterior motives, they just get blurted out. And my mother was very happy with that remark because, after all, it's a sign that I felt at home where I was.

But then I said, "I think my mother and father were mean to have left me all by myself." I saw myself as a baby with parents who went away and left me there alone.

"What you're saying is wrong," my mother told me. "Who knows what trouble and grief it meant for those people to leave you behind— what it cost in courage and self-restraint to keep you, at the last moment, from the hands of that filth." Today, because I myself have children, I can see that you don't leave a child of yours to a stranger just like that; at the time, I was still too young to fathom it all. But when my mother had explained it to me, I accepted that it must have been very difficult, the way children accept that things must be as Mother and Father say even if they don't understand.

Mina says she is pleased to have been told of her background at an early age, as she believes that "the younger children are, the more easily they can accept." But Mina's own reaction to the news seems to have gone well beyond mere acceptance. "From the very moment that I knew it at all, I always felt Jewish in my heart," she recalls, even if she can only guess at what might have been behind the strength of her feelings.

I had already heard what had happened with Jewish people in the concentration camps and seen those horrid photos of the skeletons all piled up, and I can say without any hesitation that it had shocked me. To me, nervous and oversensitive as I already was, that was so horrible, so frightful. And then to learn—afterwards—that my parents had also died in that manner or a slightly different manner in such a camp, and that I might just as easily have ended up that way myself . . . Perhaps that is one of the reasons I thought, "Yes, you belong with them, among this people that has suffered so much." But I may still have been somewhat young for that; I don't know whether I'd thought it through.

Despite this somber background, Mina instantly became "very interested in everything surrounding Jewishness."

While I myself was merely average, I thought Jews were interesting people: that they were nice, different, and all very good-looking and smart. I found them special; and I don't know why, but I myself wanted to be something special, to be different from the rest. So when I suddenly became aware that I belonged to them, it was all very romantic to me. I too was interesting, I thought.

Whenever the word *Jew* was dropped, I would prick up my ears. And while I had never been in the company of Jewish people, I could always tell whether someone was Jewish or not. I might see somebody on TV and say, "This has to be a Jewish man!" And it would be, too—there's a certain feel for it, and I had it. If I heard of some scientist, a well-known doctor or professor, whose name was something ending in *-witz,* I thought, "See that! He is a Jew and he's so famous—something special, just as I figured!"

I was crazy about Jewish humor. When I heard Jewish jokes, I tried to imitate them, and I clowned around a lot at home. I liked Jewish children. I didn't see them all that often, but there was a Jewish family with a clothing store in Heerlen, and the children had lovely black curls, and such eyes! "Just look!" I thought. "What pretty children—they are

Jewish children. If only I looked like that!" I confess that the first time I had matzos I said to myself, "Just make mine a piece of bread and butter." But that's a question of taste, and it seemed so strange to me then.

I cloaked the whole thing in a childlike romanticism. To anyone who would listen, I said, "I come from a very distant, warm land—from Egypt." The Jews come from Egypt! Can you imagine? "And my mother and father and everyone, we came here on a very big boat." It was an excuse for me to tell stories, to be interesting, and I felt, "See, they think you're something special—you *are* different from the rest."

But Mina's enthusiasm for the tale of her personal Exodus sometimes made her a little more conspicuous than was convenient for her and than her mother felt wise.

Once, in an argument with a playmate from the neighborhood, I said something that wasn't so nice. Her mother got involved in it and said to me, "Get out of here, 'Jewish-People'!"

I ran inside, bawling terribly, and my mother said, "But why do you have to take it so to heart? We aren't, after all."

"But *I* am."

She said, "We know it, and you know it, and our family knows it, but you don't have to go around showing it off. Don't you go telling all those crazy stories in the street. You're telling it totally differently than it really was in any case, and you're bringing these things on yourself. It's your own fault."

My mother didn't do this out of shame or anything, but simply to protect me, or so I presume. And because I so idealized the whole image of Jewishness, she sometimes said, "Jewish people are just ordinary people. They are people with problems, with worries, and with nastiness, not only goodness. They are not all first-rate. So you mustn't idealize so," my mother would say, "because Jewish people are also people who make mistakes. Just like everybody else."

Despite the revelation of her Jewish origins, Mina remained a practicing Christian, and life in general went on much as before. As a teenager, she says, she was "lacking in direction." Her performance in school, which her parents "worried over all the time," was inconsistent: In some subjects she "shone," but in those that did not come easily she simply gave up. "I wasn't dumb, but I didn't like school much," she recalls. "I went only to have fun; the minute I had to apply myself, I had no use for it anymore."

Her interest in things Jewish, on the other hand, was abiding and did inspire her to effort.

I really wanted to know what the situation was in the war, so I read some of Anne Frank. When I was perhaps eleven or twelve years old, I didn't understand much of it—that girl was very sophisticated for her age, and there were difficult words and German phrases I couldn't get—so I put it away for a while. Then I read it again, skipping over everything that was too hard. I kept reading that book, over and over, so that I understood more of it. Whenever I thought, "Now I feel a need to find out what it was like," I picked it up again.

When Mina was in her late teens, she was invited to the home of her cousin, who had figured so prominently in accounts of the custody fight but whom she could not remember meeting. The cousin, the daughter of one of Mina's mother's sisters, had dropped in on the Heemstra household when Mina was a young child; as she "often came unexpected," the two had repeatedly missed each other. In the intervening years, during which Mina's cousin had married and been absorbed in starting a family, contact had been all but broken. But when the cousin discovered Mina was entitled to a share of an inheritance that had made its way to her—"it was also from someone in the war," Mina explains, "and was to be distributed among those still there"—she and her husband, a non-Jew, had notified Mina and asked her to visit.

From her cousin, Mina learned her true date of birth—which was nearly two months earlier than the "birthday" which had been picked arbitrarily for her by the Heemstras and which she had celebrated "for years." Her cousin also provided an important "piece of evidence" that firmly established Mina's origins in her own mind.

My cousin had a photo with my mother in it, a beach scene with her sisters. I picked myself out, exactly my own face—and it was my mother. So even if they can't say with 100 percent certainty "she is Wilhelmina Elzasser"—my passport was marked "Parents Unknown" until we saw to having it changed—for me, the testimony of my cousin and that photo closed the case.

Mina's cousin also offered impressions of the Elzassers. She had liked Mina's mother, calling her "nice and pretty, a darling." But of Mina's father, a "hypernervous" man who "could be very unpleasant," she said, "He didn't seem to me like a nice person." In addition, the cousin provided a disturbing description of how Mina and her parents had been discovered in hiding.

It appears that they had a very good address but that my father's nerves were shot. At a given moment he couldn't hold out anymore and—saying, "I have to get out, I have to get out!"—he abandoned caution. He was spotted outside, and that seems to be the reason the whole setup was denounced.

My first reaction was to think, "What kind of a thing is that? That must certainly have been someone who was not at all nice, and completely out of control, to do such a thing while he had a wife and child." I thought it was awfully irresponsible, and it troubled me for a time.

Around the period of her visit to her cousin, Mina was taken over by a desire to marry a Jewish man. What she describes as her "wish-dream" had been kindled by a pubescent infatuation some years earlier, but with time it had taken on the aspect of a duty.

When I got it through my head how much had happened, how many millions of Jews had been murdered, I thought, "So many Jewish people lost through the war, so many children, so many people from one race." And I somehow thought—although this may be idiotic—"You should actually marry a Jewish man. Everyone of my age who is left ought to do that—Jewish boys with Jewish girls—and so build up that race again. What a pity it would be," I thought, "to marry a Catholic; my children would probably become Catholic as well, and then it gets all watered down and nothing remains of that Jewishness anymore. But the few we still have left just must regroup," I thought. "And if I marry a Jewish man, I will have a bunch of Jewish children and make a small contribution to scraping it all back together again."

But there wasn't much chance of getting to know a Jewish boy in Limburg: There were so few Jews left and, besides, I was in a Protestant orbit and didn't go around in Jewish circles at all. I had a boyfriend at a certain point, but he was a Catholic. I talked him into going with me to the Protestant church—I, a Jew, persuade a Catholic to go with me to the Protestant church! He went, against the wishes of his parents; today they all go to one another's churches, but in those years it was still unheard of. I got engaged to him as well, but on the night of my engagement I wept in my bed. "You are completely spineless," I thought, because I still wanted a Jewish man. "But that was a dream," I told myself. "You'll never get one, and you have to have something." So this fellow was a substitute.

In the end, that came to nothing anyway. I then had one boyfriend after another, merely for the fun of going out once in a while, to pass the time, nothing really serious. I didn't see that as my goal in life; I still had the hope that a real Jewish boy would come along one day. I was actually waiting for that alone.

But then Mina, who in the meantime had become a resident nurse in a hospital a dozen miles from home, decided to take steps: She applied for immigration to Israel and placed herself under an "ultimatum."

"If I don't meet a Jewish boy within three months," I promised myself, "I'm going to Israel." Of course, that's not the right reason for going to Israel, because you ought to be idealistic and ready to devote yourself totally; but I thought, "I can do that as well," my idea being to work as a nurse in a hospital. "And you're sure to marry a Jewish man then," I told myself. "There are so many, all you'll have to do is pick one out."

But what was really difficult for me was that I was very attached to my parents, very much tied to home. My father and mother had always spoiled me rotten and taken care of everything for me, and I was still very dependent. So to leave all that behind and go so far away from my parents bothered me a lot; I couldn't do it just like that. "But I'll do it all the same," I thought. "After all, I have to stand on my own two feet at some point. And I want to meet a Jewish man, and perhaps the experiences I'll have working in the hospital there will be good for me. Perhaps I'll want to stay there—who knows? And if, after I've been there a while, I get so terribly homesick, then I'll figure out some way to get back and my parents will help me again as well."

Before the ultimatum had run out, Mina met her husband-to-be. One of her patients, noticing the Star of David pendant peeking out over her uniform collar, offered her an introduction to a Jewish woman with an eligible son. Thinking, "Well, now—this is it!" Mina accepted; and when the evening of the initial meeting rolled around, she found it was all she could do to hold her enthusiasm in check.

It was a really nice evening, but I still didn't want to lay it on too thick. I told myself, "Keep your distance a bit. It's as if you were throwing yourself at him; you're being a little silly." But I really did like him—and he me as well. And this is strange, but I swear it's not romanticized or fantasized: More or less from that moment, I thought, "That's him. I'll marry him." Even though I actually didn't know him yet. But I had a feeling.

I dropped a note to my parents the following day: "I have met a

Jewish boy, and I'm head over heels in love. We are going to see each other often, and he'll become my husband." They tried to slow me down, because I was rushing things so much: "Take it easy," and "You don't see the whole picture yet," and "You're half-married already and you've seen him only once." Then they actually did try too hard to restrain me, in my opinion—but that's another story. When I told my future husband that I was working on immigration to Israel, he said, "Now you have to choose: Either Israel, or me." Well, that was not such a difficult problem anymore.

Once she was engaged, a new problem arose. Although Jewish history as she had learned it in Protestant Sunday school had sometimes given her pause—"I did think that it was mean of them," she recalls, "nailing Jesus up on the cross like that"—Mina felt no conflict being at once a believing Christian and a Jew. Before her wedding, however, Mina had hardly set foot in a synagogue, and the abrupt switch from Christianity to Judaism proved difficult for her.

It was logical that I couldn't keep going to church and go to shul [synagogue]: I had to choose. But I was used to going to church regularly. I didn't go every week, rather I went now and then, when I myself felt a need for it. Pressure had never been exercised on me, but I had experienced enough of a Christian upbringing that at a given moment I would think, "Now it's about time that you went to church again." I was serious about my religion, too—I listened attentively and didn't just go in a perfunctory way, because he or she was also going.

But now it was expected of me that I drop it all at once. I couldn't do it gradually, I couldn't get used to it, no. All at once that was no longer allowed—which was absurd. I loved my husband, and I was happy to belong, but I thought, "What have you actually given up? And what are you getting in its place?" And I did have the feeling of missing something.

Because, if I may put it this way, I didn't get any satisfaction from my new religion. When I'd met my husband, I'd gone with him a few times to services and found the whole thing really strange. Everyone was talking and laughing, and the chazzan* seemed to be singing more or less for himself. It was certainly different; to me, it seemed peculiar, disor-

---

chazzan: cantor (Yiddish and Hebrew).

derly, profane. Since I didn't understand it so well, it all had to be explained—why there was no reason you couldn't have a chat with the person next to you, that it was more a meeting place than something where you had to sit still as a mouse—and then I did see it in a somewhat different light.

But my husband couldn't convince me sufficiently of some things. He had learned everything as a boy for his Bar Mitzvah but had forgotten it all again, and he wasn't such a faithful synagogue-goer either. Besides, he didn't really appreciate the difficulty I was having with the transition; and I didn't feel that my father-in-law and mother-in-law, who were still old-fashioned in their views, showed proper understanding for the fact that I hadn't grown up in a Jewish atmosphere, that it was a total change for me. They expected me just to accept everything that was dished up without questioning, and I had trouble with that. But then my foster parents said, "Why wouldn't you go to the synagogue and simply do as your husband does? You are Jewish by race, after all. That shouldn't be such a problem for you." So they helped me at that point.

At the time of the interview, Mina was able to say that her earlier "wish-dream" had been realized. She and her husband, a businessman old enough to remember living hidden in Belgium during the war, seemed comfortable and contented in their suburban home in the southeast of the Netherlands. They had three bright-eyed children—Mina, backing away from her earlier ambitions, had decided that three was "plenty"—and the elder two were already learning Hebrew. Mina seemed touched that her twelve-year-old daughter was reading The Diary of Anne Frank *and "skipping over the difficult passages," just as she herself had done at that age. And she enjoyed her son's enthusiasm for Jewish jokes, though she warned him about telling them in school, much the way her own mother had cautioned her not to be so open with the story of her voyage from Egypt.*

With the years, Mina says, she has "gotten over" the difficulties she initially had in "letting go" of her Christian faith. She becomes "furious and defiant" upon hearing that her children have been told by classmates, "You Jews were meanies, murdering Jesus"—a charge whose validity she herself once earnestly pondered. And, believing that "the way you live your daily life is more important than the number of times you set foot in church," she says that the feeling that she might be "doing something wrong" in not going to church has gradually abated.

I don't have any problem with no longer belonging, no longer having anything to do with it; in fact, I never go to church anymore unless I have to go for a wedding, and I don't feel the need to go either. We do have a Christmas tree every year. My husband didn't want to when we first got married; somehow, he didn't dare. But the next year he brought a bouquet, which I thought was terrific; and the year after that a few branches; and the year after that a little tree, and so I'd won. I'm crazy about it: It was something I was used to, and when you leave home or get married, you like to take along something of the atmosphere of home. A Christmas tree is for the ambience, the conviviality; to my mind, it has nothing to do with religion.

In any event, I don't have so much conviction anymore. It was taught to me, and I didn't know anything else, but you don't remain a child forever, you become somewhat more realistic and down-to-earth in these things. I now have a lot of doubts about everything. Sometimes the children ask about God and about what happens to you after you're dead, and then you ask yourself, "Does God really exist?" I tell them, "I could say, 'Yes, dears, God is up there taking care of you' to make you feel secure, but I don't know myself. And I don't think it would be honest to say that just to be done with it, or to set your minds at ease." Because you're not going to say it, after all, if you yourself don't know.

Another change which has come with time is that Mina's attitude toward her Jewish father has softened.

You go through phases in which you reflect more deeply on certain things. I talked it over with someone, with my cousin or my husband, who said, "Considering the situation people were in during the war—with the tension, and the terror, and all that went with living in hiding—you can't pass judgment." Nonetheless I sometimes thought, "If only my father had been less short-tempered or less lacking in self-control, who knows then?"

But there were so many who went in any case; and second-guessing is useless, after all. I've now gotten to the point of recognizing that if someone who is nervous to begin with and is living under stress then has his nerves go, you can't hold it against him. It appears my father was unwell, that he'd had a stomach operation that had kept him out of work for some time. This, and the war, and being in hiding—and then the fact that I was there—certainly all played a role. I can well imagine that sitting there, stuck for a long time in a small space, he might have said, "I must have fresh air, and I'm going!"—at a certain moment, it can get to be too much. I know that I too can become pretty quick-tempered and impulsive, and I was sick for a time myself. Perhaps I would have done the same.

In contrast, time has not done much to wash away either the discomfort that Mina felt upon first entering the Jewish community or her nostalgia, if not for the Christian religion then for some of what she associates with living in a Christian community. Although realizing that she may have a "skewed picture" owing to the sparsity of the Jewish population in the region where she lives, Mina can't help feeling "disappointed."

When I had just started going with my husband, I got a royal reception in Jewish circles here: "Great—he's found himself a Jewish girl!" Everyone was kind, and friendly, and interested in me. I was again something special, and I liked being something special.

She has since found that, aside from the High Holidays and the Saturday morning services that she herself rarely attends, "there is simply nothing to do." She misses, to some extent, how "the parson came by now and then to have a chat," and the way her church congregation rallied around fellow parishioners in need. "I don't know whether that's done among Jewish people as well," she says, "but you hardly see any of it here—there's so little Jewish life."

And much that she has been exposed to within the Jewish community has left Mina feeling out of place or even angry. About those of her age-group who serve on the board of her synagogue—which, like most in the Netherlands, is Orthodox at least in name—she says, "I feel Jewish, but they are super-Jewish—so Jewish that I'm not at ease with them." Her reaction to the "convivial ladies' luncheons" to which she has been invited is somewhat stronger.

As far as I can see, it's not only a matter of a convivial luncheon, it's a matter of showing how chic they are. They all come in their diamonds and their mink, and what they have on their hands! I can't make such a show—it's either that I'm too simple for it or else that it just disgusts me.

And there's so much fuss and boasting: "How's the store?"

"Wall-to-wall people, you couldn't move"—while there wasn't a soul at the door, they'd hardly sold a thing.

I don't like dishonesty, I don't like pretense. And that exaggeration: so false, so deceitful. "You are a Jew, but at this moment you're a goy [gentile]," my husband says to me then. "It may be that you have a bit of a goyish streak after all, from home."

Nor, frankly, can I really see the Jewish religion. The Jewish traditions do move me, but to do all that yourself—it asks so much of you, it's so demanding, and I'm actually too easygoing for that. Besides, with the exception of the few elderly, most of them don't have any idea what they're talking about. My husband says if you let go of this and let go of that, the whole Jewish religion falls to pieces, it's no longer truly Jewish. But when from time to time he's asked to do something in shul, he has to learn it by heart, and I think, "What a tremendous effort just to memorize a few little phrases." I say to him, "I think Hebrew sounds pretty and everything, but do you actually know what you're saying?"

"Gosh," he says, "do you think I still remember all that?"

So I tell him, "I couldn't say anything that I didn't stand behind or whose meaning I didn't know. After all, you wouldn't sign a letter without knowing what was in it either."

"Sometimes you seem anti-Semitic," my husband tells me. But my feeling Jewish—my being Jewish—and the Jewish religion don't have anything to do with one another. Besides, I feel just as Jewish, it's remained the same for me, only I have become more down-to-earth. I still think that if Jews are good in something, then they become particularly good—after all, there are exceptionally intelligent people among the Jews—so there is a little something left of my ideal. But I have come to see Jewish people as they are, which is just like other people are: In certain things they shine, and in other things they are, at times, not so great.

In the old days, Jews for me were wonderful, perfect people. But now, on occasion, I'll see a Jewish woman or a Jewish man and I'll say, "What a mies ponem!"* Formerly, I would have thought, "That is a Jew!" and I would have built something up around it; that was so special for me that it was good, period. But today if someone who is Jewish doesn't seem to me like a nice person, I am able to say, "He's a rotten apple."

Then my husband says, "Now, now—but he's a Yid."

"So what!" I say. "I still think he's a skunk!"

Mina's more sober perception of Jews and Jewishness seems to coincide with a lessening of her tendency to romanticize her own life.

---

*mies ponem: ugly face (Yiddish).

I do wonder on occasion what it might have been like with my own parents, and I think it's a pity that I'm going to die without ever having known them. But that may be overdoing things, because I'm thankful I was so lucky as to have good foster parents and everything—I might just as easily not have been so lucky. So everything worked out well: I have a normal family life, nothing extraordinary, everything very average. And as important as I used to think myself and as interesting as I wanted to be, that's how little I think it all is now.

I used to be a dreamer, someone who idealized everything, and I didn't really stand with my feet firmly on the ground. But through experience, through marriage, through getting older, you become more serious, and I've become very down-to-earth.

My husband says, "Boy, you're no longer romantic at all!"

"No," I say. "What I like is being straightforward, knowing where you stand, no frills."

Yes. A person can change.

AFTERWORD

Mina Landau's conclusion, "A person can change," rings with a conviction born of many years of soul-searching. But it is not necessarily possible to put one's finger on change with the same assurance that marks Mina's pronouncement. To what extent experience reflects who a person is and to what extent it causes that person to become someone different—how much experience is shaped by what the individual brings to it and how much it shapes that same individual for the future— may not always be easy to discern.

Was the effect that the narrators' encounters with persecution had on their identities mainly to reveal what and how much being Jewish already meant to them—to bring into the open feelings, perceptions, and attitudes they would have had in any case? Was it to intensify these feelings, perceptions, and attitudes, to render them not merely more visible but deeper, better defined, more compelling? Was it to alter them in some way, modifying more than just their level of definition or intensity? Or was it to bring into being entirely new feelings, perceptions, and attitudes—to produce connections, whether intellectual or emotional, where none had existed before?

Had Isaäk Feldman's ambivalence about the world of his youth— about that Jewish society in which he felt safe and protected but also stifled and misunderstood—actually made of him the "Janus figure" of later years long before his arrival at Auschwitz's gate? Could it have been nostalgia for his old neighborhood that caused Isaäk to envy the Jewish inmates for what he imagined to be their togetherness, even as a less explicit memory of the limits imposed upon his young nature led him to press on alone? Were these feelings simply revealed or intensified as he stood at the barbed wire? Were they, in ways that would be fundamental for Isaäk's future experience and sense of self, altered there? Or might the split he felt later have been totally absent from his life had he not volunteered to work in the German Reich?

Hélène Terlinden, recalling the tears her classmates shed upon first seeing her with the yellow star, observes, "From that moment on, something was changed in my state of mind." But could the change have been less in what determined Hélène's attitude toward being Jewish than in how she perceived her attitude? Was being Jewish no longer "totally negative" now that it had begun providing her with the social acceptance she had felt it denied her before the occupation? Was it because the non-Jews' attention and sympathy had faded that, after the war, Hélène again bore her Jewishness as an unwelcome burden? To what extent did Hélène change, then change again? To what extent did her life take its shape from two forces that had always been in conflict: her desire to fit in to the majority society and her feeling that the Jewishness she saw as preventing her from doing so was as inescapable as her own mortality?

When does change come? For Walter Roth, was it when he reached "the fork in the road" at which he decided "to become a Jew"? Or was what he saw as a "conscious choice" determined, unbeknownst to Walter, somewhere along the road that brought him to the fork? In declaring herself a member of the Jewish community in 1933, was Hilda Dujardin taking leave of her nonsectarian upbringing? Or was she simply doing what she had done every time she had seen Jews threatened since her scolding in the streets of Oderfurt: taking her "stand alongside [her] Jewish father"?

What constitutes change? Was Romulus Berliner a different man once he was dressed in an SS uniform? Or was he still the fellow who "couldn't allow [himself] to notice" conflict, who feared that acknowledging it would inevitably "come to no good"? On her journey from Judaism to Christianity and back again, did Dvora Goldenberg break twice with her past? Or did her foster parents' rigorous Calvinism keep alive, even reinforce, the religious feeling of her early childhood, providing a bridge to the orthodox Jewish milieu she was to seek as an adult?

What, ultimately, is essential? David Kornbluth insists it is being Jewish that is essential to him, and he was apparently willing to risk his own death and that of his family to prove it. But might it not be whatever impels him toward the position of the outsider, whatever fuels his inclination to play the role of "heretic," that is truly at his core? Etienne Lenoir declares that Jewishness "is nothing" to him. But how different might have been his view of the world, and how differently might he have approached his choices, had he simply not been of Jewish descent? Leonore Hoffmann avers that her time in concentration camps is what "made [her] as a human being." But might not qualities she already possessed have enabled her to overcome a separateness that led many others to isolation and death, helping her to make her experience of persecution a positive influence on her life?

Pavel Balázs believes that "if you as an individual want to know what your life is, what you have done, what you may be doing in the future, what the problems are which confront you, what the meaning is of being alive, then this problem of belonging ... becomes very important. [It] comes in to amplify our knowledge of ourselves—what we are, why we act like this and not like that. And it's important to know."

But for the conviction that Pavel is right—that self-examination can make a difference, that there is value in explicit understanding—this book would not have been written. Still, what is essential may simply be that which does not change because it cannot change, and in that case there are limits to what knowledge can do. After all, is it not Pavel himself who observes, "I've always been like this without knowing it"?

ACKNOWLEDGMENTS

Hundreds of people contributed time, effort, and understanding over the decade and a half it took *Embattled Selves* to evolve from an idea into a published work. I always looked forward to retracing my steps and thanking them all in person. This dream has never come true, and the best I can do is to offer my gratitude on these few pages, in these inadequate words.

Even if there were space here to name the 280 people who allowed me to record their life stories, I would be prevented from doing so by the promise of anonymity I made to each. But I am aware of how large an emotional undertaking the interview could be, and I am filled with admiration for those who agreed to attempt it.

Finding people to interview required speaking with hundreds of others, many of whom proved willing to contact friends or relations on my behalf—a mission that, considering the delicacy of the subject, promised an awkward moment at the very least. I refrain from listing these people here only because there were so many of them and not because I fail to recognize that, without their help, there would have been no book.

Scores more went out of their way to give me other kinds of aid: They taught me their languages or reviewed my transcripts and translations; they stored copies of my interview cassettes in their homes or let me use their office equipment; they lent me money or gave me a chance to earn it; they introduced me to foundations, agents, and publishers. Among those who helped me in such ways in Europe, where I collected the life histories, were Louise Bosschaert, H. F. Gans, Maya Gordon,

Gundl Herrnstadt, Serge and Beate Klarsfeld, Riet Lamers, Erika Lu-
dolph, Elisabeth Meter-Plaut, Myriam and Gérard Rodach, Michael
Seiler, Nel Slis, Paul Syrier, Richard de Weger, Walter and Patricia
Wells, and Annette Zaidman. In the United States, where the manu-
script was produced and revised, I received similar help from Abby
Collins, Patricia Crisafulli Commins, Susan Daitch, Galia Hanoch and
David Roe, Jerry and Sarah Jacobson, Veronica Jochum and the late
Willo von Moltke, Michael Johnson, Larry Joseph, Veronique Keeley,
Eve Jacobson Kessler, Bill Kosman, Fritz Krachtowil, Andy Markovits,
Frank Mecklenburg, Peter Merner, my former colleagues at *Metals
Week*, Cullen Murphy, Martha Palubniak, Victor Peeke, Lise and Nick
Peters, Rabbi Alexander Schindler, Joanne Wang, Betty de Weerd, and
Richard Woodward. Many of these people provided me with compan-
ionship as well as aid, and the encouragement I got from their selfless-
ness is a most important form of sustenance for one who is embarked
upon a long and uncertain course.

In addition, people on both continents opened their homes to me,
many for weeks or even months. This took special generosity, and in
most cases either reflected or became the basis for special friendship.
Over the years, I stayed in the homes of Susan Becher and Bruce
Gilbert, Elie Benchetrit, Bob Dorang, Monica Fischer, Blanche Katz and
Sandor Tamasi, Tim Keeley, Betsy and Stan Lampe, Günther and
Ursula Mähner, Andreas Meyer-Hanau, Robertine Nabarro, Is Reece,
Ruud Ronteltap, Brigitte Sturm, Daniela Thau, and Jack and Ria Weil.

Several foundations helped me as well. I received grants from the
Gustav Würzweiler Foundation, the National Foundation for Jewish
Culture, and the Memorial Foundation for Jewish Culture. I would like
to express my gratitude in particular to Dr. Fred Grubel and to Rabbi
Robert Jacobs, the former and current executive directors of the Leo
Baeck Institute, and to Abraham Atik, the former executive director of
the National Foundation. I also received aid from the Centraal Isra-
elitisch Wees en Doorgangshuis "Machseh Lajesoumiem" in The
Hague; for this, I owe special thanks to Judith Belinfante-Cohen of the
Jewish Museum of Amsterdam.

Historian Michael Marrus personally helped me with some fine
points of the history of northern France. I am also indebted to three
published sources: Jacques Presser's *Ondergang* for historical events in

the Netherlands, the *Encyclopaedia Judaica* for background on centers of Jewish population in pre–World War II Europe, and Raul Hilberg's *The Destruction of the European Jews* for the general history of the period 1933–1945.

Before I had embarked on this venture, Brian Backman told me that it was not madness to consider writing a book; he was wrong, but without his encouragement I might never have learned the truth. From the beginning, my father, Norman Jacobson, urged me to put notions of practicality aside and supported me in the single-mindedness with which I pursued this work. Herb Lewitz and Ken Betsalel had been with me on the excursion recounted in the introduction. Herb's own belief in this project often provided me a much-needed lift; Ken's lending me the notes he had made after our visit to the cemetery proved an indispensable aid to my efforts to describe it.

Silke Bernhard and Ruth Neray made me party to their unusual insights, which added dimension to my understanding of how it felt to face persecution and to live with the experience afterward. Sam Crawford, Anna di Lellio, Geoffrey Hawthorn, Hartmut von Hentig, and Joshua Sherman made me the gift of particularly sensitive readings of my manuscript; their responses helped me to hold on to the conviction that it was worth trying to communicate the power and meaning of the life histories in writing.

Gail Greene spent a great deal of time going through my very lengthy first draft, and her advice shaped my sentences, as well as my contacts with the publishing world, all the way up to the book's acceptance. Faith Evans gave me valuable editorial guidance as well, and both Dorothy Markinko and Lester Strong made helpful suggestions. Henk Figee and Marijke Bartels, my editors at the Dutch publishing house De Boekerij, put much effort into helping me find a publisher and an agent in the U.S. and much care and comprehension into preparing the Dutch version of this work. My agent, Heather Schroder of ICM, has brought to all our dealings a highly appreciated combination of enthusiasm and professionalism. My editor at Atlantic, Anton Mueller, truly understood what I was trying to do and has spared nothing in helping me get it done; I count myself enormously fortunate to have been able to work with someone of such patience and perspicacity.

Many, many friends—some of whom I met in the course of this

enterprise, others of whom I knew before, some of whom fall into the categories of those named here, others of whom do not—stood by me through all of this, their loyalty providing both comfort and inspiration. Of all those who contributed to this project, however, a handful seemed at times to live with it as intensely as I did; they made extraordinary efforts in behalf of the book, my well-being, or, usually, both. For this, to Jane and the late Reinhard Bendix, Harvey Goldman, Ursula and Dieter Goldschmidt, Christine Muck and Thierry Guérin, and Bruce, Jacquie, and Kenny Parker, I shall always be grateful.

Finally, these acknowledgments would not be complete unless I expressed my thanks to my mother, Jean Jacobson; to my sister, Ellie, and my brother, Matt, and their families; and to my wife, Cecilia. All have shared with me some of my darkest and some of my brightest hours, and all have done so with unfailing generosity and love.